WORLD WITHOUT A ROOF

World

Without a Roof

AN AUTOBIOGRAPHY

BY *Hassoldt Davis*

DUELL, SLOAN *and* PEARCE ～ NEW YORK

FOR ALINE

CONTENTS 〰〰〰〰〰

viii

ix

WORLD WITHOUT A ROOF

1

Treasure trove—a boy up
a tree—poet with ghosts

NOW IT IS LATER, and a somewhat darker time than the midnight when I was born between the third and the fourth of July in 1907. It was an old-fashioned time which still permitted fireworks in Boston. My mother's window was brightly webbed with them. I didn't care about them really, in that comfortable womb of my own, and it was only by hours of persuasion, with the aid of forceps and such, that I was induced to come into the gleaming world.

A sorry thing, my father recalled, reddish and wet and with a head as flat as a book. It is a defensive consolation to know now that my errors of later life may have been formed by the hands of Dr. Cauldwell, who took my poor head between them and gently molded its soft skull to what he felt was the acceptable style in heads. I have never since been quite happy about this. Nor was I then. The whole business bored me to the extent that I refused to come alive. They held me by the heels and spanked me and held my blind eyes to the fireworks.

"William," they said, "come alive. See how dandy it is," and they must have grinned.

But I was against it. I wouldn't even breathe this alien air. Discouraged, Dr. Cauldwell wrapped me in a towel, dropped me into a dresser drawer, and returned to Mother who was doubtless regretting the folly of this dead issue.

It was then that I met my first explorer, a redheaded nurse who for the rest of my fifty years was to be known fondly as Aunt Louise. The young Louise came into the room in search of something, explored the dresser drawers, explored the contents of the towel, and acted promptly.

Some say that she sprinkled a few drops of ether on me, some say alcohol. But the result was electric. I took a deep breath and howled. I kicked half the cover away and emerged to a world, which never was to change for me, of milling, excited people, of fireworks spangling my horizon.

I coughed, gargled, hiccuped. "Zut-zut!" I said. "Zut-zut et zut."

"Little booger speaks French," said my father.

Nurse Louise, very proud, took me to the window, and family legend has it that I reached for the bright horizon. "Zut!" I said.

Childhood is rarely happy. The world is too immediately with you, a world of hard objects and stark admonitions, of barriers, fences, walls, tight cold sheets, the hand clenched over yours, a world of repression and frustration which rests longer in the memory than the bubbles of ecstasy you enjoyed. Childhood may be fun for everybody but the subject of it, and the child who is scolded for saying "I didn't ask to be born" is perfectly within his rights.

I, the first of my family's three children, remember little of my parents during the so-called formative years. My father loomed over me from time to time, a large bald man whose egg-shaped head wore such bushy eyebrows that I could stretch them out two inches or more. He had been a poor boy whose father had died in poverty after inventing, patenting, and selling the floating-ball water closet, but the spirit of invention had continued in my father; he invented the greeting card by the simple expedient of putting a postcard into an envelope, and thereupon founded the largest greeting-card industry in the world. My mother was a dainty girl of southern lineage, given to cooing, I recall.

But less vivid than they was an imaginary monitor whom I dreamed of recurrently when I must have had less than three years of life and

4

adventure and love, though this may be refuted by the analysts. She was a girl grown, whom I loved and hated, and who possessed an ironing board immensely tall, which I assume to have represented the far, lost places which as an explorer I have sought ever since. Night after night I climbed the legs of the ironing board, slipping back, falling, climbing again until I fell exhausted on its white snowy plateau. Then the girl would come, singing, with the hot iron in her hand, and put it on my heart. And new life would come into me with the sweet pain of it, and I would reach my hands into the chestnut-brown jungle of her hair, and bury my face in it, gasping the rich scent of it, the musky dank scent of the jungles I would later love so well.

I remember my first physical adventure and first crime with a clarity confirmed by my mother. I was in love with Marion Fowler who was four and played the piano. I felt it would be a splendid thing to live forever with her harmonies, but away from our parents, of course, so I abducted her from her summer home beside the sea.

There was a brisk curly breeze along the shore that evening, whistling adventure to us. The tin can with my father's treasure was heavy inside my shirt, and I must have looked strangely potbellied for a little boy. The hood of Marion's cape flew back, and her golden hair whipped against my cheek. We held hands tightly, running into the wind, running from the hard folk behind us. The wet sand trapped our feet.

"Come on, girl, come on!" I yelled. "You know what they'd do to us, don't you?" We staggered along the beach which we did not know, while the sun was swiftly leaving us to the night and the pursuit. Marion sobbed. "Don't be a baby!" I said. "You're older than I." A white comber came roaring at us and chased us to the main street of Winthrop.

"Let's rest," I said, "and count the money." Marion held her red cape around me, because I was shivering now, from the sea's cold and the chilling apprehension of the thing we had done. Looking down inside the cape, smelling her sweetness, I pried up the lid of the old tin can and touched the wonderful money which would get us anywhere. I didn't know that this was a collection of my father's antique coins. Cheek to wet cheek we laughed, for we were very rich. We could have castles and horses and at least one bike.

5

"Most of it's gold," said Marion. "There's so much of it we ought to give some away."

"We'll catch that old man. He looks poor."

We caught him beneath a gas lamp and, running past him, thrust a couple of coins into each of his ragged pockets. They may have been the nomad money of Thebes or Carthage, come to rest where no one would trouble it any more.

We played a game now, the reverse of pocket picking, slyly giving away a fortune in coins which were useless to the tramps we met. This was my first self-taught lesson in generosity.

"But we must save some for us," I said. "We must find a high house to live in."

"The highest house," said Marion. "Look." There was a thin apartment building dominating the town. We ran to it eagerly and up the stairs to the very top. And at my bold knocking the door was opened by an ample woman who smiled at us.

"Why . . . how do you do?" she said.

"We would like to live here," I said. "Do you mind? Are you nice to children?"

"Why, of course," she said. "Won't you come in and try my cookies?"

I recall a room luxuriant with flowered chintzes and loud with birds, but most marvelous of all was the view of the night-lit town as from a mountain castle. Never had I been so high. For the first time I saw a world unlimited, and my breath caught like a claw in my throat. I have since seen Aleppo from a minaret, Khatmandu from a peak near Mount Everest, a jungle full of temples from Kintomani, but none has widened my world so suddenly and with such a jerk as this view by night of a country town. The little sponge of my mind absorbed a broader beauty that night. Did I know then that I must always travel, that even the most fey of high houses would never hold me for long?

Our ample lady had returned with cookies now, but we had not eaten half a dozen of them before there was a knock at the door, and in came reality, long and blue and helmeted, our favorite policeman, Frank.

6

"Would you like some money?" Marion asked, with a precocious instinct for bribes, jingling the tin box.

Frank settled for cookies and our custody home.

Life achieved momentum now. I, the recalcitrant at birth, began to learn of love and war and beauty in Parley Vale, near Boston. It was a pleasant place, pleasantly named, of green-and-gold flickering shadows beneath the trees and a veritable mountain of rock dominating the old houses of our little community isolated from the grim apartment buildings of the town. Parley Vale—I saw my ancestors parleying there with the Indians who had come leaping over the Rock to steal some fair grandmother away. Lying on my back on the tickling grass, I squinted through bits of broken glass I had collected from the dump heap and saw the world in sunrises, sunsets, and I knew its nightmare terror through green bottle glass, while the Indians screamed from the Rock, not yet knowing that the screams were real and came from a primitive insane asylum across the way.

It was years later that I found another little boy, in the shape of an aged sculptor, a hermit on a mountaintop of the Ivory Coast. We were filming the distant forests of Liberia with red, green, and yellow filters, and he was as entranced with them as I had been. "You have given me other worlds," he said. "You must leave them with me and I shall be lonely no longer. I shall be a wandering man again."

The facts of war and love in Parley Vale were brought to me by Philip, a neighbor's adopted son. This alone was dramatic. He was a traveler from places unknown even to him. He was tense, thin, spotted with chicken-pox scars, which he claimed were made by the curling irons of his foster aunt who once had chained him to a bedpost for her delight.

Philip was horrendous but fascinating. He led us forth to war against the Green Street gang when they came swarming with their knives across the Rock. We drove them back with switches and slingshots, sped them howling to their lairs. We were self-righteous but well-organized little snobs and were hated by the Green Streeters because even though we were clean we could beat them at their own dirty tricks. And we fought only in self-defense, we never invaded.

It was Philip who led me into the torture garden of sex long before

7

I was ripe for it. We were sitting in a cave we and the woodchucks had dug into the hillside. It was fetid, musty as was our small boys' talk. I had confessed to my hero the humiliations I had suffered at Miss Seeger's private school, the matter of my velours hat with the bright silk band around it, which I carried like Christ his cross, the mottoes I had to recite before the mothers' meetings ("Habit is a cable; we weave a thread of it every day, until it becomes so strong we cannot break it"). Suppose, I thought, I got into the habit of reciting mottoes whenever I saw a few women together?

But my serious woman trouble, as I confessed to Philip, was Mary Williams, a blond, plump, ringletted type, in the grade ahead of me, Grade Two. How could I love her if I was always hoping she would fail when she stood up to answer the teacher's questions?

"Girls shouldn't know no answers," said Philip sagely. "Why don't you feel her up?"

The brutality of this shocked me and I spat into a woodchuck hole. Philip was relentless, sadistically enjoying my embarrassment. He elucidated. "First you gotta get through them drawers," he said. Then he described all kinds of things, including the manner in which babies were born. "All blood and guts," he said. I thought of the pink purity of my baby sister Aline, whom I had often seen nude, and couldn't believe that such ugliness could afflict her. I felt sick.

"I'm going to climb a tree," I said, and went out running to my best tree, a magnolia, a very feminine tree which I could violate cleanly. I climbed it with hands made gentle by Philip's crudity, stroking the smooth bark, laying my cheek and its tears tenderly against it, until I reached the highest branches where I sat through the afternoon. Before me was the monstrous Rock, below the green valleys scabbed with houses, and everywhere around me were the magnolia buds pink and white and pointed like young girls' breasts. I held one in my hand and put my lips to it, but reverently, not as Philip would have done. I could imagine his long yellow teeth tearing a bud in two.

Here was a high place which was home to me, I thought. There was no evil here. In peaceful community the ants went up and down the branches, and the breeze whispered. I sat there till the sun was setting, and felt I must hurry now to walk straight into it before its red door closed beyond the horizon. Ah, if I could fly! I ignored the

8

obscene whistling of the housemaids to their swains, and stroked my flowers happily until my door to the horizon had closed and I had to return, cold, to the house.

Aunt Kate, a dark gaunt Irishwoman, was our governess. Her face was terribly scarred from some fire which she explained, being a good Catholic, as God's visitation for her sins. She told me Bible stories and tales which she believed of the wee folk in the Irish bogs.

"You tell me of faith, Aunt Kate," I said, "and that if I had faith I could do anything at all. Could I fly, perhaps?"

" 'Tis a lot of faith you'd need for it, Billy boy, but you could do it easy then."

So I was armed with faith in the morning, having spent half the night awake, praying. I was up before sunrise with a scarf packed full of my treasures for a long journey to the horizon's red door. I climbed the Rock and stood on a ledge which faced the brightening east, and hoped that my built-up faith hadn't slipped in the night. I spread my arms wide and saw God, and myself held up by strings like a marionette. I don't believe I thought of the world I was leaving, nor that I was now to escape from its cramped quarters. To me it was not escape; it was aggression upon the alluring unknown.

"Now I shall fly," I said aloud, clenching my eyes till I saw stars. I stepped out into space and landed on my head about twenty feet below. The garbage man brought me home.

By trial and error we learn, I suppose, more securely than by rationalization. My faith in blind faith had been shattered on the Rock, at a healthy age before I might come to depend on it in times of trouble when the problem was really mine, not God's. I learned gradually to foresee consequences and temper my faith in accordance. I learned the falsity of my hero Philip's dirty love, when a little girl named Ruth Mann (she later became a champion high jumper) kissed me while we were skating one night. It was a good clean kiss which I would have improved had I not fallen through the ice. I learned that I couldn't chase Aunt Kate around the garden with a log of wood almost too big to carry, for my father corrected this with a razor strop. And by similar instruction he taught me not to bust my brother

9

Milton on the nose. It took an afternoon to find the lenses of his glasses in the snow.

I must have been an unconscionably selfish brat, sensitive and belligerent both. My family attributes whatever success I have had in life to an attitude clearly exemplified by the legend of our nursery bed.

Milton, with whom I shared the bed, got up one night and called to Mother from the balcony which overlooked the great living-room fire where our parents were wont to sit tenderly together.

"Why, Milton—what are you doing there?" she cried.

Milton blubbered, "Bill wants half the bed!"

"Seems fair enough," said my father. "What's wrong with it?"

"But it *isn't* fair. He wants the *middle* half!"

I began writing poetry, or at least verse that rhymed, at about the age of six, on the moonlight equivalent of my sunset door to a better world. On the wall above my bed was a rectangular patch of light projected through the open window. Tree limbs wove lovely silhouettes upon it, and I could make shadow plays with my fingers there. But most fascinating was to envision my own handwriting upon the wall, and this, oddly enough, was musical though it made little sense. It was a tremendous and joyful discovery, equal only to that of a day years later in high school when I discovered I could wiggle my ears. Here was still another door, within the door of moonlight, through which I could pass to a world musical and of my own making. I had no slightest notion of what poetry was, not even the name of the thing I did, but I knew vaguely that this was a free and self-induced adventure, personal as my own blood.

It served me otherwise, for I was afraid of the dark and buried my head beneath the bedclothes on the nights of the waning moon, imagining that my golden square was with me still and that I wrote dreams across it, until my father would come into the room and rip the sheets from me and I would waken, shaking.

This was dubious therapy, and I couldn't understand why my father didn't frighten the bugaboos and not me. Alone in the dark again I waited for them. The air grew thicker about me, with dark bodies moving. Every breeze was their whisper or their stinking breath, and when their pressure became intolerable I knew what I had to do. I must bait them in their own den, in the attic from which they came.

I crept gelid out of bed, my shoulders hunched to their fangs, slipped to the hallway quietly, climbed to the attic, and shut the door behind me. They were there, all right, as I fought against drowning in this very sea of night, but I got my back to the wall, my fists clenched, and challenged them in a creaky voice.

"O.K., ghosts, I'm here. Just try and get me, ghosts!"

But they wouldn't, so I marched triumphantly back to bed. For the rest of that night I was unafraid. I scared the daylights out of quite a number of ghosts when I was young. I cleaned them out of nearly all of Parley Vale, I thought proudly as my fears diminished. I was the Ghost-getter.

2

My father's toes—a rope in
the night—the flying carpet

I MUST HAVE been about ten when I met my first explorer, Colonel Charles Wellington Furlong, a crony of my father. He looked like an explorer, rangy and tanned, with an Indian's face that could cleave the wind. He had been in mystic Turkey and the storms of Patagonia. He had ridden wild bulls at the Wyoming rodeos. He had been scarred in passing through the sunset door and returned to tell us of the wonders beyond.

On Sunday nights he would come to the house with Uncle Bill, my father's artist brother, and the beloved but fictitious uncles Bill Brown and Hank. Bill Brown was a little pixie of a man who illustrated my father's greeting cards. Uncle Hank was a huge German designer for a printing press. And around the fire in the evening, with their pewter tankards, they would tell us three children a round robin of a bedtime story, never ending, to be continued on Sunday next.

My father would lead its hero through a maze of adventures to leave him strapped to the back of a tiger.

"Now Uncle Bill will tell you what happened then," he would say, and Uncle Bill would have to get the hero out of that predicament and put him in a worse one for Uncle Hank to solve. Thus around the circle it went before the great log fire, better than any television, until it was time for bed.

"Don't forget now," Uncle Charles, Colonel Wellington Furlong, would call to us as we backed slowly up the stairs, "there's our Aladdin whom they've hanged in the well by his heels. He's still got the lamp, but it's flickering, it's going out . . . it's going out. . . ."

When we moved to Wellesley Hills I was unaware that my father had prospered to such an extent that he could build the enormous mansion there. He was a millionaire at thirty-five, and I received a good allowance on condition that I work, too, at school, which I detested, and at driving a horse and buggyload of newspapers on Sundays. My school friends jeered at me, the poor little rich boy, but they were happy to pay a nickel to ride with me, particularly in winter when I drove a sleigh. The snows were deeper then, the telephone wires had great spikes of icicles on them, the trees were crystal jewelry. Business with beauty, it was.

At our summer place, built on the rocks of Maine on Penobscot Bay, I spent my summers mostly in the treetops, for I had been reading Tarzan, and even then had Africa as a goal. From the time I could stand, my father had made me do setting-up exercises. We had trapezes and rings in the bathroom ceiling, which occasioned my first loss of faith in the adult word.

"Now swing, Bill," my father ordered as I clung to the rings. "Now toss your feet through your hands, let go the rings, and land on your feet. You'll see how easy it is, and if you miss I'll be here to catch you."

But he didn't. Down I came on my nose, with a startling gush of blood all over the bathroom. The pain was bad enough but not nearly so serious as my loss of confidence in the sacred parental word. It was my father who was to be pitied.

My admiration for him was in considerable abeyance until another morning in the same bathroom when for some reason I counted his toes. Darned if there weren't only eight. Surreptitiously I counted them backward when he stood still for shaving, and they still were only eight.

"Look, Daddy, I know I'm bad at arithmetic. But do you have only eight toes really?"

"Of course," said my father. "Much better, too. Leaves more air in your shoes." And he told me that when he was a boy my age he went barefoot to a country circus, and got so close to the fat man that the middle toe of his left foot was crushed beneath one of the giant's shoes.

"Have to amputate," said the doctor.

"Then do them both," said my child-father boldly, "the other foot, too, or I can never get shoes to match."

I then understood the courage and foresight which had made my father a successful businessman.

Undaunted by the plunge on my nose, encouraged by Tarzan, overwhelmed by my sissy devotion to poetry, I was determined to be the strongest boy in the world, and spent my allowance and newspaper money on physical-culture courses by Charles Atlas and Lionel Strongfort, with the result that I did actually win the *American Boy Magazine* competition for The Best Developed Boy in America. My picture was published and very proud of it I was indeed, until I found it was inciting more challenges from the toughs of the neighborhood than I could cope with. It was a relief when my school voted me First Poet of the Class.

But what I wanted most was to be alone on the sea or in the woods. Before I had learned to swim I set off for the islands in a baby *Kon-Tiki* of a raft which I had made of boxes, and was towed ignominiously back by my father's cruiser. I built a fine platform in a tree and again was thwarted by the family, who wouldn't let me sleep in it. I built a proper hut in the woods, spent a sleepless night in it, and returned to my habitual spanking. I was getting nowhere as an explorer.

I was lonely because of a complex knotted by poetry and physical hazard. None of my small pals would run away from home with me, to live amiably with the animals of Maine or Africa. No one but my brother Milton, who was two years younger than I (which is very young, when you are), would join me in making ladders of tarred rope to escape from the house in Wellesley and visit Howard's Athenaeum Burlesque Show fifteen miles away in Boston, or climb by moonlight through the abandoned quarry, or swagger scared down the street where the tough gangs lived. Milton, the sprout, was sometimes my companion, and though I loved him he didn't quite see that there were drama and beauty in the audience of a burlesque show, and rhythm in the rusted machinery of the quarry at night, and a singing that my heart made alone on a hostile street. To the few of my chums who had any appreciation of beauty, adventure was vulgar; and to those with the raging of blood in them, beauty was stuff for the girls.

I must get away. Life in suburban Wellesley had become intolerable, and so had, doubtless, I. I parted my hair down the middle with Stay-put. I grew pimples. I fell in love successively with Marjorie, Elinor, Rosalie (blessed be they wherever they are), and was spurned by them all. And I was so stupid as not to know until thirty years later that Marjorie Osborne had saved every poem I had anonymously sent her; she was too lovely to approach.

On the night of my third Boy Scout meeting I was so disgusted by Honor and Righteousness and Purity that I fled by moonlight to the hills of Wellesley, where Babson had started the construction of his great Institute. I climbed high into the skeletal structure of one building and sat on a girder about forty feet above the ground, miserable to find no place but such as this, away from the carping and querulous world. Looped around my girder was a rope which hung to about ten feet from the ground, and I knew that somehow it might serve me in the dark of my loneliness. I pulled it up and tied it tentatively around my neck. I tugged on it, and didn't like this much. Obviously there was a better use for such a beautiful new rope hanging loose in space. You could swing on it, I thought, but not by the neck. You could swing into life on it, if you had the courage for life.

With my heart beating so hard I could barely tightrope the girder, I carried the end of the rope around and over to the girder opposite, tied a knot for a seat, and steeled myself to the crazy project of swinging off into space and the night. It would mean a sheer drop

14

of half the rope's length, I knew, before it would stiffen to bear me through that arc of the night.

I was frightened, because I had an inalterable choice now, to swing to death by my neck, or into a bolder life by my own strong hands. I made the decision quickly, sat on the knot, grasped the rope, and kicked off.

Straight down I flew, like a gull diving. There was a jerk that nearly tore the rope from me, then I was swinging up again, spinning like a top in the night nearly forty feet above the ground, then down and up again, a pendulum measuring a small boy's courage.

The earth which I had despised was good again when my feet reached it and took me buoyantly home. I had vanquished fear. I had vitally vanquished boredom which might have hanged me a moment ago.

Now it was time, I thought at thirteen, for a serious incursion on adventure. I was standing then on a height again, dropping the cut glass of my parents' wedding presents on the brick walk below. This was paid labor. My father had offered me a dollar to drop it, sweep it up, and bury it far away.

Smash went a decanter, and my father behind me howled with glee. Crash went a hideous salad bowl. "Bully, Billy boy!" my father yelled. "You got it in bits! You can have a quarter extra for that monstrosity!"

I thought of Tarzan of the apes dropping coconuts on the enemy, and knew instantly what I must do. I must go to Africa. Now.

So I set about it methodically, boning up on the Tarzan books and an atlas, planning my itinerary and equipment. Into a small felt bag I packed, if I recall rightly, a large carving knife, a compass, a slingshot with marbles for ammunition, a map of the Congo copied from the atlas, a packet of bouillon cubes to eke out a Tarzan-berry soup, and a mighty document written by me in longhand.

This was in the form of a dialogue between me and the captain of the ship which was to take me to Africa.

I: "I should like to work my way to the Congo, Captain."

Captain: "But you're far too young, my boy!"

I, showing the magazine photo with all muscles strained: "Will you look at this, sir?"

Captain: "Hmmm, you do look strong."

I, letting him feel my biceps: "I can do the work of two men, sir. I'll challenge any of your crew right now, and beat him to a bleeding pulp, sir."

Captain: "Oh no, don't do that, but I like your spunk. I'll sign you on, young man. What's your name?"

I: "Victor Vitalis, sir. Thank you, sir. Right-ho, sir."

That was a pretty good name, I thought. The "Vitalis" I had got from a hair lotion.

I had confidence that I would get the job, but nonetheless I would need a little money before I learned to earn my dinner with slingshot and spear, so to this end I cast about for something of the family's which I could sell. Jewelry would be difficult, I knew. I chose a very small Persian prayer rug which lay at the foot of the stairs, and with my savings bought a train ticket to Boston. Up and down Tremont Street I wandered, seeking the courage to enter a rug shop.

A very pirate of an Armenian fixed me with a baleful eye as I loitered before his door.

"You buy rugs, mister?" I timidly asked.

He grunted and unrolled my package. "Where'd ya get it, kid?"

"I . . . I found it."

He caressed it, examined its back. "Your name isn't Davis, is it?" he roared at me, and I felt my knees buckling.

"My name is Victor Vitalis . . . sir."

The pirate looked at me askew. "I'll tell you this about rugs, son," he said more gently. "Each rug is different, and a man who knows one and has sold it—oh, maybe ten years ago—to a different sort of man like this Davis, ain't likely to forget it, see? Now take this back where you found it, Mister Victor Vitalis, and give my regards to your dad."

I had sneaked into the house and barely replaced the rug when Aunt Kate's angry brogue called out to me from the kitchen. "William, did you steal a rug today?"

"How silly! Aren't they all here?"

They were, indeed, when she came to the hallway. "Ah, my old eyes," she said, kissing me. "I could have sworn that one of them was

16

gone. It's the leprechaun's curse," she said, sitting beside me on the step to tell me about it.

It seemed that her mother in the Auld Countree had known the only way to catch a leprechaun, and when she saw one once beneath an apple tree she crept on him fast and spat in his eye. Then when he was blinded she pounced on the wee mannie and carried him home between finger and thumb and locked him in a chest. He made a terrible racket there. "Let me out! Let me out, woman Katie, and I'll tell you where's my pot of gold!"

"For sure?" she demanded the next day when hunger must have chastened him.

"For sure, and a gift for the bairn ye be carrying in your belly, too." With that she let him out and tied him to her shoelace, and off to the apple tree they went, the leprechaun riding on her shoe, but just as they reached his hole among the roots, zip! out came the shoelace and from the safety of his hole he spat straight into her eye. "That's for thy bairn," he screeched. "May ye neither of you see a leprechaun again!"

"And I haven't," said Aunt Kate, wiping her glasses. "Faulty me eyes have always been."

But not really always. A few days later I went to look at my African equipment where I had cached it behind the music cabinet, and it was gone. Neither of us mentioned it. It may have been filched by leprechauns.

During the next couple of years my interest in exploration was temporarily halted by literature and romance. I was reading the fantasists mostly, Cabell, Lord Dunsany, James Stephens, Oscar Wilde, and Donn Byrne, and at the expense of my Latin instruction wrote poems in school. The Latin teacher, Miss Molloy, was a plump and pretty little thing supposedly about to get married, which incited the incipient lust of us young blades. To keep my eyes off her and Cicero I wrote little love poems, two of which were published when I was fifteen in sensational magazines named *Hot Dog* and *Captain Billy's Whizbang*, at ten dollars each. The pity of it was that I couldn't mention this literary and financial success to my father, who became aware of my scabrous authorship only when a friend sent him a clipped poem from *Secrets* signed Hassoldt Davis, impugning him as the writer who had combined the names of his and Mother's families.

"Now look, Bill," he said. "This won't do. It would be bad for the greeting-card industry if people began thinking I was responsible for this crap. Use another name, or write something serious. I know true poetry doesn't pay, but if you get a non-paying acceptance from any respectable magazine, *I'll* pay you for it. Matter of fact, I'll start now."

Rather shyly for a brusque man, he reached beneath the desk and pulled out a portable typewriter in a cowhide case. "That's yours, poet," he said. "Now get on with it."

I needed no urging. The beautiful machine, which made my poems look so much more impressive in print, was an incentive, and the curly-headed Rosalie another. I was tortured by my need to love her even more than that she should love me, and in my long, dark, gabled room at the top of the house I paced the nights through between the window that framed the stars and the small lamp by the typewriter that framed my words of love. I suffocated literally. My chest hurt. My stomach rolled over with revulsion at my timidity the last night when I had sat on the sofa with Rosalie in her blowsy living room. Ty Cobb had kissed her, I knew, so why couldn't I, Victor Vitalis, who was afraid of naught? Let no one scoff at puppy love, for none other is so poignant ever.

Poems came from this torment and I placed them, usually without payment, in the little literary magazines, *Tempo, S4N, The Dial, Rhythmus.* But my joy in them was solitary. With the exception of Uncle Bill, the artist, none of my family knew what they were about, and I was sometimes unsure myself. As there was not another adolescent among the high school's thousands who was interested in the arts, I felt more than ever a freak and fought for normalcy in the gymnasium or with the tarts of town whom I didn't have to love. I shudder at the memory of the nights when our chauffeur and I would cruise in the magnificent Pierce-Arrow to pick up floozies in the adjacent towns. Lulled and at ease with their sweaty flesh, rolling on the green and dewy flesh of the golf course, I could laugh at my mother's asking so often, so wistfully, "Bill, Bill, why don't you know any clean, *wholesome* girls?" Why didn't I? They were so dull. What could you

18

talk to them about? School scandal? It bored me. Poetry and the bright adventures in worlds far away? It bored them. The richness of the flesh and the vital earth were a bond sufficient between us.

But for the moment only. I would sneak into the house feeling naked and ulcerous, abhorring myself. I would take a shower, scrubbing my skin nearly off, put on fresh pajamas, and seek the purity of my four-years-younger sister Aline. I would sit hunched at the foot of her bed while she slept gently, and I would begin to compose a whispered fairy story.

"There was once a dragon. . . . Do you hear me, little sister? And he had a bold armor all around him, and no one could guess that he had worms in his heart." I would raise my voice slightly and touch her foot.

"And what then?" she would ask. "Where was the princess?"

"The princess, now, was disguised as a worm, and *she* had little dragons nibbling at her heart, so . . ." and I would tell her as she sat up now with her knees poking high the sheets, and her arms around them.

"Look, Brother Bill," she would say finally, "let's sneak down and get a drink." So in nightgown and pajamas we would tiptoe to the long, curling banister of the staircase and slide down it, but sitting on it, mind you. The belly slide was just for kids.

And feeling the walls we would reach the refrigerator at last and drink our fill of blood.

It was cow's blood which our family doctor, Wescott, had drained himself at the slaughterhouses and dispensed in brown bottles to the children in his care. Usually it was mixed with milk and called by my mother, a dainty sort, "pink milk"; my French Aunt Adele called it "the ruddy gore." A wonderful thing it was, mixing protein and calcium and vitamins, a perfect nutriment, as I was to learn later, among the Masai of Tanganyika, who live on it exclusively. They slit the jugular veins of their cattle, stopper the wound with manure and mud, and when hungry bleed a cow into a gourd, filling it with milk. The Masai are the heartiest warriors of East Africa.

We three children were raised like cannibals on "pink milk." We were healthy and, as our thirst grew with us, we put less and less milk in the blood, until we wanted blood straight.

Aline and I would sit on the floor before the refrigerator, with its door open to cool us on the summer nights, and sip blood as we later would sip champagne, grinning at each other with smeared ruddy mouths.

"And what happened to the princess then?" asked my little vampire.

"Ah, she perished of drinking champagne in the middle of a sultry night. . . ."

All the while my grades at school were diminishing and I was on the way to becoming a very bum of a poet, I was spending night after night with, at last, "a Good, Clean, Wholesome Girl." I helped her to waste one or two of the best years of both our lives. Elizabeth was peace, a pillow, warm and benign, into which I could bury my dreams without an echo. I was fast becoming a *bourgeois gentilhomme,* sinking into a torpor of bovine love, when the family decided that I was a disgrace in high school and had better be moved to a private one of military discipline at Powder Point in Duxbury.

This was a huge colonial building on the edge of the sea. It looked like an asylum. Discipline stuck out like spikes all over it. There was a football ground and a track for wearing down recalcitrant little poets, and I was lodged at first with a nice humdrum character who wasn't interested in raiding the larder at night to cook canned soups on my clandestine electric stove, or in the rope ladder which abetted my escape to town. Paradoxically I was so bored that for the first time I worked at my studies, getting honor grades, and became champion of track and boxing.

Compulsory football and compulsory church bored me, so my father got permission for me to skip them for my extracurricular but still admissible pursuits, poetry and a desperate reading of the philosophers whom I have quite forgotten by now. The happiest memory I retain of Powder Point is of my escape from it in the early mornings, when it was still dark, to run by the sea's edge to a sand spit where, with a book of poetry and pencil and paper, the fog caressing me like the breath of ghosts, I could divulge the daemons that beset me. When this truancy was discovered, my admirable father once again backed me up, roaring into the telephone that he insisted on my using my free time as I wished.

20

This I took quite literally and pointed it out to the English teacher who caught me one night seated on the floor before his room. Harlow his name was, a dark, blunt Irishman whom one would never suspect of playing the violin exquisitely for himself alone.

But I exceeded my latitude on the night of the episode of Dunham's door. Dunham was a history instructor whom we neither liked nor pitied. We, the younger boys, knew that his buxom dark wife was sleeping with our older schoolmates, and we were properly piqued by this. The Dunhams lived in a room at the end of our corridor which contained twenty rooms, each with a door transom, and each had an eye at it on that night when the Dunhams turned in for bed. When our spies reported them sleeping we spread flypaper before their door, quietly poked the fire hose through their transom, aiming it to where we knew their bed was, and turned on the water full blast. We were back at our transoms again when Dunham came out roaring, slipped on the flypaper, rolled and floundered imprisoned in it as the malicious laughter of twenty adolescents followed him in his panic. Weirdly we were avenged.

My mother, who was a formidable correspondent, concluded each letter with what seemed to me a wistful postscript, "How is your ukulele?" This saddened me, too, for I hated to admit that it wasn't going well at all. I should interpolate here that since about the age of five I had been subjected to continual and various music lessons. Music, as an avocation, had never had the same appeal as magic, for instance, did, and it was always when I had my hands in the rabbit bag that I would be summoned to my piano lessons with Aunt Adele. They were a great trial to me and cost me dear, for I was fined a dollar whenever I missed one.

After several years of this grueling practice, my grandfather's violin was given me with accompanying lessons, and these I slaved on for a year, until I could play Kreisler's "Souvenir" so badly that my father, in self-defense, bought me a mandolin. The instruments were gradually reducing in size and dignity, but, dauntless, my parents paid for mandolin lessons, too. It was no go. So they gave me a ukulele with a book of charted chords. But the trouble then was that I had no voice to sing with the ukulele.

My mother spoke to me sadly when she came to Powder Point.

"But Bill, you always *said* you wanted to be a musician when you grew up."

"Mother, no. I always said I wanted to be a *magician.*"

This was the end of my music, and it was thus by the aid of the gap in my young front teeth, by the malformation of a cogent word, by assiduous practice and self-denial, that I eventually became the champion sorcerer of the Ivory Coast in cannibal Africa.

Powder Point was followed by Allen Military School, which was closer to home and the benign Elizabeth, then the swank Stone School on Beacon Hill where we were taught at a fancy fee the tricks and dodges of College Entrance Examinations without labor unbefitting gentlemen's sons. When my learning was sufficiently riddled with ruse, and my first novel, *Danse Macabre,* half done, my father sent me, at the age of nineteen, to Paris with just enough money to avert starvation.

I was to live the artist's life, grubbily, and either achieve true art from it or discover for myself that I was deluded by what I and even my father thought was a rather gruesome talent.

3 ~~~~~~~~~~~~~~~~~~~~~~~~~~~

Paris—the comestible cats—
the mountain lady—I go to jail

PARIS, the old eternal virgin, took me to her bosom and coddled and excited me by her beauty, her warmth, her pathos, her confidence in being the only habitable city in the world. And through my years of deserts, jungles, mountains, seas, there has been only Paris as a city where I could feel at home.

I began the artist's life, wore a black shirt and frail mustache. I sat with lemonade in The Dome, which was the intellectual Café de Flore of the twenties. I didn't drink or smoke, for I had been tough and sensible enough to accept my father's offer, made years ago, of a thousand dollars at twenty-one if I should abstain from tobacco, alcohol, tea, and coffee. There had been no stipulation regarding love.

But love for a shy youth quite alone in a new city is hard to come by, and the counterfeit of prostitution was the best I had. There was a jaunty wench named Dodo, an artists' model whom I picked up one rainy afternoon while wandering by the bookstalls along the quais. We found ourselves reaching for the same book, and suddenly were hand in hand walking happily along the banks of the Seine. Dreamily we walked far south through the shining streets to the Port of Alesia, and into the Impasse de la Roulette (the Blind Alley of the Spinning Wheel) where she had a room among a jerry-built clutter of artists' studios. One of these I rented, a barren big-windowed room with only a cot, a chair, and a table, and there began the life of the struggling writer.

I worked hard and gloriously at my novel which, if I recall correctly, concerned a young poet with a withered arm, his father who was a leper hidden in the attic, a ball at which love and murder ran masked, and necrophilism in the family tomb. There was little of the sensational that I missed, nor hardly a vivid adjective. The passages that weren't purple were ultra-violet. But to me it was Art, for my mind was tumid with Baudelaire, Huysmans, Poe, and the privately published curiosa of Ben Hecht. Joyfully but very briefly I became a Decadent. I was pleased to have so many real live arty bedbugs in my cot that I had to lave myself in kerosene each night. The smell of me was not pleasing to Dodo, but she suffered me with bated breath, which was just as well since we couldn't understand each other's language anyway. This did not at all deter me from reading aloud to her the more poetic passages of my manuscript while she sat, nude and by candlelight, on the one bugless chair.

"Is it about *l'amour?*" she would ask, and if it was she would listen attentively, understanding nothing, sighing. If I read a non-amorous bit, for what I thought the fine swing of it, she would grumble and clack her high heels until we were back with the bugs again.

My neighbors in the next studio were Sascha and Sonia, Russian

23

artists whose poverty I aspired to live down to. Sascha was cadaverous, long-haired, with thin lips and a complexion of gray-green. He was nearly decomposed, but I imitated him, pulling in my lips to a thin line and sucking hollows into my cheeks, slouching with the weight of beauty and death on my broad shoulders.

Below us lived the completely mad Baroness Elsa Von Freutag Loringhoven, an idol of the Surrealists and the contributors to *transition* magazine. She had been a model, an abstract artist, a lunatic but published poet. Now she was ancient and alone, a bedraggled creature with close-cropped dyed red hair, and not a franc to her name but the occasional one that dripped in from a lover of forty years ago. I never saw her out of her bed, where she lay as translucent as wax, wearing a man's felt hat on which she had stitched spoons and forks.

"Come to me," she would plead. "Warm my old bones with your youth." And I would sit in fear and fascination at the foot of her bed, caressing her skeletal toes.

"Can't you see it? Can't you see it?" she would scream, pointing to an upper corner of the room. "The green mist, the green mist of death. Oh, you stupid American! Even the cats see it now!"

And truly her seven alley cats would be staring at the corner where even I seemed to discern a floating mist of green. The toes of the baroness contracted in my hand, and my spine went chill as the cats, looking over their shoulders, sidled to the round hole in the door to the back yard and slunk through it.

"There will be death here," said the baroness, shivering, pouring us wine in beautiful crystal glasses.

And there was. I thought at first it might be Sascha, for though I had lent him a little money he and Sonia had been living on bread and bananas all week.

"Ah, meat!" he cried, pinching the thick peasant thigh of Sonia. "I love thee enough to eat thee, my dear." And he crumpled over, breathing stertorously, with his head in her lap, biting at her dress.

It was in the evening that, continuing my role of Florence Nightingale, I visited the baroness with a bottle of wine and Gaulloise cigarettes.

"You spoil me," she said, "but I will teach you in exchange a most

24

precious thing, that you must never grow old. I will teach you the courage that I lack—for the knife on the wrist in your prime."

"Cover yourself," I said. "It is cold here." Indeed there was a wind blowing, swinging the music of guitars from the gypsy encampment in a vacant lot. The kerosene lamp flickered in its dirty chimney, and all but one of the cats sat in a huddle, licking each other. The seventh was drowsing by the hole in the door.

We were talking without much enthusiasm of Miro's painting when the baroness sat up suddenly, spilling her wine. "The mist!" she whispered. I glanced quickly at the corner, saw nothing, then looked at the cats which were all regarding the ceiling. And then I, too, saw Death, a gnarled hand and hairy forearm sliding through the hole in the door. Before the seventh cat could move or cry it was strangled and drawn through the door.

I rushed to it. It was locked. "I'm sick," I stammered, and rushed through the front door and around to the yard where I found no one. Slowly I went up the stairs, past Sascha's studio to mine, and sat limp at the typewriter, daring neither to speak to Sascha nor to tell the baroness what I had seen. Maybe she wouldn't miss the cat; there were so many going through her room, and if she knew, I doubted that her remnant of sanity could stand it. I was conscious of the distant gypsy music, and of Sonia singing with it just beyond my wall. After half an hour or so as I sat there, lonely and comatose, I grew aware of the smell of frying onions in the next room.

There was a knock on my door, and Sascha came in, his sleeves rolled up above his hairy forearms. "Bill, my little Bill! You must eat with us! I sold a sketch to a tourist and bought a little rabbit. *Allons!*"

"Ah, Sascha, I'm sorry, but I've eaten too many bananas. *Bon appétit!*"

As photography was one of my many hobbies, I roamed the streets of Paris with a camera and the only flash attachment available in those days. This consisted of a chromium pan which one filled with magnesium and set afire with flint and steel. It went off with a bang, an immense cloud of smoke, and usually scared my subjects witless as well as bringing the police at a trot. With an energy which it wearies me to remember I crisscrossed Paris on foot from the Porte d'Orléans to the Porte de St. Ouen, from Maillot to Vincennes, photographing churches, tramps, tree branches, cafés, whores. Instead of walking, I usually ran with the long stride I had learned at track in school, for life and drama were always just around another corner and might vanish before I arrived.

Once of a night I was rushing through Les Halles, the great market district, when I dived headlong into what was virtually a human mattress. As I pulled myself out from this woman's gigantic breasts she said with a titter, "Were you looking for me, *chéri?*"

I backed off, shaking the perfume from my nostrils, gulping air. She simpered and stroked my face. It was incredible, but unquestionably this monster was a prostitute. "Come home with me, *chéri*. It's only fifteen francs and five for the room. You'll *like* it, *chéri*."

With my French bogged in amazement but an eye for Art in the Lower Depths (a book of photos I was contemplating), I stuttered, "Yes, look, but I don't want to—to make love with you, madame. I—I'm married." Her fat painted eyebrows went up. I was against the wall and she moving in on me like a pneumatic tank. "Will you just pose for me, for my camera?"

"Anything you like, and you'll *like* it." She shooed me ahead of her as one would a fractious goose, into a *maison de passe* where I paid five francs for the room and a towel. Up the stairs I was shooed, while she followed sideways, and into a room that barely fitted the two of us and the bed.

Quickly, for such a behemoth, she undressed, and bolsters, bulbs, and balloons fell out. Her belly was a blimp, and I stood open-mouthed with the wonderment not only that anyone could want to make love to such a hulk, but that it should be physically possible. She must have weighed four hundred pounds. Nodding her ringleted head pertly, she pulled a batch of old newspaper clippings from her purse, and they acclaimed her to have been once the fattest woman in the world.

"Oooooh," she moaned, and tears stained her rouge. "Until just last year I was champion and then, zut! an Armenian came to beat me, and out I went into the cold with my savings and the appetite of champions. It has been hard, *chéri,* to be a has-been, to walk the streets on my little feet—see how dainty they are?"

26

"You have your memories, madame," I said, setting up my camera on the folding tripod, attaching the flash.

"Shall I pose like this?" she asked, wiping away a tear and holding her chemise above her head.

"No, no, just sit still, with your knees, er, crossed." This was accomplished with difficulty.

Hah, I thought, here was truly a document of life in the raw. I snapped off the light switch, opened the camera diaphragm, and exploded the flash. Vesuvius must have been like this. Madame screamed and in the dark and the smoke there was a crash of furniture. My camera went over as a monstrous moist bulk landed on me, flattening me to the floor. I gasped, poking my elbows into resilient fat. The screaming went on, shriller and shriller. The door was flung open, slammed again, and now there was screaming in the hall. Suffocating, I fought with this female Moby Dick, choking on magnesium fumes, and was just pulling my last leg out of a sort of quicksand— God knows what part of her it was—when in burst the door. The lights went on before two brass-helmeted firemen from the station next door. I saw them in the blue haze which looked like a fire, all right, then I was past them with my camera and twisted tripod, and down the stairs and into the street.

"*Le voilà!*" someone shouted. "There he is! Get him! The arsonist!"

A kaleidoscope of harsh voices exploded behind me, and I fled into the dark alleys of Les Halles, twisting, falling, a fugitive from an innocent but grievous error. I tumbled over beautifully piled mounds of market vegetables, ran smack into the carcass of a cow on a butcher's back and got spattered with blood.

Then I saw a refuge, La Grappe d'Or (The Golden Grape), a doss house I had heard about but vainly sought. I plunged down its basement stairs into as evil a crypt as the movies could invent. It was a long room filled with benches, tables, and silence. The raggedest tramps of Paris sat asleep on the benches with their heads on the tables. There was barely light enough to see the brute of a barman who stopped me, assessed my filthy and bloody clothes, and demanded seven francs. This would purchase a glass of *casse-patte* (footbreaker), a night's sleep, and a bowl of onion soup in the morning.

27

Cheap enough, but I refused the liquor and sat in a dark spot between two snoring *clochards*.

But I couldn't sleep, lice leaped at me regardless of my stench of kerosene, and in the corner of the floor at my back a hag of a whore plied quite publicly her five-franc trade. Once I tried stretching out on the table between the rows of heads, but that didn't last long. I was picked up by half-a-dozen apaches, carried to the door, and flung with the other garbage into the gutter. And I ran all the way home.

It is odd to remember now my obsession with the underworld of Paris, and my refusal to be discouraged by the spiritual and physical revelation of its sordidness. I suffered with it; I was masochistic in the cause of what I thought was Life. I lived in dramatic squalor and wouldn't have been caught dead in the luxury of Versailles. I was tough, I was still Victor Vitalis, but I ached with the impact of beauty I was busy kicking down upon my head. I decided I was a Nihilist.

With some confusion as to what this really was, I joined the mob on the night of its protest against the execution of Sacco and Vanzetti, although the American Embassy had warned all Americans to stay indoors. I didn't know much about Sacco and Vanzetti, except that they were rebels and oppressed and were coming to a sticky end, so I put on my black workman's shirt, sucked in my cheeks, pinched my lips to a thin grim line, and went out to join the crowd which was expected to demonstrate at 10 P.M. in the Place de la République.

There they all were, the conspirators, jamming the alleys that converged on the Place, and I, tense with excitement, joined them, ready to do any desperate revolutionary deed, so long as it didn't hurt anyone. But the crowd was suspicious of me, despite my grunts and glowering. Someone said, "I saw him get out of a taxi!" They drew away from me, who might be a police spy, and when a great cry went up and they rushed rioting into the Place, I ran along eagerly but alone. I didn't know much about rioting, and I saw no point in breaking windows as the others did. I let out a whoop or two and was writing notes for a possible article when there was a scream of brakes just behind me as a police truck ran into a lamppost.

Out came the *flics* like spilled grapes, and I was caught in the mob and flung into a subway entrance just as another contingent of police

28

came up the stairs. We were surrounded and I was quickly subdued, ducking wallops, while attempting to explain that I was a simple journalist, out for a story.

"Your papers?" I had cautiously left them in the studio. "Come with us, *gamin.*"

Through the dark streets they led me, sputtering in my wretched French, to an ancient stationhouse dating from the considerably greater Revolution. My belt and the humble contents of my pockets were taken and I was kicked into a true cell, dank, dark, windowless, and swarming with other prisoners whom I could see only as they passed the little two-inch porthole in the door. We screamed out of it, demanding to telephone, but no one heeded us. We watched men being brought in and beaten before being flung into other cells. We fought for place on the one stone bench and slipped in the ordure around the corner hole. And every fifteen minutes a church clock boomed the time.

We had no food, no water, for twenty-four hours. We talked in whispers, for whenever we raised our voices a *flic* would dash in among us, belaboring us with his club. Once an old man's glasses were broken, and he wept. Once the door was snapped open and the *flic* yelled, *"Qui est le premier?"* We all shouted that each of us must be the first, supposedly to be freed. But it wasn't that. One after another we were snatched out, and at the porthole we watched the man spread-eagled against the wall by two policemen and beaten with a club by a third. When he fell, he would be tossed back among us, muttering, as ordered, *"Vive la police."*

I was number six. I was beaten. A tooth crunched out. I vomited and said, *"Vive la police."*

We lived in a Goya painting of twisting foul bodies, of hate and hunger, of a listening silence that was almost like a noise when we awaited the quarter-hour strokes of the clock. But there was pity with us, too, when a boy was beaten so badly that his cheek was ripped through to his teeth; the stronger ones on the bench stretched him on their laps and held a cloth to the bleeding wound.

The next night, when our whispered talk had turned to suicide in a crowded cell where there was apparently no means to commit it, the door was whipped open again and we were ordered into the harsh light. Taxis were waiting for us, and out of the money taken from our pockets we paid to be transported to the Palais de Justice on the Ile de la Cité.

One by one we were pushed before a sleepy vulture of a judge. And the awful thing was that we kept saying "Thank you" to everyone who abused us.

"Stand up!"

"Merci."

"Sit down!" With a clack on the head.

"Merci." We were filled with a whimpering gratitude for this moment, no matter how short, of freedom from the dark. The clean faces of policemen were as refreshing as fruit to see.

"You," said the judge. This was I, and I explained that I was an American, a journalist. . . . "Wipe your mouth!" My broken tooth was bleeding.

"Merci."

I was given a slip of blue paper which I had to have translated for me. It stated that I must leave France within three days. Life came into me, and at the risk of anything I shouted, "I'll be back! I'll be back! I love your France!"

And I walked free into a misty morning, a skinny kid in a crumpled black shirt. I walked down the quai beside the wise and tired and gentle Seine to the open flower market, where the perfumes, condensed by the mist, washed the stench of the cell from my memory of it, and the blooms were bright in the darkness I had still to shake away. I could move freely among those smiling merchants who made a place for me, their guest, not hostage. So whimsical is fortune that I, now deported as an undesirable alien, should devote most of my life to France.

There was an old horse in the flower market, and I put my arm around it and laid my face against its bony jaw. I hugged it close, close, loving it, while the blood from my broken tooth ran down its nose.

30

4

The leprechaun, my Uncle Bill—
Suzanne of the gay garret—
I leave through the sunset door

SO I RETURNED to the duress of studies at Harvard, an institute of learning which interested me socially not at all. Fraternities and raccoon coats were abhorrent to me as affectations. Football was a scrambled exhibitionism. I drove from Wellesley to class in my Chrysler roadster, worked hard at metaphysics, which I flunked, at ethics which aided me later in the jungles, and at English composition which was not work but an avocation of my own determined trade. Only one course did I love, the Theme a Day, and that I would recommend to every aspiring author, for it taught diligence in writing, the necessity of organizing into form the nebulae of idle dreams. Writing, I was to learn, was work, and lonely work, and through the happy combination of my social timidity and the aberration of my still not drinking or smoking I achieved a loneliness that was productive of poetry and short stories, some of which I sold. The novel, *Danse Macabre,* remained impaled on the last purple passage written in France.

I became about this time the Tough Poet, writing quite ethereal things which I defended by boxing for the featherweight championship of Harvard. Probably I didn't realize that boxing was a sort of ballet for me, with grace and rhythm, the swinging counterpoint of punches, the exultation that came with the effect, often grisly, of executing a graceful and precise maneuver. But I hated being hurt as I hated hurting the naked flailers who lumbered around before my Art. I hated the stink of dressing rooms. I was nauseated by contact with male flesh. Though we all read Rupert Brooke, I detested his implication of homosexuality, of the "rough male kiss of blankets," and was infuriated with the Freudians who maintained that such a passionate revulsion must indicate a concealed inverse desire.

31

So I became absurdly tough. I wore a derby hat, chewed a toothpick, picked fights along the water front, made love like a madman—or a frightened little boy—and returned with confidence to my poetry or the studios of Uncle Bill and Tommy Atkins.

No two artists could have been more dissimilar. Tommy was a very successful sculptor, short, tough (like me), broad-shouldered, a radical in revolt (like me) against everything, including himself. My uncle Bill was the gentlest and most gallant man I ever knew and, because his example to me was even more important than my father's, I should like to write fully of him here.

My uncle Bill was a leprechaun, a long one, and an artist. He cobbled, as leprechauns do, beneath the great trees which to him were the slightly hostile world. He cobbled his paintings, patched them, repainted them endlessly, and timidly sold them for pots of gold as the leprechauns do their shoes.

You can see him easily, the lank, gray, balding man, his kneecaps so big that they made lumps in his trousers and were hard to sit on when I was young. His white hair was tufted above his pointed ears. His Adam's apple bobbed perpetually, his eyes were spiderwebbed around the corners—because he was always laughing shyly, his chin in his collar and his eyes slanting up at you. He would sedately stop laughing if you looked at him.

He hadn't much of a chin, and his shoulders sloped smoothly to his elbows. He was afraid of loud winds and of the sea, for he had been tubercular as a boy, but even then he had been a terrible fighting man, my father said. When they both were young, and my father, the younger, was bullied by boys at school, Uncle Bill would always arrive, somehow, consider the conflict, take off his coat, fold it carefully, hang it on a fence or a wall or a hydrant, and attack the enemy of my father, his little chin drawn in, laughing.

"Biff! Biff!" my father told me, and a "Boof!" and that was all. Then Uncle Bill, always meticulous, would shake the dust from his coat, put it on and button it, and forcibly lead my father and the enemy to the ice-cream parlor.

I recognized him finally, at about the age of five, for the gentleman he was, the wizard gentleman, when he pressed a dime to my forehead for a minute or two and then asked me to shake it off. The coin was no longer there, of course, but the feeling of it was. I shook my head till it was dizzy, and for my innocence I got two dimes from Uncle Bill.

He was a son, like so many, who devoted and sacrificed his life to his mother. He spent sixty-five years in attendance upon her. There was the *Mayflower* behind her and she couldn't forget it. Her ancestors were her only friends, for none of us were very fond of her. Above her bed, above her pathetic, bitter head, was suspended a little sack containing a hundred dollars to insure her burial.

Grandmother Davis was stark as driftwood. Grandmother Hassoldt was plump and chortling and took her brandy neat. They didn't see much of each other. As a child I was grateful for the shining Lincoln penny which Grandmother Davis gave me on my first birthday, and for the ten shining pennies when I was ten years old, and for the twenty of them, tied up with fancy ribbon, when I reached the age of twenty and had no money at all.

Uncle Bill stayed by her, in the grayest house of Boston. It had sparse little windows, mean, and steep stairs. She was always falling down them, and we would say, "Poor old thing, with her arthritis, bursitis, neuritis, nephritis, she will be better gone to a kindlier land." But she wouldn't. She persisted. She recovered always to invite us to the grayest turkeys and gigantic tough peas on Thanksgiving Day.

Uncle Bill, during these many years, painted landscapes, portraits, and nudes. They were the neatest nudes. They danced through an aspic pastel. I would come to his studio on Boston's T-Wharf and find a live nude on her perch, and Uncle Bill with his left eye modestly shut and his right clamping a smoked monocle, through which he considered his model respectfully. I was too young to know how to do this then. His gentle paintings are in many of our museums, and sometimes they are signed Will R. Davis, sometimes not.

I wanted to become an explorer because I was curious about the people, the weeds, the animals, and the gods beyond my horizons, over the hill, so Uncle Bill and I would set out from Boston like vagabonds, tramping through the good wooded country toward the mountains of Vermont and New Hampshire, thumbing rides along the dull highways.

Uncle Bill didn't smoke—except on Christmas—but he had pockets full of Havana Havanas which he would give to the truck drivers who

33

helped us along. He would pull one from his tweed pocket, holding it as though it might explode, and ask, with his stammer, if the driver, who had been so kkkkkkind to us, would like a ssssssmoke. Then he would search desperately through all his other pockets for his sweet-potato flute, and play it like mad to relieve his embarrassment.

Once we found an abandoned schoolhouse and slept on two shelves of its closet, with the door shut because of the mosquitoes, and in the morning stole the top of the teacher's antique desk because it was wonderfully made of spruce planks two and a half feet wide. There were three planks, and Uncle Bill computed their value at a dollar a foot, sidewise, and so we, or he, dropped seven and a half dollars with a courteous note through the window of the modern schoolhouse in the valley.

The schoolmistress caught us, a long and a little shadow, as we ran down the road in the morning twilight. She was pretty, much too young for Uncle Bill, much too old for me, and spry. She and her tremendous family had a house in these hills, she said. Her husband tended his maple trees. The sap was flowing now, rich and good, into the buckets, and they boiled it in great pans. She took our hands, as she would her scholars', and led us home.

That night we dined on hot maple syrup poured over the coarse country bread, in her shack lit by candles made of bacon fat. I remember that her husband, clean and smartly bearded, who had just arranged five children in a single bed, came into the odorous candle-light saying, "Thieves of good wood are friends of mine."

Our schoolmistress, without a word, gave him our seven dollars and a half and he put them without apology into a book which was called, I think, *Recreations of the Soul*. Uncle Bill drew portraits to give to those nice people. As I was a little less timid I reached up to his shirt pocket for the Havanas. A few years later, when I was those years older, we came back through the mountains to spend a few days with them, and Uncle Bill, as we left, sneaked a bottle of true French Cointreau behind the six books above their fireplace. He scared me because he was trembling so.

Then Grandmother Davis died. She stumbled down the stairs again, and died without pain and politely, as those of the *Mayflower* should.

34

Uncle Bill spent the sinister hundred dollars, hung above her bed, on orchids for her funeral.

And suddenly, at the age of sixty-five, he was free. No one to tell him to turn the front of a nude to the wall. No one to interrupt his painting with cambric tea. No one to ask him unappetizingly at breakfast if he had scoured his old skull with the circular, toothy, Chinese device which he had obediently used these many years, scrubbing his hair away. He didn't brush his teeth with plain soap any more. He didn't write me cramped invitations to adventure on sheets of cheap paper economically torn in half by his mother's fingernails.

His paintings sold profitably, and with the money from them he began to wonder about Mildred whom he had known and loved in art class forty-five years ago. The renaissance of my Uncle Bill appeared when he sent detectives throughout the United States, at a fee which would have killed his mother quicker than the stairs, to find the lovely Mildred Barnes who had painted well and loved him well so long ago. They found her, painting quietly, and very well indeed, living with the memory of Uncle Bill, not far from his grim house in Boston.

So they were married, just before I went to the last world war. My news of them then was tenuous. I had one note from Uncle Bill which was tossed up to me when I was on a camel's back in the Tchad Desert. It said, "You can drown in that damned desert. Me, I'm learning to live in the sea."

And there was a note from my mother saying that Uncle Bill, who had never liked surf bathing, was now plunging through the combers of Rockport, Massachusetts, with no very obvious encouragement from Mildred. He was healthier and happier than ever he had been.

The war went on apace, with Uncle Bill's romance galloping faster than we. Mildred, it seemed, had won his youth again, and she not far younger than he. My camel, meanwhile, developed some illness which made her lose her hair, and I thought of the tortuous device of my lesser Grandmother for the scalp of Uncle Bill. It was just when my cruel saddle was slipping one night over my camel's balder spot that a Senegalese orderly galloped up to me with an unhappy, and still a heartening, note from home.

It said that the tap-dancing lessons, which had always been the desire of my uncle Bill, had been accomplished now. He had started

35

them at the age of sixty-seven, with the sea's salt and with Mildred in his great old heart, and had died happy as a leprechaun in golden shoes.

By my junior year at Harvard I was leading a triple life. Usually I slept at home in the sumptuous Wellesley house looking over the golf course, far over its rolling hills and beyond suburbia. Sometimes I shared the studios which my father and Uncle Bill had taken side by side on T-Wharf. Uncle Bill painted in his. My father sat in his with a rictus of a smile, fighting migraine headaches, dreaming my dreams for me as we watched the gaudy Italian fishing boats returning, singing, crystallized with ice.

"Now there's one that has rounded the Horn," my father would say, gritting his teeth against the pain. "It has been through the straits and —see the patch on that sail?—has suffered the arrows of the Yaghans and Alakalufs of Tierra del Fuego, which Uncle Charles Wellington Furlong has told you about. More probably it's running rum."

My third habitat was a proper poet's garret in Joy Court, Beacon Hill, the Greenwich Village of Boston. This I had rented without even my father's knowledge. It must have been about twelve by twelve feet square, and you couldn't stand up in it without poking your head out the skylight. There was a double bed taking most of the floor, a tiny sink, and a harmonium. My Paris photos were tacked to the sloping eaves. Each Thursday there came here the dozen or so writers I knew, and soberly we read aloud the many vibrant words of our last week's work. Norman Fitts, editor of *S4N*, played the harmonium to accompany old French ballads, while Harold Armitage, a poet who had already sold to *transition*, lay on his belly pumping the instrument, or sat up, silencing us, to recite T. S. Eliot.

There, too, came the poet Suzanne, whom I was to love my life long. Apologizing to Eliot, we read Swinburne and Browning and Conrad Aiken. We wrote poems together, alternately line by line, lay hot together, laughing with love, or climbed from the harmonium through the little skylight to sit, nude and hard as youth must be, beneath the stars over Beacon Hill.

On the roof, in spring, we learned the ardor and tragedy of romance through the lighted window of a tenement opposite where a blowzy

36

wench, the wife of a butcher, made love to another man. As Suzanne's husband was a brute who beat her, we didn't disapprove of this. One night the butcher erupted into the room while his wife and her lover were busy on the couch. He didn't kill the man. He did far better. With his cleaver he severed the uppermost Achilles' tendons of his rival. There was a blur of twisting bodies, and a great screaming, and a few minutes later the awful sound of a man crawling, thump, thump, on his hands and knees through our alley. I rushed down to help him, but the police were there first. The newspapers reported that he would never climb illicit stairs again.

Suzanne's and my love became intolerable. I skipped my classes at Harvard to spend most of my days and half my nights with her, until she would have to return to her baby Donald and the drunken banker who was, after all, her legitimate spouse. He found my letters and threatened murder, and at last, when he was out of town, we decided to drive away forever—to live on God knows what. She had written him that she was going to their summer house in Vermont, that Donald, two months old, would go ahead of her with the governess. Actually she sent the governess to Vermont and kept Donald to go with us.

Suzanne was asleep that hot summer afternoon when I let myself into her apartment with the key she had given me. Baby Donald, naked but for a diaper, lay in his crib. I took off my clothes quietly and lay down beside Suzanne, to sleep a little before our long journey to, I think, Maine. But Suzanne abruptly wakened me, flinging my clothes at me and then Donald into my arms. "Quick, get out! It's Junius! He called from the garage!"

Naked and with my burdens, I climbed into the dumb-waiter which went from kitchen to kitchen the length of the house. Suzanne, struggling into a dress, slammed the door on me. I pulled the rope to descend as I heard the doorbell ringing. There was no time or space to get into even a shirt. I pulled the rope again, and we came to rest at the second floor just as the door to the dumb-waiter was opening. A Helen Hokinson woman, complete with funny hat, stood staring at a naked man sitting cross-legged with a naked baby in his lap. She seemed to have a thick whisky soda in her hand, and she didn't scream but, with a look of some distress, quietly closed the door.

Gently I pulled the other rope and we went up again until I could hear the voices of Suzanne and her husband arguing. Had he beaten her again I would have seemed a fine gallant knight, naked as a worm, coming to her rescue. "All right, I'm off," he shouted before slamming the door. "I'll see you in Vermont tomorrow." And he did.

Wisely or not, in the interest of my writing I played hooky from Harvard in the second siesta of my junior year. My father had given me an ample allowance to pay my tuition fees, on the theory that anyone as impractical as a poet and a potential explorer had better become accustomed to the vagaries of money early in life. But I was more prescient than he thought and for years had been saving a few dollars a month in my bureau drawer. Though I loved my mother, my brother Milton, and my sister Aline, there was gradually growing a tension, for no reason I knew, between my father and me, and I saw that one day soon—but not before I should win the thousand temperance dollars at twenty-one—I should have to go my separate way.

This tension probably was the outgrowth of a terrible night when I was fifteen. I had come home from a dance wearing my first tuxedo, obviously a man grown at last, and proud. My father met me at the door.

"Take off those clothes and come into the bathroom," he said gruffly. Puzzled, I did so and found him waiting with a razor strop in his hands. "You lied to me," he said. "When I went to return your mandolin they gave me a dollar more than you had told me it cost. I don't give a damn whether it came out of your own pocket. It was a lie. I was embarrassed. I told you what I would do if you lied to me. Now take this, and this, and this!"

He slammed me all over the bathroom with the strop, and I was so shocked that I put up no defense against him, though I probably could have knocked him down.

"Coward!" I shouted at him. He flung me from the bathroom, and I spent a wretched night because of the injustice of this beating, because of the inexcusable humiliation to which, denuded of my man's tuxedo, I had been subjected. I would have run away then, but for two cogent deterrents: I hadn't any money, and I knew I would be running blindly into a world which might be just as unpredictable and cruel as my father tonight.

Mother was sitting golden at the piano in the morning, playing softly. She knew. "Bill, go see your dad. He's in bed and miserable."

When I saw him there, a huge man weeping, my hatred changed to pity and I sat by him. He flung his arm around my neck and held me so tight that I didn't know whether it was affection or some new torture.

"Bill, you did a terrible thing to me. You called me—me—a coward. You don't remember the days when we lived in a cold-water flat, and you were then my only child, and I fought for you and your mother. I used to kneel beside your bed and hold your hand until you went to sleep. We had no money and I was not a coward then. . . ."

I was touched, but Christ, why couldn't he say he was sorry for last night? He wanted me to approve of it. He wanted pity now.

Gradually the tension had grown and we laughed no more together and broke no more cut glass on the sidewalk. There was always that shameful night between us. We had to separate, and in preparation for this I no longer paid my tuition to Harvard, but hoarded it carefully. I paid only, and extracurricularly, Professor Thomas Hood for criticism of my writing.

I was now working on a biography of Ambrose Bierce, that trenchant old journalist, purist in English, who found what he called euthanasia in being shot during the Mexican revolutions. I set off from the house in the morning, ostensibly for classes, and went instead to the garret, where I wrote the day through, except for my conferences with Hood and my research in the libraries. Strictly, it wasn't honest, but surely it taught me more about the essential lonely discipline of writing than the required courses of chemistry and mathematics would have done in school.

During this time I made the acquaintance of Rupert, a scientist who was my father's colleague in one of his various ventures: the impregnation of cotton fiber with rubber latex for use as shoe soles, tires, and possibly paving blocks. Rupert was a gigantic worldly man in his middle forties and led a life of what I thought was creative

39

glamour. He kept a plain but brilliant mistress in a quietly lighted apartment adorned with hundreds of photographic nudes. There was nothing erotic about them. Many he had taken himself by a camera he had made without a lens; a minute drilled hole replaced it.

Ruth and Rupert intellectually adopted me, and I found with them a sympathy for my odd ambitions which was warm to my heart. It was stimulating to know that they were so eager to read what I wrote, to see my photographs, to hear my dreams of Africa and the South Sea isles. They were equally interested in my love life, in the very details of it, and as I had never had a chance to talk about this startling volcanic phenomenon, I talked to them boastfully, without thought of spicing their appetites. From time to time they showed me beautifully bound and illustrated editions of pornographic books. I didn't like these and was confused by the feeling that somehow they must be art. After all, James Joyce and Henry Miller were accepted by the intelligentsia.

The climax to this phony friendship, as well as my home life in Wellesley, came on suddenly. I had spent the night at my father's T-Wharf studio and got up early to walk in the fog of the docks, watching the fishing boats come in and go out, and the bright gulls wheeling. There was the mooing of foghorns, the lap of water against the piles. "The fog comes on little cat feet" I remembered from Carl Sandburg, and indeed I was full of poetry, with a sweet nostalgia for my romance with Suzanne, who was still in Vermont. I was wondering whether the ache in my chest was truly physical when I saw a small dark girl leaning against a dock post. She wore an old yellow slicker, a startling contrast to her long black hair.

"I think I was waiting for you," she said in a rich, deep voice, strange for such a little body, and put out her hand to mine. "The fog," she said, "on its little cat feet . . ." She drew to me and kissed me. My head reeled. This was the romance I needed, even though it did smack of the Little Theatre, for it was obviously no tart I held in my arms but a simple and exquisite and intuitive person molding the fog, as I was, into viable substance.

We walked back, not to my father's studio but to my own garret, and spent most of the day simply holding hands and staring like blessed idiots at each other, saying again and again, "This is too glorious to be true. . . ." And what I had never thought possible to happen to me, a platonic and mystic and perhaps foolish love, grew great around us. One day, we said, we would consummate it in sunlight beneath a tree where the wee folk would hum our nuptial song, but there was no physical urgency in this. We rarely even kissed, we were so sick with love.

Though I talked of Rupert and Ruth she did not tell me that she knew them nor, what I learned later, that Rupert, too, had long ago been impassioned by her. I noticed uneasily that my welcome at his house was not quite so cordial as before. He criticized my photos perfunctorily. "Why don't you try nudes?" he asked. "You couldn't have a better model than your sister Aline. I've admired her at the beach."

Aline readily posed for me, wearing a scarf around her loins and balancing a hoop. It was a beautiful photo, and Rupert approved and encouraged others, with an ethereal fair quality which I obtained with lens screens and an opal printing paper.

My term at Harvard, such as it was, came to an end a few days before my twenty-first birthday, and my father invited my friends to celebrate the occasion when I should have my first drink, tobacco, tea, and coffee.

It was an all-male party. My mother and Aline were in Europe. My father, after being assured by most intimate witnesses that I had strangely enough kept the pledge, gave me a thousand-dollar bill, a cigarette, and one of his home-brewed cocktails which he called T.N.T., a sprightly potion which prompted me to stand on my head in the crowded dining room, to show how sober I was. And I coughed pretty good smoke rings.

The first few days of my coming of age went by rather dizzily as I sampled various drinks and tobaccos. One night I received a telegram from my father at the garret. "COME HOME AT ONCE," it said.

My reception at Wellesley was funereal. My father and Rupert, both big men, stood before the fire which cast their titanic shadows from wall to ceiling. God, I thought, somebody is dead; I couldn't know that for them this was I.

"What has happened?" I asked, standing before them, but withdrawn from them, for there was hostility in this shadowed room.

41

Rupert's mustache seemed thicker and longer, dropping, my father's egg-shaped bald pate abnormally high. The cuckoo clock made a sullen sound.

"I would never have thought it of you," said my father.

"Nor I," said Rupert, looking at his slender pointed shoes.

"Thought what, for God's sake?"

Neither of them moved or spoke, apparently waiting for me to recognize some sin. I could think of none. As they both held glasses I went to the desk and served myself a rum, and stood before them again.

"You'll leave my house tomorrow," my father said.

"That I will," I said, "but why, for God's sake, why?"

"Rupert," said my father while Rupert's big body squirmed, "has told me of the pictures you made of Aline."

The choking in me subsided. "What of them, Dad? Do you want to see them?"

"I have found them in your darkroom. I have destroyed them. Can't you realize this incestuous damn thing you've done?"

"Incestuous, great Jesus, did you look at them? And you," I yelled at Rupert, stepping quickly to him, for the rum had warmed me, and I could have taken on both these inquisitors now, "it was your idea that I should have the sweetest body we knew to pose for me. Damn it, neither Aline nor I saw any evil in it."

"Her breasts were exposed."

"And you, Rupert, what the hell business was it of yours to bother my father with what I never could have imagined would bother him?"

Rupert drained his rum rapidly. "I might add that Cecile, whom you met on the docks, has promised me not to see you any more." So that was it. In the shadows were the receding shadows of both Aline and Cecile. The prurient old man smirked behind his mustache.

My head reeled in the red cloud of fury which I hadn't known since childhood, when I had chased Aunt Kate with a log of wood and my brother with an ax. "You treacherous—bastard!" I said to Rupert.

"Enough of that," said my father. "You can have your choice. You can go as far as possible from your sister and Cecile, to California perhaps, or we will have you certified to an asylum."

42

It was incredible. It was ludicrous. I walked out at last through the red sunset door of my own anger.

5 ⌁⌁⌁⌁⌁⌁⌁⌁⌁⌁⌁⌁⌁⌁⌁

Ambrose Bierce—bootlegging on Telegraph Hill—mayhem on a mustache

I WAS ON MY WAY at last, with a few clothes, camera, typewriter, and manuscripts, including *The Shadow-Eater, the Biography of Ambrose Bierce,* half written. The little green car had never run so well, with more enthusiasm than I, despite my freedom. What would I do? How could I live with no training but that of an amateur free-lance writer? In the hot deserts I was cold with anxiety. In the dunes of Nevada I came upon the wreck of two cars with three men dead and a fourth barely living. Putting him across my lap, I drove on wildly again, digging the coagulated blood from his mouth with my free hand. He died before I could reach the doctor of the nearest village.

I drove on frantically through the night, along that tape of desert road, until through exhaustion I began to see the dead man before the headlights, his mouth a gaping red hole, another sunset door to me, the door of death. I would stop, try to sleep, fail to sleep, and tear on through the violet night again until the corpse would return before me. I smashed through it and came over a hill into sunrise.

This was a curiously cathartic experience. The poisons, the fears and self-doubt left me, driven into that red maw of death, and when I reached the enchanting city of San Francisco, I loved it, loved the world, and had even a sort of suspicious affection for me.

It is hard to convince those who do not know San Francisco that there is unmistakably a difference of temperament there in a warmer,

43

quieter, and more trusting people than one finds in the cities of the East. I arrived as a brash kid with the nerve to write a biography of the great Bierce and barely enough money to support myself for the next few months. Within the week I had (1) contracted scabies in my lodginghouse, (2) nearly been raped by a fat female spiritualist, (3) got a sporadic job as book reviewer on *The Argus,* (4) met George Douglas, editor of the San Francisco *Chronicle* and (5) Bert Caldwell of Telegraph Hill.

I went to the office of George Douglas because he had known the literary crowd of San Francisco when it had culturally rivaled Boston. Ambrose Bierce, Jack London, the poet George Sterling had been his cronies, and he took the paternal interest in me that Bierce had taken in Sterling. I was always welcome at his home, and sat in awe and devotion as the old man discussed with flourishes the literature of his generation.

"Ah, the good old days! I was there when Jack ate the live lizard, when Bret Harte ate the tuppenny nail!"

I assumed he felt that we new literary aspirants were something less than the men of old.

The physical charm of San Francisco is that one always has a view of it, looking either up to its residential hills or down to the city and the sea. Telegraph Hill in 1929 was the precinct of poor writers, artists, and the Spaniards who lived in the jerry-built huts looking over the bay. It was honeycombed with speakeasies, chief of which was Myrto's tavern where I met Caldwell, an architect of monasteries, who invited me to share his Spanish shack. This consisted of one L-shaped room with a fireplace set into the inner angle and its walls covered with Chinese gilt paper.

Bert was a plump, jovial character with whom I got on splendidly. He performed his work or pleasure at one leg of the L, I at the other, both of us convening before the fire with the others of the hard-living, hard-working group on the hill. Because we had little money for firewood, we first cut off the lowest step of the back stairs, then the next and the next until we had to jump into the back yard to hack up the fences.

But we lived high and drank well of the gin and sherry we brewed not merely for ourselves but seriously to rumrun to Los Angeles.

44

Ethel had a roadster and a baby who served as sufficient camouflage for our bootleg load. We prospered for a while, and even paid for firewood.

Meanwhile my biography jogged along. I met Ambrose Bierce's most helpful relatives, and George Sterling's innumerable mistresses, each the only one and blowzy now, referring to him ad nauseam as The Master. Charmion London, no longer young, came curvetting on a wild black horse to meet me at her ranch and talk with me of Jack and the suicide he had already suggested in *Martin Eden*.

"It was here on the porch," she said, serving jasmine tea, "that I found him contorted in his last wrestling with the world, Jack who loved the world and hated its puppet people. Here in the Valley of the Moon he renounced us all."

I finished the book, a tremendous documentary job, and had it rejected by a publisher's representative sitting drunk in the bathroom while I paced back and forth in anguish as he flipped over pages. "Fancy writing," he grunted. "Won't do." And reading over my opus until dawn, I knew that he was right. It was verbose, pretentious, slavering. Though it was by far the most complete biography of Ambrose Bierce, filled with anecdotes unpublished and letters given me by his friends, it was a book too adulatory to be good. I had made Bierce, the writer, the soldier, in my own image, but I had learned a great deal from him by studying him and his work so minutely, a way of living life hard but sensitively, and a clean way of death which I should attempt and fail to imitate some years later.

Meanwhile I had to eat, drink, and pay for the merriment of love. My book, conceived and born in exactly nine months, was now a dead duck, especially dead in that another biography, an excellent one by Carey McWilliams, was published just as I was finishing mine. I said, as Ambrose Bierce so frequently did, "Nothing matters," and abandoned literature to muster whatever other money-making talents I had.

So I boxed, for five dollars a bout, win or lose, and this wasn't the boxing at Harvard. I usually lost to the leathery bums who had done little else all their lives. Fighting in carbarns or workmen's clubs, I was sometimes lucky to win an imitation gold watch to pawn for medical expenses. I was an eager boxer, bulging with good will, which

45

was as poor in fighting as it was in writing critical biographies. One of my alternate jobs was posing in the art schools, nude, for a dollar an hour, and I improved on this when some instructor noticed that I had excellent feet. Thereafter I became a footmonger, a specialist with feet, to sit clothed and comfortable with a book while those treasures I hadn't recognized, my feet, were painted. It was like farming out your pet to the movies while you sat back and garnered the fee.

Through George Douglas I got a column in the San Francisco *Chronicle* called "A Book a Minute," reviewing a few books there once a week. The pay was small, but I could sell the new books for about a third of their price. Encouraged by this, I ran an advertisement offering my criticism of young authors' writing. Brash was indeed the word for me, who could scarcely qualify as an author myself, but the manuscripts came in, mostly from country housewives, and were so bad that even I could cope with them.

But my champion job was as a sculptor of death masks, which I became, as I became a writer and explorer eventually, simply by impertinent practice. Jerry Donnelly was one of the good companions who came to the house on Telegraph Hill, to sing like an angel as we bottled gin for our trade downstate. Jerry was a tall pink young man in his twenties who had inherited his father's undertaking business with as few qualifications for it as I had for any of my crafts.

He looked up one night to the wall of our gilt-patched room where the firelight flung the shadows of the andirons, and saw there a life mask in plaster which Uncle Bill had made of me years ago.

"Got it!" he said, thumping down his glass.

"Got what?" asked Bert.

"Money," said Jerry. "Do you remember how your uncle made that mask? Think, Bill, think!"

I recalled that I had been stretched upon a table, my face greased, my eyebrows done up in toilet paper. Straws had been inserted in my nostrils before the moist plaster of Paris had been folded over my face. There I lay for half an hour while a pellet of plaster bobbed up and down in one of the straws. I couldn't quite blow it out without warping the mold which Uncle Bill removed a long while later, pouring into it fresh plaster to make a positive mold and varnishing it. Very simple.

46

"Could you make one?" demanded Jerry. "Look, I've got Italian and Spanish clients who would pay twenty-five dollars for masks of their dear departed relatives. We'll put up a sign: 'Get Your Ghosts Plastered,'" said Jerry.

Here was a new field which sometimes, stumbling over the impediment of words to make a sentence and a living, I regret not having developed further than our initial attempt.

Jerry phoned me in great excitement one night. "Time is of the essence! Get your plaster and vaseline and come hopping. We bury him tomorrow."

"Bury whom?" I wasn't quite awake.

"My Dago. Shot himself in Golden Gate Park. Wife wants a death mask. Thoughtful bugger put the bullet in his heart. Face intact. Come fast!"

One doesn't hop on Telegraph Hill or find plaster of Paris readily at midnight, but in a short time I was at Jerry's Funerary Studio, which was his quaint appellation for it. Even an undertaker can't live on the Hill without going slightly arty. "Most of us," Bert had said once, "can't tell our art from our elbow."

Jerry's "studio" was fairly crawling with cupids. Cupids were his hobby, and friends all over the world collected them for him. He had ancient ones from Renaissance Italy, Surrealist ones made of cubes. Everywhere above and around you in the anteroom were these pudgy little monsters beckoning you to Heaven.

Jerry's voice roared from the back room, the workshop. "Ho, it's Bill! Come in, I've started the plastering!" That he had, with a bottle of my best six-dollar gin and a putrid pipe which half obfuscated with smoke the cadaver on the marble slab. Coughing, I found a chair and a glass.

"Wunnerful model," said Jerry, "big as death and half as handsome. Have a drink, me sonny, and get to work."

I had one and sat on the slab, studying my model. He was a thick-haired, square-headed Italian with only one defect from my point of view as a sculptor of death. He had a tremendous walrus mustache. This, the eyebrows, and the front hair of his crew cut I wrapped carefully in greased toilet paper, then plastered him to the ears.

"He's got time," said Jerry, when we sat down to wait. "Have a

47

gin?" We had a gin and passed the time of night pleasantly with Jerry's reminiscences of cadavers he'd known. One, a Hawaiian hula dancer who had collapsed on the stage, had been carried to him in only her grass skirt. She had come alive when he had been about to give her, rather intimately, the embalming fluid. We drank my bootleg gin and talked of the gaieties of death and sang a sea chantey or two, while the plaster hardened on my model's face.

"Shouldn't it be set by now?" asked Jerry.

"Let's be sure it sets hard. Let's have a gin."

When that bottle was emptied and I was beginning to worry about killing my favorite undertaker and inheriting his business as he had promised me, I lurched to the death mask and began to pry it loose. The side came up, the top and bottom, but the center was firmly fixed by the mustache.

"Jeez," said Jerry, "that walrus! We're in for it now." We tugged and pried with his mortuary instruments, but the mask held fast in the middle. "Let's think and have a gin," he said, knocking off the neck of a new bottle against the marble slab. I made a note to rectify my ingredients, for this one did smell very much like Jerry's embalming fluid.

"Heroic measures!" said he, lunging at the patient corpse. "Heave-ho!" said he, shutting his eyes and pulling at the mask. It came off, and half the mustache with it.

This was sobering. Most of that night we spent digging mustache from that mask and sticking it back on the corpse with rubber cement. By morning our customer was presentable, and I had molded and varnished a positive mask which delighted his wife and earned us twenty-five dollars.

By now I had fought everybody in San Francisco who was willing to break my nose again. The art market had had a surfeit of my feet. Ambrose Bierce, in my effigy, was still making the hopeless rounds of publishers, and I had achieved no fame as a death-mask maker, though I did improve my gin.

There were two things left to do before my money ran out, get a regular job or a ship to Tahiti. The only advertisement that seemed promising requested a writer at $3.60 a day. I should have assumed

48

that there might be a turnover weekly, or more often, of personnel, but I went to the address given and found it to represent *Who's Who In America*. From a dozen applicants I was taken, on the strength of my published book reviews and probably the fact that I seemed to be the only writer who had brushed his teeth.

Immediately I was placed at a long table with nineteen others and given the homemade biographies of *Who's Who* characters to rewrite intelligibly for inclusion in the book. At the end of an hour I was chafing under this drudgery. At the end of the day, having completed the only day's office work I was to do in my life, I collected my $3.60 and resigned. "Thank you also," I said, "for having made up my mind for me. I'm off to the South Seas next week."

The rewarding sequence of this occurred many years later, when for some time my name, too, had been included in *Who's Who*. I had written the annual revision of my listing and in a moment of whimsey had written on the back of it, "Dear colleague: Once I sat at your desk, rewriting as you do the biographies of people who have achieved a certain notoriety in their work. One day of it sufficed me, and I went to Tahiti the following week. Boats with third-class passage still leave once a month, I believe. Best wishes."

Six months later I received a postcard from Tahiti. "My dear savior," it said. "Thanks to you I made it, and oddly enough I'm writing a book. As my name, too, is Davis I hope we shall meet as neighbors in *Who's Who* before too long."

6 ∿∿∿∿∿∿∿∿∿∿∿∿∿∿∿

*To Tahiti with love—the eels
with ears—ghosts follow me*

I SAID GOOD-BY to everyone and spent a week in
bed recovering before suddenly discovering my presence on the high
seas, with all bridges burned behind me. I had sold my car, my
other suitcase, and a poem for third-class passage to a world without
a roof.

Tahiti seemed to sink from the clouds as we came to meet it on an
early morning, withdrawing its great peaks of Diademe and Orohena
from the pink and silver sky. To our starboard rose the serrated
crags of the island Moorea, which was the Omoo of Melville, and
slowly, as we slipped through the pass in the foaming coral reef, another island, a mere fragment of sand and palms, detached itself from
Papeete, the port. This was Motu-uta, where the royal belles of ancient
Tahiti repaired occasionally to bleach their skins beneath its shadows.

Scenically Tahiti was no disappointment. I adapted myself very
well to it in a hut whose floor boards were so rotten that I didn't
trust a bed upon them. Gingerly I would pace across them and make
a leap into the hammock where a lovely lass named Tiare was already
installed.

Papeete now is a compromise. It is not the town of gay laughter
and beauty which the Spaniards discovered in the seventeenth century, of which Captain Cook, that dear varlet, later told so pleasantly.
There is laughter, but the tone of it has changed; it is cynical, embittered. On the southern part of the figure-eight-shaped island, on the
Presqu'ile, there still exists shyly somewhat of the primitive charm
for which all voyagers hope, but even here it is sullied by the frowzy
plantations of the white man. Papeete itself is colorful and cosmo-
politan, with the brilliant glint of rot that is seen upon many moldering
things. It has the charm of its vices and the pathos of its tourist-
beaten beauty, but with acquaintance more than the superficial even

its vaunted vices become rather drab to a young man of twenty-one. There is little for its populace to do but work lazily and drink and make love, and none of it is done well. The sinister coconut radio of gossip buzzes back and forth as in any East Burlap of America. Your secrets are known, relayed, corrupted before you have even formed them. There are the same political squabblings and social knifings in the back.

Every noon, with the sun glaring hot and pitilessly down upon Papeete's pettiness, I vowed to move by the next boat to the outer islands, Maupiti, Huahine, the Tuamotus, and every night I vowed to stay forever, here in my rotted hut with my trim trollop. When by some subtle alchemy the day's brass was changed to the silver of night, I went with Tiare for long walks about the town, wandering up little back streets past the open doors of houses from which plaintive singing and the thrumming of guitars flowed liquidly to dissolve in the night. We walked hand in hand beneath the slim arcs of coconut trees and the tangles of hibiscus, while the flowers fell twisting like ghostly pinwheels to the ground and the dark was redolent with them.

"Do you love me still?" Tiare asked. "I am so old now. In another month I shall be eighteen. Will I have many presents and some dollar bills so I won't be too unhappy?" More than anything, then, I loved her mercenary little self. She would run from me to hide in a thicket and when I caught her, with her shoulders to the earth, she would have woven fireflies in the mesh of her black hair.

Unsteadily on our feet again, we would pass groups of singing Tahitians who would call to us, *"Maitai oe? Are you well?"* or *"Haere oe hieh? Where are you going?"*, but seeing the live jewels in Tiare's hair they would know we were lovers and laugh us on our way. We would walk along the water front, stopping to shine the flashlight at the marvelous fishes of sapphire and yellow spinning belly up like the native girls for no reason of locomotion but simply for the fun of it.

It is a very odd horror which nice civilized people have for the phrase "going native," a horror which is baseless and mistaken and slightly prurient. No, you haven't gone native any more than you might have gone French in France or gone peasant in the rural hills of Ireland, adapting yourself to the customs of the autochthonous peoples and trying not to make yourself obvious by being different from them. If you are interested in the Tahitians and wish to know them as well as a white man may, you certainly live among them in a house like theirs, eating food like theirs (though it may gag you), taking unto you a girl of their race (though she will probably milk you dry).

You wore a *pareu* when indoors and white ducks when out. You drank the illegal orange beer or a sort of honey mead. You did not, of course, go barefoot in town or become as drunk as your neighbors, or worship graven images. You lived sensibly and quietly and, above all else, unostentatiously.

Two men whom I was to love and revere in Tahiti were Charles Nordhoff and James Norman Hall. They were poor at the time, for *Mutiny on the Bounty* had not yet been written. Both aces in the Lafayette Escadrille, they had come to the islands when the first war ended, married girls from the upper-crust Tahitian families, and built houses on opposite sides of town. Each morning, like disciplined commuters, they rode their bicycles to their halfway office and sat down to write, Nordhoff doing one chapter, Hall the following, then each polishing the other's script until the style of it was harmonious. They knew better than the schooner captains the outer islands, as far away as Pitcairn, and it was always Hall's project to write for once a book independent of Nordhoff, *An Adventure in Solitude*. He knew an exquisite island—no, he wouldn't tell me where—which had not a person on it, and there he would like to spend three months alone living by his wits and with the dreams he found in them.

"Nevair," said his wife Sarah, serving the rum punches, "until he gives me the automobile and the radio for my company." Both of these Jimmy detested as impingements upon his self-sufficiency. He and Nordhoff were the warmest and gentlest of men, constantly beset by young writers like me whom they would counsel and encourage. When I showed my *Danse Macabre* in progress to Nordhoff, he said discreetly, "Maybe it isn't as good as you will write sometime, but somebody has got to buy it! Think of all those words for two dollars and a half!"

It was in Papeete, on the aromatic veranda of Sophie's ramshackle hotel, that I first met Bob Flaherty who was justly known as the father of the documentary film, for he had already made *Nanook* and *Moana*. Now with Fritz Murnau he was to film the beautiful *Tabu*. He had come on ahead to seek actors and locations. Driving the biggest car on the island, he would load it with a dozen fair candidates and spin at a tremendous clip to the black laval beaches where, a rubicund and cherubic figure surrounded with bottles, he would put the girls through their paces. I was enchanted by his explorations in the Far North, his ethnological researches in Samoa. That was the life for me, and the life that mine became, due largely to the inspiration of Robert Flaherty. Twenty years later he introduced me and my films at the Screen Directors Guild and the Explorers Club.

"You want adventure? You want beauty?" Bob asked me once. "There is an island named Bali in the Dutch East Indies. So far it is practically unspoiled. But get there quick before another old beachcomber like me gets his film made. He is Andre Roosevelt." Andre became the other mentor of the two who shaped my career at the pliable age of twenty-one.

I fished for my supper as did the natives, with diving goggles and a simple spear, for this was long before the popularity of skin diving. Only a few feet below the surface of the lagoon you could see the blue and yellow and scarlet coral, unimaginably gorgeous. There were fantastic castles of coral, jagged mountains of it; there was coral that seemed to be monstrous filigree and embroidery woven by the shuttling of fish through it. Shaped like wedges, hearts, daggers, colored every hue of the spectrum, the fish swam lazily before your nose.

Once I met another diver under water, hiding on the other side of a coral buttress. He smiled as well as one could and put out his hand to shake mine. We lunged together to the surface.

"*Iaorana,*" I said. "My name is Davis."

"Mine is Gauguin, Paul."

The son of the painter Paul Gauguin lived like any native in a simple hut, undecorated by a single example of his father's work. "The popaa, the white people, came in after my father's death," he said, "and offered my mother as much as three dollars for a little scrawl he had made for me. The last we knew of in Tahiti was done on the glass of a hotel bathroom door. Somerset Maugham bought it, probably for the sixpence in the title of his book. *Ita pea pea!* What the hell! We still have the moon!"

In the evenings, in our hut on the sea, Tiare and I would hear happily the whistle of Uncle pedaling down the road on his high bicycle. Uncle was an ancient and wizened American Negro whose chief occupation now was the making of pies and imaginary love. He had been everywhere, done everything. He had been a boxer in Siberia, a poet in Chicago, a pimp in China. He had traveled for years with circuses and still occasionally gave stilt-dancing exhibitions at native festivals. He was respected by everyone for it was thought he had occult powers and could cure fe-fe, elephantiasis, and coconut, gonorrhea, and could raise the dead. His debut in Tahiti thirty years before had been sensational. Arriving from California, where he had had a thriving bootblack business, he set up a very throne of a shoeshine chair in the market place. It was a splendid thing of brass and glossy leather, and despite his first disappointment that white men wore canvas shoes or sandals and dark men none at all, he waited patiently like a king on his throne until some imaginative native offered him a franc to sit in it while his girl walked by.

Quick as a wink Uncle whipped out his brush and shoe unguents and polished the young man's feet to a gleaming brown. Whisk, whisk, he went, and the client giggled as it tickled. Such resplendent feet had never been seen before in Tahiti and Uncle said modestly, "That will be one more franc, please."

The vendors of fish and fruit and vegetables came flocking then to sit in Uncle's throne high up above the crowd, while their huge, flat, calloused, spatulate feet were made to glow. The mode lasted a month or so, with natives padding in from as far away as Tautira to be king for ten minutes and mince home on polished feet.

Then Uncle was advised by a colleague in the States that there was a gross of no longer fashionable brown derby hats for sale cheap. Uncle imported them, modeled them in the market place, and sold every one. The good natives must have been handsome in their pareus, polished feet, and brown derby hats. This traffic gave Uncle sufficient funds to set up his pie shop.

As we sat on my veranda, smeared with papaya pie, the neighbors

54

gathered around us, in awe of the great lies which Uncle told so well. "... yes, and so I pulled the rope out of the well on the fourth day. There was a crowd of Malays at my back, each one with a kris, a long knife. The Sultan, damn his guts, was there, too, and he told me (there, there, little Tiare, what are you looking so sad about, me?) and he told me, the Sultan did, that if I didn't catch the Thing this time he was going to use me (my, but you're a well-built little gal... young Davis doesn't merit you) for bait himself. And so I pulled and pulled, and the rope was heavy at the end, and at last, b'God, I pulled the Thing up. It was awful; I tell you it was something frightful (now, now, don't be shy, ain't you more cozy with my arm around you?) to look at, and the Thing was all swelled up like an octopus, with rubbery feelers and five red eyes on the top of its head. We got it killed after a while, and zowie! its belly was full of pearls (come on now, be a good girl and come with Uncle; I'll give you a pie *full* of pearls)."

There was peace for me in Tahiti, and good companionship. I wrote poetry without a thought of selling it, for the sea was as full of fish as I with love, but gradually Bob Flaherty's ferment began to bubble in me and I began to dream of farther islands. Tiare, knowing my need to be sometimes alone, sent me off on therapeutic adventures. I climbed to Lake Vaihiria, high in the mountains. It lies encircled goldenly by orange trees, and from its depths rise ghosts and *tupaupaus* that are most wisely left alone when the sun sets over its rim at four in the afternoon.

Giant eels with ears live in it. The gills at least look like ears. The legend of it is that many years ago there lived a tribe on this lost lake, a strange people unlike the other Tahitians, a dark and evil people. The king, who was known everywhere as a great magician, became tired of his wife and took unto him the wife of a neighbor. One night when these two were together they heard a sound outside the hut. The king rushed out and found there his old wife and his mistress's young husband, with their ears pressed tight against the bamboo wall, listening. The king was furious, of course, in the way of righteous men, and changed them both into large eels with enormous flapping ears, and threw them into the lake, vowing that their children and all their children's children should be like them.

I brought back one of these monstrous eels to Tiare, who screamed and flung it into the sea. "You don't know what you've done," she cried. "The tupaupaus will get us now and, my God, it's the third night after the full moon, *their* night tonight."

No old-timer of the islands will scoff at the tupaupau as an ignis fatuus or will-o'-the-wisp. Every old-timer, every missionary, will admit on the evidence of his own senses that there are extra-normal happenings here which he cannot explain. There was a magnificent house, built by a white trader over an old graveyard, which had killed one member of every family that had lived in it for generations. There is the abandoned House of the Stones where I once spent a night. In the middle of the night pebbles began flicking from wall to wall, though all the thatch windows were shut. The old-timers knew the house quite well ("It's just haunted, old boy,") and averred that my particular pebbles were found only on the other side of the island.

On the night of my return from Vaihiria I slept well and dreamed of nothing more disturbing than that I soon must set out in quest of new islands at the earth's end. Then into my dreams there came music, faint at first, that gradually grew louder until I wakened. But still there was music, a strange whining tune such as the Tahitians, as reported by sailors, used to make on their nose flutes a hundred years ago.

Tiare, shaking, and I rocked out of the hammock. There was no sound. I put my ear to the canvas and it returned distinctly. Only through the hammock could it be heard.

"Look," I said boldly, "there must be a hymine, song fest, nearby, and the vibrations are caught in the cloth. You know, when you put your ear to a railroad track—"

"What's that?" asked Tiare reasonably.

The nearest hut was half a mile away, and there was no light anywhere other than that of the full moon. I looked again. There were *two* of them, two full moons, and the larger one was moving slowly down the mountain, following closely the path I had taken from Vaihiria. Holding a hard grip on my sanity and trying to remember how many rums I had had before dinner, I walked to the nearest hut and dragged the Australian, Bobby, from bed.

"I've got a tupaupau," I told him.

"Don't bring it in here!" yelled Bobby, trying to crawl under the mosquito net again.

"No you don't. You come with me. You say you've seen them. This one is musical." We marched back to the house, and there was my tupaupau, all right, balancing in all its golden glory upon a nearby palm.

"Well, what do you think of it? It isn't the moon, as you see. Over there's the moon."

"Nervy blighter. Son, I'm going back to dear sane old Australia by next boat. Two tupaupaus in a month is an epidemic to me."

The weird globe had now slid down the trunk of the tree and approached us so closely that we could discern the form of it, a round luminous mass shading to blue at the edges. We could hear the whining now, asthmatic and sibilant. It hovered for a moment, expanding and contracting slightly—breathing, you would say—then slowly withdrew up the mountainside and disappeared.

"He's got his bloody eye on you," said Bobby as he started off homeward. "He's looking you over. You ain't been up to any hanky-pank with the native customs, have you?"

"Ee-yah!" Tiare howled.

7 ∿∿∿∿∿∿∿∿∿∿∿∿

*Fiji, Australia, Celebes—shark in
the night—the lost Roosevelt of Bali
—the quicksands of Mont St. Michel*

SUDDENLY I WAS on a ship again, and Tiare and
Tahiti had been kissed good-by. I had in my pocket a startling letter
from my father, saying that he missed me, that Rupert had turned
out to be a scoundrel, that here enclosed was a modest letter of
credit which I should use as sparingly as possible on a trip around
the world. Travel the hard way, he advised, and see more. Write, and
earn as much of your deck passage as you can.

There was a great fellow, I thought, to admit tacitly that he recognized some injustice in my being flung out of home; and my old love
for him wished that he might be with me on the road to adventure
now.

I traveled deck among the Annamites, stopped at Fiji to do a
monograph on a group of ancient petroglyphs, cut down to Australia
to sell it for enough shillings to take me nearly to the Celebes in the
Java Sea, deck passage still, sleeping in my hammock (ah, where
was Tiare sleeping now?) amidst a populated rainbow of Malays, with
their brilliantly batiked sarongs, their babies, their gaudy parrots.
I must get to Bali, to Bali soon.

But there was Macassar in the Celebes first, among the Spice
Islands, where the Dutch and the Spanish and the Portuguese had
fought for herbal jewels as precious as gold, where there still were
marble mansions sinking into the muck of swamps.

I slunk from shadow to shadow in the lilting littered streets, waiting for a boat, eager to stay, to go on, to live as vitally as these hot
people, to die, like Conrad's Lord Jim, in the great opulence of spirit
that was theirs, panting behind their bullocks, puffing to their temple
heights.

Of one shop, in the saddest slums of the city, I was particularly fond. The proprietor, an ancient Chinese, had for many years sold nothing but beer and arrack to his customers. Recently, however, he had expanded, moving the "beer-garten" to a tiny windowless concrete room in back and filling the shop with a really notable display of made-in-England chamber pots. He had salvaged a shipload of them and was exploiting them in the manner of Uncle's derby hats in Tahiti. Macassar was going wild over chamber pots. They were the rage, the mode, the *passepartout* in sophisticated society. Macassar had become pot-conscious overnight. If you didn't have a made-in-England pot, one worthy of display, your reputation wasn't worth a damn.

To get out of the heat of 105 to 115 degrees I made it a daily custom to visit this wizened purveyor of social luxuries, to watch some young bucko, perhaps a connoisseur, weighing a pot in each hand, appraising them, clinking a gold ring against them to test their tone. Or there would come a young girl who liked her pots tinted, and would arrange a dozen of them in a row along the counter, to compare the color schemes of this golden one, say, which was striped pink inside, with this black one (perhaps for mourning) which had a painted rose within it. And here would come the aged dandies who didn't trust these newfangled contrivances but who nonetheless, if society so decreed, must have them. They usually bought the ones with two handles.

It was with some difficulty that I proved by purchase that I was sociably eligible for the crowd in the little back room where the heat couldn't reach me. It was a murky den, blue with smoke, raucous with argument, jammed with Dutch officials and high-caste Malays, and containing, to the best of my perception in the half-darkness, no means of ventilation other than that afforded by the quickly swung bartender's door. Ventilation was sacrificed to temperature.

It was not in the Governor's Palace but within the four blank concrete walls of this room that the affairs of Celebes were settled. This room was the fetid heart of Celebes, from which, upon waves of München beer and Dekuyper gin, the executive pulses sounded. The native and the white man met amicably here, on a parity of pots.

You sat here, with your beer or gin or whisky soda, listening to such racket as you never imagined beyond the clubroom of Babel.

59

Large Dutch faces swung through the smoke, mouths askew, roaring. Lean faces of Malays, hinged to the table top, nodded periodically in deference if not agreement. Chinese faces, like stoic masks, drifted through the swirling lamplight. You saw hands, seemingly detached from their invisible bodies, lifting glasses to what seemed the mouths of other men.

"*Apa mau minum?* What will you drink? It's hot outside."

"Shark fight tonight," said someone. "Cinema's too hot."

We sat and shouted around the table, eating ya-ko-mein and sati as our supper. Sati, which doubtless means molten lava in Malay, consists of chunks of pork or goat on sticks anointed with soya and Lombok pepper sauce. You hold the stick erect before you, so that the sauce can run down, and bite off the uppermost sati. This, the first bite, would boil the saliva of a Mexican, but as you progress downward along the stick from sati to sati that is progressively more hot with the settling of the sauce upon it, and when you swallow at one fell desperate gulp the last ardent tidbit, you drink many a whisky soda, not caring a damn whether or not they are tepid.

One of the merchants packed us into his car and we drove to see the shark fight at Agoeng on the edge of town. Already a crowd was gathered upon the shore, around a twenty-foot-square coral tank which had been built in the harbor. Rows of lights upon the four walls of it illumined a gray darting body within, a six-foot shark. Our old Chinese was passing a chamber pot for money.

"Secareng! Now!" called a voice, and a lean but well-built young native pushed through the crowd. He stood for a moment on the edge of the tank tying up his sarong into a sort of swimming tights, stretching the muscles of his arms and back so that they resembled small snakes twitching beneath the skin. He looked around him. "*Made Rei, dimana?* Where are you, Made Rei?"

"*Sayha dateng.*" A pretty Javanese girl stepped from the crowd. The boy spoke to her softly, touched her hair, and exchanged his small knife for her large one.

We watched with held breath as he slipped into the tank with that furious creature that had been starved for days. We saw the flash of a fin, zipping like a buzz saw. We saw the boy dive deep while the shark churned the water to froth in its effort to find him.

60

Round and round the brown body and the gray one plunged, playing hide-and-seek, swimming a dance of death. I saw that the boy's whole effort now was to keep the shark's back turned toward him, for the mouth of the shark is underset and it cannot bite without turning its belly to its victim. When the shark rolled mouth upward, the boy dived beneath.

It was a beautiful exhibition of gladiatorial courage, to which we cheered as weaklings cheer any battle which they are personally too craven to join. We yelled for blood. This was grimmer than a bullfight. The boy was tiring and it was time, now or never, for him to ride the shark, and kill it.

The boy heard the cry of the crowd and laughed; he glanced once at little Made Rei on the shore, then set to business. The shark shot toward him across the tank and, as it rolled belly up, the boy dived beneath it. We could see a dark whirling in the depths of the pool, then the surface was streaked with crimson. Blood. Was it the boy's or the shark's? We leaned far over the edge, shouting hysterically.

The water split wide as the figures smashed up through the surface of it, and we saw now that the boy was riding the back of the shark and that the blood had come from the ripping of his leg along the sandy hide. For a minute or so the crazed monster darted and rolled, swerved viciously, leaped clean from the water and plunged, while its rider clung to it, the long knife raised. Then there was a greater convulsion, too swift for the eye to follow, and the pool became a well of bubbling crimson. The game was over; the shark was dead; and little Made Rei was calmly helping her bloody lover to shore.

Boeleleng, the northern port of Bali, gave little promise of the beauty which began immediately beyond its shattered temples and Armenian shops. Up into the mountains I was lugged in a native lorry and deposited aching at the Kintamani pass where I ate ancient Chinese eggs and raw heart of palm. It was sunset. Far below and ahead was a tiny village of crazy-quilt roofs, some of them purple, some black, and one of new thatching that was still a dirty ochre. From among them, clearly and richly, came the gong notes of a gamelan, a Malay xylophone, pushing gently with dull points of tone through the fog that veiled the valley rice fields and hushingly swathed the town. It was a melodic but doleful magic, as though for the quieting of convalescent gods.

A group of Balinese passed us leading heavily laden small horses, the women pacing stolidly on mountain legs, nude to the waist, bearing on their heads great mounds of rice. It is because of their straight posture necessitated by these head loads that Balinese women have the most beautiful breasts in the world. Now twenty years later the Indonesian government has decreed that they be covered with the blouse-like badjoe.

Again we started, and by now it was dark with the intermittent sprinkling of rain on the lorry roof. We roared rocking into the valleys, and the rain suddenly heaved down upon us. The men jumped out of the truck and attempted to fasten the flapping curtains. It was like doing calisthenics in a cataract. The little Balinese women laughed and chattered as they were drenched. Those prim ones who wore blouses took them off to put over their heads, and we all stripped down, and in the red glow of cigarettes sang sadly the wailing songs of Bali. Thunder plunged howling down the sky. The windshield was splotched lavender with lightning, but we rocketed along, empty of stomach but cheered by the lights of Den Pasar.

It was Andre Roosevelt who dislodged me from a crevice in the Chinese boardinghouse which was the best I could find. This Roosevelt, this cousin of old Teddy, this astoundingly gifted black sheep, was born in France and lived a life as checkered as a paddy field. He won championships as an athlete in both Europe and America. He had grown rice without profit in Texas. He was a bluff man of little patience, immense vitality, buoyant enthusiasm, and the endearing capacity for wonder and surprise that children and true explorers have. When he heard, as few people had in 1929, least of all Thomas Cook, that there was an island named Bali in the Malay Archipelago, that it was unique among the many islands of this chain, he rushed off to find it. Scientifically his imagination was piqued by Wallace's Line, which divided Asiatic from Australian fauna between the adjacent islands of Bali and Lombok; they were utterly different in a

62

few miles' space, tigers on one side, giant Komodo lizards on the other. Aesthetically he was lured by tales of the most beautiful scenery, temples, music, dancing, women in the world, and he was not disappointed. He rather neglected the fauna.

He spent five years on the island with little money but the dream currency of sometime making a motion picture there. And eventually his daughter Leila and her husband Armand Denis came out to join him in the production, on a shoestring, of the film *Goona-Goona,* on which I, too, worked later.

On Andre's advice I took a house in Kedaton with a gloomy neurotic writer named Jeff who, although a competent author of Western stories, had fled here to write a psychological novel. We were equipped with two serving girls, Marini, eighteen, and Rinpiog, fourteen. Our concrete mansion had been the residence of an Ida, a high priest, before he died and was removed to a tomb in the back yard, where he was to wait until a suitable mass cremation occurred. Surrounding the house was a garden of orchids, surrounding the garden was a tropical orchard, and surrounding the orchard was an actual moat in which the water flowed green and venomous. We were wellnigh impregnable but for the ghost of the second wife of the corpse in the back yard. We met her soon.

The gray lizards wriggled over our floor, watching us with brilliant wise eyes which must have divined our moods and our secrets. A huge tokeh lizard in the next kampong, or village settlement, blah-blahted seven times which meant good luck. There was a welcome wind in our garden, a wearied wind out of Asia, which tossed the orchid blossoms to and fro as if tolling from them a music inaudible to our obtuse Western ears. And I knew how relative a matter was beauty, and how its only appreciation was by those who were alien, as we were alien, to it. Little Marini, who lived in its envelopment and bore the pulse of it in her blood, neither knew of it nor cared.

"Listen," I said, "the water circling through the moat makes a pleasant sound, don't you think?"

"*Tida! Buang ayer darah!* Why no! It is full of dysentery!" said Marini. Then she turned to explain at last to Jeff's wooing that, since Rinpiog was still under age, she, Marini, would divide her nighttime

63

services between us. That would be a guilder, or forty cents a week, more.

On any day the streets of Bali were festive. The files of market maidens came swinging from the woods, bearing temple offerings upon their heads or simple produce for the market which was just as beautifully arranged. Behind a lattice of shadow on every road were the gray piles which were the fabulous Balinese temples, devoted to a combination cult of Hindu polytheism and Malay animism. But they were empty temples, courtyards whose walls were intricately sculptured to the gods' terrible heads, of Garuda, the bird, and Durga, goddess of terror and death, of Bormah, the giant whose legs straddled the archway, and Brachma and the goddess of rice, Batara Istri.

The market was the secular temple, a riot of strange folk, a jumble of color, a hashing of tongues beneath the square batik parasols that tipped toward the sun. In less crowded corners were rings of squatted men gambling for corroded brass coins, betting on the number of them that was in a closed fist. Everywhere sounded the kachik-kachik of ice being grated for drinks, and suffocatingly about you was the shuffling, the panting of sarongs on the hot thighs of the Balinese.

An old herb doctor perched sedately as a mandarin behind his terrifying paintings of what would certainly happen to you if you ignored his prescriptions. Spread thickly beneath every parasol were curious fruits, the grapelike langsap, the spined and stinking durian, the applelike mangosteen with seven snow-white pips which were cool to suck under the hottest sun. Bottles of the native drink, toeak, burned orange with the reflected sun within it.

"Could I sell you a fairy tale?" asked a sweet voice in English behind me. Sitting on the ground with a pile of oranges before her was a blond American girl. "Have a seat. Help me sell these. Your name is Davis, of course, and mine is Julia Adams. Boston, too."

"What the devil are you doing here?" Her face was freckled and her nose turned up.

"Odd business," she said, "quite odd for Boston. I collect exotic fairy tales. Write 'em. Sell 'em sometimes, and sometimes have to sell

64

the oranges from my garden or the fish from my sea to make ends meet." Her eyelids crinkled into little slits of laughter.

"Do you know a tale of elves," I said eagerly, "which I just heard yesterday?"

"But I want to tell you mine!"

She did and I did, and people bought the oranges without consulting us, throwing a coin to our cross-legged laps. We were holding hands now like children in that kaleidoscope of a sun-stifling market, interrupting each other.

"I can juggle oranges," I said. I had learned this in Tahiti where one of the sensible courses in the schools was for coordination. There was scarcely a scholar who couldn't juggle at least three oranges at a time. So I juggled oranges, and the crowd collected about us, and we sold them all.

"You'll come home and help me pack," said Julia. "I'm leaving for Paris tomorrow."

"Julia, you can't."

The gaiety, the nonsense had gone out of us as we walked slowly through the fairy world of the temple market. The world of Boston was far from us until suddenly and properly I was bitten by a horse.

You must get on, said my conscience, you must get on or be mired in the hot beauty here, writing a page a day at dawn, protracting siestas nearly until dark and the gamelans call you to another Legong or Djanger dance, wrapping night and music and lust around you as a baffle to your own world. This is euthanasia. Get on to Paris and Julia and juggle your oranges of phantasy with her. If you don't, you're sunk, you're sunk.

I sat on the terrace looking through a ravaged garden, for the locusts had come this week and we had spent it imprisoned while the smashed and smashing small bodies mottled our windows. When we went to the well for water, it was all we could do to fight our way against the billion insects which battered and burst upon us. Those were nightmare journeys, in which we staggered through a world unrecognizable. It was streaked and flickering like a sick television screen.

Marini and Rinpiog were sweeping the debris of corpses from the veranda when the gongs began lugubriously in a neighboring kampong, a thanksgiving, Marini explained, for the end of the terror. I should have been writing but I sat in apathy. I must get away, but I was ashamed to leave Bali, like a mistress whose charm was gone, even though I knew that with the briefest of tropical rains she would be as though by magic rejuvenated. There was the trouble; she was a mistress stronger than I.

I tried to continue reading *Tristram Shandy* but it was no use. It was impossible to concentrate on Sterne's subtleties with that gong punctuating them like a comma more cogent than the text.

"Something eating you, Bill?" said Jeff, fishing a locust from his drink.

"Me." I got up, threw my drink into the garden, and wandered off to follow the gong beats past clamorous kampongs and fields of rice which were ruined and piteously stirring in the thick night wind. Past the stinking Cave of the Sacred Bats I walked and through a dimly lighted gate in a mud wall, and there we all were, we worshipers, the gamelan orchestra, the white-and-black-swathed dancers, the old men chanting together beneath a contorted great banyan tree, the gods. Incense lay heavily upon us like a pall.

The girls in tall, tinkling headdresses danced three at a time, weaving in geometrical patterns through and around each other, their faces as expressionless as masks. Each bore a pot of flowers or smoking incense held high before her. Suddenly they would turn on the gong note and stride off to a little temple. After making their offerings they would slip back again into shadow while other groups took their place. Constantly the old men moaned and the gamelan played softly. Four women on a high roofed platform beckoned to me. I climbed up and sat among them, drinking arrack with them as we watched the ritual. One made a fire of coconut husks and roasted paper-thin wafers of beaten rice.

Gradually the crowd increased, squatting before the little temple. All eyes were upon an old pedandah, a priest, and a boy of about twenty who sat in the front row, their hands lifting now and again to flutter over a large pot aflame with incense. The dancing girls were changing; they were becoming older than they should be to dance the Legong or Djanger, and soon the crones of the kampong were

66

dancing, trying to remember the lost steps and forgotten graces with which they had formerly charmed the gods.

"It is the invocation of the goddess Durga," a woman whispered to me, "Durga, the goddess of madness and sudden death. Look."

The old priest and the boy in the front row were trembling. Their eyes were closed and their heads tipped back in a state of true trance. Their entire bodies shook as the goddess filled them and possessed them. Suddenly the priest screamed and flung himself into the crowd, and as if in defense of them, a man swathed in black scarves danced from the temple door and circled him. The priest snarled like an animal, his mouth slobbering, and slid on his belly toward the dancer, recoiled and leaped again, catching a foot which he tried to tear with his teeth. He darted insanely about the abandoned space, intent upon carnage.

His adversary, the interpreter of the gods, called out loudly to Durga, and the woman beside me translated: "Why do you afflict us so with locusts? Why do you thus torture our priest?"

And Durga answered aptly through the slobbering lips of the madman, "Why do you bother me with your prayers? Have I not been good to you? It has been very long since your island suffered misfortune. Why do you bother me?" The priest leaped into the air and fell back to earth on his head. And after a moment the goddess spoke again, demanding food.

The interpreter rushed forward and broke an egg into the old man's slavering mouth, pushing it in with a stick, then gave him arrack from a banana-leaf cup. The priest reeled to his feet and fell fainting into the arms of Durga's dancer, who carried him away.

Now the boy before the pot of blazing incense was trembling more violently, his hands clasped before him and his uptilted head jerking as with palsy. This had been going on for at least an hour. No man conscious could maintain that terrific tremor for such a time. Certain of the Balinese, to whom the gods have given signs, are trained from childhood for this role of sangkiang, intermediary between the kingdoms of gods and men, and, like the priests, they must live under the most rigid discipline. They can eat but one meal a day; they can unexceptionally have no more than four wives.

Now a girl and an old woman were shaking slowly, and now an-

67

other girl, a child, had caught the divine palsy. She was beautiful in a ghastly way, with her bare young shoulders throbbing and her hair flung across her face like dark rain. She flounced about in a fury, beating those who were near her; she moaned and sobbed the convulsive words of Durga, which the interpreter called nasally to the crowd.

The gamelan had steadied to one iterant gong note; the old men whispered their dirge. And suddenly the boy fell forward with both hands in the blazing incense pot. Women rushed to him with a gigantic dragon mask of green and gold and red, and fitted it upon his shoulders. His hands were still among the coals, and the horrible mask bobbed above them.

There was a tremendous report and a blinding flash, then a war of explosions as a long string of cannon crackers tied to a banyan tree was set off. Sprayed with fire, the sangkiang leaped into the midst of it, howling and stamping madly upon the spurting flames. And suddenly he stopped, limp, blubbering, the awful dragon head swinging from side to side. Arrack was poured by a dozen hands between the tusks of it, and the boy lifted his own hands to the sky as he keeled over, and I could see that they were unburned.

Now Bali and its magics were far behind me, and so were Singapore, a jumble of stork's-nest junks, of glittering jackstones flung on the tip of Asia, and Colombo, with its couchant idols a hundred feet long. Traveling third class on a German freighter, I passed through the Maladive Islands where the sails of the boats are upside down, point at the bottom, and brilliantly stained. I rounded Socotra where the natives only a few years ago had saved the passengers of a sinking ship to bury them up to the eyes in sand, with the ants and the vultures coming. I fled from Port Said to Jerusalem and Damascus and Aleppo, a grim whoring town, and across the deserts populated by people who were blue-tattooed, living in beehive huts of sand and dung. The spires of Istanbul remained like spines in my memory as I rushed by train across the singing of Budapest to Munich and finally Paris, which I entered lovingly and cautiously as one who had been deported from it a few years ago.

It was unchanged, as it forever will be. I found a better studio, with

68

no windows but a skylight opening to the neighbor stars, and there was Julia who brought a housewarming present of three oranges. Still she was a pixie, plumper now, and her fairy tales of Bali were sometimes sold. Our couch was too narrow, so we slept on the floor before a roaring fire in the iron stove, wakening to nudge one another with a dream we might write tomorrow, if we should have an interval in love.

The interval came, but there was no writing in it. Julia, in a sarong, turned from the stove one morning. "I'm worried about these sores," she said. "Are you sure you are all right?"

"I'm worried about mine, too." We looked at each other's legs. They were covered with pustules. "Look, I've some on my back, new ones."

"You know what I think it looks like?"

"I do," said I, going cold, "and I think so, too, but it can't be, darling."

"How—how careful in Bali were you, Bill?"

I thought of Marini. It couldn't be. "Fairly," I said with an honest groan. "And you?"

"It was much too hot," said Julia. "It must be something else, but we better have tests taken. Anyway syphilis, like murder, never happens to people like you and me, of course."

"Yes, yes, I mean no, of course."

We went to the American Hospital and had Wassermann tests, and spent a ghastly night waiting for the analysis. "I hate to tell you this," said the doctor on the telephone, "but it's positive, for both of you. Sorry." He hung up with a clang, like dropping an iron curtain between us and the world. He didn't even invite us for treatment, or a drink for our last long mile.

I poured us one, thick. "The cure," I said (this was 1929), "takes years and is apparently terrible. Isolation and no love, dearest. Are you for it?"

Julia flipped a pancake so high it hit the skylight and dropped back in a mess on the floor. "I'm for the other way out," she said. "What about you?"

I scraped up the pancake and ate most of it. I could have eaten dirt. "Me, too."

69

It was decided. I had thought of suicide before, as everyone has, but here was the only defensible propulsion to it. The problem was to leave no messy pancake on the floor for others to clean up.

I solved that one. We took the morning train to Saint Malo, very coolly, as if we, old blasé travelers, had nothing to be excited about in visiting another land. But we neither read nor talked on that long journey to the coast, for we knew that from our ultimate goal there was no return to the sweet countryside of France. I thought with amusement that I would need no passport this time. I could not even be deported from the free land of death.

At Saint Malo we chased down Brittany Calvados with sparkling Normandy cider in a little inn at the edge of the quai, while waiting for the bus to take us to Mont Saint-Michel. "It is over there, in the Manche," said the patronne, patting our shoulders. She couldn't know that we were exactly the reverse of a honeymoon couple. The famous Mont, one of the world's seven wonders, was obscured by fog. The bus came and took us jolting along the beach road to the causeway connecting the ancient island to our shore. And there the fog lifted, or rather settled into the sea of sand, so that first we saw the golden archangel Saint Michel on the spire of the abbey, then the huge stone church around it, then the town of pointed roofs and the fortress walls plunging into the quicksands.

Julia stared at the quicksands, and not at the magnificent pile of the Mont, as we ran above them along the causeway. It was low tide now and we could place them among the healthy sands, for they were deceptively glazed and crusted over. Her hand tightened in mine. No one who had sunk beneath these crusts had been seen again. There were no broken bodies to recover, to embarrass a ghost.

"So this is it," she said, and she added, "It's clean. Thank you, Bill."

We took the best room in the Hôtel de la Mère Poulard, for money didn't matter now, and spent the week we had promised in cuddling before the fire while old women cooked the famous omelette in long, wooden-handled frying pans, and walking always up and down the titanic stone staircases of the town, and visiting the fortress and the abbey, the Perrine Tower, the Merveille, the Great Wheel, the women's prison where in 1817 that corner of the mount subsided, taking the wall of the jail with it, and the women screamed at the freedom which was open before them, with a straight drop of several hundred feet.

"This," said Julia, "is what you and I, my Bill, have before us now."

"Darling, we have three days of love and happiness and beauty before us—before Monday." Seated in the gay chintzed armchair, she crossed one knee over the other, and the golden dressing gown fell away. She pulled it back quickly to cover the sores. My own were no better. They had spread up my back by now, making it hard to sleep. Julia's face was still unspotted; its loveliness remained, but it was ravaged by worry and pain, and I looked and felt like a leper, half-covered with white calamine lotion.

"Let's have another split of champagne, and walk."

We walked along the gray ramparts of the fortress, holding hands gingerly, for even that hurt. We stepped across the rooftops of the cramped little houses, four hundred years old, and down their outside stone stairs to the one precipitous narrow street, lined with souvenir shops and restaurants, Le Cheval Blanc, La Tortue, Le Gai Cavalier. Carefully we walked across the sands, avoiding the shimmering, quivering places where the treacherous sands had formed. I flung a piece of driftwood at one. The sands billowed out around it as it was slowly sucked under and disappeared.

"It looks comforting," said Julia, "like sinking between giant breasts."

Above us rose the beneficent Mount of Saint-Michel, supported by its tremendous walls and buttresses, at peace, slumbering in death but for the ratlike gnawing of the tourists. The gulls wheeled keening over it. The winds, whistling past us, cooling and caressing our sores, smashed like waves against that crenellated pyramid and tossed the birds back to the distant sea, as the ancient armies had been repulsed by the serene might of Mont Saint-Michel.

"Once," said Julia, "there were two sick baboons in love . . ."

And Saturday passed, and Sunday, when twice we dined on lobster and champagne and returned through secret walled gardens to the great fireplace and held each other like two sick baboons.

"Tomorrow is Monday," I said, pulling back my ulcerous legs from the heat of the flames.

"I know," said Julia. "Watch the fire. The flames build up like a golden Saint-Michel. Let's remember this tomorrow."

It was a glorious sunlit morning, and we were up early to see through diamond-leaded windows the dawn pulsing behind the spire of the abbey. It was just the morning to take a nice long walk across the sands. We were not hesitant. We were going through with it without dramatics. We were so much in a hurry that we didn't notice at first the letter on the breakfast tray. Strangely I had left the forwarding address of this point of no return.

I thought vaguely that this was the penultimate curiosity I should have in life as I opened a letter from Andre Roosevelt, from America. I read it aloud to Julia, jumping passages.

". . . Leila, Armand, the twins, all of us got it when we returned to the States, the same thing as you describe. Terrible! I was on a train to a lecture engagement in Chicago and scratching my leg when an old Negro porter said, 'Boss, if you'll give me a quarter I'll cure that at the next station where there's a drugstore next the depot.' He came back with a little yellow can of Dr. Sayman's Healing Salve, evidently a patent medicine, but I rubbed it on because it soothed the sores. In three days the whole family was cured. . . ."

Leaving the breakfast untouched, we packed, paid the bill, which was enormous, and rushed to the causeway, laughing through the cracked sores around our lips. By a freak of chance there was someone's taxi waiting, and by the persuasion of francs we chartered it all the way to Paris, where we found an English pharmacy on the Rue de la Paix and returned to the studio holding a dozen golden boxes with the bearded face of that magician, Dr. Sayman, on them.

In three days the inflammation had subsided. In a week our sores had closed. Because it was so absurd I phoned the doctor at the hospital who had unwittingly, but with our deliberate connivance, condemned us to death.

"I've been trying to find you all week," he said placidly. "We made a re-examination of your samples with a tropical consultant and found it isn't syphilis but a skin disease, called paroo, which also gives a positive Wassermann but which you can get innocently in some hot countries. . . . You did? Never heard of the stuff. Some quack medicine. . . ."

"It just occurred to me," said Julia, flipping pancakes cautiously, "that we never finished reading Andre's letter."

It continued. ". . . and I need you at the earliest over here, if you still want to return to Malaya for the new expedition. . . ."

"Don't be an ass! Of course you must go," said Julia, "but not before we have a sentimental holiday on Mont Saint-Michel."

That we did, and we were very happy, and I got under way with my first travel book, *Islands Under the Wind,* though somewhat discouraged by Julia, who thought I should cleave to poetry and fairy tales. When I wrote my father that I should soon have to return to America and join Andre Roosevelt, he wrote that, by God, he would come and get me.

It was a gray morning when he came. Rain stung the skylight, but our little stove glowed red. The landlady pounded on our door. "I have seen from the window," she babbled, "a handsome monsieur of a certain age with a gold-headed cane and the eyebrows of the devil. . . ."

I was down the stairs in my shirt sleeves, and there on the shabby sidewalk, looking it up and down, was my most elegant father. We were embarrassed and clung to each other, each trying to squeeze the harder.

"Christ, it's cold!" he said. "Let's have a drink."

Never had the corner bistro seen such sartorial chic in the company of one of their least pretentious customers. *"Bon jour, Jacques,"* said I. *"Bon jour, Jacques,"* said my father. *"Deux cognacs, doubles."*

We tossed these off without a word and ordered two more doubles. "Forget the past," he said, wiping a spot on the zinc with his glass. "It didn't happen."

"I know. I've missed you."

"Let's see what kind of a barracks you live in, son."

He diminished our tiny studio to barely room enough to hug Julia in before being introduced. "Knew your grandfather in Boston when I was a boy," he said. "Quite a character. Painted his horses green."

Most of the conversation that morning was between him and Julia. He was shy of me, as I of him. He took us to lunch at Foyot's, that grand gloomy Paris restaurant, now gone, and to the Tour d'Argent for dinner. "Forgive me, Julia," he said. "You're probably the finest thing that ever happened to Bill, but I'm taking him on the *Ile de France* tomorrow. He's got work to do. Join us when you can."

8

Hinny—romance in the desert— Mallorca—my hat's in the soup

THE NEXT SIX MONTHS in America were divided between Andre's farm in Connecticut, the family house in Maine, and a weird studio without windows which I found on Beacon Hill. With Andre I worked eagerly on two-reel movie scripts which we should film in the Dutch East Indies, when we got the money. I remained alone at the house in Maine after the family had returned to Boston, writing furiously what I thought would be a great book, a biography of the god Pan as I imagined it after that tragic cry rang out along the shores of Greece, "Great Pan is dead!" It was a poetic book with what I thought a sly Cabellian naughtiness as I made a great wanderer of the scapegrace Pan, chasing him through fantastic adventures, mostly amorous, across the world. He met other gods. He was the respected companion of Jesus. Through Balkh and Samarkand he went limping to find absolution in a convent of Tibet.

Alone but for a dog in my cabin on the cliff, surrounded by books on history, geography, religion, I lived my narrative and was never lonely. With no literary discipline at all, writing was not the structural tedium that it later became. I read Pater, Addison, Donn Byrne, the Bible to get cadence in my prose, and finally achieved a flowing phony pseudo-biblical style which pleased me very much. Half my sentences began with "And" and were slippery with present participles, to help the sweeping hypnotic cadence I desired.

74

I took the book to Boston at last when Maine grew too cold for me. By one lamp in the windowless studio I continued it, seeking the bright adventure for my poor boy Pan, drawing him from one crushed breast to another, driving him to Herculean labors and constantly greater magics. So completely swallowed by the old world was I that I rarely thought of Andre Roosevelt, in Paris, supposedly paving the way with gold bricks for our expedition to the East. This was the third of my first three books never to be published. I took small solace from Burton Rascoe's remarking that it was the finest imitation of Cabell he had ever seen.

Andre had guaranteed no expedition, and he was as financially myopic as I was, but we had several qualities in common: tremendous vitality, limitless enthusiasm, and a lust for the unknown though it might be the death of us. Without any particular faith in him I loved the old pirate. Without half believing the offhand assertions in his letters that the Rothschilds were coming in on this, that he had met a countess who, et cetera, that it was imperative to reach the Dutch East Indies before the rains, I caught a boat for France within three days of receiving his cable saying simply, "COME."

There he was, up five flights of stairs, snuggled into three over-furnished little rooms which could barely hold the bulk of him.

"Scenarios, my son! We've got to have 'em quick. Our producers are panting for them." I realized soon that only I was panting here-abouts as I typed on the balcony of the Hôtel St. Yves. Andre was supervising the French version of *Goona-Goona* which he had filmed in Bali in 1929. I wrote the commentary for it and made a thousand enlargements for publicity. Andre took me with him to pad out the non-existent expedition when we went to see the countess, the Roth-schilds, and the others who were unanimously—but not at all finan-cially—interested.

"Wait till the Colonial Exposition is launched!" It was launched with a dozen of our own dancers from Bali, and in the middle of winter their pavilion burned down, leaving them starry-eyed in the first snow they had ever seen.

"Wait till the film comes out!" The film had its premiere at the

75

Théâtre Marigny and was received triumphally, as it deserved, but still no backers hounded us for a share in our new expedition.

I was considering this with some asperity one afternoon, walking up and down the balcony with an unlighted cigarette in my hand.

"Must you drive me crazy, or may I give you a light?" asked a voice behind me, from the balcony next to mine. I slid out of my dream of a debtor's prison to examine the very gypsy of a girl with her black hair to her shoulders, earrings that tinkled, and a dress of India print. Attractive as she was, I would never have divined that we would be together for the next nine years.

Now there are various problems in writing an autobiography, the worst of which is people, for if you write anything of anyone he will undoubtedly be disappointed and may, indeed, be angry. If you don't write of him he will be doubly hurt. And the worst of people are the women who formed and deviated and transformed your life, as Hinny did mine, and the causes of the changes in it you often cannot properly tell.

But Hinny said, half a night later, "When will you start collecting me for your autobiography, boy Bill?" She was six years older than I, of Russian Jewish descent, and the most exciting, perverse, stubborn, passionate, and unpredictable person I had ever known. We moved together to a gaunt studio on Rue Vaugirard. There was a table and a bed in it. Georgette, the concierge, lent us her grandmother's rough linen sheets.

When Hinny wasn't packing bags in a Russian fury, to leave me forever, we were happy there, entertaining Andre and his cotillion of countesses, who doubtless thought us quaint, and Rose who had come to France with Hinny to go bicycling through the Alps. I had fortuitously put a crimp in this, but I gained the lasting friendship of the always-sparkling Rose, who was to bear with fortitude our future follies. Rose was the anchor we clung to in many storms.

We three, one murky afternoon, were looking at a map of the countries bordering the Mediterranean when I saw a small speck of blue in the desert country somewhere south of Algiers. Hah, in this month of July what could be sweeter than a lost lake in the Saharan dunes? The Djelfa Oasis?

"Bill, let's go! Let's all three go!" said Hinny. Rose cocked a well-

turned eyebrow and opined that as Andre's expedition was still somewhat less than foetal, the change might do us good.

"A Rose is a Rose is a Rose," said Hinny. "She clinches it." There
was no need for further deliberation by me.

The train took us third class to Marseilles, and the boat third class
to Algiers amidst a gross of vacationing deaf-mutes. Like a menagerie
we in third seemed to serve as entertainment for three priests on the
first class above. But our deaf-mutes were unabashed. Gesturing like
mad to one another and occasionally pointing to the proud priests,
they broke into awful silent laughter. They bent double with hilarity,
slapped each other on the back. It was a most disquieting hysterical
pantomime.

"What's so funny?" Hinny asked their guide, the one man who
could talk.

He burst into audible gales of laughter. "Madame, I regret that
I can't repeat it to you. They are telling dirty jokes about the priests!"

We were halfway to Africa when we made the acquaintance of an
English girl named, marvelously, Peonie. Thin as a rail she was, with
long, unevenly cut blond hair to her shoulders and a large leather
belt which must have tortured her duodenum. She spoke in gasps, but
always ecstatically. She was a student of anthropology and needed
notes of a sexual nature for a thesis. Such was her enthusiasm, even
into inquiring by rather lurid sign language into the wooing customs
of deaf-mutes, that Ruth and Hinny became fond of her, and I said,
sure, she could come with us to Djelfa, a sterile land, I said, no
research for her there.

So we landed together in Algiers and were respectfully treated by
the Arab customs officers as an American sheik with a woman's club
in tow. Ya Allah, I was no longer to be master in my house.

Algiers fascinated my girls, with its smells, its oriental clamor, and
particularly its tribesmen from the desert who swaggered through the
crowd, their hawk eyes burning. We had found a little Swiss hotel,
respectable but not far from the Casbah. At the mention of that
wicked word Peonie was determined to go there. Now the Casbah is
a city within a city, sharply delimited by the Algiers police, for its
walls hide the most compact vice in the world, traffic in women, little
boys, drugs, murder. It is a warren of stinking clay tenements reached

77

by tortuous stepped and vaulted alleys so narrow that two people can barely pass. The prostitutes squat in doorways three feet high, easily defended.

"Ah, how exotic!" Peonie raved. "Those smells, ah!" An urchin, crowded, was peeing on her foot.

We found a cavernous restaurant lit by kerosene lamps and sat down to dinner of couscous, spitted lamb and millet. The shadows lunged across the walls as gaunt desert men swung in and out in their flowing robes. Next to us was a group of them singing drunkenly, and signal among them was a very tall, very handsome young caid, or sheik, as his headdress indicated.

"Do you have a cigarette?" he asked Peonie, flashing teeth like a wolf's. She gave him one, trembling with excitement, and the rotten ice was broken. Speaking in quite good French and totally ignoring me, he told the girls of his wealth, his women, and asked where we were off to. "Ah, Djelfa." He grinned. "I should like to take you there. It is the town of the Ouled-Nails, the holy whores. They have a school there to teach the arts of love. They will ask no money from a man, for they believe that to make him happy will secure for them a better place in heaven. Very nice, huh?"

I kicked Peonie under the table and Hinny poked her, for the caid now had his brown hand on Peonie's pink arm. I didn't want any trouble in this dim den. I paid the bill and with difficulty pulled the girls to the street, the caid's party following. We turned down the steps which should lead to the harbor but didn't. We turned into tunnels which had no lighted exit. We skidded in the slime and passed through courtyards I had never seen before, and always we were followed by the Algerians, laughing as if certain that the girls would soon abandon their stupid lost American guide. And Peonie and Rose and Hinny encouraged them with glances and smiles over their shoulders. "God damn it," I growled, "be sensible. This can end up being no fun!"

Miraculously we found our way to the boulevards and then the hotel, where I rushed my charges to our rooms. Without turning on the light we leaned from a window, and there were our buccaneers calmly waiting before the hotel door. "They're waiting for us!" Peonie giggled. "Oh, Bill, don't you think . . . ?"

78

Furiously I filled a pitcher at the lavabo and dumped it accurately on the Algerians' heads. The street became turmoil, a bedlam of howling natives who in an instant had leaped through every doorway. They milled and screamed up at the hotel, not knowing from which window the water had come. They stormed into the lobby, up the stairs through the corridors, banging on doors, including ours which I locked and barricaded. Terrified, we heard murder howling. My brass knuckles felt like a toy in my fist. We scarcely breathed as we stood in that steaming darkness until nearly an hour later when the crowd had given us up and dispersed.

"A Peonie is a Peonie is a Peonie," said Hinny, snuggling into bed.

We made the trip to Djelfa, by train to its last stop, then by lorry across the practically roadless desert. "Where's your lake?" asked my charges. Blue on the map it was, but it was absent here. "Does anyone know of a lake hereabouts?" I asked the passengers. "You know— water." They pointed over their shoulders to the distant Mediterranean. I was a hell of an explorer.

On we jogged, eating dust, seeing nothing, for there was nothing to see, not even the road. Hinny, true gypsy, sang Russian songs and seemed not discomfited, but Peonie had read Edith M. Hull and was beginning a disillusionment with desert romance which reached near catastrophe a few days later. Rose's smile was a mirage.

We were approaching a group of half-a-dozen mud hovels when I demanded of the driver, "Where in Allah's name is Djelfa?" We jerked to a stop before a two-story mud mansion about thirty feet square.

"Here is Djelfa, monsieur. Here is inn."

We were stuck with it, with a week of it until the return bus came. The filth was indescribable, the W.C. a mounded mass of ordure, the food a garbage of beans and goat which would have been just as appetizing with the hair left on. There were only two things to do in Djelfa, drink anisette during the stifling daytime on the rickety porch, and at night, since our lamps were not meant to read by, sit in the walled compound and watch the "holy whores."

These Ouled-Nails are a curious tribe, and from them are garnered the best dancing girls in Algeria. At the age of puberty an Ouled-Nail

79

maiden is given a mattress by her mother and taken to a boarding "school" where she studies the arts of dancing and love until she is expert enough to go out on her own to the cities. She earns her living by dancing, but her carnal favors are free, for it is an act of devotion to Allah to bring joy to men. Presents she may accept, but never that gross thing, money.

I and what must have seemed my harem of Hinny and Rose and Peonie would sit in a dark corner of the compound. The girls sat cross-legged on one side of it, so heavily robed that you couldn't guess their figures, though you could assume correctly that they were mostly corpulent. There wasn't one, I thought, pretty enough to whip up the lust of anyone but these old desert goats who sat on the other side of the compound, facing them and drinking beer.

One at a time they danced to the music of drum and flute, though it was less of a dance beneath those voluminous costumes than a vertical imitation of birth pangs. To me, young and susceptible, God knows, there was not even sensuality to it, but the customers cheered and sent beer bottles to the ladies of their choice. Some had dozens of bottles between their knees and drained them like bilge pumps. Apparently the caid who sent the most beer to any girl gained her for the night.

The only rival for their services was the dwarfed, hunchbacked homosexual flutist who bounced from knee to knee of these desert chiefs, tootling wildly at their groins like a fakir trying to make a cobra rise. It seemed to be very funny until one of the caids went off with the musician, and the dancing had to stop until he returned. The holy whores were furious.

Nothing troubled the dull and dusty tenor of our days until two evenings before the lorry, that blessed lorry, was due. The four of us lost souls were seated at a round iron table on the porch, drinking anisette and reading glumly a French newspaper several months old. When one of us finished reading a sheet he would pass it on, in exchange for another, hoping that there might be something in it, an obituary notice, or an ad, which he had missed before.

"I think that big fly is a new one," said Rose, pointing with a circling finger.

"And there's a lizard I don't know," said Hinny. Her long black hair was gray with dust. "My, what can happen next?"

That was quickly answered by a rumble in the sands to the south. "The lorry!" we cried, but it was more remarkable than that. Spinning toward us with a plume of dust behind it came a tremendous motorcycle, ridden by a man in a flying burnoose. He skidded to a stop beside us, and Peonie said, "My God, it's my caid!"

"Keep reading your paper, gal," I said, pulling a bottle within quick gripping distance.

Indeed it was our handsome swain whom I had doused with water. He showed no sign of recognition as he sat at a table a few feet from us and yelled for anisette. I read the obituary notices again and didn't discover mine.

The caid leaned toward Peonie, staring at her with sand-burned eyes that looked like stuffed tomatoes. "Have you got a cigarette?" he demanded without a smile. Peonie dropped one shakily into his long, gnarled hand. He crushed it, threw it away, got up, and started his motorcycle. His eyes had never left Peonie's.

"Come," he said. As if in a trance Peonie stumbled to him, flung a leg over the back saddle. The bike roared, and away they went in a cloud of sand which obscured them instantly.

Hinny and Rose and I hadn't moved; we had had no time to. "That!" said Rose. "Is she mad?" She was certainly mad, but there was nothing we could do about it, with no telephone, no conveyance but a mangy camel nearby.

"This may be romance for your bird-brained Peonie," I said, "but it may be damned serious, considering our last encounter, which was, to coin a phrase, all wet. The little idiot, she should be spanked."

Hinny sighed. "She probably will be, and she'll be back in an hour with sand in her pants, no worse."

But in the morning Peonie had not returned, nor in the afternoon. The caid was only known to the Arab hotelkeeper as a nomad whose motorcycle had been seen all over the Sahara, from Laguat to Dakar to Meknes while his wives—wives, mind you—followed on camels a week or so behind. Poor Peonie, our passion fruit. There was nothing we could do but take the lorry tomorrow, if she didn't turn up, and notify the police fifty miles from here. Frustrated and furious, we sat and watched the holy whores dancing again that night, and suddenly above the drum and the hunchback's flute came the roaring of a motorcycle.

We reached the street just in time to see it barely slow down before us. The caid with a backward swipe pushed the limp and bedraggled form of Peonie into our arms. "*Kelb!* Dog!" he said, and drove off.

Now Peonie was never kempt, but as she lay on the bed, drunk, torn, black and blue, she looked like a hideously broken marionette. "I'm cured. God, am I cured!" she moaned. "Know what happened?"

I said I could guess. Did it? "And worse!" she wailed. "Do you suppose I'm going to have a dozen little sheiks, one after another? Oooooh! Hinny! It was awful, and"—her voice sank to a drunken conspiratorial whisper—"rather wonderful, too. . . . I was in a trance. The moonlight . . ."

"Damn it, there wasn't any moon!" said Rose.

"The perfume of incense, and," she shook her matted curls, "burning camel dung in that tent, and, oh, God, the sweat of those three women's bodies, and the sick smell of the arrack Yussuf forced me to drink. I must stink. Give me a drink."

Hinny was bathing her, so I turned to the window. The tethered camel made an obscene blubbery sound.

"Yussuf flung me down among his women and fell upon me. I screamed. He kissed me—what a breath! I bit him and the women cheered but he gave me an uppercut to the jaw. When I woke up I bit him again, gently like you're in love, and the women howled with laughter again when he tried to get his lip from my teeth. Hah, they were on my side! 'Arab women don't bite!' yelled Yussuf.

"That's the way it went all day long. Yussuf gave me a bowl of some nauseous soup once and lots of arrack. The women took me to a wet spot in the sand where we strained water through a cloth, while they laughed and patted me, making snicking sounds with their teeth. 'Bite him again,' was what they meant. I didn't have to wait long, for Yussuf was on me again in that damned so-called oasis. You'll see what I write to Mrs. Hull and that phony Burton Holmes!"

"Now, now," said Hinny, giving her a couple of aspirin, "it's all over but the—"

"But the baby sheiks!" Peonie screamed. "They'd rape me even

82

before I got them out! All day he kept at me. It was awful, and sometimes when it wasn't so awful I bit him gently, while the women cheered. He beat the daylights out of me and finally flung me at the motorcycle, while the women begged me not to go. *'Ne vais pas!'* they said. *'Reste avec nous!'* But it was too late. And I hadn't bit him very hard. Ah, Yussuf! Yussuf!"

Rose took Peonie, perplexed, back to France, and Hinny and I went to Mallorca on the counsel of Andre, who wanted me to get a Spanish governmental subsidy for a film on that exquisite island and to round up non-professional actors. It was to be a documentary film to inspire tourist interest, and of course I could write the scenario. . . . He said nothing about the Bali expedition.

I got the promise of a subsidy, but actresses seemed a problem insuperable. Spanish girls, non-professional, hid behind their iron window grilles and just didn't act. In desperation we went to the brothels.

When it was known that we merely wanted to look around, probably as *voyeurs* with the pretext of seeking actresses, not even to enjoy the facilities of the house, we were charged admission, Hinny twice as much as I. These desperate visits imperiled my government sponsorship when it was noted that I was visiting four and sometimes five or six bordellos a day. It was costly to pay for pleasure unachieved, for merely a line-up of tired women among whom there might be a film star lurking.

It is due to the one-track mind that is the single genius of explorers that I finally rounded up five auto loads of conceivable actresses and conducted them, singing like parrots, over the mountains and swiftly past the monasteries and down to the plain of Alcudia, where I had virtually stumbled into the very cave my scenario required.

It was a hole in the ground, perhaps thirty feet across by fifty deep, and bulging pear-shaped at the bottom. A flight of old, well-hewn stone steps led down it to a floor strewn with fallen rock. Three passages led from it straight to hell, and between two of them stood a great rock carving, a monumental bas-relief depicting Saint George and the Dragon.

All my ladies trooped tittering down the stairs and made a play of putting tiny handkerchiefs over the rock to sit upon. I had thought

83

it a great idea to have a picnic here, on location, and try each heroine out in her part before the audience of the others.

The sandwiches, wine, and the pot of almond soup were coming down the stairs, when one of them said, "This is a bad place, it is haunted. I know because I was born right over there," and she pointed diagonally at the sky. "They say this cave was used as a church when the Romans were persecuting the Christian martyrs. The Romans finally found them here. Those tunnels are full of bones!" A ripple of pre-prandial indigestion went through my cast.

"Maria," I said, "now I want you to be a Christian martyr. You stand by the tunnel here."

"Ah, no, you look into it first, señor!"

With a match for guidance I stepped into the tunnel boldly and followed it for about twenty feet, until the flame diminished and there was unmistakably what I had always imagined to be the smell of sulphur and brimstone. It was the breath of hell, all right. A fresh match burned bright for an instant and suddenly died out. The fumes of the place caught at my lungs and I staggered, coughing, back to my picnic of movie stars.

"Nothing there but a bad smell," said I gaily.

"Bones," said Maria. "Count me out. I like work in the bordello better."

Steaming in the midst of us was the iron kettle of *sopa de almendras,* the spume of it redolent with almonds, chicken, basil, cream. Antonina was cutting the peasant bread, chipping garlic on it, folding it over golden slices of saffron-flavored Spanish sausage. Saint George and the Dragon were menacing each other through the rising steam of the soup, and I was on the way to becoming a motion-picture director when the mouth of the cave above us darkened with a cloud like a cork, and a clap of thunder deafened us.

My dainty ladies screamed and staggered among the rock shards. There was an answering rumble in the tunnels branching from our central cave. Grit fell from the walls. I flung my hat over the soup tureen, calling to the girls to be calm. Then a sound like "whoosh" came from the tunnels and with it such a Stygian stench as to propel the girls screaming up the stairs and into the rain, which was lavender-lit by lightning.

84

I followed cautiously, cursing, with the hot pot of almond soup swinging against my leg. A shard fell and chipped a piece from Saint George. I crawled out to the field where the high grasses were bent and racing like horsemen, but swifter than they were my movie stars, their shoes in their hands, racing to the cars.

I am not one ever to abandon an almond soup. The kettle so encumbered me that all the cars but mine had sped from that cave of hell before I reached the road. Exhausted, embittered, and hungry, I sat down in the back seat, watching the whipping grass, watching my first expedition return through the mountains to the brothels. I burned my hand fishing my hat from the depths of the almond soup, which I drank gingerly, sadly. It tasted like sulphur and brimstone and hat.

Hinny I loved, but I was too young to know her. Moody was the term we used in those days for women who bounced from the abysmal to the ecstatic capriciously. When I was working on *Islands Under the Wind* in the hot attic of the hotel in Alcudia she wanted me to be working on my story of Pan, and when the travel book was finished and I was delightedly working on Pan, I should, said she, be writing Andre's Mallorquin scenario, though several months had passed without a word from him. He was a great man and dear to me, but my slight funds couldn't keep pace with his projects' vagaries. The thought of quitting him appalled me, but I realized at last that I was using his dreams as a float for mine and that sometime soon I had to learn to fly for myself.

"I'm going back to Tahiti," I said one night as we sat in a quai-side café frequented by smugglers. It had been a day of wrangling over trifles, and I was fed up with caprice. "Do you think you would like to come?"

"We'll see," Hinny answered, with that vague, arrogant phrase which infuriated me.

While waiting for her to see and Andre to write, lacking companionship, we pitched pennies against the back of the concrete church, and soon interested half the smugglers of Alcudia in our game, which was a childish one but seemingly unknown here. The pitcher of the penny landing closest to the wall won all the others pitched. Thus were we occupied one Sunday during mass, with the congregation gradually

85

slipping from the church to join us, when the priest, rotund and raging, gave up his service and appeared waving the collection bag.

"Sinners! Blasphemers!" he shouted. "If this is what you do with the money you should be giving to God's work, there will be no more masses until God wins!" With that he, too, pitched through the hot morning until his bag was emptied. Hinny said he showed talent as she, invariably the champion, collected God's loot.

During the following week, night and day, we heard clicking sounds in the priest's house, and our fellow urchins explained that he was practicing pitching pennies. On Sunday, sure enough, there was no mass, but the congregation and more than had ever attended assembled behind the church. Father José asked the blessing of God and pitched with the devil's accuracy. Everyone joined, and tourists, hearing of the strange game in Pollensa, came. Hinny did her best but it was insufficient. When the clock struck noon, Father José had the pennies of us all. He clinked them into the sack.

He blessed us. "Next Sunday at six," he said, "we shall resume mass and pitch pennies afterward. I, your humble servant, will of course be with you. Thank you very much."

Zigzagging through Andorra, the world's smallest republic, between France and Spain, and the Alps of Haute Savoie for a needless cure of Hinny's imaginary tuberculosis, we returned at last to Paris. Georgette, the concierge, met me at the door. "The police want you," she said, shuddering. "You must go to the Sûreté."

I shuddered, too, remembering my expulsion from France in 1927. Desperately I sought my way through the dim corridors of the Palais de Justice and was directed to a little man in black at a little desk cluttered with handwritten papers. He let me stand. "Not Hassoldt Davis," he said, "but that same William H. Davis who was expelled from France on September 3, 1927." He didn't look at a note. "Since then, you returned in 1929 when you lived at 14 Rue des Plantes with a woman named Julia Adams, and you did not take out a carte d'identité. Am I right?"

I was dumfounded. All my sins of omission were catching up with me. "Yes, but . . ."

"No 'buts,' monsieur. You have been under observation. You are now living at 128 Rue de Vaugirard with a woman named Esther Girsdansky Squires who uses the aliases of Hinny and even Jim. Right?"

This got me in the pit of the stomach. I must be considered an important criminal if this little agent knew my dossier by heart. The French Sûreté was living up to its reputation as the equal or superior of the FBI and Scotland Yard.

"Furthermore, your little friend is of Russian origin, and her parents were intimates of the Socialists Bergman and Goldman, eh?" I seemed to remember that Hinny had mentioned this, though she was no more revolutionary than I.

"Let me explain . . ." I began desperately.

The little man smiled. "Andre Roosevelt, a respected citizen with whom you are associated, has already explained satisfactorily your indiscretions, which we will consider innocent. You will be fined, of course, for not having taken out a carte d'identité. Get one soon. That is all. Happy sojourn in France."

I could have planted a kiss on the bald black top of his derby hat.

The swinging pendulum of Hinny's humor was up again and she agreed to Tahiti. No "We'll see"s. No "What are we going to do for money?" She had a little of her own, and by now, I knew, sufficient faith in my writing to take a chance with me on that far island where I wanted to live for years, not merely visit. For me the decision was momentous, the choice between a static settling down to books and the frantic living on hopes of adventure with Andre. Ruefully I said good-by to him, like a sailor taking off in a leaky lifeboat from a ship indefinitely becalmed.

"But, you idiot, the expedition is just around the corner!"

Hinny boldly, to save money, went to America steerage. I took a Messageries Maritimes ship bound from Marseilles for Tahiti, and picked her up in Martinique. Off we went again, through the Panama Canal and the beautiful Gatun Lakes in the midst of the isthmus, filled with just the sort of tropical islands we would live on during the next two years. She loved them.

"Do you realize, darling, that we shall have almost no white companionship but you and me?"

87

"I can stand you, if you can. But ... what are we going to do for money?"

"We'll see," I said snidely.

It was the morning of our approach to Papeete Bay, after seven weeks of travel, when we were leaning over the bow watching that mound of glistening emeralds that was Tahiti rise into the dawn, that a steward passed me a telegram. I opened it shakily.

"Islands Under the Wind accepted," it said.

9 ∿∿∿∿∿∿∿∿∿∿∿∿∿∿∿∿∿

Return to Polynesia—adventure together in solitude—the hounds of the sea—we lose a son, and I my father

TAHITI WAS UNCHANGED. Hall and Nordhoff were writing a book about Captain Bligh's mutiny. Tiare, now living with a Swedish millionaire, refused to remember me, which was just as well. Hinny kept looking for two-year-old babies with bushy eyebrows and a turned-up nose, but there seemed to be none. She was delighted with the climate which was never hot, never cold, the beaches of black laval sand, the quiet friendliness of the natives. Everyone, even the men, wore flowers. Everyone sang.

We would live here forever, we said positively, and to that end went about the building of a house in Paea, eighteen miles from the port, on a plot of land which I leased for one dollar a month. It was an acre wide at the sea front and ran twenty-two miles up the mountain until it encountered the property of a district chief on the other side of the island. Nearly all we needed for good living grew wild upon it—coffee, oranges, limes, breadfruit, vanilla, ginger root, taro, coconut, and three huge trees of avocado which was so creamy the natives used it instead of butter. There were wild pigs in the mountains, shrimp in the streams, every imaginable fish in the lagoons.

88

Our house was built in a month, mostly by my own hands and those of a leper who was not supposed to leave his plantation. It cost four hundred dollars and was a proper house, not a shack, of wood and bamboo and galvanized roofing. The ceilings were of native woven straw mats for coolness, and the interior walls of reeds. I made its beds, chairs, tables, bar, and furnished it comfortably with goods from the weekly auction in town.

We lived two years in it, still unmarried but socially admissible to our French and native neighbors, though the bachelor whites candidly wondered why the devil any young man should bring a white woman to Tahiti unless he, poor dope, was legally bound to her. *"Il y a un tel embarras ici!* There is such an embarrassment of love that one cannot cope!"

"Ah, the long-term view," I answered smugly. "Your lovely Tahitian is aged at thirty."

"But with such craft, my son, as to make noodles stand up in the soup!"

There I wrote my fourth book never to see the light of publication, but *Islands Under the Wind* was doing well, and encouraged by its editors I attempted another novel, *Save Me the Sun,* which I was to rewrite completely three times in the years before it would be accepted.

Our friends were many and various. George Bowles, first press agent of Barnum and Bailey and inventor of the Anna Held milk-bath story, had retired to Paea at seventy, and at his seventy-third birthday party broke his leg playing leapfrog. None of us doubted his authenticity as a father when a little while later his native girl bore a stalwart son. Erii, the girl, bore the child in the usual way. When labor came, she sat on a stool in a thatched hut with a pile of tapa thatched mats beneath her. The old midwife sat on the same stool behind, her legs around Erii's hips, her hands folded over the pregnant belly, gently kneading it and pushing down. Whoosh! the child landed headfirst on the tapa. The cord was tied, the baby bathed, and within the hour Erii was back at the ironing board, pressing her champion white master's shirts.

Jerry Tittell had done the reverse of most of us; instead of coming from civilization to a relatively primitive land, he had come from the primitive to Tahiti, for he was one of the few who had lived as the only white man on Easter Island, that fabled place of the gigantic statues in mid-Pacific. For twenty-two years he managed the cattle ranch there and fathered twenty-two children. "Damn it," said Jerry, "there weren't many distractions and I couldn't teach those heathens to play cards!" Eagerly he had looked forward to the arrival only once a year of the ship with provisions and mail, and particularly so on one occasion when he had a throbbing tooth which must be extracted. A little Chinese who served as doctor came ashore in the dinghy, braced Jerry against one of the grim monoliths, and tugged and heaved and pried and hacked in Jerry's mouth. After an hour the ship began tooting for him, and with a violent effort he tore the tooth loose. "Back to see how you're doing next year," he yelled as he fled for the boat. Jerry sighed over the memory of this. "He did his best, the little heathen Chinese, but unfortunately he pulled the wrong tooth."

Down the road lived our carpenter, Zuki Swizloff, who was afflicted with, reputedly, leprosy. He was confined to his plantation by government decree as he had threatened to shoot any gendarme who came to fetch him to the leper colony, and for twenty years he had not set foot outside the district of Paea. No one feared him, for leprosy is hard to contract. Hinny and I had him in for drinks when we were tired of hammering and sawing in the sun. His story was an ugly one.

Twenty years ago the young Zuki, a Pole, had come to the islands and prospered so well that he could buy a plantation and erect on it the huge square house where he still lived. It had two verandas completely circling it and water piped from a mountain stream. The best was none too good for Zuki, so he married Teiuna, who was one of the loveliest of the district Papara, to the grave annoyance of the government doctor who itched for her as a subsidiary wife. There were rows in the bars over her. The doctor hurled Zuki over the balcony of the Cercle Concorde, broke his leg, and, of course, treated him.

Now this wily fellow announced to the governor that, according to a smear of Zuki's nasal mucus, he was afflicted with Hanson's disease, more often called leprosy. He told it as well to Zuki's wife, with no effect advantageous to himself. When Zuki was condemned to the leper colony he and Teiuna barricaded their great lonely house and shot at the gendarmes. As these were few and precious in the islands, the governor finally marooned Zuki for life on his own plantation, never to come into town, never to come closer than shouting distance to another man. A sign was nailed to his gate: "LEPER—KEEP OUT."

But Teiuna, unaffected by the messages the doctor managed to pass to her, remained faithfully beside her man, who never showed a sign of leprosy. It was the type that attacked the nerves, the doctor had said, without skin lesions. And Zuki continued to thrive among the friendly folk of Paea, though he yearned to see Papeete once again.

"Where is this doctor?" I demanded one day.

"Oh, he died about ten years ago."

"And you've not gone to a new one?" No, the inertia of his long ostracism had been too heavy for that. "Damn it, do you *feel* sick, Zuki?"

"Me? Never sick in my life, but I'm a leper to the government just the same."

It wasn't hard to arrange. One of our friends was a French military doctor who consented to see Zuki in our house and examined him thoroughly. Next week he brought out a colleague who put him through other tests, while I thought of Julia and me and the quicksands of Saint-Michel. Every test was negative, and the administration sent Zuki, in my care, a formal paper stating that he was free to travel as he chose.

Never had Paea known such a celebration. Their dear Zuki was free. We danced on the beach between fires of fronds, roasted pigs in the uma, the oven of earth, covered the poor bewildered Zuki with garlands, and drove in a fleet of three trucks to Papeete where there was another crowd to meet us. Lazarus, returned from the dead, had no welcome like this. Zuki and Teiuna and Hinny and I went finally to sleep on the beach, holding hands.

It has been remarked by bolder men than I that living together requires considerable adaptation and compromise under the best of conditions. In the cities or their suburbs there are theaters, movies, parties, people to serve as buffers between man and wife, there is escape into other worlds and fresh conversation when one returns. On a remote island with few social distractions it is far more difficult. Native entertainment becomes monotonous. One's few white friends run short of repartee. Mail comes but once a month. And friction inevitably grows between the most loving couples.

It had seemed odd to me that most white women disliked Tahiti. Men explained it facilely as due to the obvious competition of the young Tahitian female, but it went deeper than that. Monotony was largely responsible for it, and the sense of insular imprisonment. One woman who had lived for years on Tahiti felt an almost physical oppression from the mountains which were always just at her back, towering, forever about to break, like a jungle wave, driving her into the sea. The only habitable land in Tahiti is along the shore; you have but two vistas, that of engulfing blue space before you and that of the green wall at your back. There is no escape but into the sea.

Hinny loved Tahiti, and it may have been that her ill ease was fostered by the even greater love which I had for it, that she felt the greater tranquillity in me when I was in the forests. We weren't enough together, for I was writing in a separate shack down the beach, so we had picnics whenever we could, bicycling to Papara or Mataiea to roast a fish in banana leaves by one of the streams where Loti saw his visions of loveliness, or to the pathetic abandoned estate of Donald Duncan.

Duncan acquired a transient fame during World War I. He was a British preacher who wanted to write and did produce the book *Exits Anonymous,* which was considered audacious then. He abandoned the ministry and retired with all his earnings to Tahiti, to enjoy what beauty he could before his eyesight wholly failed. He built a huge splendid house of native woods and pandanus thatch, horseshoe-shaped so that its hidden garden courtyard faced the sea and England, which he could never quite forget. Nostalgically he built a great stone fireplace to remind him of his country home, and so as not to feel but merely see the flames in that hot climate, he contrived a glass door that could be lowered on brass chains before them.

Such a catch as Duncan was not long in getting caught by a half-caste girl named Ana, a canny courtesan whose art since the age of

92

twelve had been the solacing of aged lonely wealthy men. But Duncan thought he was happy with her as they sat by that false fireside, or she leaned over him, her dark hair tickling his throat while he wrote. It wasn't long before they had a joint account, and it diminished, though with his failing eyesight he could no longer see what money remained.

He would fumble for her hand before the fire, and often it wasn't there, and when he became stone-blind little Ana left him. She went to the Riviera. He died, stone-broke.

The house was empty now, but the glass still hung before the fireplace, and though vandals had stolen most of the furnishings, there still remained hundreds of worm-eaten volumes of Duncan's library. It was neither a theosophical nor worldly library such as one might expect of a renegade clergyman; it was devoted to black magic and witchcraft, and its walls were scribbled over with cabalistic charms and pentacles for the winning of love. Some of these I copied and Hinny hopefully embroidered them on the canvas backs of our chairs, but they were not very useful. Briefly we would wrangle, then fall headlong into the suffocating silences.

"What's wrong, darling?"

"Nothing. Nothing at all."

I was delighted when Hinny at last found an interest privately, her own, bookbinding, and took the Chinaman's bus every morning to study under the Tahitian bookbinder who worked for the administration. I carpentered a sewing frame for her and a screw press. The tensions in her eased as she produced beautiful books, learning to tool them and stamp them in gold. And we helped ourselves somewhat by celebrating all the holidays, and as we enjoyed giving and getting presents, no matter how trivial, we invented a monthly fete to bridge the gaps between Christmas and birthdays. This occurred on the first Monday of every month, on Moonsday, and then we gave each other presents which we had collected during the last month long, a chisel for me, a stone idol for Hinny, a rum for me, an aspirin for her, each one wrapped carefully and beribboned.

Silly as this may seem, it was anodyne to our chafed emotional sores. There was always the imminent holiday to look forward to, and no matter how sour the evening before, the morning of Moonsday brought us together again, grinning at the trick which with our knowledge and consent we had played upon ourselves.

But even this palled as the dry season came on. Hinny went into what the Victorians called a "decline," with slight fever. I wrote poorly. One Moonsday I received a package with nothing in it but the scribbled message, "I've missed a period." Hinny watched me closely as I read this.

"Wonderful!" I said. "Miss another. Miss eight." She bounced like a rabbit into my lap. All our stratagems seemed puerile beside this solution by childbirth which we had never considered, poor and unmarried as we were. I wrote to my father cheerily, and he, the illegitimate Boston grandparent, sent us his blessings and a check.

It was in the fourth month that Hinny said, "Bill, we have barely time for the trip to Maupiti. God knows when I'll be free of your son again."

It was folly, but Hinny would not be refused. "We pregnant women have our whims," she said. "They must be pampered. Frustration is bad. I might, after all, be asking for strawberries."

Maupiti seemed nearly as unattainable. It was a tiny island on the northern edge of the Society Group, with no European on it and no regular trade communication with the other islands. There would be no facilities at all, and we would have to live on our addled wits, I pointed out. "Good for them," said Hinny, packing. "They may get to know each other out there alone. They may get to love each other again. Love is a good thing to go with babies."

Our schooner, the *Potii Tubuai,* was jammed to her gunwales as we prepared to cast off from the Papeete wharf. There was a fine mist slinking down from the valleys as the hupé, the dusk wind, pursued it. It veiled the top of the red church steeple, spread like softest tulle above the galvanized iron roofs and balconies of the shops, yet the mountains remained clear above it, patched with golden green and the shadow of lesser hills. Last-minute passengers scrambled aboard. Aged Annamite women with faces like walnuts bade stoic good-bys to sons who were leaving for Raiatea or Huahine or Bora-bora to start little shops with the savings their mothers had earned by repairing the roads. Two huge lads from Fiji whammed each other on the back, yelling foul jokes in excellent English. Hinny and I, exhausted, sat down by the rail on the mattress we had rented from the Maori captain. The twelfth of a dozen pigs was hauled to deck and tethered amidst us, feeling one of us, no doubt, in our floating sty.

We sailed under a brisk wind past Motu-uta, that fairy islet, and in an hour Moorea lay abeam westward, lifting up to us as upon a jagged crown of iron mountains the most exquisite sunset the world contains. Now in a moment it was gone. There was no twilight, no amber dusk of northern evenings; the day was eclipsed suddenly, the stars shot into their places, and night dropped like a bowl upon the saucer of the sea.

I watched the bustling life aboard ship, the cattle and swine on the foredeck, stamping their hoofs indignantly as we rolled, the natives wrapping their heads in pareus like flowered tablecloths as protection against the night wind, the poor-white-trash family with their tongues and noses in sardine tins. The luggage was piled so high on the main hatch that the helmsman aft could not possibly see where he was steering. But that made no matter. Reason was a white man's toy; ships were propelled by faith in Polynesia. Hawaii had been discovered by outrigger canoes, sailing through three thousand uncharted miles.

It was too hot to sleep now with the great wind full of heat blowing from the north. Hinny put her head in my lap, and I was grateful for her quiet presence there. It was not worth wondering, on such a night, how it was, in what curious manner, I did love and need her, but I knew that without her I could not so thoroughly have enjoyed the little sparklets of rain flashing against the sea from a vagrant cloud.

Quite innocent it seemed, but the wind rose suddenly and the whole sky was blurred with torrential rain that banged like bullets against our lumbering ship. The passengers screamed and struggled in a knot to find shelter. Hinny and I beat them to the cabin, but the tiny room was soon packed with steaming natives; there was barely space to breathe and it was impossible to sit even on the floor amid that trampling herd. The wind roared. I could hear the cattle thumping against the deck as the schooner lunged and wallowed, and through the porthole, in a glare of lightning, I saw them wrenching frantically at the ropes which tied their horns.

"Attention!" yelled the lieutenant. Beneath the door slopped the vomit from the pigsty forward. There was no avoiding it. It was impossible even to bend to clean the nauseous mess from our ankles.

"I suppose," Hinny yelled above the roar of rain and sixty hysterical voices, "this is what all adventure is, half real discomfort and half the fiction you make of it afterward. But it's fun if you can live the fiction while it's going on. Hell, isn't it fun?"

At daybreak the storm collapsed as suddenly as it had exploded, and the sun swooped up over the horizon to light the three azure islands.

We stopped for the morning at Raiatea, where once a priest of God Hiro had stolen a hammer and saw from Captain Cook and planted them that they might reproduce. Beneath the shadow of a blue mountain and a corrugated iron roof we lunched on coffee and beans. From Raiatea to Huahine we sailed in sunshine. Huahine was all that a South Sea Island should be, except that there were almost no people on it, for it was evilly reputed to be a haven of elephantiasis. In Tahiti I had seen one of the more famous victims of it, an old man wheeling his testicles in a wheelbarrow.

Then jutting from the sea was the great obelisk of Borabora. Our little boat shot through the pass in the coral reef, between breakers that howled and crashed on each side of us, and immediately was in the smooth water of the lagoon. There was another little boat in the harbor, a curious little moon-shaped galleon with a high poop deck surrounded by a balustrade.

"You're in luck," said our captain. "It's from Maupiti."

We walked silently along the water front beneath the shadow of that impossible mountain that hid the moon so barely that its gilt touched the beach and not our path. The large white houses built during the brief vanilla boom lay abandoned. Only one shop was open, and its light made grotesque froglike silhouettes of the Chinese squatting on its porch. There was a smell of moss and lichen, of rank and fabulous weeds. pushing down from the mountain jungle to stifle the village.

By midmorning our new craft had taken us within sight of Maupiti, and our half-mystic decision to come here, to live here, to resolve our problems alone, was justified by its beauty at least. It stood like a fortress upon the sea, its gray cliffs rising a thousand feet above the four low islands surrounding it. Two of these, two round flat islets (like biscuits spread with parsley, I thought), marked the passage in the silver reef which encircled Maupiti.

Here was the paradise that poets dream, a lost island, a splendid verdant land completely isolated by leagues of water from the rest of the world that man had plundered.

Our little boat skirted the reef with slackened sail, awaiting a coincident wave and wind to carry us through the narrowest and most dangerous pass, a mere slot between two enormous scrolls of green water that shattered into powdery spray on either side. The captain stood above the tiller, clutching its handle between the first two huge toes of one foot, gazing critically at the monstrous seas which hove beneath the boat and suddenly into the gullet of the pass. The boat balanced uneasily. No one spoke. A dark gull swooped from a cloud into the brilliant sunlight, and the captain waved to it, grinning idiotically as one might to amuse a child, for the bird was the euau, the shadow of God Stability, Tu-ta'iri-moana, the Smiter-of-the-Sea.

The bird looked back over its wing and darted through the pass, streaking the water with a white wake where its claws touched it. "Uh!" the captain grunted, for the wind rose at that moment, and I saw a mountainous wave bending over our stern. The boat slipped sickeningly backward, then lifted and fairly soared into the pass. The coral flashed past less than a fathom below. Minor waves assaulted us, and the reef thundered as if in anger that this morsel should slide so dauntlessly through its teeth.

For a dozen seconds the boat skidded irresolutely from side to side as the seas caught it and tried to hurl it against the gaping reef. The captain swung the tiller firmly between his toes; he was not concerned with danger; his body rose straight and towering above the sea's tumult, and the butt of a cigarette, glued to his lower lip, swung synchronously back and forth with the tiller's sweep. Then we were in the harbor, slipping smoothly over soft billows toward our conquered fortress island.

Never had I met a people with such assertive hospitality. We were given a faré himiné, a communal song house, and sufficient food for several days. Most of this moldered on the doorstep, for old Chief Tamano had summarily adopted us. He would rouse us before dawn and lead us like children, one on each hand, to the home of some relative where a meal was already spread upon the floor. We three sat alone while the host and his family squatted by the walls watching us, marveling at the table manners of white folk who did not know how to eat properly with their fingers, but required the crutches of forks, which Tamano carried for us from house to house, polishing them upon the seat of his pareu.

Breakfast began with scalding coffee, which was followed in rapid succession by roast pig, roast fish, roast breadfruit, taro and other tubers, mostly roasted. We quenched our thirst with young coconut, but it was not usual that we reached the coconut, which was brought in last, for Tamano would snatch us up in midmeal and shepherd us outside where we must sit a few minutes, rubbing our stomachs and grinning, and repeat the phrase of gratitude our tutor had taught us. Then we would be dragged to another breakfast, exactly similar, and when this array of viands was half-eaten we would be dragged to another still.

This continued for our first three days. Our throats were parched with the salty pork and the miti ha'ari sauce, composed of coconut milk and lime and sea water. The unexpected lack of water was torture. There was but one thin spittle of a stream in all the district.

When the novelty of us had worn off and we were on our own, we learned how callow was our independence. I had to climb into the mountains and then up the thorny tree for oranges. Fishing, too, was a chore of time wasted for very little food. I found that during daylight I had few spare hours in which to write, and that at night I often was too tired to do so. "Go back to the land and find freedom," we have heard, but there is no freedom when one's every moment must be devoted to just staying alive. Freedom consists of the corner grocery store, the telephone to reach it with, the available doctor and

98

his car, and, most of all, emotional tranquillity, which Hinny and I had lost.

Now for a long time we had been to each other no more than understanding companions, continuing friendship with the courage that we must succeed because we were too lonely to fail in it. Reaching brusquely in the dark, or turning carelessly, Hinny would reply with the proper routine answer to my gesture, and no syllable more. I ached with this, knowing that I must constrain these gestures to the progress of what might be our renascent love, which our child might weld. And I despaired because we both were clumsy, and both afraid.

My friend Hae was a mighty fisherman, a mighty husband. We were taking a rest from goggle fishing one day. "You've got to be strong," said Hae, "to be a good fisherman like me. That's why they call me Hae-i-te-oa, Fierceness-of-Blackness. What does your name mean, Beel?"

"Redness-of-Awfulness," I said, without a smile.

"Uh," said Hae, slugging down half a gourd of orange beer. "Let me look at you." I turned around, white and probably shaky from my chores beneath the sea. "It doesn't show much on the outside. You're married to that pretty little brown girl, I suppose?"

What the hell? I thought. Does he mean am I married to her? "Why, yes," I began.

"Me," said Hae, "I've killed all my wives. At least they've all died somehow. Five of them, not counting the one I've got now. She'll die soon though, I suppose." He shook his head and smiled wistfully. "My blood is too strong for them. It eats them up, boils them. You've seen the little concrete house in the district of Mahaena?"

I remembered it as a curious haunted shrine of which the natives would not speak.

"Well, that's the tomb where my five wives are buried, in a row. Years ago, when my second wife died because my blood was just too strong, I saw how things were going, so I went to Papeete and worked a while to make me feebler, and I brought some cement among other things. When I came back to Maupiti I made the tomb, capacious. It's a pretty one, don't you think?"

99

I avowed that the spare hunk of concrete was very pretty.

"Well, I put them all in there, side by side, for they were good wives and I wanted them to be comfortable. And it wasn't their fault that my blood boiled them." He sighed. "I guess I'm cursed by being a strong man, Beel. You're lucky, I guess."

I chuckled. I was fond of old Fierceness-of-Blackness. He sprinkled slowly the butu seeds upon the water to drug the fish, a lazy man's way. "Lots of people," he said, "have offered me as much as thirty-five francs to be buried in the tomb. But I won't have it—unless perhaps you'd like to raise it to seventy-five francs?"

"Thank you, Hae, but—"

"Just a thought, but my wives probably wouldn't like it, for one thing." He laughed. "I suppose they like to talk about me and the old days, comparing notes, and they wouldn't want you, you pale Redness-of-Awfulness, there listening to them. And it might embarrass you. But as for your wife? A hundred francs, say?"

Sunstroke got me and I couldn't shake it. Maybe Hae was right; I had so little strength that even to husk coconuts had become an exhausting effort, and they grew too high, and the roots of taro grew too low. Bananas, even when I soaked them in sea water, took too long to ripen, and every fish in the whole damned lagoon must have thought I was sent to them to play with.

Writing was an almost intolerable effort; the words tangled in the keys of the typewriter. I procrastinated, avoiding the machine by finding a hundred urgent jobs to do, none of them well. I salved my conscience for a while by making things for Hinny, trinkets of wood and seashells, since that, I convinced myself, was at least a worthy incidental means of making her happy. But I knew she understood the ruse, though she wore my earrings and odd bracelets until I couldn't mistake that they hampered her and were grotesque.

So I would attack the typewriter again, each morning writing furiously whatever came into my head in the hope that I could swing from that facile nonsense to a proper story without a jerk, but it didn't work for me as it did, I had heard, for Mr. Maugham. There was no easy way to write. I only crippled the typewriter and therefore found a new excuse for not writing in meticulously repairing it.

At night we walked together along the quiet path and were startled to discover that this journey had never seemed so beautiful before, not even yesterday or our very first night in Maupiti. The water was alive. As we shuffled through it the little waves wrapped our ankles with ripples of brightest phosphorus, and when, leaving our scant clothes on the shore, we ran into the sea to swim, the churned and shattered water fell about us like opals, and we dived beneath this beauty, spreading it everywhere around us.

Often now the night fishermen would be coming home, their torches extinguished, and there was a crowd ashore, waiting with guitars and patient songs to see the catch. The children rushed out to drag their fathers' canoes through the shallows; they wrestled and splashed, covered with a foam of phosphorus, and as they helped to load the fish into palm-frond baskets sometimes they cut off a tail or a head and rubbed the phosphorus, which had permeated the flesh, upon their bodies, so that they looked like tupapaus, or luminous ghosts. The young girls properly screamed at them, greenly glowing and prancing fiendishly, then rushed away to the security of their lovers' arms. And as Hinny would pretend to be afraid, she would sometimes rush to mine.

It was on one such night, when we were happy, that a weird and inexplicable tragedy occurred, inexplicable to us but, as I have written earlier regarding the supernormal in the islands, perfectly acceptable to the natives and the white old-timers. We were unloading fish when we were alarmed by the howling of dogs. Tamano dropped his basket. "That's death," he said. His companions and the girls on shore set up a fearful cry, "A-ué, a-ué!" and down the path came a pack of dogs, rushing as though on the trail of some invisible prey. They swooped off up the valley and down again; they doubled on their tracks and redoubled, their noses to the ground in silence or lifted, howling again.

Then we saw their prey but dimly. It was the wraithlike figure of a fleeing child, racing faster than they. "Titiri," said Tamano. "She was sick . . ."

I jumped into the path to stop her, but I was flung on my back by a dozen hands. "Leave her alone! She's not dead yet!" I struggled to my feet to jump aside as the dogs rushed in circles around us and the little girl. Hinny held to my arm, her mouth agape. I leaned back on a solid wall of wet bodies. Suddenly the child, screaming clearly, broke through the circling hounds and rushed into the sea, the dogs still pursuing her. She didn't try to swim, but the dogs did, slowly. She just walked and walked, stumbling over the coral, until the water rose to her chin, and to her mouth and eyes. Then she was gone, and the dogs, whimpering, swam back to shore, nosing out their masters. We stroked them, calmed them. They were real.

Real, too, was the body of little Titiri when we went to find it in her mother's house.

The better my work progressed at last, the more our affection was re-established, the worse seemed Hinny's health. First she got dengue fever and fought it valiantly. Of course there was no doctor here. Then the glands beneath her arms began to swell and turn purple. This frightened us, for it indicated lymphangitis which might well turn into elephantiasis; her arms would become as thick as bolsters. But the worst was that she was having pains in her abdomen, where the baby was kept.

There were no two ways about it; we had to get to Tahiti, to the hospital, but with no communication between the islands there was no way of divining when a boat might visit Maupiti, and none of our little outriggers could hope to reach even Borabora.

It must have been an ironic god who sent us the missionaries, French Protestant, none of them medical, of course. They were purely tax collectors, with the nerve to solicit an innocent island where they didn't even have a chapel. But our native friends chipped in. "Who knows," said Hae, "but that sometime our gods may want to borrow money from your god, and we shall have given them a reasonable argument, yes?"

Furiously, Hinny and I had refused to attend the prayer meetings which bled our friends, so it was quite reasonable, if not quite Christian, that the missionaries should refuse us passage back to Tahiti.

"Are you married?" they demanded.

Belligerently, stupidly, I said no. "But listen, my girl is ill! She must have a doctor." The pale, thin, black-habited men shook their heads.

"Pas de savon," said Hinny, but we moved aboard their boat while they were collecting funds, and kept Tamano and Hae as musclemen until the boat set off for Tahiti, where I paid them a normal fare and became heathen for life.

Hinny had elephantiasis, and there was no known cure for it. It was thought to have been arrested in changing to a temperate climate, but in the tropics it would surge and thicken until one or two or more members of her slender body became elephantine. No one was sure of the cause of this hideous disease. The natives believed it emanated from certain soils. The doctors of Tahiti assumed variously that it came from water, flies, mosquitoes. They were only in accord that we must leave Tahiti soon. Retreat after retreat, I thought. But we couldn't leave now, with the child to be born in less than three months. Hinny was advised to go to bed and stay there, but with her great vitality and facility of being bored, it was impossible. If I served her dinner in bed, she was soon up to wash the dishes. Then there was the bookbinding; we must float paper on oil paints in water to make the swirling endpapers. There were our two pups to be cared for, both with cankerous infections of the ears, the result, said our housemaid Lola, of listening to ghosts; dogs should turn a deaf ear to ghosts.

"But those dogs of Maupiti, do you think they all—"

"Every one of them! Do you remember the night of Monsieur Moses?"

It had been a very odd night, a few weeks ago, when we had had eleven people, the entire white population of Paea, for cocktails on our porch. We were sitting on the L-shaped divan at one end of it, talking idly, when suddenly the two dogs got up and walked stiff-legged, their neck hair bristling, to the Dutch door. The top half of it was open and they put their feet on the closed lower half staring into the night. All of us noticed this, as we did the reason for it, the quiet appearance of Charlie Moses, bigger than life with beard. As Charlie was a constant visitor from his house nearly next door, we paid him no attention but kept on talking.

But the growling of the dogs made me look at them again. Charlie was gone and the dogs were backing up, still bristling.

103

"That's funny," I said. "Why didn't he come in?"

"For God's sake!" said Cas, jumping up. "He isn't here! It just occurred to me. He's in town! Eighteen miles away!"

"Didn't you see him? Didn't you?"

"Of course, we all did. What's he up to? This is a bit on the eerie side."

We hurried out-of-doors where the full moon illumined clearly my property as far as the road. The dogs would not go out. There was no Charlie. Cas bicycled to Charlie's house. He wasn't there. I snatched the bike from him and sped to the nearest house with a telephone. I got Papeete, then the Hotel Tiare, then Charlie, sleepy and truculent.

"Damn it, you spoiled a good cocktail party," he growled. "I was just dreaming that I was sitting on your porch, drinking mead."

Hinny had fever now, and her glands were ferocious as ulcers, purple and throbbing as they calcified; she had to walk with her arms stretched out as if about to take flight.

"This worries me less," she said, "than the pains I'm getting in my belly. Don't like it."

I had bought at the Papeete auctions the nineteenth-century book by Dr. Conquest, *Outlines of Midwifery*. To divert Hinny from her troubles I read to her the chapter on the Ideal Accoucheur:

"While the patient and her friends are all bustle, consternation, and despair, his countenance and manner must never express alarm or want of resource under the most trying and adverse events."

"Give me a drink," said Hinny, trying to brush off a shadow which weighed on her stomach. This I did, and had one for me.

"Neither his hand nor his heart must, for a moment, lose its firmness; but with a mind unassailed by fear or doubt—"

"That, my darling, I have both of."

"The customary practice of taking off the coat before the operation of turning often disgusts and alarms the patient, and cannot be necessary if the sleeve of the coat be made sufficiently large to admit of its being slipped above the elbow. . . ."

Hinny's dark hair tossed from side to side as she turned on the pillow. The candlelight cut caves beneath her cheekbones. "I'm both disgusted and alarmed," she said through clenched teeth. "Something's wrong here. I feel I'm in labor now."

The neighbor's telephone was out of order and there was no other way, in that wilderness, of getting a doctor. I pedaled the bike to Papeete, eighteen miles away, returned with the doctor and his car, and rushed Hinny howling to the hospital. We had barely got her to bed when our boy was born, in the sixth month, and I held him in my hands for a moment before he died. I placed him carefully upright in a chromium jar.

There was then the problem of burying the poor little bastard, for bastard he was, ourselves unmarried, and no church on the island would permit his burial in its cemetery. Days went by as I sought a means of lodging my child, and the doctor said, "Look, you must get a permit soon, for you know, in this climate—"

"But can't I bury him in the sea? Or in the mountains? He's mine, isn't he?"

"Ah, no. Tahiti is not yours. I can arrange perhaps for you to inter it beneath a path in the public cemetery, with a tip to the guardian, of course."

I made the coffin of redwood, with brass screws, and then found that no taxi would transport it, as it contained the corpse of an illegitimate child. At enormous expense I could have a bier, carried by four black-gowned men, but we had scarcely enough money for hospital expenses now. "And the climate," said the doctor.

I took the minute coffin beneath my arm on the bicycle, and pedaled up that nightmare road, and with every bump there was a loose bump within the coffin for my son had been poorly packed.

We reached the cemetery, and the guardian with a huge cigar buried the coffin, with no headstone, beneath the path. He was a fanciful character. "He'll not be lonely," said he. "It's the best spot really, with people always coming and going above him. Thank you, monsieur. I'll drink to his happiness with this."

Every door we opened, I thought, split on its hinges and fell upon us. Carefully and cooperatively we would build new doors to shelter us in the dark, to open in Tahiti's sunlight to a good world where we might walk together in love and tranquillity, and again they would come crashing down. The gods of Tahiti were like landlords trying by negligence, by contrived inconvenience, by threat, and by shock to evict us as unwanted tenants of their house.

We had no money. I sold a short story from time to time, and my book was doing well enough, but royalties were paid semi-annually, and in any case wouldn't see us through a year. My father, having lost his fortune in the crashes, was in a hospital, meticulously printing his letters to me. Yes, he might come down, but the news from my mother and Aline was not encouraging. Obviously we must return to America.

Hinny's glands grew worse, purple and big as grapes, and there was no question now that we must admit defeat before everything. We were broke, homeless, ill, and not even very much in love. But, oddly, though we admitted defeat we were undefeated. We laughed. We slept snugly together. We watered our rum. Life is so simple in youth that mistakes and misfortune, even if they are intimately emotional, can be complacently shrugged away. Whistling round the corner is a wind with new breath for you. There's a sun to seal your sores. Look, there's all the ocean that is yours.

We sailed across it to the fabulous Marquesas with their tremendous cliffs, their turrets of lichen-green rock, their wild dogs hunting in packs against the wind, their silent villages—for in the last hundred years their population had dropped through tuberculosis and leprosy and venereal disease, brought by us, the white conquering cankering races, to reduce it from one hundred thousand to six hundred inhabitants of the lush valleys.

We sailed on toward Panama with the consciousness of death around us, past Easter Island and its tilting dead statues, past the Galápagos and to Cristóbal on the isthmus of Panama.

We were sitting in Dempsey's Bar drinking white rum at ten cents a shot, laughing at an experience of the afternoon, when a whore had tried to snatch me from Hinny. "You may be a five-dollar gal," she had shouted, "but I can do better for a buck"—the nicest compliment, said Hinny, she had ever had.

One of our hotel porters in fancy uniform came into our grubby bar and handed me a telegram. It was from my sister Aline in New York. "Dad is dead," it said.

10

Marriage and the death of it—
girl with apple—exit to freedom

DESOLATELY, lost, we landed in New York to sleep on the floor of Harold who had guided my poetry on Joy Street. My mother, still pretty as a dryad, and Uncle Bill and Aline came to meet us, and were a little startled by the bronze skin of Hinny. "Good heavens," they said, "it's beautiful, but Grandmother Davis will be sure she's a native. Can't you at least marry her?"

It had never occurred to me. We sat up together like twin dolls on the floor that night, and I said, "Why not? What have we got to lose? Maybe marriage is an island which will help us more than Maupiti to live happily together."

"There might even be love in it," Hinny said, giving me a ghoul's cold kiss.

So we got married and found a magnificent unfurnished apartment, which we could barely afford, for forty-five dollars a month at 226 Fifth Avenue, a house built by President Polk as his private mansion in the days when this section of New York was a hill with trees. Then Waterman, the penman, bought it and built my two top floors for his daughter who needed skylights for sculpture. There was said to be a green ghost in the attic.

Richard Harding Davis lived here, and the actor Richard Mansfield, and finally I on my wedding night, curled with Hinny on the floor of that immense studio without a stick of furniture. It was a desert of a house, and our future seemed a desert, and we didn't give a damn, sitting arm in arm on the floor with our backs to a cracked wall and a bottle of Scotch between us.

We were toasting the ghost in the attic when Teddy came up the stairs. Teddy was an old friend of Hinny and a brigand, a Robin Hood who robbed the rich to indulge the poor. Platonically he had loved Hinny since she was a child, so when he tossed his broad shoulders through the door he looked rather quizzically at the single acquisition she had in this apartment, me.

"Back in a few minutes," he said, and back he was, bumbling up the five flights of stairs with an enormous green armchair on his head. "Wedding bed," he said. "I think you'll do," he added to me, and took off his shoes and socks to treat his athlete's foot with mercurochrome. Hinny and I spent the night in the chair which he had casually removed from the Prince George Hotel—he was the upholsterer, he said—and Teddy spent the night on the floor of a back room. He was gone in the morning leaving another memento, a telephone book torn in half, an obvious suggestion that I had better treat his old girl well.

Bit by bit, with the help of friends and my mother, we got to sleeping horizontally and eating at table. Teddy was invaluable. He would take us to Macy's or Hearn's or Gimbel's, ask our needs, and plunder the store. "Don't bother me," he'd say. "Just watch, by the elevator." And I would watch in wonder as he filched pots, pans, sheets, got them wrapped, and incredibly walked away without paying for them. "Just hold these, son. I forgot the rug."

I became a book reviewer, modestly, with the *Saturday Review* at first, then the New York *Times,* the *Tribune,* the *Atlantic Monthly, Nation, New Republic,* finally the Book-of-the-Month Club, until I was reading and writing of a dozen books a week, and making a decent living. But this was escape from reality into the secondhand lives of other people, and I had little time for creative writing. Hinny was binding books again, but desultorily, matching bindings to the wallpapers of Park Avenue matrons, and she, too, was cheating, farming out her jobs to others. The Rockefeller Foundation treated without effect her incipient elephantiasis, and eventually, miraculously, it was cured by Dr. Arthur Grace who had spent years in South America studying the disease.

But it was no cure for the greater ill which beset us, which has no name, the simple and inexplicable drifting apart, for no overt reason, of people who had lived so tightly and so alone together over so many years that this attrition had worn off surprise. Physically and intellectually we were, to each other, neuters. Hinny got a job selling exquisite glassware to an apathetic public. I got Carmine, a charmer who resembled and replaced my own wife, and I would slip out at five in the morning to sleep and wake with her again, to see a dawn we could share in lust and tenderness, the same birds in the same branches of the park, the same tramps to whom I would give more money than I could afford, guiltily, and rush home up the steps like a comic-strip character in my stocking feet, sick with infidelity and nauseous with a phony love for my own wife.

We gave tremendous cocktail parties as an escape from each other, and Sherwood Anderson and Fannie Hurst recommended me for a Guggenheim Fellowship which I didn't get. Charles Studin brought us into the warm circle of his salon. There was a good man who should be remembered by the young aspirants of New York in that day. Slowly on the way to death, he decided to do what he most wanted to do, to give parties, and three times a week he would flick through his card index of friends, divided into categories of Art, Literature, Science—there were no politicians among us—and invite us to his cocktail parties, from five to seven, when the Filipino houseboy, Pedro, opened the windows and blew us out so that his master could eat and go to bed by nine. Never has there been such a lavish and considerate host; he would move from group to group of people talking over their drinks, and say, with an arm around you, "Hassoldt, what are we talking about?" and let you conclude, when he would move you to another group where possibly, if you were a writer, he would introduce you to a publisher.

I found two like this, the first by Charlie's whispering into the publisher's perfectly good ear that he should meet me and talk quite loudly as I was quite deaf. He had told me the same about the publisher, and so we met and bellowed before a company of fifty or so people.

"I HEAR YOU'VE WRITTEN A BOOK ON THE SOUTH SEAS," cried the publisher.

"I HAVE BEEN HOPING TO MEET SOMEONE WHO KNEW THIS," cried I.

"You don't have to shout. I hear quite well."

"So do I," I whispered, and we had a drink to Charlie's caprice.

Half the literary world was there, Gunther, Sheean, Dos Passos,

Dawn Powell, and I would return from them limp at the knees to review their books.

Hinny was more realistic and forthright than I. "To hell with it," she said. "This marriage is poison to us." Courteously we gave up all pretense that it wasn't. We slept in separate rooms, but I still brought her breakfast in bed. We had elaborate Moonsdays, birthdays, Christmases, but as we sat on the floor amid all our presents we would try to achieve a pretense of ecstasy with our arms around each other, and fall back into the castoff wrappings of our gifts to find again that our love was mechanical. Every few weeks she would pack her bags, knowing that I would unpack them and rearrange her things meticulously while she was downstairs looking for a cab. We didn't want each other, but loneliness was the colder choice.

There came a New Year and its midnight when, in evening clothes, we were about to go to a party, given by one of her old loves. The cuckoo clock struck twelve.

"We're late," said Hinny. "Let's call now and wish him a happy New Year."

I dialed his hotel, standing, Hinny waiting at the door. "Hello . . . hello, Joe?"

A woman's rich voice replied, "Hello, is this you, Eric?"

"No," I said, "it's not. Apparently we're both calling the same hotel. We're on crossed wires. If you're not in a hurry, may I put my call through first?"

". . . of course . . . I just wanted to wish Happy New Year to a friend." Her voice had timbre. It was slightly unsure, with a foreign accent which I couldn't place. It was a strangely thrilling voice.

"Well, happy New Year to you," I said.

There was a pause. "Happy New Year to you, too . . . ghost," she replied slowly. I sat down at that word "ghost." Hinny was tapping her foot in the doorway. The voice continued, warm, caressing. "I haven't had a New Year since I don't know when. They have all been old years and very much alike. Good-by . . . ghost."

"Wait! Wait!" I clenched the telephone as if to prevent her slipping through it and away. "What do you mean? Tell me who you are?"

Hesitantly and excitedly we talked. She was Russian. So I was a writer? Curious that, because she was, too. She had been four years in America and knew only Eric. "You are kind," she said. "But no, not tonight, that would be asking too much of luck. Call me at this number . . . if you want to. Ask for Lisa."

I called the next evening, and she called the next. For a month we held nightly rendezvous by telephone, telling each other far more intimately of our lives than we could have done without the dark of space between us. She was young, so she said, twenty-seven, a year younger than I. She was beautiful, she said. No, not yet, dear Bill; we should create a New Year carefully.

I was so excited I could barely work, and Hinny took this odd affair with delight, for it might solve her problems in giving her the freedom to leave me. She seemed now to be trying to whittle down our remnant love and need of each other, but we temporized, for the alternative to our cool companionship was the lonely void. It was winter now, with snow caressing the skylights, and hail beating them, and as we sat together with no new words the storms around us were no longer like those of a winter ago when we had laughed at them and loved them, thumbed our noses like children at them, for they couldn't reach us in our attic island. The fury on the roof was hostile now.

Lisa telephoned. "I will come to see you tomorrow night at ten," she said. "But you know that this may ruin all of it?" That was what I was afraid of, the almost certain disillusionment if we met, the clumsy pretense of the hour before the whole thing shattered, to leave us deprived even of the memory of our enchanted hours by the banal telephone.

"Galahad," said Hinny, putting on her gloves, "I shall be doing the town with Teddy until about three A.M. Believe me, for my sake I wish you luck."

At half-past nine I was pacing the floor with a whisky and soda, stealing nervous glances at a mirror as I passed. I certainly wasn't vain; I was acutely conscious that it might be I who would smash this lovely unimaginable rendezvous. At ten the bell rang, five flights downstairs, and up them came heavy footsteps. Oh, my God, I thought, I've a dulcet-toned, literate washerwoman to deal with.

I believe I was suddenly calm, almost resentful of this stranger's intrusion. It was like the old boxing days, just before I entered the ring. What the hell? Can't you take another bruise? But too soon she was rounding the last newel post and coming up to me, eating an apple.

"Hello, I'm on the dot, I think."

I took a gulp from the glass in my hand before putting it around her back and leading her into the studio. She stood against the bookshelves and we looked at each other bravely without much breath in us. She was exquisite, despite the lump of apple in her cheek. Her long black hair was glistening with snow, her eyes smiling wisely as an elf's.

"I think I like you, Bill," she said, nodding and taking another bite of the apple.

"You are lovely . . . lovely." I took the red rain cape from her shoulders and put my arms gently around her. She shook her head strangely, as if shaking away tears, and kissed me quickly. Her red mouth was moist and apple-scented. I felt I had known her always, the taste of her, the clean, certain movements of her hands. As if we were rejoining now after some stupid separation of years. As if she were a wife returning.

Time went by with the ugly years of the early thirties, the century's and my own. Lisa remained a faithful and exciting friend, Hinny a correct and casual wife. I flourished modestly, with fat, and one day was contemplating a slim Hollywood contract on the piano when salvation came by telephone from Armand Denis, the husband of Leila Roosevelt, Andre's daughter. I hadn't seen them since Bali.

Would I join them as photographer, writer, publicist, and whipping boy on an expedition to Burma? Would I? It was deliverance. I left Hinny the bank account, with all but twenty dollars a month of my future salary to be paid directly into it. She had easily the means to run away if she must, I thought, going down the stairs with no good-by kiss, feeling lost and sick, but with space before me again. Years ago I had been one of the first volunteers for the rocket to the moon, among the other possible suicides. This, for the moment, would do nicely.

11 ～～～～～～～～～～～～～～～～～～

Burma and the great gray gods—magical tattooing—the hill of the cobra

IN FOUR DAYS we had flown across Europe and the Middle East and old India to Burma's Rangoon. We were to drive up the then-primitive Burma Road into warring China, filming as we went, to Chungking, possibly Tibet. Burma was a land of green and gold and gray, the green of its jungles and lush paddy fields, the gold of conical temples and the pongis', the begging priests', robes, the gray ruins of cities like Pagan.

We were five on the expedition: Leila Roosevelt, Armand Denis, Roy Phelps (cameraman), Jack Kenney (mechanic), and me. Aside from the fact that each of us was a specialist in his field, Denis had chosen us among his many applicants because we were uninterested in cards, politics, and hunting. We got along admirably well through nine months of frequent danger and, what was worse, monotony.

We drove in our truck and two cars slowly northward and came to Kyaukpadaung and Mount Popa, the home of the most powerful nats, ghosts, in Burma and descended to one of the branches of the Irrawaddy River which was running thin over quicksands. We yelled at the native Karens who were watching us from the farther shore, offering them money to guide us and help us across. "Three hundred rupees!" we yelled. They didn't budge. In the shelter of a lean-to they stretched out at full length puffing gigantic cheroots into brass pots to protect them from the rain.

"Five hundred!" we yelled. That was a lot of money, and suddenly, in a splotch of lightning, we saw a strange figure stand up amid the Karens. It was nude but for a loincloth and a feathered war bonnet. This was incredible, I thought; an American Indian, in costume, in Burma. He raised his hand dramatically and bawled orders to the natives who immediately produced wide planks with which to make a bridge over the quicksands. Buffaloes were harnessed with fiber rope to our cars, and in a few minutes we were safe on the other side.

"You American?" asked our apparition with the rain-drenched feather bonnet. "Me Chief Michael Joseph Thunderface. California Mission College, '21. Do not think this masquerade. It is my forefathers' feathers. It scares people." He grinned broadly. "Forget the money."

He led us to a typical canvas wigwam in the center of a group of huts. Buffalo and bear were painted on the walls of it, and inside it was cozy and warm with the small fire ascending straight. We sat on hides while Thunderface carefully dried his forefathers' feathers, one by one, then wrapped the bonnet lovingly in a soft deerskin envelope.

We blinked at one another, and Thunderface explained that he had traveled through India to Burma with his own Wild West Show some ten years before, and bad luck had progressively befallen him. Finally, with little left but his tent and headdress and a bag of conjuring apparatus, he had worked north from Rangoon, shopping for a village worthy of him, until he had found it here. After various vicissitudes he had become its headman. Unlike a European gone native, however, he had lost none of his racial pride, and was making an honest living guiding cars across the quicksands—for a shocking fee, of course.

"What's this exhibition of yours trying to do out here?" he demanded, crinkling the leather creases around the predatory nose.

"We are looking particularly for the Hill of the Snakes," Armand said as a starter.

"You mean serpents?" asked Thunderface.

"Snakes," said Armand, who dislikes a quibble. "The snake, specifically, called the King Cobra or Hamadryad or, sometimes, Ophiophagus, because it eats its own kind. There's a legend, you know, of a sacred hill where the snakes were, and may still be, worshiped."

Thunderface was adamant. "If they're cobras they're serpents. Serpents is to snakes like trousers is to pants. They're higher class." While we were assimilating this aphorism the sound of temple bells a long way off came tinkling to us, which meant the rain had stopped. "I've heard that story," said Thunderface, "but I never believed it. They tell me that Naga worship died out in Burma a thousand years ago. Still, there are two old temples, which they call snake temples, at the dead city of Pagan. There's always a monk hanging around them. And he might know. The rain has stopped now. I'll go with you, if you like, as Director of Exhibition, heh?"

We jumped at the chance, for this was the most likely lead to the sacred hill we yet had had. We set off immediately, munching green coconut strips, for Pagan, the city of the dead.

Thunderface rode in my car, befouling the night with his cheroot, blowing embers like comets from it. Within an hour he halted us atop a bare little hill. "Look," he said quietly. "The old city, Pagan."

Bleached as bones beneath the moon ahead of us lay the ruins of what had once been Burma's capital city, five thousand stupas, pagodas, temples dating back to A.D. 108 and spread over a hundred square miles. We stopped the cars and turned off the lights. I felt cold before such desolation. A fruit bat, as big as a movie vampire, lumbered across the sky. A jackal nuzzled what at first I took to be the whitened leg of a man, but it was that of an old god only, torn from some alabaster idol. As far as we could see in that greenish light stood the crumbled ruins of brick and marble, littering the jungle with holiness. Something was watching me, I felt, and turned to meet the leer of a griffon on a stone pillar beside the car.

Thunderface, the stoic redskin, grunted, "I like it better in the day." So do I, I thought.

Even the great lost cities of Indo-China cannot boast the multitude of stately ruins that are found at Pagan. The temples of Amanda, Ta-pyi-nyu, and Gawdapalin, built in the vaulted cruciform style of Marco Polo's day, had not suffered too seriously, but around them rose, as far as we could see by moonlight, wasted towers, terraced shrines of ethereal fretwork, huge bulbous onions of architecture through which the jackals slunk to disappear in their cores and appear again, like worms burrowing.

So thin are the alabaster walls, striated with shadow, that they truly do resemble the skins of an onion, through which you can almost see, layer within layer, the Buddhas enshrined. Leogryphs stand stalwartly above the debris of their crumbled temples. Crippled Gautamas of all sizes lie splashed by the droppings of the magical mango tree. Great arches lead nowhere but to a shadow where men walk no more. Dragons, once magnificent, lie disarticulate, vertebra from vertebra sundered, whiskers dead and limp as ancient roots, teeth spread helter-skelter like the seeds of Cadmus, waiting for a new culture of Pagan to water them.

The cart road we followed led down to the Irrawaddy River, then back for a mile through clumps of tamarinds to two temples which were set alone on marshy ground. There was movement on the top of the smaller one, vultures waiting, and at the pagoda's edge shone the vertical eyes of a dying goat.

These two ruins had once been the Nagayon Pagoda and the Aveyadana Temple, built by King Kyansittha in A.D. 1084 to commemorate the time when, as only a servant of the previous king, he had had to flee the royal displeasure. No one now knows why. But he fled to the jungle and there a cobra, the great Naga itself, shielded him from the storm with its hood.

Thunderface called softly at the temple door, and a saffron-robed old priest came out with a taper. Holding it close to one eye, as if its flame were a lens, he examined us suspiciously, sighed, and ran a lean hand across his shaven head. He accepted one of Thunderface's thunderbolt cheroots, and we sat talking there, winding our words through devious paths until we could state our errand.

Did he know the village that was once called Kensi, Kansi, or Kunsi, according to the old historians, on a hill? And was Naga worship still practiced there? Or anywhere now? Fear and cunning shone in the old man's eyes and he turned them quickly away toward the Nagayon Pagoda, the dead shrine of a cult that was dead—perhaps. There was something snakelike in that quick, ancient, shaven head. He could be descended, I thought, from those Tantric priests, the Ari, who had come from Bengal through Assam and Manipur, bringing their unclean worship, the perversion of man's love for even the amorous gods.

But his face was candid, bland with kindliness, when he turned it back. Secrecy didn't matter any more, he said, since the cult was formally dead in Burma. We might go to Kya Lap Sing, the Black Valley or Valley of Night, where we might find a pongyi to guide us to Kensi.

We crossed the parallel ranges of central Burma, where the Taung Thu women wear earrings the size of carrots, and for a while we

116

filmed the neighboring Padaungs, the giraffe-necked people, whose throats are stretched and encased in spirals of brass. And we lived with the tattooed Karen people whose men tattoo full-length pants upon their legs and insert talismans of gold, the hkaung-beit-set, in slits beneath their skin. And we came over sweet rolling hills into the Shan States where the people were light in color as the Chinese, and afflicted by nats, the demons. There was a nat in every letter to us out of China, saying that, in spite of the letter we carried from Franklin D. Roosevelt, Chungking still would not receive our expedition.

The farther we went from the Irrawaddy, the main route of travel in Burma, the better and brighter became the tattooing of the natives. The old men of the Shans were the most decorative of all, with almost solid trouser tattooing from feet to navel. Most of the charm patterns tattooed are protective, of the a-hpi-se sort which is known even by the monastery schoolboys who have it incised where they are generally caned, as they believe it lightens the weight of the rod. And when they are grown to manhood a sprinkling of these charms over the body is supposedly efficacious against blows, bullets, and slashes of the dah, that herculean razor which the professional murderers, the dacoits, employ. For this reason the a-hpi-se is usually tattooed upon the belly, throat, and top of the head. The only imperative charm, to my knowledge, is the a-nu-se, which insures that the love of the bearer will be returned. This consists simply of a dotted triangle, and is most often placed between the eyes, though its use on the lips for the cajoling of kisses and even on the tip of the tongue to form honeyed words is not uncommon.

Gloomily we went on, fighting for film to justify the great cost of our journey. A simple travelogue wouldn't do for the makers of *Goona-Goona* and *Dark Rapture*. Desperately we filmed animals and bubbling miniature volcanoes until we came to Lake Inle and the Princess Golden Nest.

I lost my heart to this fair princess of the peach-bloom skin and almond eyes as we walked in her palace gardens without time, without clocks. Only at three-hour intervals a group of musicians somewhere in the depths of the palace played soft Burmese songs, night and day. I sat comfortably among the red-velvet cushions of the private gondola of Princess Golden Nest while the boatmen, the first leg rowers I had

117

met, propelled us across Lake Inle. These men were Inthas, I learned, a curious race from the Arakan Islands in the Bay of Bengal, enslaved long ago.

Balancing on one foot on the slippery edge of the canoe, the Intha grasps his paddle with one hand at shoulder height and with the opposite foot drives the blade backward through the water, an incredible, ludicrous performance, I thought at first, but the paddlers make excellent time and are accustomed to trading voyages of a hundred and more miles in length.

While the Princess Golden Nest told me legends in excellent English I watched two strips of sparkling water which rapidly approached from the other side of the lake. That would be Armand and Leila in the gigantic canoes paddled by ninety leg rowers each. On they came at a hell of a clip, like galvanized centipedes, and tore past us as I filmed them.

My princess snorted at this industry. "You do not appreciate a fairy tale," she said. And I sat down abashed to listen. We passed floating marshy islands with small shacks and gardens upon them. They actually floated and so could be towed from one part of the lake to another.

"It is said," said my princess, "that the ancestors of Hsa-pu, the priestess of the King Cobras, in Kensi . . ."

I stopped gazing at the orchid in the jungle of black hair above her ear. Rupturing dreams, I asked, "Do you know where Kensi is, where Hsa-pu is?"

"Of course, Beel. If you'll come back soon I'll lend you my elephants." I kissed her hard, and the mosquitoes bit me hard while I recalled the report of an old missionary named Hurston, a hundred years ago, who visited the animist tribes at the foot of a bare black mountain near Kensi. He described a narrow serpentine stairway which apparently wound up the pinnacle but which he was forbidden to approach. Up there, he was told, the Naga, the snake cult, was practiced. Other investigators, chiefly military men on holiday, sought to identify the district from Hurston's notes, but they met with such hostility on the part of the natives who admitted the legend but refused guidance that they never got even as far as Hurston's Kensi.

Erig Gongue, the manager of a nearby teak plantation, confirmed the princess's opinion that Kensi was called Kawmyo now. "Full of crazy people," he said. "Live on opium and bhang and stuff. If there is snake worship there, it probably came up the Mekong River from Cambodia, where the Khmers, who built Angkor, used to practice it, rather than directly from India across Burma."

"Fare thee well," said Princess Golden Nest in her meticulous old English, and we rocked away on elephant back through the forest of teak, its broad leaves curtaining the sun. We climbed gradually; the teak was replaced by pine; the shrilling cicadas were left behind and in the absence of their stridor our presence was heralded by a symphony of birds, the crows and the crow pheasants, the cuckoos, quail, hoopoe; and when we came to a clearing atop a hill a male peacock shot into the sky, dangling the ponderous beauty of his tail. The smell of the linden trees was as thick as an air full of cheap talcum powder.

North of us rose a mountain to about six thousand feet, and west squatted a number of lesser hills, their jungles folded about them like the cloaks of trolls sleeping with their heads on their knees. Armand in the lead suddenly flung up his arms and tried to find a footing in the teetery howdah, the elephant saddle. "There it is! That's Hurston's black mountain!"

A great swab of cloud erased it for a moment, but when it had passed we saw a black nearly symmetrical pyramid of a mountain which seemed to correspond exactly with the one Hurston had described. The village at its foot was almost indistinguishable, but over it streamed the long cloth serpentine pennants, the emblems of the Naga and the token of our goal.

We yelled at the mahouts, our elephant chauffeurs, and the mahouts prodded our colossal vehicles. We went down that hill like an avalanche, loped across the plain regardless of clattering teeth and pounding posteriors, and only slowed when we heard a terrific din coming from the village. Drums and flutes and weird stringed instruments were playing all together to accompany a moaning melody which seemed to be made by human lungs.

We entered the village slowly, with the dignity befitting white men. The musicians, beneath their central tree, didn't pause; they scarcely looked at us. Some had kidney-shaped violins, some had the common narrow drums with clay daubed on the heads to raise the tone, and some were playing floppy flutes which seemed to be jointed.

The half-naked village men, their long hair twisted into topknots, had eyes only for this procession of musicians which was winding through the single muddy street, and the women, wearing embroidered red skirts, sat before their huts and moaned. Only a few of the younger men, who looked less entranced than their elders, reached for pellet bows—which shoot stones, not arrows—and watched us suspiciously.

"Don't stop," our interpreter advised us. "Follow the procession slowly." But my mahout waited to point through the open door of a hut.

"Bhang!" he said. The old man of the house had been smoking Indian hemp, I judged from the sweet stink of it, and was now lolling on a filthy mat. At three more huts I saw the same sort of decrepit addicts to the drug, and when my mahout pointed at one after another of the procession, saying, "Bhang! bhang! bhang!" like a boy cowboy shooting Indians, I assumed that most of the village was drugged. He spoke to one of the older men.

"Great fortune!" he said. "Not one son has been born in this village for over a year, and they are going to try to get their serpent god to fix it up."

"Great fortune indeed," said Armand. "Will they mind us watching and filming them?"

"We can try. They don't seem to have spirit enough even to be curious about us. This race," he said pontifically, "is decayed."

When we caught up with the twelve musicians we noticed that a woman was now leading them, a woman who might well have been a creature of the infamous Dr. Fu Manchu. She was dressed in the purest white from throat to ankles. The *lonngyi* skirt was wound tight around her waist and the long-sleeved blouse fitted like a dazzling skin, a strange contrast to the somber nudity of her companions. Her face was farded white with some heavy paste, and her agate eyes were those of a snake. She was evil and sensually exciting.

"Hsa-pu," said my mahout, the name passed down among the priestesses of Naga, so Hurston had said.

120

Riding my elephant beside her, and staring fascinated at her, I had forgotten the sacred hill ahead, and it was not until she had left her musicians and started off alone that I looked up. It was Hurston's hill and no mistake. Before us was the serpentine stairway, a foot wide, winding into the clouds, and slowly along it climbed Hsa-pu, followed by a fattish youth who bore a roll of mats and a tray with offerings of coconut and fruit and rice.

We knelt our elephants and got down. Hsa-pu was far ahead by now and we followed hurriedly in single file. Each step of the stair was shaped like a scale of the Naga, crudely cut of flagstone, and where the rain had settled on it and thin moss grown it was slimy as a serpent's skin. I turned to look at the musicians and the half-drugged villagers with their pellet bows held indecisively, but they made no move to stop us. We climbed for half a mile, slippery step by step, until we reached the lowering mists.

The stairs leveled here and seemed to go directly into the solid earth. Before us was a low precipice honeycombed with caves. There was just light enough to see, far in the depths of the largest one, a low cot woven of vines, and flower garlands suspended from pegs above it. Hsa-pu went in slowly, followed by her servant, and in a moment he came backing out, looking neither to right nor left but abjectly laying the mats straight before him. My mahout was whispering to me. Hsa-pu had gone to propitiate her god, Hsa-pu, whose ancestors for centuries had exclusively had the knowledge of the snake and the secret of placating him.

And it must be Hsa-pu of this generation to discuss with the god all matters of fertility, whether of crops or beasts or women. This year no sons had been born to Kensi, and so Hsa-pu had come to exert her powers.

We could dimly see her raise the tray of offerings to the level of her eyes, scoop a fistful of rice, blow upon it, and flick it in all directions, to appease the other gods or nats, I assumed. Then she put the tray upon the cot and knelt beside it. It was nearly too dark to film, but Roy and I chanced it. The sun beyond the mist was sinking, and the orange light that reached the cave was whitened suddenly with a flare of lightning. We could hear the music far below, muffled by mist, and from the cave came strange noises, alternately sibilant and explosive, that sent a shiver up my spine.

Hsa-pu was squatting, backing toward us, talking to the snake god that lived within, drawing him out along the mats. We, too, backed off and stood breathless before the creature we saw. This was the King Cobra, or Hamadryad, at least fourteen feet in length, as long, I believe, as they ever grow. His hooded head arced four feet above the ground, on a level with Hsa-pu's breast as he wove after her.

"My God," said Armand, who cherishes snakes, "look at its fangs!"

My interpreter-mahout was whispering hoarsely. These snakes, he said ("serpents" he corrected himself), were caught in the jungle and brought once a year to the sacred mountain, where Hsa-pu made a pact with them, promising to return them within twelve moons to their homes. She would be bitten, she knew, if she broke faith.

The snakes were content to remain within the cave, where she fed them frogs once every five days, and besought their boon when the need arose. The fangs and the venom were untampered with—you can't pull the teeth of your god—and since the King Cobra, because of his enormous secretion, carries more than a hundred times the lethal dose of poison, I realized that we were filming perhaps the most dangerous ritual in the world.

Now the woman and the snake were upon the mat before the cave, Hsa-pu squatting, approaching, and backing with quick, smooth movements of her heels, drawing the attention of the god with her left hand and striking it lightly with her right, as a boxer might do. Now she rose to a crouch and curved one arm over the snake farther and farther back. The snake followed her arm until it was erect as far as it could reach—approximately one third of its body length— and Hsa-pu could gently bring down her hand upon its head, forcing it flat upon the ground. She would humble it thus, remind it of her power before she wheedled it for the village sons.

The snake, the god, sprang back hissing when she released it. Squatting again less than three feet away, she tempted it with her knees, swinging them together from side to side, opening and closing them until the snake lunged and she could catch it beneath the throat with the side of her open hand. Lightning forked across the dusk like a snake tongue threatening us.

Hsa-pu backed round in a circle now, always squatting, and the huge snake pursued her. With forefinger pressed to the thumb of her left hand, she seemed to draw it toward her, as if by a thread, while with her right hand she made curious lithe gestures similar to those used in Tibetan Lamaism. Her face was set hard as a mask. Sweat beaded her forehead and ran down in gray lines across her powdered cheeks.

Roy was beside me. "This is incredible!" Leila started to speak, then suddenly pointed to the cliff. From the holes beside the cave of the god three common cobras were slowly emerging. I reached for a boulder but the mahout stopped me. A fourth cobra, six feet long, had raised its head within striking distance of his thigh. The mahout nodded reassuringly.

The music from below grew gradually faster, and Hsa-pu's movements quickened with it. Rain was falling now, and the great snake glistened as he tried to get close enough to his tormentor to strike. She bent forward, protruded one knee, and when the snake flung toward her, half its body off the ground, she received its fangs in the taut skirt which her knees had spread. A stain grew slowly there.

I could hear Armand muttering, and from the corner of my eye I saw his finger point. "There's another." Another cobra, a small one, was within five feet of us. This was getting a bit thick, I thought; we were interested in strange cultures, but . . . but I was as fascinated as the snakes by this amazing woman. I scarcely felt the rain that was flailing against us now.

Hsa-pu lowered her head almost to the ground and looked sideways at her god; and he rose and remained motionless above her, hood expanded and jaws wide to strike again, while she talked to him gently. She laid her hand upon her abdomen and then upon the earth, and along the muddy print where the snake had fallen when he struck at her she drew her two hands caressingly, then cupped her breasts with them. No ritual could be more explicitly phallic.

The rain was blinding. We shielded our eyes and leaned forward, trying to watch the other snakes and the god at once. The lightning was continual, and the thunder drowned out all the music with the exception of the whining flute. I realized with a sudden chill in the marrow of me that neither Hsa-pu nor the snake had moved in a very long while, but had remained watching each other's eyes, she crouched and he overlooking her like a god.

Then with an almost imperceptible motion her head was rising. Her head was tilting across the green, lightning-lighted sky till it was level with her god's, and slowly it came forward. There were but two feet between them now. And now there was but one.

Hsa-pu, her hands behind her, leaned slowly down and pressed her mouth against the poisonous mouth of her great god, and the trembling that ran through her whole body seemed communicated to his before he swung his head to one side and slid off into the cave.

Hsa-pu remained kneeling, her forehead in her hands. My breath came slishing out and I was aware suddenly that the storm had swung with all its fury upon us, lashing leaves in my face and pressing me toward the stone stair that led to supper and sanity and a long drink.

For weeks there was no news from Hinny at home, then a curt, cool note came saying mostly that she had decided to walk the dogs on the fire escape instead of the street. She hoped I was doing what I wanted to do.

I wasn't. Fascinating as Burma was, and charming as were my companions, an odd emotional metamorphosis was going on within me; I wanted Hinny now, none of the others. I wrote true love letters to this wife who loved me no longer, and sent them by every mail truck to Rangoon. It was idiotic. I could remember her beauty, her bravery, the alluring caprices of her mind, but I could remember no tenderness ever, not a gesture of love which was spontaneous. If I had been unfaithful it was because I sought the duplication and perfection of her who had rejected me. I hungered for her to such an extent that I would waken sweating in the night and hold my palm to my lips to warm her cold absent kisses. Unashamed, I would wish on the first star of twilight that this separation had done to her what it had to me, that she would love me and write me in tenderness, to tell me she was well and missed me and had beautifully bound a book.

I bought exotic presents for her next Christmas—bracelets, earrings, silks, and gritted my teeth as Armand went through the mail at each administrator's residence: "Leila, Jack, Roy, oh, here's a postcard for you, Bill."

"Hoping you are doing what you want to do—Hinny."
I was, of course. I was having half the bed, the middle half.

12 ∾∾∾∾∾∾∾∾∾∾∾∾∾

*The valley of the shadow of
death—the master of gold*

WE DROVE UP through Lashio, the border town
between Burma and China, where we were forced to accept the
services of two of the dreaded Black Guard of China, "to protect you
from bandits," they said, but actually to see that we didn't photograph
the Burma-Yunnan road. Through Musé and Manwhé it rained continually, yet there was no water but the rain to drink, for the streams
were polluted and the one pure river was thousands of feet beneath
our cliff. We argued our way through Wan Ting, the border customs
station, and into China. Now the monsoon rains were upon us and
we could barely distinguish the mountain villages of Chefang and
Mongshih.

This was the Valley of the Shadow of Death. The Japanese had
already bombed the convoys here, but of more immediate concern
to us were the roving bands of dacoits, professional assassins. As
defense against them we camped one night in a Chinese cemetery,
knowing that the bandits would be afraid of ghosts. The cemetery
with its paunchy little tombs seemed cheerful in comparison to the
view that greeted us in the morning.

Two hundred munitions trucks squatted in the mud ahead of our
cars; three hundred more were jammed behind. Between here and
Lung Ling, we learned, there were two great landslides that the rain
had gouged from the mountains and spilled across the road, and the
two bridges had been sloughed away.

Expeditions are often the fun that the hammock explorer imagines

125

them to be, but they are often composed of mud and rain mounting above the floor canvas of your tent, and a diet of cabbage soup, and a distant ennui like an itch which comes from invisible dacoits, and the persistent vacuum of no letter from the Chinese government permitting us to wait a while and finally continue along their bitter Burma Road, to Kunming and Chungking and Tibet as we had planned.

We gave up. Sopping, dispirited, running out of conversation in flabby tents, we said to hell with it, we would try another terrain, perhaps the impossible Nepal. And away we turned like bats down the bitter Burma Road, the road to Mandalay, to Rangoon where we took back the blessings we had given to the great golden cone, three hundred and seventy feet high, of the Shwe Dagon Pagoda, and drooped into an establishment which advertised: "All Kinds of Eatable Can Be Obtainable."

A walloping huge wind blew out of Asia and hurtled our plane nearly into Calcutta's Great Eastern Hotel, which we ascended in an elevator with a sacred bull. As all bulls in India are sacred, you are as likely as not to meet one sitting on your doorstep or blocking the road in front of your car. And you will either go around him carefully, or wait for him to move, knowing that if you should hurt a hair of the arrogant creature's tail the swarming crowds would tear you limb from limb. And defile your remains unspeakably.

This bull which roamed our hotel, and which none dared evict, must have been a joy and a vengeance for the Indians who were forbidden to enter the snobbier British clubs. The Great Eastern had for years been his home, the elevator his sanctum. We and the bull traveled up and down for weeks, all of us praying for anything better than this. The bull probably wanted to be a horizontal, not vertical, traveler, but he had no place to go. Nor did we, until out of the dusk of a cocktail party bloomed one of the princesses of Nepal.

We were shameless in pursuit of her, we married men, and I became her personal plague.

"Foreigners are simply not permitted in Nepal," she stated. "My father is very reasonably worried that they would infiltrate as they have in India, with the same resultant discontent among our people.

126

The poor Oriental is happier when he is not trying to imitate the rich European's ways."

She was a grave little princess. Blandishment got me nowhere, but gradual attrition did, and she sent a telegram to her father, the Maharajah of Nepal, to be taken by runner from Raxaul on the Indian frontier across the Himalayas to Khatmandu.

We waited, remembering that only one hundred and forty-nine white men had ever been permitted into that Shangri-la more forbidden than Tibet. And lo! there was magic in the East! On wings of what must have been the bird-god Garuda came the message that an expedition good enough for Roosevelt to sponsor was good enough for his august majesty the Maharajah of Nepal. We could come in.

This time I kissed a princess's foot.

We were at a loss for gifts worthy of the Maharajah of Nepal. Armand had found gifts of ivory, but Leila and I searched Calcutta for Goldwasser, that clear, sweet fluid made in Germany which has flecks of real gold floating in it. "Regal," I said, "beautiful, original, dignified, useful. . . ."

But as there was none in all the town we boldly decided to make it with sweetened vodka and gold leaf, stoppered with gold sealing wax, hand labeled by Leila on torn brown paper, and aged with adherent dust like many an expensive cognac bought in Paris.

We sought gold leaf from one jeweler's shop to another up and down Chowringhee Road, through the jammed lanes by the river ghats where the dead were burned, even in Kariah Road where the dainty prostitutes of India and Japan leaned like massed flowers, russet and pale yellow flowers, from rival balconies. We met encouragement at last from one leprous artisan who suggested that we try, of all places, a pharmacy.

There were no windows in it. The spaces where they might have been to allay the stench were hung with the dried or cooked carcasses of animals, birds, insects, snakes, withered or bloated, but all very dead. Boiled iguanas hung by their tails; the skulls of men and beasts were impaled on spikes jutting from a cluttered wall; stiff skins, haired and hairless, were tacked to the ceiling. One corner with a wire net around it was filled with precious aphrodisiacal litter: a couple of

127

rhinoceros horns, half a dozen antlers of Mongolian deer, the manure of owls, the red-and-white rock salt from Kalabagh, the black salt, of especial virtue, from Kohat. There were noisome piles of beetles similar to the familiar Spanish fly, and other piles which seemed to be composed of the pale headless corpses of dwarfs, their long legs agonizedly twisted; these would be mandrake root, the sovereign aphrodisiac of peasant belief.

We were being glared at by an old wizard who was grinding some hell bane in a mortar.

"Look," said Leila, "gold leaf!"

I bent down to see that the wizard was mashing together the skeleton of some rodent and the brittle skin of a frog. To them he added a yellow ointment. He mixed the mess thoroughly and put dabs of it on small squares of gold leaf which he folded over into parcels like ravioli.

"Now what do *you* want?" he demanded in perfect English.

I nearly stumbled with surprise. "Why, a little gold leaf, about three sheets like those."

He peeled off three sheets. "Three rupees," he said.

"By the way," said Leila, "if you don't mind my asking, aren't you English?"

The old man stared at her for a long time, his lip curling. Leila is very pleasant to look at when there is not a dried iguana like a sword of Damocles hanging over her head. "Perhaps I was," he said.

"May I ask," I asked, "why you wrap your medicines in gold leaf?"

Wearily he leaned back into the gloom of that demon's cavern and gave us a scholarly dissertation on the curative values of gold, as adjudged by Pliny, Constantinus Africanus, Henry IV, Roger Bacon, and fairly recent members of the Pasteur Institute. Syphilis, scrofula, leprosy, juvenile diarrhea, women's periods were all alleviated by it.

"Hell," he said, drawing his finger across his forehead where the sweat had made mud, being careful not to disturb the trident of Vishnu painted there. The finger had plowed to the subsoil of pink English skin. "Let's have a drink." We had swallowed already too much powdered snake skin and owl manure and bone dust to object even to a decoction of these, provided it be wet.

We followed the old man through a grim passage, turned a corner, and stopped in sunlight before a scene that literally staggered me. "Please make yourselves at home," he said, standing between us, very tall now, looking with pride at the lovely walled garden we had entered. Java fig trees and the stately peepul shadowed the benches by the wall. Orchids grew from wicker baskets. A small fountain played at one side of the garden, sending a jet of blue and silver before a shrine where Vishnu, his four arms extended, sat uncomfortably on his merman's tail.

It was idyllic, a cloister of dreams impossible to imagine as the home of the grisly wizard who owned the shop beyond the passage. I exclaimed with delight at the beauty before me, and when Leila, wordlessly, touched my arm and indicated by a lift of her chin a gleaming metallic statue on the other side of the court, I spluttered honestly, "That's the loveliest thing I ever saw."

"It is my wife," said the wizard. "Literally my wife." I had a shiver at that. "She is my Tita-Bhai, sheathed in copper now, but soon she will be sheathed in gold."

I examined the statue. It was of an Indian girl seated with her legs curled beneath her. She was quite nude, and every detail of her body was superbly modeled. I could not detect a single seam left by the casting.

"Exquisite, isn't she?" the old man asked as we returned to the table under a lavender jacaranda tree. "Inside the casing is the true body of Tita-Bhai."

"Impossible!" said Leila.

"Ah! You'll have to hear something of a story then. If your forbearance is as great as my pride is small, I'll tell it to you. I'm surprised that you haven't heard it somewhere before, for it was the scandal of Calcutta once." He dug a grimy forefinger under his turban and drew out a louse.

"I came out here as a boy of twenty-three, just graduated from Oxford with a degree in chemistry. I had no interest in making a success in the world. I only wanted adventure and the means to hunt tiger or serow in Burma. A generous inheritance lasted me for quite a time, and I added to it considerably by my work in the Government Assay Office, chiefly by assaying gold. But I squandered my substance very merrily. I lost money at the races. I drank too much. And because

I was healthy and imaginative and deficient in what you nice people call a moral sense, I spent more money than you'd believe possible on the little Hindu girls. Not the hetaerae and lustrous courtesans you'd find at the races, decked out with authentic diamonds, but the low-caste dassis, the lovely poisonous little girls of the randi-bazaar.

"However you may explain it, I simply could not have these youngsters for a night or a languid afternoon, then return them to their huts. Whenever one was especially nice to me, and seemed to understand not merely my need of her comfort, but my need of the romance which she as a woman represented and I as a transient adventurer could only buy, I set her up decently in a decent quarter of the city and paid her rent so long as she remained a decent girl. Each time I would think that this Magdalene I had saved would love me as very shortly I came to love her, for I could fall in love to order then and needed to, but each time I would find that the chaprassi at my gate, or some snide young subaltern I had been having drinks with, had cuckolded me under my very nose.

"This virtually drove me to drink, or so I believed, in fear of my incompetence to hold even a girl of the bazaars. It was silly reasoning, but it served as an alibi on those mornings after when I was too sick to go to work or on those nights when I behaved like a boor in the homes of good people. One by one I lost the girls I had tried so hard to exalt and to love. I lost my inheritance. I lost my friends and their respect. Eventually I lost my job, and as I had to stay clear of the authorities for fear of deportation, I rented a room from a pimp in the randi-bazaar.

"I made a meager living by compounding drugs from the native pharmacopoeia, to which I added doses of calomel, acetanalid, sulphur, and whatever contributed to man's happiness by taking pain out of it. I catered to the people's faith in magical potions, simples made out of the rotted junk you saw out there. And I gave them gold leaf, which really does a great deal of good, psychologically, at least, when wrapped around a pill."

The sun was setting. The mina birds were still, and the only sound in the garden was the bubble-bubble of the old man's water pipe.

"Meanwhile I was regaining my health and was finding life again adventuresome. From time to time one of the girls whom I had helped with my pills would of her own accord come to pass the evening with me, and though they were professionals they would never accept an anna as a gift. I learned their language easily. I learned their beautiful faith. I became a Hindu and worshiped with them, these soiled children who had taken me to their breasts when my own world had cast me out.

"But occasionally I would be puzzled by some girl out of their class who sought me and achieved no joy of our union. More and more of this strange sort of girl came to me, not for my drugs, but for love, if I may call it that. The odd thing was that they were all of them superb physical examples of young Indian womanhood.

"Puzzled, I began turning them away, for this wasn't the sort of love I sought, but they kept coming, never happily and as if by some compulsion outside of themselves. And one morning, after one of them had gone, I discovered this incredible thing, a small chunk of gold on my pillow. And then I began to find gold regularly there, not much but always a crumb or two after one of these strange, joyless, perfect women had gone, none of them returning ever. I tested the gold; it was real.

"Then one night as I lay in bed smoking the huqa and pondering on the amazing turn my life had taken, the door opened quietly and into the path of moonlight stepped the most exquisite lass I had ever seen in this land of beautiful girls. And she was sobbing. Slowly she took off her sari to reveal a figure which must have been sculptured by the gods themselves. And still she was sobbing, almost mutely, in an anguish too great for sound.

" 'Child, what is your name?' I asked.

"I could barely hear her answer, 'Tita-Bhai.' I made her sit on the bed while I sat on the floor, holding one of her small feet in my hands.

" 'Why have you come here, Tita-Bhai?'

"She did not hesitate to answer me, except to swallow the tears. 'For the baby,' she said.

" 'For the *what?*'

" 'The baby.' Then she went on to tell me of the atrocious business in which I had unwittingly become involved. Somewhere in the province of Behar, she said, there lived a man who was called The Nail.

131

He trafficked in whatever would foul the hands of decent men: drugs, women, stolen goods, counterfeit rupees, but chief of his trades was that of supplying, to wealthy Hindus, white or nearly white girl babies.

"You understand? The traffic in white women had been a prosperous one in India before the British put it down, for dark men of most southern races prefer their mistresses blond. But this monster with the awful name of The Nail went the trade one better and by a method not easily discernible to the official eye: he found stranded white men like me, the blonder the better, down on their luck and in the ill graces of the government. He supplied us with the choicest damsels he could lay his paws on, and if we balked, as I had done finally, he paid us in gold nuggets to breed white baby girls for his debauched customers. Infant boys were disposed of."

"I can't believe it," Leila said.

The old man's face crinkled in annoyance. "You don't have to, but consult the Criminal Records of India, if you are interested. You will find there that I testified against The Nail. . . .

"Little Tita-Bhai stopped sobbing finally. Five years ago, she said, she had been sold to The Nail by her father when her mother died, and apparently he had nurtured her carefully for just this vicious job. She was light in color, like the aristocratic women of Nepal; I was pink and white, with red hair. The Nail was astute in judging that we might have bred a most valuable daughter.

"But as I looked at Tita-Bhai and held her warm bare foot to my heart I knew that it was she I had always been seeking. She smiled in a little while, for she, too, knew that now we must always be together. It was a gay joke on The Nail.

"We were happy. I bought this house with the gold I had earned by my involuntary partnership with The Nail, and in the shop I prospered, though you might not imagine it, and in this secret garden we lived like great Siva and his bride, sufficient in ourselves. At the end of the first year we had a child, a baby girl almost as blond as I and as lovely as its mother, but within a month it died.

"Then one evening we were sitting on this same bench and I was trying to divert my wife from her sorrows. I invented a game, but she played half-heartedly; we would try to flip pebbles from where we sat so that they would fall straight into the well, all the way to the water

132

without touching the sides. My servant called to me softly, 'Master!' and brought to us a black Madrassi boy with a letter. It was from The Nail, demanding that Tita-Bhai come back to him, with the white child he had sent her to conceive.

"I wrote back angrily that the child had died and that Tita-Bhai would stay with me. I thought that would be the end of it, but within the week Tita-Bhai saw The Nail at the market and fled back to me. And in another week she thought she saw him peering at her from the balcony of that house over there. And in the third week it was the same; she saw him, or thought she saw him, everywhere. She was nearly insane with fear. She must go back, she said; he would kill us both in some horrible way. I told her to wait, and when he came I should deal with him, for although I was an orthodox Hindu now I still had the white man's confidence of superiority.

"But Tita-Bhai could not eat for fear of The Nail, and she could scarcely sleep. She would spend half the night wandering in the garden, to the well and back again, and to the well.

"It was on such a night that I wakened to a cry in the garden; a night bird, I thought, and went to sleep again, knowing that Tita-Bhai would come in and sleep beside me when she was so tired that the fear was numbed. But in the morning my hand reached to an empty pillow. I rushed to the garden. Tita-Bhai wasn't there, but there were other visitors, the vultures sitting in a ring on the edge of the well. They hopped away as I approached, and I looked in. There on the water lay Tita-Bhai."

The bubble-bubble of the huqa was a stream of soft round sounds like a cascade of little opals poured from hand to hand. I sought something to say, but any phrase would have been futile now.

"It was the very next day that I read in the *Statesman* that the case of The Nail was coming up for trial. He had been in prison since a few days after he had sent the letter. Tita-Bhai had imagined seeing him, and had died when at last she was safe."

After a moment the full horror of it burst upon me, and I felt cold sweat running down my spine. The old man's voice had changed when he went on. The anguish had gone out of it, and a brave sort of pride had entered.

"I have shown you my Tita-Bhai," he said, with a gesture toward

the shadows where the statue was softly glowing. "That is truly she.
. . . Hindu that I am, I could not bear to have her body burned at
the river ghats, her sweet skull beaten open and the remnants of her
flung into the Ganges for the eels to feast upon. I am a scientist, and
so I have preserved her scientifically, in a manner which I hope will
bring comfort to thousands who have lost the ones they loved."

Was he mad? I wondered. He couldn't mean this.

"That statue," he said slowly, "is Tita-Bhai sheathed in copper,
not yet gold, unfortunately. You are amazed? Did you never study
chemistry or physics in your great American schools? That is Tita-
Bhai electroplated with a film of copper which fits and conforms to
every pore. Tita-Bhai will be forever with me."

I thought, uneasily, was this possible? Could flesh be electroplated?

"Yes," the old pharmacist went on in a voice that was very tired.
It seemed he read my mind. "Yes, it is possible. You can electroplate
almost anything, you know. You wouldn't understand the details of
it. The essential thing is to coat the flesh with graphite or bronze dust
in an adherent ointment, then pass your current through it from the
copper anode. It requires care, and devotion, but it is not hard to do."

The combination of my respect for this old wizard, aversion to the
life he had led, and compassion for the lost loveliness of Tita-Bhai
was not a comfortable one. I was relieved when he rose to dismiss us.
We passed the statue and furtively I touched a shoulder. The copper
was as smooth as flesh and warm as flesh with the heat retained from
the afternoon sun.

The old man paused before we entered the tunnel leading to his
hellish shop.

"She is only of copper now, but she must have gold. It takes a lot
of gold for even so small a girl as Tita-Bhai. But she shall have gold.
Every year brings us closer to it. One after another of the Calcutta
pharmacists is being convinced that it is better to accept my annual
fee for the right to handle his gold leaf than to take the chance of
making that much money by handling it himself. They send their
clients to me, with bare pills to be wrapped in the magical gold, hundreds of them already, and there will be more. I am prospering, by
gold leaf alone. If the cancer gives me time, if Kali will be forbearing,

134

in a few years I shall have such a monopoly that Tita-Bhai may be invested with gold as she is with copper now. It is a blessed thing, the gold. . . ."

13 ~~~~~~~~~~~~~~~~~~~~

The Himalayas—Nepal—my miraculous
little girl—the sacrifices in the temple
—African safari—farewell to Hinny

NEPAL LIES BETWEEN India and Tibet in a nest of the Himalayas, banked by mountains five miles high, plus Mount Everest. We drove toward it with awe and incipient heart failure as far as Patna, where the good rice comes from, took a toy train to Raxaul, switched to a toyer one to Birganj and Amelekhganj and a beat-up Buick into the Himalayan foothills of Bhimphedi. From there, on our more reliable feet, we climbed toward the resthouse on the eight-thousand-foot pass of Disaghari. Our sixty coolies had contracted to carry our equipment over the mountains for three rupees, about a dollar, apiece—seventeen miles of terrible travel along a rocky footpath.

Pilgrims from India, hastening to salvation, passed us occasionally. There was a woman large with child which would have birth on the banks of the sacred Baghmatti River, three old men plodding hand in hand, a sadhu with his begging bowl and iron tongs. And climbing among them like an inch-worm was a naked and ulcerous Hindu, measuring his length on the ground, standing, falling, stretching his claws as far as they could reach, then rising to walk three paces and repeat his penance. His eyes were staring; he was blind, but nonetheless he would make his pilgrimage across the mountains, groveling toward his gods.

We climbed straight up for two thousand feet past small clouds like islands against the green sea of the mountain jungle. The hundred-pound loads of the coolies seemed to inconvenience them not at all, and even the shaggy, bearded ancients and the children tubercularly coughing passed us by. We, the hardened explorers, plodded. I felt my heart pounding against my Adam's apple.

When we reached five thousand feet and sprawled along a ridge while our boys boiled tea, we saw the valley for a minute clearly, the thatched cottages and shoestring streets, the golden roofs of the little shrines. Then swiftly they were obliterated by soft gray clouds, and the tops of pines on the mountainside showed mistily, floating.

I felt my joints had welded when we got to our feet again, but gradually we caught up with the Indian pilgrims, and felt considerably better about our prowess. The three old men were still hand in hand, a senile ballet, and the pregnant woman was bravely climbing, her hands clasped about her abdomen.

The fog cleared sufficiently for us to see that we had a small valley to descend before climbing the final ridge, but it still hovered over our path. Suddenly a scream came slashing through it like a blade, Leila's scream. Armand reached her first, then the rest of us in a stumbling mob.

"Look at him!" she cried. "He'll go over!" Inching down the valley path ahead of us was the blind Hindu who was measuring his length to Khatmandu. He lay flat on the wet and jagged rocks, his blind eyes staring over a precipice and his arms like tentacles groping into space.

I thought the roaring in my ears was of my own blood, but the fog swerved again and beyond the prostrate pilgrim I saw a torrential waterfall, an intricate braid of silver hurtling straight down for a hundred feet. The man was too far for us to reach him in time. We yelled, we five and all the coolies, but our many voices must have been incoherent. He lifted his head, listening. I could see his naked body trembling as he clawed with one hand at the air and with the other at a mossy stone.

"Oh, lord, he's going!" Leila groaned.

We watched fascinated, futile. If the stone would hold . . . it was slipping. . . . "No! No! Don't move! Wait! . . ." we shouted, staggering toward him. One of his legs slipped over the edge. He clutched at the stone and it began to revolve.

136

"Bandkaro! Bandkaro!" the coolie yelled. "Don't move!"

His brown arched body vibrated against the blue white of the waterfall. The stone slowly turned beneath his fingers. The mossy side disappeared as it rose from its hole. Then the man was gone.

The fog filled the valley again. The waterfall that had swallowed the man gleamed faintly, phosphorescently, and I hoped that somehow it might flow to one of the two sacred rivers of Nepal, to carry its pilgrim, less arduously now, the rest of the journey he had so faithfully begun.

We passed the bitter night in the resthouse of Sisaghari, and the next morning continued more comfortably to the pass of Chandraghiri, for the Maharajah had sent dandies to transport us. The dandi is a sort of litter or roofed palanquin which is carried, with you in it, on the shoulders of eight coolies. Poorer folk, even fat ones, are carried in baskets on the backs of these prodigious little men. There were no roads leading to Khatmandu, though in the valley itself we were to find some five hundred automobiles, all transported by coolie back.

An icy wind whipped over the Himalayas and whirled fog around us in great clots as we bumped along in the dandies. At one minute you were lying on the nape of your neck, at the next you were falling forward over your feet. Most of us gave it up to climb and slide. It was on the seventh day when we were resting to burn leeches off each other with cigarettes that Brahma, tired of hurling fog at us, let it lapse for a moment, and suddenly the valley of Nepal shone clear below us, a lambent jewel box of a country touched by the last light of the sun.

Four thousand feet below us and four thousand five hundred feet above sea level lay this enchanted place, its three major cities gleaming where the shadows had not yet reached the palaces of marble and the temple roofs of gold. There was Khatmandu, whose very name was awesome, and Bhatgaon and Patan, jeweled miniature cities snug in the folds of green velours. We had reached journey's end.

During the several weeks which were permitted us in Nepal we saw wonders and miracles, beauty and horror, which we assiduously filmed

137

in so far as we could. Always with us was our official guard, saying, "No, so sorry," that we couldn't enter here or film this, making notes of our every movement. After many days of snubbing us, the Maharajah invited us to film his palace of marble imported from Italy, block by block, on the backs of the mountain coolies, and to admire his million-dollar hat (so it was assessed by Lloyd's) composed of diamonds, emeralds, rubies the size of grapes. Blood and beauty were everywhere, flowers and the blood of sacrifices before the thirty-foot-high statue of Khal Bhairab the terrible who wore a crown and necklace of skulls. We went to Tantric temples, the abode of a cult which had spread secretly through India and Nepal and Tibet, a temple of ardent and obscene worship, as the temples themselves proclaimed when the sun struck into their niches where congeries of men and women, wonderfully wrought in painted wood, writhed together in amorous ecstasy. Beasts and men, beasts and women, all of them laughing, performed romantic gymnastics for the delight of the Tantric alumnus.

We filmed the burning of the dead, the Devil Dancers brought over the mountains from Tibet, the sacred monkeys that nearly tore Leila apart when she tried to help one of their hurt babies.

And one day we came to the pool of Narain. There seemed at first to be a gigantic corpse in the pool; so cunningly sculptured was the god and so cleverly placed, half in and half out of water, that the movements of the goldfish and the wind ripples gave a semblance of life to it. He reclined full length upon a bed of stone serpents which seemed actually to writhe about him. Here was a place of pilgrimage, and among the pilgrims was a pockmarked little girl with eyes as sweet as pansies who tried to straighten her crooked legs when she smiled at me with those soft eyes. One of her legs was so short, the result of polio, probably, that her body was pitched to that side at an angle of nearly forty-five degrees. I took her hand in mine and led her within the walls, where she seemed timid to trespass, to the reputedly miraculously healing Narain pool, the Lourdes of Nepal.

We wandered idly within the enclosure of brick and moss, not looking at the pool just yet, but growing accustomed to each other, I to a girl of about ten with a horrible deformity, she to a pink alien whose language sounded like monkey chatter and whose innocence

138

was so pristine that he could look straight at her and apparently think her beautiful. She could never have known that beauty was implicit in her.

We wandered among the mass of God Narain's devotees, among the gowns of gold and violet, of black and silver. Large and little bells were suspended everywhere. She rang them devoutly, and rang them again for me who could not touch them with my strange hands. Once when we stood still, gobbling chapatti, she leaned her cheek quickly against the green moss of the soft red brick wall, and once, squeezing my hand a little, we passed a dribbling idiot and she looked up and smiled, shaking her head in pity of him.

There was the sound of musical instruments at the entrance to the walled garden. The bells stopped ringing. The shush-shush of whispering died as all heads were turned toward the gate. Three elephants, caparisoned in gold and red velvet, with embroidered masks over their faces, lifted their trunks while from the central one an old prince descended. He was simply dressed in tight-fitting black trousers and long black jacket that buttoned to the throat, and there was great dignity to him as he paced to the pool of the god. Attendants followed with tall fans of peacock feathers. They flung sandalwood incense into the air, where the rich scent of it was spread by the fans.

My little girl made a tremulous sound and led me to one corner of the pool. She smiled; it was glorious when she smiled. The old prince went slowly from bell to bell, making obeisance at each, until he came to the steps leading down to the pool. A servant followed him, a young man with a goiter, as he descended to the feet of the great god sleeping in his bower of snakes upon the waters.

The old man removed his shoes on the bottom step and flung the garlands which his servant carried upon the stone figure. He kissed the feet of the god three times and cringingly crept up its gigantic body, dropping flowers the while, until he reached the forehead which he marked with the three white parallel lines that are the insignia of Siva. Then all over the courtyard rose the chant, "Narain! Narain!" while he backed slowly to the steps again, sprinkling rice on the god and the water that was his home.

Then the old prince was gone to the sound of Gurkha music and the faint plod of elephants down the road. I turned at a choked cry

139

behind me. My child had stumbled into the crowd of the goiterous, the monstrous, the dwarfs. She groped her way forward, clutching blindly for the wall by the pool, and the crowd parted before this deformed and humble peasant girl.

She groped for the great bell and rang it weakly. It nearly jerked her off her feet. She fumbled, step by step, to the supine god of the pool and made her way along its body until she reached its head. Hands pressed flat together in the prayer gesture, she bowed her forehead to touch that of the god, then held the gray cheeks tightly with her small fingers. Her body began to shake; sobs rushed through it; she trembled so violently that I feared she would fall into the pool.

As suddenly as the tremor had begun, it ended, and from all the crowd burst the glad cry of "Narain! Narain-ah!" The child turned and moved down the body of the god, up the steps, toward us, and as she passed into the press of the street my heart thudded.

She was limping no longer. She was healed.

There were two cogent reasons for the Maharajah's requesting that we leave Nepal. First, he had received the news on September third that World War II was launched, and foreigners with cameras and curiosity were no longer welcome in his peaceful land. Second, the great gory festival of Dasehra was about to begin, and it might be unwise for the world to know that such religious barbarism existed in Nepal.

We wheedled, we cajoled, we begged the Maharajah to let us film this ceremony, but he was adamant. Only when he realized that we couldn't get coolies to take us over the mountains in the next festive ten days and that there was no way short of imprisonment to prevent us seeing what went on did he give us permission to witness the affair, on our promise that we would take no photographs.

The guide and spy officially allotted us was a whiskery young man named Thapa. "Your little girl, who was healed by the favor of Narain, will be made a living goddess at the Dasehra," he whispered to me, so close his mustache tickled and spit got in my ear.

The Dasehra, or Durga Puja, was originally a Hindu festival to commemorate the victory of the goddess Durga (one of Kali's cruel avatars) over the monster Maheshur. The slaughter of thousands of

140

buffaloes is the ritual which chiefly distinguishes it from its counterpart in India today.

Khatmandu had been bedlam for nine days now, and we had remained discreetly inconspicuous, but on the tenth night we slipped into the kot, or temple courtyard. Leila had said that she would stay at home, thank you; massacres left her cold.

It was a nightmare scene into which we came and unobtrusively merged; the stench struck us first, the stench of steaming blood, then the charnel-house heap of decapitated buffaloes. We separated so that we should be less obvious and kept to the shadows at the back of the kot courtyard. I pressed hard against the spike of a golden dragon's mane, hoping the pain of it would keep down my heaving gorge. Try to be objective about it, I said to myself; it has nothing to do with you; the knife doesn't hurt you; the gushing blood of men smells worse, and you've endured that. Breathe deep; immunize your fussy lungs to it.

The court was a furious din of sound, of bands playing and guns being shot in volleys, the groans of the struggling victims, the crazy ringing of bells to drive off the evil spirits, the monotonous mutter of prayers lying like a spine at the base of these ribs of sound. The color of the scene was kaleidoscopic, for around the kot were ranged the flags of Nepal's seven regiments, to be blessed in blood. In the center was an enormous statue of the goddess Durga, leering with fanglike teeth and her three awful eyes upon the butchery at her feet.

The buffaloes, garlanded with flowers, were pushed and hauled before the goddess and given into the hands of the Kassais, the butcher priests. The beast's head was quickly fastened to a post, its nose to the ground, and stretched backward by a rope around its loins so as to extend the neck. The priest raised the curved and dripping khukri and sliced it down with all his might, to decapitate the buffalo with a single swipe. Usually he succeeded; the body flopped over, kicking, and the crowd shouted acclamation. But occasionally one blow was insufficient, and the priest would then be set upon by the good-natured but scoffing worshipers and his face smeared with the hot blood spurting from the partially severed throat.

My stomach felt like a washing machine, churning my dinner in blood.

Immediately after decapitation the carcasses were dragged off by the military servants and porters, who had this meat as their pay. If they were orthodox and couldn't eat it, they would sell it to the wild Gurungs and Tcherpas of the hills. In one corner of the kot sat a Brahman, the officiating priest of the ceremony, chanting incessantly from the Hindu sacred books, yet weaving Buddhist gestures over the little flame which had been brought from the eternal flame of the temple Swayambhunath.

I moved to get a better view of the shadowed figure behind him. My moccasins squished with blood. The erratic electric current flared the lights for a second and I saw the shadow's face, the face of the child at the Narain pool, my lovely youngster who had been miraculously healed. A hand closed on my arm then. It was the guide, Thapa.

"They will not hurt her," he said. "They will test her, and she may be the living Kumari, the daughter of Kali, tomorrow. Don't worry, sahib, she will live. It is an honor." He paused. "She may be quite mad, of course, but that with us is an honor, too."

My eyes were jerked back by the fearful wail of a buffalo which was being led to the post by two stalwart priests. These were of the other, more ancient, tribe, the Newars, whose method of sacrifice was horribly different. Both jugular veins were slit open and the blood geysered forth in jets across the loathsome image of the goddess Durga and over the mounds of rice which had been offered it.

Again came the cry, *"Main bookhi hun! Main bookhi hun!"* as the Newars rushed to scoop up the blood-drenched rice.

"They will eat it!" said Thapa, his mustache in my ear. "It is an honor."

I was conscious suddenly that the voice of the old Brahman had risen from a mutter to an urgent chant. He rang a bell—it was clear and cold as ice water in that fetid place—and at once the servants began lugging off the several hundred buffalo heads and piling them like an inner wall within the torch-lit shrine where the sword of Durga stood. The priest turned to the shadow behind him and drew gently from it my little girl. She seemed dazed; she was drugged perhaps. He put flowers in her hair and a necklace of them around her shoulders. He touched her lips with gentle fingertips which had been dipped in holy water from the Baghmatti River.

"They prepared her for the Rathjatra," Thapa whispered. "She may be Kumari, daughter of Kali, if she is brave."

The Rathjatra was a relatively modern festival, dating from the reign of a king of Khatmandu (Jayaprakasa Mala, A.D. 1740–50) when a young Banhra girl claimed to be possessed and asserted in her ravings that she was a Kumari or deity. The king, considering her an impostor, banished her to the jungle. And for a long while the doubt of her divinity beset him, until the doubt became a sin to him, which only one Kumari, even though she might be a false one, might absolve. So he sent his tiger hunters to find her where she lay starving in the jungle, and after offering her his homage and worship and being forgiven by her, he endowed her handsomely and instituted in her honor an annual festival at which she should be drawn in an elegant chariot through the streets of Khatmandu.

The festival now was in commemoration of this, except for the gruesome method of determining each year which young aspirant is actually possessed by the Kumari. It is a test of courage; if the child can endure it, as the original Kumari endured the king's cruelty, she will be known as a goddess, feted splendidly, and supported at government expense.

I got Thapa's mustache in my ear again before he asked me, "Do you watch now? Do you attend?"

"Yet . . . yes. . . ." Most of the crowd, with the exception of the priests, had left the kot. The child was finally decked to the satisfaction of the old Brahman, for he moved behind her, made prayer gestures with his hands, rang his brazen bell, and uttered some word of kindly command. Slowly she moved toward us and a light of recognition came to her eyes. Her hand brushed mine lightly.

"Salaam," she murmured. *"Ap ma-bap hai*. You are my father and my mother." Damn, I thought; I can't let Armand see me cry.

We followed her with the priests, who showed no interest in us, to the shrine of Durga, ineffable Goddess of Terror and Death. The old Brahman put his lamp in her hands, bearing the eternal flame of Swayambhunath. She did not hesitate as she walked between the torches and through the low door and into that reeking Bluebeard's

143

chamber of a room, a cage. The grilled gate clanged shut behind her, and the priests settled themselves on their hams, careless of the blood, to watch her for six hours through the only openings, the meshes of the grille.

"She will be a goddess," said Armand thoughtfully. Yes, she would be a goddess, when the heart had withered in her; so she would.

I moved to the grille. She was sitting on the pedestal that supported Durga's upright sword, one hand resting on the bright blade of it. Her face was aglow with ecstasy. The flame of the small lamp wavered, waving shadows across the piled heads of the sacrificial buffaloes, striking sparks in a hundred dead eyes, but she seemed unaware of them, so terrible and exquisite was the thing that was happening within her, the withering of the heart to the stony kernel that would be a god's.

Faintly another light slipped through the grille and touched the hair of the child. It was sunrise. Her forehead was bathed with it, and between her eyes there glowed like a ruby a single drop of bullock's blood, like the tikka of Brahma who created the world and the goddesses of it. I turned away to rejoin the group of my own people. The sun emerged suddenly from the Himalayan snows and slid down the gold roofs of the temples, skimming the homeward road which we should this day follow. My back was turned to Nepal and to my little girl, as it forever must be. So help me.

Once again we were quagmired, now by the war which had gotten off to a serious good start, and no one knew how far it might spread. India didn't want us. Armand said, "We might as well go home to Africa," and we rushed to Bombay, a dry city where we got drink only by signing certificates averring that we were chronic alcoholics. And we sailed to Mombasa in British East Africa, and climbed to Nairobi, one of the world's loveliest cities, where we engaged a gnome of a white hunter, the great Al Kline, to guide us to the animals.

Even outside the protected reserves they were plentiful. Traveling in the cars across roadless plains, we filmed lion, cheetah, baboon, elephant, the weirdly sensual giraffe. Lions, the most stupid and craven creatures of all, poked their noses between our tent flaps at

144

night. They wouldn't come in for they saw no other way out, and we would drowsily drive them away by whispering a sinister "Skat!"

Elephants were a different, so to speak, kettle of fish. All one day we had sought a camp site with water in the Tanganyika plains and found it just at twilight when the sun was being impaled on the thorn trees. There was a little water hole, obviously used by elephants, which we had our boys clean out, and we set up our tents around it, dined on the kongoni antelope, and went to bed, lullabied by the roar of lions in the dongas, the dried river beds. It is the male who vaingloriously makes this racket to scare game into the jaws of his lady; a perfect pimp is the lion.

Toward midnight we were awakened by the screams of elephants. Their voice is a scream, a neigh, a whinny like that of a horse. We jumped almost straight from our cots to the roof of the truck, itself an unstable fortress, while the boys shinnied up trees.

"Just don't breathe," said Al Kline calmly, balancing his heavy rifle on his knee. When I did come up for breath a dozen elephants, trumpeting indignantly, were in the camp headed for their water hole which we had appropriated. They marched like tanks in a parade, deliberately across our tents, to their water hole, drank, and went off into the night, screaming their disdain of us, the intruders.

The lions were sociable. They soon learned that our cars on the horizon meant that we were the lunch wagons, and they would come galloping in droves to tear at the gazelle we tossed them, while Roy, intrepid, filmed from the truck's roof.

The rhinos were recalcitrant. We wanted to film a rhino charge at one of the cars, and the one elected was that which I drove with Roy filming through a hatch in the roof. There was no lack of rhinos. We bumped across the plains trying to avoid the wild-pig holes, chewing on salted slices of coconut, and suddenly there would be mama and a kewpie of a child rhino, a mass of tonnage that would certainly have knocked us axle over elbow, but art before axle was our axiom here. The procedure was always the same. I would grind my teeth, wondering how long I would have them, and charge the car at the rhino, which would charge me to a distance of ten feet or so, skid to a stop when it saw the large glass eye of the truck, and spin like a bulldozer

145

in another direction, whirling its tail in what seemed complete circles and glancing, left, right, left, right, over its shoulder apologetically.

But soon there were no animals at all on our plains, for the drought had come and everything alive had gone south for water. There was no question but that our expedition was petering out, and Armand agreed that I should return to New York with the film and start publicity for it. The others would follow in a month or so.

I flew through the Rhodesias to Capetown, and took a freighter to Boston, with a million dollars' worth of supposedly secret gold ingots on board. There was, of course, a little mutiny by those who discovered it and wanted to take over the ship for somewhere on the South American coast, but we quelled that quickly, with only one man knifed by his own colleague, and reached Boston at eleven o'clock on New Year's Eve.

I landed on the dark dock with a ton of baggage, including three cages of African birds, one of monkeys, one of Scaly Sun-worshiper lizards, and found a cheery Irish customs man to welcome me.

"It's New Year in fifty-bloody-nine minutes," said he, "and we'll both of us confiscate that flask to drink the New Year in, and if ye'll give me a bird for the wife I think we can understand each other. Happy days," said he. "Now will ye fly the coop before me conscience gets the better of me? Me wife is expecting me to buss her before twelve. Same to you," said he.

I returned to New York and Hinny as no hero but a vagrant, I who had childishly wished on stars that Hinny and I should want none but each other again. Perfunctorily I was kissed; it didn't taste right; it was like a bad martini. We had a better one and sat on the floor, the two dogs lapping my ears, and unwrapped the fabulous things from Asia I had brought to her. They were very nice, acceptable. I was home at last with my wild gypsy wife, who tried on the bracelets politely, and said, "Look, I'm in love at last. Do you mind if I divorce you promptly?"

So we were divorced, and a war was on, and America mobilizing but still isolationist. I had articles on the expedition published by *Life*

146

and the major newspapers. The telephone rang. "Bill? This is Armand. We just got in. Have you developed your Leica film?"

Hesitantly I said, "Yes. I'm ashamed to tell you that all the African stuff came out absolutely blank. Damned if I can understand it. I couldn't have left on the lens hood. . . ."

A six-foot-four groan came from the other end of the wire. "Hold on to your hat," said Armand, "for the following announcement. Forty thousand feet of our movie film—India, Nepal, and Africa— are as blank as yours, which was cut from the raw movie film, remember?"

He gave me time for a five-foot-eight groan. Ye gods, the first film ever made in Nepal! A two-hundred-thousand-dollar expedition gone down the spout.

"My poor old Armand! What do you make of it?"

"I make nonsense. For some reason that God only knows the company furnishing the film sent experimental stock not only to us but to two other important expeditions which had the same experience as ours. When the film was sent back by air for development, as ours was in Burma, it was all right. When we sent it by boat, the latent image simply disappeared during the time lapse. All we have left of the expedition is the Burma film, your negatives developed en route, and the book you are doing. We are suing, of course, but that won't give back to us Africa and Nepal."

We had enough on Burma to make the film *Dangerous Journey,* and during the next six months I wrote a book on the expedition, *Land of the Eye,* which was published in New York and London, and did well.

But I didn't. Writing is the loneliest job in the world, and let all aspiring writers realize this. You sit by yourself all day long and, if you get tight enough, half through the night, living with the ghosts of memory or the imagined ones of fiction, hoping the telephone will ring, that your most calamitous friend will drop in on you, forgetting your work to call up women you really don't give a damn about, even in bed. You work yourself into a state over them, and when they are there you lose interest in them and hate yourself because now you want to write. They sleep peacefully and you return like a faithless, feckless lover to your typewriter, and try to seduce her, too, in the

147

trance state of exhaustion, which often makes for fine, unself-conscious fluid prose with no body to it.

I was bored. I had everything a young man of thirty-two could want—health, proper literary acclaim, money in the bank, a multitude of both men and women friends, a devoted family, but life had no savor to it; the gusto was gone.

One roiling emotion alone remained to me: fury that France should be invaded and that America should sit back on its hams, when it should be obvious to the dimmest-witted citizen that here was a world war growing apace. I don't think I really cared whether or not we might be invaded, though it seemed unlikely. But that my lovely France should be invaded and that still there was a General de Gaulle and his volunteer army of Free French were enough to stir me howling from my apathy. By hook or by crook I would join the troops of De Gaulle in Africa, and by crook I did, getting Washington's permission to visit a war area with a journalist's credentials from NBC, NANA, and the *Saturday Evening Post*. Once I reached Brazzaville in the Congo I could join as a soldier that fantastic little band which had rallied to De Gaulle from all over the world. He had said, "France has lost a battle, but she has not lost the war," and fanatically we believed.

There were three cardinal principles of a sensible suicide, I thought: you should do some good to somebody; you should leave no mess for your friends; and you should enjoy it. This, I thought glumly, was going to be fun.

14

*War—the Free French—*mon général *Leclerc—the girl who whistled*

SO IT WAS that I paid my own passage across what I thought the Styx of the Atlantic. I had given away my more important possessions, and I intended (what I later did) to give to the Free French half of any soldier's or correspondent's pay I might earn, for I wasn't coming back alive, or coming back at all. First I would help the Free French with the publicity they needed, by radio and writing, and then I would join their tough little army and shoot some Germans for them and get decently shot myself. For this last I was to show no talent at all.

General Sicé, High Commissioner of French Equatorial Africa, received me in a bewilderment nearly equal to mine, and I went to live with his two aides, Richard de Roussy de Sales and Henri de Mauduit, to work particularly with Dick on information. We wanted Vichy France to know that we the Free French still believed that France was not hopeless, and we wanted Roosevelt, who didn't like De Gaulle, to recognize us. The spontaneous hospitality of the general and his aides was surprising only on my first evening in Brazzaville, for it was common there where lodgings were nearly impossible to find, where most of the Free French were working on lean salaries to save every possible sou for their proud young army. Nothing was asked of us except sincerity and competence in our jobs.

The long, thin house in which De Sales, De Mauduit, and I lived had been dubbed La Bonbonnière, the bonbon box, by some ironic guest. It was black as night inside, as some protection against the drenching heat of Brazzaville. The walls, from floor to ceiling, were papered with maps of the French Empire, and grisly ju-ju idols with arrows sticking in their bowels grimaced at us as we tried vainly to sleep in the afternoons. Above us rose the dim white cones of mosquito netting; below us were the puddles, never dry, of our own sweat.

There was little rest for us at the Bonbonnière, which was a sort of annex to the high commissioner's office where we worked. At any hour of the night black hands would shake the mosquito nets to deliver telegrams which required immediate response, or the preparation of propaganda to be released in the morning by Radio Brazzaville or printed as leaflets to be dropped by plane over French West Africa. The informality of our jobs left all of us a considerable latitude in which to work, and General Sicé was canny enough to choose his staff with few mistakes and thereafter trust its confidence in its own talents. The office closed at no regular hour, and no one left before the general, who was not infrequently there until nine or ten at night. And no one arrived later than he in the morning. The volunteers working with Lieutenant Desjardins, Chief of the Information Service at Radio Brazzaville, were equally conscientious. Desjardins, who preferred to drive a tank, loaded his collaborators to the ears with papers, films, recordings, and though they bent, they staggered through their tasks uncomplainingly.

All the death was washed out of me by the spirit of this band of heroic volunteers. I wrote articles for the *Saturday Evening Post* and the North American Newspaper Alliance, and then confronted a terror worse than any other I met in the five years I spent with the French at war: Radio Brazzaville.

I had flunked public speaking at Harvard and had nearly fainted when I once broadcast over WQXR for the *Saturday Review*. Now, night after night, stripped to the waist in the palm-thatched "studio," shaking like an epileptic, I broadcast news of the Free French. My voice, said the reports, came through beautifully, but why didn't I lay my script flat on the table so it wouldn't rattle in my hands?

It wasn't merely stage fright; it was more that these Fighting French had injected a frenzy in me which I hadn't known since I was adolescent and wanted to be a hermit with a harem. By God and by Jesus, I wasn't going to die! I would see France restored.

Bill the dog came out of the Congo to live with me and chide me and lap my jaw when times were bad. He was only a speck on the great river when I discovered him; flotsam, I thought, and that is what he was. He drifted nearer and I saw the good shape of his head turning from one side to the other blindly, as the current shoved him down-river toward the cataracts below. He swam a little to the right, then to the left, seeking the shore, and I realized suddenly that he was blind.

I whistled at him frantically, and his head lifted. I ran down the shore beside him, whistling through my fingers and stumbling over roots, and slowly he moved toward me, following the thin thread of the whistle. His head went under water once, and I thought he was gone, but he came up again as a small whirlpool caught him and spun him helplessly around. He broke away suddenly, touched bottom, and lunged toward the shore, and in the shallows he smashed against my legs. He was too tired even to whimper. His breath came racking from him, and his eyes, gray-blue with blindness, looked up to where my own might be.

There was one short shake left in him when he reached the shore, then we sat down together and I tried to warm him against my ribs. He trembled and leaned against me with his great body utterly spent, and that was terrible to see, like the sight of a grown man crying. He was a slim, gray, noble-looking hound, nearly as big as a Dane, and the pride in him kept him somehow aloof as he leaned against me, as though to imply that although it was nice to meet me, I shouldn't think that he couldn't have reached shore alone. It was obvious that some native had tried to drown him, probably because he could no longer hunt with his old blind eyes.

I called him Bill, which was my name, too, with some vague idea that we might serve as scapegoats for each other. His blindness troubled him very little, for his sense of smell was developed extraordinarily, and his nose wiggled like an anteater's when he raced after my bicycle. He was an independent old dog, except for his compulsion to sleep on my bed at night, which I let him do after he had clawed his way through three mosquito nets. In that climate he was hot as hell. He also snored.

Smack in the middle of Africa is an enormous desert region called the Tchad, the capital of which is Fort Lamy. The fabulous General

Leclerc had assembled his troops there, planning to liquidate the Italian forces in the Fezzan.

General Sicé, after months of my apprenticeship in Brazzaville, asked Leclerc by wire to accept me: *"Homme determiné robuste santé dont esprit sacrifice total."* My total sacrifice was nearly achieved with dysentery and malaria before Leclerc wired curtly, *"D'accord."*

There was only one plane a month to Leclerc's headquarters in Fort Lamy, and I had to miss the first as there was but one free seat in it and the Deuxième Bureau, the Intelligence Office, thought it more important to get rid of an indiscreet young journalist, with advice to Leclerc to return him to Egypt, than to send me as a propagandist north.

General Sicé couldn't say outright that Leclerc had a new campaign in preparation, but we sensed it, and I did not want to miss the show. I missed it. Leclerc wired a modest announcement of his success in taking five Italian outposts in the Fezzan. There were no details, and naturally no indication of his next move, but I made certain of a place on the plane for March sixteenth. This was an ancient Farman, a flying booby trap.

The night before my departure, Henri bought twenty pounds of Roquefort cheese for me to take to his underprivileged friends at Fort Lamy. "Give them more or less of it, according to how they receive you," he said. I climbed carefully into the plane with the cheese and a hangover, and we taxied back and forth and couldn't get off the ground. At 6:00 A.M. I returned with the Roquefort and was admitted to the patient welcome which is the lot of frustrate prodigal sons.

The loyal companions got up with me again at 4:00 A.M. and waved me away. Somehow we rose, and the plane burrowed like a mole through the thick air above Brazzaville. That didn't last long. Smoke was streaming behind us and petrol was shimmering across one wing. So we landed, the Roquefort and I, and again returned shamefacedly. Henri wrung his hands and smelled the Roquefort without much effort, for it was getting pretty high by now, and swore that the plane mechanics should work all night. The cheese must go through.

I greeted the next dawn with a groan. I slunk aboard the plane, trying to give the impression that I was a man who didn't carry a, by now, very tropical cheese. We put down at Bangui in the plate-lipped-lady land, where the fumigators attacked the plane savagely as I sneaked the cheese off. In the morning we were up again, over plains country growing rapidly more barren, flying low enough to see occasional elephants and lions. We dropped lower and the heat baked through the aluminum, and my twenty pounds of Roquefort burst its veins and made a stench which the other passengers thought poorly of. I smiled bravely and apologetically like a mother whose infant has misbehaved.

No sooner did we strike the desert landing ground than the pilot lunged at the door and severely pointed the way out for me and my cheese. We landed in a gust of hot, dry air which probably blew the aroma of us half across the town

"Welcome to you and your secret weapon," said the aide to Leclerc who had been sent to meet me. Contrary to my expectations I was lodged well in that baking barbarous city, and the Roquefort didn't at all prevent me being received by the finest families of Fort Lamy. They followed me in the streets and shamelessly touched my elbow. I had been hoping they would welcome me as one who would lay down his life for Free France, but "You're the man with the cheese?" they would ask. I would lift my chin defensively. "You know," they would go on, "I'm a good friend of Henri de Mauduit. I rendered him a little service once, and I wondered . . ."

I then would ration them a few drops of that ulcerous cheese. I became a power with women, who would follow me, two and three deep, through the house to the secret Cheese Place. There I would issue each a portion, and if it wasn't measured equably there was hell to pay. It wasn't long before almost no one in Fort Lamy spoke to anyone but me.

General Leclerc returned from the north to the spartan office he despised. I craned my neck like a tourist to see him get out of his sand-colored car, a lean figure in shapeless khaki, carrying his rough habitual cane, wearing the pillbox hat which had been made of the top of a red native fez covered with khaki.

He sent for me a few days later, and received me in the office that was furnished only with a desk, two chairs, and three captured Italian flags. *"Eh bien,* Davis," he said, "so you got here at last. You're a little late." This was inauspicious, and I tried to pass it off with sincere felicitations for his recent conquests in Libya. He had no intention of putting me at my ease. His blue eyes, slanting downward at the corners, dared me either to get mad or be courteously humble. He wasted not a word, and he apparently felt any sort of interview on his personal success would be a waste of words. I gave up and we talked generally.

"Look here, young man," he said—he was only five years older than I, "we want the help of the United States, and they don't seem yet to understand what Vichy is doing. If it had not been for Vichy, the Italians would have been chased out of Africa in the first months of 1941. If the French colonies in North Africa, whose troops have always been superb fighting men, had rallied to General de Gaulle, they could have attacked Libya with three hundred thousand men from the west in concert with the British from the east, and the tanks of Rommel would never have touched African soil. The fall of Greece could have been delayed and possibly prevented, for the British would have been able to spare many more troops for the Balkans.

"Listen: if Vichy hadn't ceded Indo-China to Japan, Singapore would have been able better to have resisted, and perhaps to have avoided, invasion. There never could have been that tremendous surprise attack upon the Allied fleet if Indo-China, Vichy China, hadn't served as a base, a springboard, for Japan's offensive. The indirect aid which Vichy has given to Hitler has been far more effective than all that Italy has done for him since its entry into the war."

His head jerked back and he smiled, the heartening smile of a man who rarely smiles. "I'm flying to the Tibestis in a couple of weeks, to meet our troops on their way back and give a lift to some of the wounded. Perhaps you'd better come along. That hat's too thin," he said.

Our plane followed the winding Shari River for a while. The thin brush disappeared and a desert spattered with wind-worn pink rocks spread below us. Five hundred miles north we saw the first of the Tibestis in the distance, the great purple peaks of Yoo and Mount

154

Emi Koussi, ten thousand feet high, then, at the foot of them, Faya Oasis, our goal. From the air its houses looked like unbaked biscuits or pale cocoons.

The desert men who welcomed us bore little resemblance to the soldiers I had imagined. Some wore helmets, some kepis, some were in shorts, some in long trousers or the ballooning pants of Tchad. They were working soldiers, dressed individually for comfort, not for style, and I was struck by the cheerfulness of them all. The grim heroes, mouths drawn to a thin, hard line, live mostly in novels. A sense of humor is as essential as sweat in the desert.

Nothing, I believe, in all the African war can be compared for heroism and downright dogged soldiering with the four operations of Leclerc and these confident men. Leclerc's problems of actual warfare were severe enough, but the problem of provisioning must surely have been one of the toughest encountered by any army. It required the transport of food, petrol, and munitions from Duala, from Brazzaville, and from Fort Lamy through the unmapped region of the Tibesti Mountains. Dante's Inferno could have been no worse than that desolate land, inhabited only by nomads and baboons. And the provisions went on from there, to within two hundred miles of the Mediterranean, on the third campaign, and all the way to Tripoli on the fourth, still to come.

No one but Leclerc and his immediate staff officers had known beforehand of the attack which I had missed. From Faya, Zouar, Fort Lamy, the troops had converged in three lines upon the Tibesti Mountains. The western line drove two hundred miles through French West Africa, Vichy territory.

The moon was brilliant as the troops approached T'messa, and surprise seemed impossible. But on the night of March second there was an eclipse of the moon which lasted nearly three hours and allowed the French forces to approach in darkness. When they reached the fort, they found it in an uproar, for the half-wild native troops of the Italians thought that the blacked-out moon meant the end of the world. T'messa was captured so quickly that the Italians were unable to destroy all their documents.

The post of Tdjerri was not so easily taken. Major Diot's troops were tired, for they were operating far from their nearest base camp and had few provisions with them. Very little food had been found in the forts previously taken, for the supply trucks which the Italians were expecting daily had apparently sensed danger and turned back up the road to Tripoli. This excellent highway over flat terrain made it possible for the Italians to come from Tripoli to Tdjerri in less than two days, whereas the French, to reach Tdjerri from Faya, required two months' grueling travel.

On March first, the anniversary of Leclerc's victory at Kufra, he assaulted Tdjerri with mortars. Armored cars poured from the forts, and Italian planes swirled overhead to clash with the Fighting French planes. A few minutes later a German Heinkel appeared far above, radioing orders to the Italians in the air and in the armored cars. In every material way the enemy was far superior. It was a mad assault but General Leclerc took that post, too, with, ironically enough, Italian guns and ammunition captured a year before at Kufra.

With General Leclerc I flew north to Zouar, the French outpost in the Tibesti Mountains, and I tipped my helmet to the men who had bullied and wheedled their trucks over such terrible terrain. For this world was dead, desolate, scarred by the wind. Below us at first the khaki plain of sand neatly filled the horizon, but gradually it became ridged with rock, apparently wind-swept from east to west, judging by the crescent sand dunes between those ridges. Then jet-black peaks in clumps pushed out of the sand, like the tips of the mountains of hell seeking an atmosphere that was but slightly cooler. Next, flying northwest at twelve thousand feet, we crossed black tablelands, precipitous plateaux a thousand feet high, curved black feathers of rock, colossal clinkers balancing, until all the world beneath us, the immense lost world of Tibesti, became nearly solid black defined only by the tracings of sand in watercourses that had dried a million years ago. Southeast of us was Mount Emi Koussi; northwest, through a veil of floating dust, Mount Toussidé; both more than ten thousand feet high, and between them had somehow passed those troops of the Free French.

Leclerc quite reasonably wouldn't tell me when he planned his next assault, but he gave me permission to reconnoiter the mountains on my own, with a camel and Bill. If I was going to die of dysentery, I thought, I had better do it decently alone.

156

"The sensible thing would be to lie up for a bit," said the troop doctor in his adobe hut. I couldn't lie up for any bit. It bored me silly, so I borrowed the camel and lurched miserably into the black Tibesti Mountains, my dog Bill following close behind, for the camel was even easier to smell than I in that waterless waste. It was pitiably a hell of a home from home for these Free French, I thought as I climbed the terrible black valleys. I had crawled over the Himalayas, pressed flat against the sky, but I had never felt then as now that I had left the world entirely, that I was outcast from it and blindly alone.

But I wasn't, quite. Day after day as I explored the ridges of the Tibesti, looking for relics of nomad occupation, shards, shattered huts, abandoned unfecund gardens, I saw two figures moving parallel on a spur to my left. And at night there was the small friendly fire far away. For a while I was content with this, and I'd say to my blind dog, "Look, Bill, the ghosts are guiding us. Should we go on into this damned waste, or turn back? What do you think of life, old Bill?"

Bill's tail shuddered, and we brooded together as we shared a cup of Mrs. Parkins' Mock Beef Tea which, with a clothes brush, my Bostonian mother had slipped into my baggage. Every night the other fire was closer to us, and finally I could see by daylight that the figures were those of a girl and a goat. Loneliness and curiosity brought us together at last. Early one morning I left the black shadow of the black rock and approached the flame that was thin and transparent against the sun.

"Saida!" I shouted politely, using all my Arabic from some distance away. The Arab girl turned without surprise and ate another date.

"*Bon jour!*" she said. She was of the Toubou tribe, itinerant husbandmen who cultivated the rare earth of the Tibestis, and she had gone to Zouar alone to buy the goat. As she was recently widowed she intended to do a little business of her own. This she told me in French which was grammatically better than mine, but I couldn't find out how she learned it. She was a lovely person, with an exciting dimple set in the midst of the tattooed triangle from lower lip to chin. Bill thought she had a good smell, too. But he also sniffed appreciatively at the goat.

We traveled for two days together, the camel, the dog, the goat, Zuila, and I. We should have seemed a strange party, gathered around the fire at night, for it was cold on bare rock at six thousand feet. Zuila had a strange talent for a woman and an Arab. She whistled, a rippled silver whistle which slid exquisitely through the dark. When she was whistling one night, paying me no attention, I protested that this was a bloody country, and why didn't she, who was so independent, go south to Ubangi-Shari to live?

Her whistle thinned to a thread and tapered into silence. She said, "Parts of the Tibesti are beautiful. If you were going to stay . . . we might go to Unianga Lake, to the east of the range. It isn't very big. It's a hole in the black rock filled with pale green water, and palms grow around its edge. It is so very still that the moon never wiggles in it."

She whistled a little more then and leaned back on her elbows and put her bare feet in my lap. "Do you believe in fairies, Bill? There was a fairy who lived once at Unianga Lake. She was very pretty and always hungry, and all she ever ate was flies. She ate billions of flies. She went gobbling, gobbling, gobbling with her pretty little mouth all around the lake, like this"—Zuila gobbled—"and was perfectly happy until one day when she fell in love. One of our Youbous, a shepherd, fell in love with her, and made love to her under the palm trees where the flies were fewest. He was very clever. He went away, and came back again, and he did that often, and she nearly starved for love of him. The flies swarmed over Unianga and she scarcely noticed them because of the greater hunger in her heart. . . ."

Zuila whistled blithely and Bill the dog came galumphing out of the dark, for a whistle to him meant biscuits or adventure or Mrs. Parkins' Mock Beef Tea. I gently took Zuila's feet from my lap. Her cool, tremulous whistle and her warm feet were discomposing.

"And he came one night when she had just bathed in Lake Unianga and eaten one or two flies, more from habit than hunger, and he lifted her, dripping, onto his white camel. They lived for a long time happily there. And the flies swarmed and swarmed at Lake Unianga, for there was no one to eat them any more. And that is why the green lake of Unianga has so many flies now."

158

Zuila whistled an unmelodic Arab song and rubbed the ears of Bill whose muzzle was on her knee. And she said, "Good night, Bill, and Bill the dog. I go east tomorrow, to Unianga. I don't much mind the flies."

15

Cairo of the "Flap"—
"Black out the moon"

SINCE I COULD get no straight answer from General Leclerc in regard to anything in the shape of combat, I flew back to Brazzaville and got a letter from General Sicé to General de Larminat who commanded the Fighting French troops in the Western Desert, asking him to accept me in the dual role of soldier and propagandist. General Leclerc added a special recommendation to this, and I was practically in the war except for half the length of Africa and the usual incapacity of our hand-me-down planes to stay in the air more than a few minutes at a time.

But this was the invigorating delight of De Gaulle's Brazzaville; nothing worked but men. The Free French so-called army had practically no funds, no arms, no transport, yet daily it increased, with white men and black who believed in France arriving as volunteers from the Pacific islands, from South America, from the prisons of Spain where they had been caught en route. From the Ivory Coast, of Vichyist persuasion, came Prince Adingra marching through the jungles with two thousand spearmen, eager to stab holes in German tanks. Brazzaville-on-the-Congo was electric. You could be draining away in the sweat of fever or shaking apart in its chills, damn near starving for anything but fruit to eat, but you never were indifferent to the manic propulsion of everyone toward the rescue of France.

The war of the Fighting French began accelerating suddenly. South

Africa broke off relations with Vichy, and General Sicé sent congratulations to General Smuts. Like our own, South African troops were volunteers in the Western Desert. From there we had word that our General Koenig was putting up what would become a historic resistance on the hummock of sand called Bir Hakim.

Over the Ubangi-Shari we flew at last, to Tchad again where General Leclerc gave me his blessings in a storm of sand, and to Geneina where we settled because of leaks in the varicose veins of our antique Farman plane. On we went to Khartoum, a flat gasping city, and to Cairo at last, where I learned that the French were still holding out magnificently at Bir Hakim, and there might yet be time for me to reach them.

My reception at the Free French Information Service in Cairo was cordial enough, but I still remained what the French call a *phénomène,* neither beef, fowl, nor good red kipper, neither accredited war correspondent nor soldier. As a war correspondent I could have been accredited by the State Department, if I had not devoutly wanted to fight in the French Army. This was a problem to me. The easy way was to accept a correspondent's status, but I accepted the harder way, and was happier for it.

On August sixteenth I received my commission as second lieutenant from General Catroux and my orders from General de Larminat attaching me to the First Flying Column of Spahis. I put on my red-and-gold shoulder tabs, buckled on the Browning pistol to which at last I had a right, and self-consciously tried the vermilion forage cap of the Spahis. The mirror didn't show me much of a soldier, but I felt pretty good nonetheless, and on the drive to Mena Camp by the Pyramids I eagerly looked for any French officer I might salute. This is it, I thought. I felt pretty cocky in that vermilion hat. All soldiers should wear vermilion hats. Bill, my good dog, was chewing at the knob of the gearshift and kept his blind eyes averted.

It was dark when we arrived at Mena Camp, but the rough hut was bright with the spotted flames of lamps. Behind them moved the fabulous Spahis, wearing red scarves and red hats like mine. The Commandant de Kersauson tipped up his pipe at me and asked me in so many words what good I was. I fumbled out my papers—old diplomas from two military schools—and for the first of them he shoved toward me half a tin of bully beef. I spread my references from Leclerc and Sicé before him and eventually got some cold beans.

"I think you'll do," he grunted. "We're short of quarters here, so keep on with your work in Cairo until I send for you. Good night . . . Spahi." He grinned.

The American consul hacked my passport to ribbons, and I was no longer an American citizen, for it is written on the back page of one's passport that if the owner thereof join a foreign army, even an Allied one, his nationality must be forfeited. I was truly a man without a country; I had forfeited the right to my own, and France had no government other than that of Pétain, which of course wouldn't recognize us, or me least of all. I wasn't even a soldier of fortune, for that character makes money on his job, and I was doing quite the opposite. I should have been the loneliest man in the war, but that you can't be when you are fighting for a cause larger than even your own death, with selfless companions snug around you.

This was the period of stalemate at El Alamein, when Rommel had pushed deep into Egypt and Mussolini had already struck coins to commemorate his conquest of the pyramids, when Alexander was replaced by Montgomery in charge of all Western Desert forces, including the Free French.

The war in the Western Desert was still so precarious, the balance of craft between Montgomery and Rommel so dubious, that Churchill, ill, flew to Cairo. Costumed in a workman's blue coverall, he blithely told Montgomery that he was to take Rommel's army to pieces, and very soon now. He returned from the desert to address the war correspondents, and by the grace of Colonel Stevens, press chief, I was invited to attend this conference.

Churchill's ringing phrases were there, but they rang as though a hand had been laid on the lip of the gong, and the tough old correspondents were whispering, "He's done in. He can't last."

Now Churchill had always seemed to me the greatest man of our time, but I had neither pleasure nor pride in being told often how much physically I resembled him, taking a bit or two from girth and age. I had grown bored with strangers, expecting no doubt to please me, leaning across a bar or through the window of a taxi stopped beside mine, saying, "Did anyone ever tell you . . . ?"

On that dusty afternoon in the garden of the embassy I was introduced to Churchill who looked at me with what seemed amusement above his prematurely dead cigar.

"Young man," he said, "did anyone ever tell you . . . ?"

"Yes, Mr. Churchill. Yes."

He shook his head and smiled around the cigar which his thick lower lip had pushed up nearly to his nose.

"Then let *me* tell you that when you reach my age you will be just as ugly."

Bir Hakim was triumphantly evacuated by General Koenig before I could get my feet in the sand. De Gaulle waited, our troops waited, I waited in my own elaborate prison of the Hotel Continental-Savoy, treating my dysentery now with zibib, which is an anise-flavored drink of nearly concrete alcohol and is akin to absinthe. As it is highly intoxicating and is also reputed as an aphrodisiac, it at least takes your mind off your dolors. The hotel itself is sufficiently aphrodisiac, and its clients did a roaring trade. Girls in their snappy uniforms and sparkling independence fell easily before the terrible direct sincerity of men who had spent months in the desert, but competition was keen, for the Eastern girls were exquisite and the refugees as wily as several years of living supine upon their wits could make them.

One of them, calling herself Ludmeela the "Rooshian," had the wicked habit of rousing me by telephone from my siesta, around the hour of four when one's intentions for the evening are nebulous and easily swayed, and the half-waking state admits of improbable visions.

"Monsieur Hassoldt Davis?" the rich, deep voice would ask slowly. "Ah, Monsieur Hassoldt Davis, I've been hoping you would call me. I'm still here. I am still in the large square bed with the black sheets. . . . I'm a leetle drowsy now . . . and it's a delicious drowsiness. . . . You have never taken drugs, I suppose. . . ."

Her voice was lovely, caressing. With some dexterity I poured myself a zibib without taking my ear from the telephone. I asked gently, drowsily, too, "But where are you, Ludmeela? Why can't I see you?"

162

"Ah, that . . . I have no faith in men any more. I lie here in the candlelight, for the curtains are drawn against the sun, and I look around me at the yellow Van Gogh above the bed and the leetle Etruscan figurine beside it, at the eels swimming slowly, so excitingly, in their illuminated tank, and the marmoset chattering at them . . . and I remember the man who left me here. Yes, it's his apartment. . . . Ah, you have guessed what I am, but I hate it, I tell you, I hate it! Men only want my bod-hy and I sell it for a song."

"Would I have to sing a very big song to you, Ludmeela?"

"You are deeferent, I think. . . . I have seen you hurrying along the street, always hurrying, with one shoulder higher than the other. I think you are a man who is good . . . ah, the drug . . . I grow so sleepy now, with my golden bod-hy almost at peace for this short while, until he comes back. . . . When I was a leetle girl in Rooshia—"

This was getting pretty thick, and I could see the hackles rising on even Bill the dog. "Ludmeela, listen; why don't you come over and have a drink?"

"Ah . . . ah . . . that is the man in you, and thank you very much, but I cannot leave until this other man comes back, to pay me for the last night, the feefty pounds—"

I had a snort of zibib fast. "Did you say fifty pounds?"

"I am such a drowsy one . . . just feefty, yes. I would come to you—"

"For a song, you said? For that song of songs, my darling."

"You will call me. You will call Ludmeela at Cairo 3682. I am so drowsy now, and along my bod-hy is a teengling like leetle mice who are inquisitive. . . ."

There were many others, in that cordial hotel, who usually charged from three to ten pounds a night, with Palestinian champagne and wilted flowers. Two of them were disguised in uniform and were haughty as be-damned, though all you had to do was to follow their proud noses to the open doors of their rooms, where you were insulted and welcomed for the fee. And there were the Daughters of Doom, as they were called by those doomed, a variety troupe consisting of a large mother and five little girls of about eighteen who were never the same two weeks successively.

Sex was a problem in Cairo, where there were at least a hundred

163

men in uniform to one woman nude, and the Birka, the brothel quarter directly opposite Shepheard's swank hotel, had been put out of bounds. But very definitely. The British, with their wry wit, had simply built walls of brick at the entrances of the naughty streets, so no one could come in and none go out. But the power and the hunger of a prostitute are terrific, and it wasn't long before the walls were broken through with hammers (and in one case a wooden leg), and the streets were acrawl with starving "bint," more determined than ever. It is wonderful how food and appetite are married.

Many girls continued their business on empty stomachs in gharries, the horse-drawn hacks, into whose utmost darkness the soldier would enter and pay his pound and assuage his loneliness in the sweating venereal shade. There was not a military policeman in the Cairo area who didn't believe that the old system of licensed and inspected houses was the better one.

The Flap, which was the interim period when the Eighth Army and the German and the Italian sat trying to determine expediency, when our allied documents—just in case—were going up in smoke from every embassy, came suddenly to an end for me as I was reading yesterday's *Egyptian Mail,* thrilled by the very essence of romance in one short sentence, factual and direct: "From Lanchow the road follows the Great Wall and Marco Polo's Silk Road across the Gobi Desert to the Baboon Pass on the Kansu-Sinkiang border."

These words were magic. They held the high adventure. I read them over and over again, "... Great Wall ... Silk Road ... Gobi Desert ... Baboon Pass ..." recalling the good days behind me, the monsoon on the Burma Road, the aching passage of the Himalayas, the blood and thunder in the valley of Nepal. To hell with this stagnant war, I thought. Wherever the Baboon Pass might be, I must go to it.

There was a pounding at the door of Room 35 in the Continental-Savoy Hotel, and I opened it to two young Spahis, Vincent and Mario. Mario had part of an authoritative beard. "My respects, mon lieutenant," he said smartly. "The commandant requests that you return with us to the regiment tonight."

He was a rare soldier and a gentleman, the commandant, Robert

164

de Kersauson de Pennendreff. He went to St. Cyr with the thin and ardent youth who became General Leclerc. Here in a galvanized iron hut he offered his officers a drink and stated gruffly his confidence in us. He wiped the flies from his lips and toasted us. Captain Morel Deville, hard, blue-eyed, flaxen-haired, lifted his glass with the quick, clean motion that marked all his gestures. Captain Brunel, our doctor, champion artist and writer, smoothed a wrinkle from his immaculate uniform and turned to speak to Captain de Courcelles, who had been De Gaulle's aide-de-camp, now in command of artillery.

These became my friends, but I was awed by them now, for as an American volunteer and the veriest amateur in war, I scarcely belonged. They were as tough as the Legion and equally proud, these Spahis of Fighting France, and they had a right to be proud of their long tradition of expert warfare. They had originated in Turkey in the seventeenth century and soon moved to Algeria and Morocco. The blaze on their vermilion caps had put the fear of God into Abd-el-Krim. They were purely cavalry then. During the World War of 1914–1918 their first regiment was the only one of French cavalry to be decorated with the fern of the Military Medal. From 1916 until the end of the war they fought all over the Near and Middle East, in Albania, Macedonia, Serbia, Hungary, and Syria, where they earned the fern of the Croix de Guerre. The ladies swooned into their azure and scarlet capes, and no man smiled at them but in respect. They were brilliant as dragons, and as independent.

In trucks and lorries and armored cars and tanks we drove to Alexandria in a sandstorm, with nearly as many flies in it as sand, and they were terrible, the flies. Heroes, perhaps, ignored them, and that's why heroes are such nervous men. We simple soldiers sleeping in the desert woke up writhing.

Slowly we drove up the long desert road beside the bloody sea, to Alamein and south of it, where we camped in caves because Rommel's planes were intermittently bombing us as a diversion from the convoys on the highroad. In the mornings we maneuvered with the tanks and armored cars, and it was poor touring. What we could see through the churned-up dust was neither interesting postcard desert nor anything like a battlefield. It was dull labor, of which I understood much

165

less than I pretended. Eating dust, I squirmed like a parasite in the tight and twisted bowels of an armored car while the man crouched beside me issued and received messages in code.

"Allo Beck, allo Beck! Ici Moux! Message pour vous: arsenic, sulphate, onion. . . . Over. . . ."

"Allo Moux! Ici Beck! Tu parles comme un cul! Message pour vous: aspirin, Noel, nuts."

After half a dozen of these expeditions I began to wonder if war wasn't too complicated for my simple sort. I looked with awe upon my companions who, it seemed, had to know mathematics and various abstruse sciences for the killing of an enemy. I sighed for the days of the catapult and the simple dagger in the dark. I had pestered everyone from the Congo to Cairo to let me have a good job fighting, and now I found I lacked the military education to fight in the elaborate fashion of modern war. I felt a fraud, and it was no good consoling myself with the thought that, well, I could write books anyway, and that would help more than murder. But murder was my dish, and I slept uneasily beneath the roar of planes, worrying that my good companions should think me incompetent or insincere. It was doubly awkward, for I must have seemed a pretentious old man of thirty-six in contrast to most of them. And though my people were still their favorite allies, I still was a foreigner.

I watched American planes go over in groups of forty and fifty, to put the fear of Jesus into Rommel, and I felt apologetic, like a servant of a rich house dining in a mediocre restaurant with the servants of a house of France who had fallen on evil days.

We moved back and waited again, deep in the desert and far from the friendly masses retreating along the coast. Rommel's tanks were wriggling patiently toward our tiny nucleus. His planes spotted us and insulted us by dropping no bombs.

We squatted in the night, waiting for the attack that had been threatened for three days as the enemy advanced. This was a lunar land, scabbed and terrible, between El Alamein on the Mediterranean and the great Qattara Depression. Plateaux rose abruptly like colossal tanks on the shining desert; the sand shimmered, for it was faceted with mica. Leaning from the shadow of the 75-mm. cannon, I found

166

small flowers the size of my fingernail and gross snails like *escargots* feeding on them. We could eat the snails, I thought, if worse came to worst, for we had food left for only two days more, and no water at all, not even enough for coffee.

Our tents lay in the crescent valleys of the plateau. The trucks, camouflaged with nets, were well dispersed, their windshields turned away from the moon so that they would reflect no light. High in the cliff I could see the caves we had dug, the emplacements of heavy artillery and the niches where we had been sleeping for three nights with our guns against our cheeks. There would be no sleep tonight, for we had received word from British headquarters that El Daba, just down the line, had fallen at 11:30 P.M., and that the armies of Rommel and the Italian Bastico were pushing on.

There was no doubt of that. Over the ridge to the northwest we saw the explosions where enemy planes were bombing the allied transport along the road to El Alamein. We knew it would be our turn next and very soon. Falconet swaggered over and saluted snappily. "They're on their way, all right. Three thousand Jerry vehicles." He puffed at the cigarette. "That bloody moon."

That bloody moon, the moon of lovers, the orb of poets. That bloody moon that would mean death tonight as it disclosed the naked world to the pilots. The mechanics of war on earth were systematically controlled, but you couldn't black out the moon.

I shivered. The night wind had slit through my jacket, stabbing like an icicle through the hole in my shirt that I'd had no time to mend. Running my tongue over my dry mouth, I thought of icicles and water, of the dirty city snow we used to flavor with fruit juices when we were children, of the tart country cider which only a winter ago we drank in barns along the Hudson.

I looked up at the cave, like the lair of a werewolf, that I had spent the day digging into the cliff. It was well barricaded. I doubted that the planes could effectively strafe it. Just under the edge of the plateau there were the shadows of others. There were figures hunched in them, and against the moonlight I caught the flash of papers turning. These were last letters being written by men who had lived war since 1939 and who could measure the chance of survival to a vein's breadth.

Remembering the sixteen days of Bir Hakim, we could hope here at least to arrest the advance of the enemy, possibly to drive him back a bit at a sacrifice, but there was small chance that most of us would come through.

The moon was just over us now, halfway between Scorpio and the Dipper which were scarcely visible because of its brilliance. Our shadows were tight around our feet. A little group came sauntering up to us, young Colonel Garbet, Captain Mirkin, and a miniature man, our mascot, Lazrir, which in Arabic means The Little One. Lazrir was twelve years old, with no family but the Foreign Legion to which he attached himself in Damascus with the plea that in the first place he was hungry and in the second he was a fighting man. Lazrir cocked his head listening. "That's a Jerry," he said.

Barely audible to the northwest was the irregular beat. An instant later the horizon was lit by the pale green fan of incendiary bombs exploding. The light lifted and fell, fluttering like an aurora borealis, over the railroad line thirty miles away.

"That bloody moon," said Falconet again. "Even at fifteen thousand feet they can see every move we make. Zut! The dirty zebra! He's coming our way. . . ."

The throb of the German motor was louder, though the plane was still invisible. "O.K., Bill," I thought, "here it comes again. This is what you asked for."

To be alive. Now that was a very precious thought. To be alive, and therefore an alien here, a tourist among the dead who outnumbered us so greatly in that desert. We were loud, we were vulgarly active across the sands that housed the quiet dead. We were the intruders.

"Voilà," said Mirkin, pointing. High in the thin blue sky, slicing through the bosom of Cassiopeia and the groin of Perseus, came the German plane, its exhaust congealing in a long white wake.

"Il va piquer," said little Lazrir. It was a dive-bomber, all right. We saw it turn, nosing carefully around the stars like a dog among daisies. Then it tilted, thinned to a fine line almost vertical as it began its plunge. I knew there was no shelter within a hundred yards. For an instant my eye left the plane to glance at my friends. They watched tensely. Falconet was aiming over a rock with a machine gun, Lucot

168

was flat on his back, the tip of his rifle following the plane, Mirkin was standing stiff, a Bren gun on his hip. No one, apparently, had moved, but now they were armed and ready.

Straight down came the Stuka, straight for us, and I felt an edge of the seventy-five-pounder jabbing into my back. Then the night was solid with noise as our guns exploded, and I was reeling in volcanic space, swinging from my tommy gun like a swimmer on a straw. I heard our ack-ack bursting like quick coughs through a tin horn, then three huge blasts that shook the world. Those were the bombs. One of our trucks erupted in flame, and veering over it and back again in a horseshoe was the Stuka, aiming its machine guns by its light. There was a brief screaming as the plane climbed again, pursued by our red tracer bullets, then silence but for the low snuffling of the flames.

We rushed over to a man staggering knock-kneed around the truck, both hands clasped to a black hole in the side of his jaw. The stretcher bearers were already beside him. "Take it away!" he moaned. "A corporal of the Legion only lies down to sleep or die!" His knees buckled and he fell into our arms.

General Cazaud crossed to inspect the damage. He paused, dropped his cigarette and carefully rubbed it out against the ash tray of a hundred thousand miles of sand. We went back to our seventy-five-pounder, walking lightly with relief that the show had begun at last. Someone laughed. "Just before I escaped from Dakar I met a girl who thought a Stuka . . ." These men rarely talked of women in the desert however much they dreamed of them. They didn't talk of water either, or of their lost homes in France. Memories could poison the morale of a man. But now, with a superior enemy upon us and the chances of survival slim, we were talking all together in furious gusts of the women we had known, of the wonders of women which didn't matter any more. We talked about the damnedest things: a Teddy bear that was solemnly adopted as a son, the curl of fingers mending a trouser pocket, the songs a good wife sang badly, a ribbon, a pin.

There was peace for a moment, and I watched a star fall from its place in heaven, dive-bombing on its own. The bombs weren't bad, I thought, but the strafing curdled your blood. You didn't see the bombs at night and rarely heard their whistle. But the strafing of a plane's machine guns was a torturing, fateful thing. Up went a wing, blacking out the moon at last, and the spray of bullets with their blood-red tracers seemed to fall very slowly toward you, and the sand twitched where each one landed. You felt you could catch them like fireflies. They were leisurely and neat and terrible.

Mirkin took from his pocket one of the emergency maps printed on a silk handkerchief which each officer carried, and spread it on a rock with the compass beside it. There was a soft explosion sounding much like "Doom!" from the north. "They're after the El Alamein Station now. Listen. That bird's coming back again."

We heard the irregular "rurn-rurn-rurn" and the northern horizon was jeweled with the tracer bullets of the British anti-aircraft. We craned our necks to stare over the plateau where our caves were dug. The men in them were leaning out and staring, too, like puppets on tiny balconies. We stared between the stars, trying to thin that veil of taut blue silk by stretching it between our eyes.

"*Les voilà!*" said Mirkin. Nose to tail two planes climbed, disappeared in the dazzling aura of the moon, swerved down again with a brittle clatter of machine-gun fire. The Boche seemed twice the size of our own.

"Wheee!" yelled Lazrir.

The blue sky was rent with fire and the German plane like a slow comet flew level, toward us. We watched for parachutes but there were none. The plane lifted for an instant and plunged flaming into our camp, half a kilometer away. There was a crash, a ripping bound, a thump, a great white froth of light that was squeezed into an orange bulb, remained stationary a moment, then tapered high with black smoke. Gradually the flames subsided. The plane had shattered into burning fragments over a space of a hundred and fifty yards. There was a reek of oil and the sweetish stink of burning human flesh.

Fortunately the bodies were scarcely recognizable, burned black, broken, crusted with sand, but I could think of them neither as human ruins nor as the enemy beaten. They were men. Scuffing among the embers, we found three bodies and seven hands.

"This isn't the Stuka that bombed us," Mirkin said, bending over a bit of the motor. "It's a Junker 88."

170

Three bodies and seven hands. I looked at the seventh, a hideous bloated thing some distance from the others. There had been a mate to it and a body once. Nearby was a silver cigarette case. We opened it gingerly, for it was still hot, and carefully took out the documents that were charred only on their edges. General Cazaud spread them one by one to the light of the moon as we walked back to camp: the blue-cloth identity card of the pilot, who was twenty-one years old, born in Vienna; a movie pass for a theater in Heraklion, Crete; Greek and Italian money; photographs of two women and a little girl; an official brothel ticket.

General Cazaud hurried to meet Durant on the motorcycle. Durant talked fast: "Vehicles to the west, spread out and coming rapidly."

Colonel Garbet ordered: "Gun positions."

We separated and ran to the spots we had been assigned. My tommy gun was as awkward as a baby under my arm as I climbed up the crumbly cliff to my cave. I heard our armored cars moving behind me, the rattling treads of the Bren gun-carriers, and I reflected gloomily that our tanks had not yet arrived. What the hell, we'd make a fight for it! There were no troops in the desert more skilled, more resolute, more cheerfully courageous than these Fighting French.

The camp was quiet now. We were ready. The moonlight glinted cold on the shining mica desert, and the flames of the Junker looked cordial as campfires far away. I listened, tense, for sounds beyond the ridge, but all I heard was Falconet in the cave next to mine, gently singing, "Dear God, black out the moon. . . ."

16 ∿∿∿∿∿∿∿∿∿∿∿∿

Desert warfare—a dream to Mama
Death—the man who was killed twice

GRADUALLY WE MOVED up under the command
of General Montgomery, and we, the French orphans, moved down
deeper into the desert below the Greeks and the South Africans. But
our hopes rose when we reached a very blank spot called Deir-el-
Regel and the rolling desert dominated by Mount Himeimet, where
the enemy still had an important observation post. Mount Himeimet,
a flat blue tooth jutting from the lip of a plateau, still challenged
Egypt and the world, although Rommel's wrecks lay charred beneath
it. Not far from us was an oasis of graves sprouting black German
crosses on which were marked in gold the names and ages of those
fanatic, mistaken men.

Eight hundred others rotted and boiled while we tore at the rocky
earth to bury them, and the flies of their guts walked upon our
mouths, so that as we breathed we were continually blowing out and
sucking in gray streams of them, like those rolled paper snakes of
the carnivals.

Nothing at all happened for a very long time. The moon improved,
grew red as a new penny in the early evenings when the wands of
the searchlights passed back and forth across it, fading it to yellow
and to silver, drawing it slowly over the zenith until in the morning
it slipped away, a tissue disc, into Rommel's camp, and Rommel's
flies arched in a daylit milky way to fall upon us.

We had no tents at first; we were on five minutes' notice and there
would be no time to uproot tents and swing into the offensive that we,
this time, were preparing. We slept in our trenches with the scorpions
that were too well gorged to bother us, and we browned gently in the
sun which the more sensational correspondents had led us to believe
was intolerable.

The moon grew and diminished while we waited. Neither Rommel

172

nor Montgomery fell for it. October came in with a hailstorm, the first in this desert's history, that punctured the lighter tents. We put on tin hats and battle dress to move about outside. God, I felt, was tired of being completely left out of the war and was strafing both our armies. A week passed and we got news of the accelerated bombardment of Malta, a futile ruse to divert our attention from the supplies Rommel was racing across the Mediterranean. Now it couldn't be long, we said; the show would be starting any day.

What the British wanted was firsthand news of the lost world behind Himeimet, of those escarpments edging the Qattara Depression which were occupied entirely by the enemy. The mystery of the Depression was gradually being pared away. Our own French troops had come from the Siwa Oasis across it, proving for the first time that it was traversible for a motorized army, but most of it was still unknown. It was a colossal rift where nothing lived, a wound in the desert two hundred miles long and two hundred feet below sea level. The enemy were thickly camped along its northern edge and might well descend into it in an attempt to break through our southern defenses.

Someone had to do the dirty job of exploring not only the enemy's strength along the escarpment but of ascertaining whether it was practicable for him to come down with his armor or for us to go up after him. And that was the job for us. In a truck loaded with water and petrol, another filled with night commandos, a jeep, and three armored cars, we wove through the intricate minefields to Lake Magra on the eastern end of the Depression.

Lake Magra was not properly a lake but an incredible swamp in the sand, with harsh tufts of green sprouting from sodden dunes, and it lay in what might be called paradoxically a heavily forested desert. For miles this desert was criss-crossed with petrified trees like giant jackstraws, trees two feet in diameter, their branches crumbled to flints which tinkled musically beneath your feet, their leaves become dust. This was a wasteland dedicated to death, the corpse beneath the skin of Egypt.

Every day we made tentative patrols for the eventual reconnaissance on the cliffs, setting out at dawn in our armored cars to skirt the escarpment that rose sheer from the Qattara Depression like the lost world of Conan Doyle. In my armored car I had a theological student and a physiologist, both in their early twenties, the fightingest men I ever knew. It seemed quite obvious to them that since the purpose of this armored patrol was to find a way up the cliffs for our foot patrol later, the logical thing was to approach the cliffs as close as possible. The fact that they were teeming with bright-eyed Italians was incidental.

But we passed safely, one car at a time, to examine the wadis, the gullies in the rock, while the others trained their guns on the spots above us where the British had charted the possible enemy troops.

Crayay, the physiologist, had his head poked like a jack-in-the-box from the turret of our car. "Men moving up there," he said, pointing. "That's the path all right." We swung quickly back to camp, chased a gazelle, shot it with the 25-mm., and served it with our report to Captain Morel Deville for supper.

He ripped at the joint held in his long fingers and nodded his round blond head. "Good. We'll make them dance, those Itie chorus boys. Get to sleep at once. We'll leave at nine." The Itie chorus boys were the eleven thousand Folgores. We were to be an even dozen, legionnaires and Spahis, including, brashly, me.

It was night at last, the bright day ended, the dust settled, the flies sleeping, an hour of peace before the flying carpet of mosquitoes from Lake Magra would fall upon us. We could see at last without squinting, without sand and sunglasses. We could lie still without continually shuffling our hands over our desert sores to keep away the insects. We were supposedly at rest in preparation for the long night.

"Me, I'll drink a dream to Mama Death," said a youngster of the Foreign Legion, draining his cup and falling asleep at once. That appealed to the Legion, the legend of Mama Death dressed in clotted blood and sand, waiting on the cliffs we were to explore. They slept like bearded babies, confident that they were pets of Mama Death. My own Spahis turned over occasionally for a drink of salty water, the best we had, and I stayed wide awake, in anticipation of my first night patrol.

I looked along the sand to Captain Morel Deville, blessedly asleep,

174

propped against the tire of an armored car. As a soldier of France, Morocco, Eritrea, and Syria, he, too, had had to learn to drop into sleep at will; he couldn't be bothered with a war until he was actively engaged in it.

We woke a few minutes before nine. All Morel Deville's sociability had left him now. He tied the end of his pistol holster to his leg, put a tommy gun on his shoulder. "Grenades for you, Davis," he said. *"Allons!"*

We drove as quietly as possible in the armored cars toward the spot on the southern edge of the Depression from which we would start on foot. We didn't talk very much. We could scarcely doubt that some of us would die. I wondered if I would be afraid. Sitting on the turret of the car, my legs swinging, my arms aching with the effort of holding on, I watched the full moon come up, straight ahead to the west. Half an hour later it was so bright that I could distinguish the Fighting French Cross of Lorraine and the Moroccan star of the Spahis painted on the car five hundred feet away, and I knew that the enemy must be watching our approach.

They were. A white light rocketed from the escarpment to our right. A mile ahead another went up, drifted slowly toward a third that exploded a mile beyond. All three went out almost simultaneously, then two lights only appeared from behind and far ahead of us. This continued for the next half-hour. We were seen, all right.

Captain Morel Deville beside me on the turret was chuckling over his chart. As each new light went up he jumped off the car to get away from its magnetic pull and write down a compass bearing. "It's nice of them," he said, "to give us their exact positions." It didn't seem to bother him that the moon had given them ours. We were as obvious as flies on a windowpane. We ground out the last cigarettes and drew up at the edge of the Depression.

It was a strange-looking band. We had left our helmets behind, for we would have to travel far and probably fast, and although the wind blew cold from the cliffs we were dressed in our lightest clothes, sleeves rolled up, pants legs tucked into boots. Some of us had tommy guns, some rifles, some hand grenades. We stood around our captain, waiting for instructions. On my right was Picoux, a gangling man of fifty who looked more like a simple farmer than a professional soldier.

On my left was little Vallin, brown and neat and murderous, who had come to the Legion from China, to fight for the France he had never seen.

Captain Morel Deville spoke quietly. "Make sure that you haven't any marks on your charts that would indicate our own troops' positions, and that you're carrying no papers but identity cards. We are going to explore Point D. Now get this straight: our main job is to bring back information, so don't provoke a fight. If we do have trouble, try to take prisoners and leave no wounded to talk. If anyone approaches you to surrender with a cloth covering his head, kill him.

"While crossing the Depression we'll spread out in three lines, fifty feet apart. Men on the right—keep eyes right, on the left—eyes left. Don't forget they know we're coming, and they may try for us from any direction. If we get separated on the escarpment during the night, try to reach Point 3 where the cars will be waiting. If you can't get down before daylight, hide until night before attempting it. Understand? Let's go."

The cars swung away from us, and it was like having a wall pulled suddenly from your back. The men looked tiny separated. The lights were still going up gaily from the cliff we were headed for. I followed fifty feet behind Morel Deville in the center column, conscious of the din I was making in my Himalayan boots. The others wore crepe-soled shoes.

Most of this dead earth far below sea level was marked on the charts as impassable for cars. At each step we broke through the crust of gravel into the sucking powder underneath, and my boots seemed to clack like castanets. From time to time a man would turn toward me, making a gesture of silence, and I would try to walk more quietly, following on tiptoe in Morel Deville's footprints, balancing each step carefully. I still clacked.

For three hours we plodded through the Depression, crouched as low as we could, inching our way around ridges of sand which might conceal snipers. Occasionally Morel Deville would stop. We would sink to the ground and stare, tense, at the shadow ahead. The three men leading would crawl toward it, identify it as a bush, a rotting camel, and beckon us on. It was like "Cops and Robbers" which we played as children, but now we were playing with Mama Death. We were in the open; the enemy was hidden, holding every advantage, and I could feel my nerves jangling like piano wires. I couldn't help but think of what one glancing bullet would do if it struck one of the grenades in my loaded pocket.

Again Morel Deville stopped. I caught up with him, hoping he hadn't heard my boots. He pointed to the tracks of a large tank and beside it those of a German jeep. The Depression was certainly traversible. He turned to me, shifting the tommy gun to his other shoulder. The smile was kindly in that hard fighter's face. "I'm sorry, Davis," he whispered, "but you're making a hell of a racket with those boots. Tear up your scarf and wrap them. If that doesn't work, you'd better follow us some distance behind. Once the shooting starts you can run up."

I wrapped the scarf around my feet and trudged on like a flamingo, making almost as much noise as before. We followed the tank tracks into the thin blue shadow at the base of the cliffs, and into the gully we had found on reconnaissance yesterday. The flints were sharper here, and the wrappings on my boots kept tearing and slipping. I would have to stop to rewrap them, then rush to catch up with the others. I was beginning to feel very foolish, thinking what a fine thing it would be if I scuttled this patrol upon which so much depended.

Up and up we went, following the tracks, till we came cautiously to level ground, but the tracks ran straight north from here, so we abandoned them to look for the observation posts. It seemed incredible that we should have gotten this far without drawing their fire. Ominously, there were no flares any more. The moon was directly overhead, for it was two o'clock and we had been walking for hours. Clouds chased furiously across it, thick, tremendous, abnormally fast, like clouds in a Russian film. The whole scene was theatrical, the gray plateau, the hunched men, the spotlight effect of the moon flashing off and on between clouds, sweeping the canyons on each side of us, four or five hundred feet deep. Niched in those walls, somewhere, were the posts of the enemy, watching. We took a bearing and had a small sip from our canteens of the salty water of Lake Magra.

177

"Point D," whispered Captain Morel Deville, pointing.

We followed him on hands and knees to the edge of the plateau. Directly opposite and a hundred feet higher was a horn of a cliff, Point D. We went down quickly from shadow to shadow to the bottom of the wadi. The signs of the Italians were everywhere, boot and tire tracks, empty tins, toilet paper caught on bushes. The light at this depth was the purple of underseas, and we moved through it heavily, feeling our way like divers.

I craned my neck to look up at the new cliff, our objective, towering high above us, and wondered what sort of fighting shape we would be in if we ever reached it. I thought, "Christ, I'd love a cigarette!" Then a strange thing happened as I realized with astonishment that I wouldn't at all. There was the hankering in my chest which usually smoke allayed, but it wasn't for a smoke. I realized with a shock that made me dizzy that nothing could assuage this hunger but the killing of the men up there. It was a terrible and heartening discovery, and I felt suddenly healed of my weariness.

I was feeling pretty fierce by the time I had thought all this. Captain Morel Deville raised his hand, grinned. In single file but widely separated we began the ascent, out of the shadow and into blue moonlight again. Flattened against the cliffs, we climbed hand over hand, and every handhold crumbled into little avalanches which I was sure could be heard for a quarter of a mile. To make things worse, the rags had ripped loose from my boots, and now I was making more noise than ever. There were only two solutions: go to the end of the patrol, or continue barefoot. I got rid of the boots, and my feet winced on the cold, sharp edges of the rock.

It was fantastic terrain, grotesque and sinister. Here and there a platform of earth jutted far out over the canyon. Squarish lumps as big as houses balanced precariously upon a single corner. The whole cliff was pocked with caves like the sockets of skulls, and we wriggled past them with guns ready and grenades balanced. The sergeant of the Legion ahead of me passed back a message from the captain: three of our men were missing, he said, two legionnaires and a Spahi. It was impossible to look for them now. We must keep going.

We did, straight up. The edge of the cliff hung over us. Our hands reached it, and at the moment when our eyes came level, the sky

178

burst open with a vomit of flame. I saw black shapes humped over me and fire hurtling out of them. An Italian with feathers on his helmet deliberately took aim with a machine gun as I tore at my breast pocket for a grenade. I ducked, flung it, ecstatic with the realization that I was loving this though it scared me silly. The earth heaved and the rocks splintered around us. The Italians were screeching. Our men, old desert rats, made not a sound as they triggered their tommy guns, flung their grenades, then spun to toboggan down on their backsides along the wadis where the cliff had crumbled to dust. I spilled down headforemost, praying I wouldn't rip the rings off the grenades in my pockets, trying to keep an eye on the spurts of sand where the bullets struck.

We gathered finally in the shelter of a cave, panting and scratched but without a wound. There was still a wild chattering from the Italians, but they made no attempt to follow. They probably assumed that we were much more numerous than we were, but we knew by the din they made that we were outnumbered by hundreds.

"That takes care of Point D," Morel Deville said. "Get going. You can rest tomorrow."

We spread-eagled against the cliff again, rounded it slowly, and wormed our way into the darkness of the canyon. With our luminous compasses we took the azimuth of each important point and marked it on our charts. We entered a sort of crater where a tank had been playing; some idle Hun seemed to have attempted to cut a huge swastika in the sand with his treads.

Morel Deville whispered, "There's something funny here." We squatted around the crater while he examined those curious tank tracks on hands and knees. He passed his discovery around the circle; the whole crater was sewn with anti-personnel mines, the kind with three little whiskers protruding above the ground. Morel Deville beckoned to two of the Spahis, indicated the passage by which the tank had entered. They buried three of our own heavy mines there.

We had cautiously started down again when a fusillade of shots rang out beyond the ridge on our left. We distinguished the bark of machine-gun fire, the great cough of mortars, the harsher yapping of tommy guns. "There are our three lost men," said the shadow beside me. The valley echoed from cliff to cliff, and flat on our bellies we watched the flashes of the fight. Hell's door might have been suddenly opened. The tall shadow of Morel Deville was framed in it.

"We've got to get to them." He spoke evenly. There was no need of silence now. We pushed hard at the ground, pried our weary bodies up. We started toward the pulsing, orange-colored cave of light. We were halfway down, sliding, pressed hard to the cliff, when suddenly the shots, the flashes, withered, and the tommy guns of our own men spoke at last.

"*Bien,*" said Morel Deville. "Good job." We leaned back against a crumbly shelf, and passed a flask of whisky among us, and we toasted those soldiers who had been fighting alone in the dark.

We had nearly reached the floor of the Depression when three blobs of black challenged us over a ridge: "*Qui va là?*" Morel Deville's gun swung forward. I ripped half my pants away to get my pistol which had tangled in a pocket. Click-click-click went the rings of the Legion's grenades as they were loosened.

"France!" said Morel Deville. There, grinning, were our three lost men. They had wiped out the observation post and taken a wealth of documents.

Slowly we trudged back across the Depression, in three columns again, slogging through the mush of sand, alive to nothing but the lust of sleep. We had already done thirty miles, most of it vertical, in the past nine hours, and we couldn't have ducked very fast if the Italians on the cliff had seen us in the brightening dawn.

Coutainceau staggered along ahead of us, as he had patrolled this section before. Morel Deville and I came next. I tried to keep my mouth from sagging open, to breathe through my nose, to hold my shoulders back. Morel Deville's tommy gun hung halfway down his back, and his knuckles gripping it showed pale green in that early light. The legionnaires, loose-limbed, swung along behind us easily.

The sun came up through the morning fog and we arrived at the stony hillock where the cars were supposed to meet us. They weren't there, and that didn't worry us much, although we still were in view and range of the enemy positions. We went to the opposite side of the hillock from them and dropped down on the rocks and went to sleep. Morel Deville and I went to sleep with our mouths still full of raisins and our first cigarettes not a quarter smoked. This was the ultimate of bliss.

The sun crept over us and we wakened fitfully. A mile or so away we could see the cars searching for us, and we flung a grenade to attract their attention, regardless of the Italians. The cars came bouncing like hares to us across the corrugated plain.

Morel Deville and I crawled into the staff car, a blessed vehicle with sponge-rubber seats. We got into it with awkward dignity, and dizzily, joking at the night behind us, suddenly aware that the bedroll among the flies of Lake Magra would be wonderful. Now, I thought, I'll drain the dream to Mama Death. We spilled our grenades upon the floor, loosened our belts and slid the pistols from them, and leaned back each in his corner to sleep.

I surged up, nauseated, from sleep again, clawing my way through oily billows of sleep to reach a voice shouting, *"Avions! Avions!"* Our car was still moving, but we pitched headfirst out of it. There were four Messerschmidts plunging straight at us. I tried to run away from the cars, for they would be the target, but my legs had stiffened and I fell on my chin. I lurched on frantically, seeing the planes bloat as they dived toward us; there seemed nothing in that polished desert that would shelter me. The planes filled the sky and I fell flat with my arms crossed behind my ears. This is for me, I thought. You're a bitch, Mama Death. The machine-gun bullets raked toward me with a hundred prongs, over me and on to the cars. I heaved up to make another run for it while the four Messerschmidts were circling back. The car I had left was gushing flame.

I saw a little rock ahead of me, a cordial little rock, and jammed my head under it, curled my body around it tight. The planes returned, their motors roaring. And there was another sound. There under the rock, less than a foot from my eyes, hissing at me, was one of the horned, brown-spotted desert vipers.

It was a ludicrous situation. I didn't know whether to go in with the snake or out with the Jerries, who were diving again, but I decided on the snake though I knew this sort to be deadly poisonous. I hardly dared to move, but I did manage to flick a little sand at him and he backed away a bit, shaking his head in rather a reproachful way.

Down zoomed the planes to within a few yards of us, and I felt my buttocks quivering. You are totally impotent under the lash of an air attack. Shattering thoughts like shrapnel strike through your mind. They'll get my legs, you think, your toes burrowing. Maybe my lungs. Now it's coming, now, now. . . .

The bullets spat over us like a mouthful of rice, and I felt the shock as my little rock was hit. My companion, the viper, hissed, and I heard the bawling of young Vallin and saw him floundering with the agony of a shot through his eye. The planes swooped out of range. Morel Deville was flattened tight to the earth beside me, but he was grinning, his pillbox hat tilted jauntily on the back of his head.

Four times the planes came at us, seeking us personally, individually. Each of us, dead, was treasure. On their last circuit Morel Deville wove to his feet, lurched to an armored car, and swung the Bren gun up. The planes screamed down at it, barely over the top, then off like bats into the sun as Morel Deville fired. A misty trail of petrol was spewing from the last. If its tank was hit, it would probably land within our lines.

Our men came up cheering from the sand, and for the first time we saw the holocaust that had been our car three minutes ago, that might well have been ourselves. Even Vallin had managed to stand. There was a scarlet polyp where his left eye had been, and his grin twitched horribly beneath a veil of blood.

I nodded to the snake, which ignored me, and wavered over to my captain, thinking dizzily that I might make a dash for our gear in the burning car. But I didn't. None of us did. We were too tired.

On the bright crisp morning of October twenty-third there was little to indicate that the Eighth Army would be starting that night for Europe. It was a day like any other. We were fed up with the war and with ourselves. I had frazzled a rope into a sort of flyswish and was swishing away glumly. I painted my feet with iodine, rubbed sulfathiazole into the cuts, and thought, "Hitler's notion that war is salutary is absurd; the ejaculation of bullets is no good for man nor beast; I want to go home, and God help anyone who tries to stop me on this straight road ahead. And I'm going home, west."

"That, I suppose," said I to Bill the dog, "is what they call morale. Nuts," said I, "for morale, too." Bill wagged his tail and I turned him gently in the sand, where I sat cross-legged, so that his tail would abet the flyswish.

That night we joined the concerted offensive of Montgomery's troops. We moved quickly to some other sand which was called Qor el Labban, and waited behind a crusted hill, perfectly visible to the enemy, who shelled us, until that consummate order barked at us to attack. Montgomery's whole army moved simultaneously forward, and we at the southern end of it swung up with two battalions of the Foreign Legion to assault the plateau to the west of Mount Himeimet. Our purpose was to isolate the observation post of the mountain. The plateau was the one called El Taqa, where we had stopped during the retreat to Alamein, where Falconet had prayed in verse for the black out of Rommel's moon. The Italian Folgore Division had it now, and I resented their using the cave from which blind Bill and I had first seen this war.

At seven-fifteen we moved quietly forward. At eleven-thirty our sappers reached the first of the enemy minefields and cleared a passage in a little less than ten minutes, jabbing their bayonets into the explosive sand, ripping out the mines, and delineating the route with white ribbon. We didn't know then that deep in the earth beneath that minefield were men of the enemy signal corps, telephoning our progress to Himeimet and the El Taqa plateau. There were too many things we didn't know, but they troubled neither De Kersauson nor General Koenig, who was in command of us, nor Colonel Amilakvari of the Legion.

Amilakvari sent the first battalion forward. It was midnight now, and we shivered with the peculiar damp cold of Egypt as we followed cautiously. We heard the noise of battle which meant that the battalion was engaged, but there was no signal from them, and no sound of our artillery which should have been already emplaced above. We didn't know, despite our patrols, that the heavy guns couldn't possibly climb those crumbling cliffs.

The subterranean telephones, behind us now, reported our movements, and when the First Battalion of the Legion rushed the plateau it was met with every arm the enemy had. Machine guns, tommy guns, mortars, four 88-mm. guns, and one 105-mm. laid a wall of fire before our men, but they charged up the escarpment so fast that they actually passed some of the enemy nests and had to come back to destroy them with grenades. The Foreign Legion didn't worry much about postwar pensions, but it differed from the Legion of Moroccan tribal warfare in that it had become conscious of a country to serve and regain, and it was less reckless now. So the First Battalion, strongly outnumbered, destroyed what they could and wisely tumbled down the cliff again.

Colonel Amilakvari, a shadow without a helmet, passed almost invisibly among us, consulting with Koenig about the disposition of our—the Spahis'—armored cars and Captain Divry's tanks. We rested until 6:00 A.M., as comfortable as cockroaches on the strings of a piano in full action; then the Second Battalion of the Legion stormed the cliffs.

They went up it and reached the plateau. Two hundred Italian infantry met them there, and the Legion surged forward, shouting their simple and terrible cry, "La Légion! La Légion!"

Upon this plateau was a smaller one, about waist high, around which the battle flowed. One Spaniard of the Legion flung his grenades across it and was wounded in the right hand. Our doctor had to pull him down by force to dress the wound, and the moment it was bandaged the Spaniard popped up again with a grenade in his left hand.

A young sergeant jumped upon the plateau with a tommy gun and semicircled it with flame. His men came after him, and in a few minutes most of the defending Italians were killed. Twenty-three surrendered, waving neat little white flags, collapsible to fit the pocket. We thought we had taken this objective, even though there was still no sign of our 75-mm. guns on the plateau. Captain de Courcelle's long-range artillery seemed to be getting its targets from east of Himeimet, and the sounds below seemed to indicate that Divry's tanks and De Kersauson's and Morel Deville's armored cars were engaged.

They well and truly were. Three of our tanks and three armored cars rounded up an entire company of German parachutists plus two hundred Italians of the Folgore. Morel Deville's Second Squadron—to which I belonged—got four Honeys, one Crusader, one armored car, and put to flight a Grant. These, of course, were Allied machines which had been captured by Rommel during the Alamein push. The Grant was a proper bastard, with 35-mm. and 75-mm. guns, but it lunged away like a terrified cow from young Rouxell's armored car, with thirty direct hits from the 25-mm. in its tail.

But Mama Death on the cliff forgot about us, and Mama Death, said Gudin, was bored with this and was probably sitting weaving the veins of little soldiers into the huge jacket of war. For through the smoke screen which we had laid between the British attacking from the Northeast and ourselves, so that we couldn't be seen simultaneously, came six American Honey tanks and a bouncing brood of armored cars. The Legion cheered but shut up fast when these, too, proved to be filled with the enemy. The battalion fell back before the blasting of the tanks, for it had no guns heavy enough to fight them. Methodically the men gathered at a promontory, then plunged down it, fighting their way backward. The crew of one six-pounder found itself isolated without any sort of vehicle to pull their heavy gun, but those good men pulled it themselves, by hand, down the escarpment and for eight kilometers to safety, while shells of the German 105-mm. pursued them.

The *toubbib,* the doctor of the battalion, crawled from one tumbling wounded man to another during that descent from hell, patching them as best he could, but that was not his only problem. Continually, while he was busy with his dressings, Italians crawled out of their trenches, tossed him their weapons, and surrendered. He dressed their wounds, too. When the battalion with their prisoners finally reached the ambulances below, the Italians were very choosy about which should transport them. One ran piteously to the doctor, crying, "Major, I am your own patient! I surrendered to you personally, didn't I?" Another ran in circles, shouting, "Where is the Second Company? The Second Company? I belong to them!"

Our losses were heavy, but we lost no men as prisoners. The slope of sand below the cliff was bright with our dead and each of our tanks returning was festooned with wounded men. It was no historic action such as that of Bir Hakim, but it served. It obliged the enemy to move many of his troops from the central sector to the southern, as he had no idea of how great, or how little, was our force.

We returned through the passage in the minefields, following dizzily the white cloth markers, and the Huns of Himeimet shelled us home. And it was then that Colonel Amilakvari was, said his men, killed for the first time. The second was when a shell went through his ambulance.

17 ~~~~~~~~~~~~~~~~

Ethiopia—The Lion of Judah—
Djibouti's long teeth—Madagascar
—South Africa with Mother Smuts

ALTHOUGH WE HAD acquitted ourselves well and shown our mettle to the British who commanded us, we were moved without any but incidental actions toward Tunisia. Hearsay was that General Leclerc was angling toward us through the Fezzan, striking little resistance from the Italian outposts. And on a night without a moon we stood around Captain Brunel's ambulance, listening to the radio when the announcement was made that the Americans, with certain British elements, had landed in North Africa. The Americans, *Bon Dieu,* were in it at last! The Americans and their money, their matériel, their many men!

Being the only American available, I was kissed on both cheeks by bearded legionnaires, but their affection for me diminished during the following days when we learned that America was backing General Giraud, not our De Gaulle.

"Look, Davis," said the commandant over tea with rum one morning. "I understand we'll be bogged down here for a while, and if I know you this will drive you crazier. What I'd suggest is that you thumb your way back to Cairo, do a hell of a broadcast to your countrymen, then get the French delegation to send you, on my recommendation, on a quick flight first to Ethiopia to get a message from Haile Selassie. Remember our Spahis fought the Italians for him there. Then pop off to French Somaliland and Madagascar to feel out the attitude of those equivocal French territories. I'd judge you could do it in a couple of weeks. Don't worry; this will be a lull, I'll save you a night patrol when you get back."

Cheered by the implied confidence of Commandant de Kersauson, I left Cairo by Lockheed plane on an empty stomach. The sunlight was halfway down the pyramids as we passed over them and I was cracking pistachio nuts with my teeth. The flat land of Egypt changed to something like moldy biscuit dough.

Somewhere around Aswan we swerved unexpectedly to the coast and flew east across the Red Sea, which certainly wasn't my direction at all. Below us were the sands of Arabia, and when we landed on them I discovered that this was fabulous Jedda, the starting point for the pilgrimage to Mecca. I thought of Burton's journey in disguise to that sacred and forbidden city, and was tempted to abandon all my projects. . . . Somewhere in these deserts there must still be silken tents and satin houris and gay gallops in the night dragging a Bedouin by his beard. The Western Desert had been far below the standard of the films.

My dreams were bumped loose as we took off again. We returned to Africa, to Upper Egypt, and flew high across the mountains of Eritrea. We came to a rolling plain of clouds, and then, jutting through them, the great Asmaran plateau like a secret world far above and invisible to the men who lived beneath the clouds surrounding it.

This was the time of the little rains, the gentle, modest rains of Ethiopia, before the torrents of spring. I watched the drops smash slowly to death, firm small bodies flattened against the mechanical drive of us. Below our plane wound the magnificent mountain road from Asmara to Addis Ababa, swinging neatly around nine-thousand-foot peaks, falling headlong like a cataract into valleys where the Shiftas, assassins, still were attacking British convoys, not because they disliked the British, but simply because they had an excess of energy and arms, and nothing to do with them.

The rolling mountains of Eritrea had now flattened, separated, become the modern, functional plateaux of the Ethiopian highlands, fertile tablelands where the peasants could raise their crops against the sun. It was through this dour country that the Emperor had come home in the spring of 1941, paving the road behind him with the bones of fifteen thousand camels which had made up his desperate caravan.

We flew still higher. Clouds as bright as snow cuddled in the valleys, and as we approached Addis Ababa the plateaux were assembled and merged, squeezing the clouds from between them, until the region of the capital spread beneath us clean and green. Here was legendary Addis Ababa, but it was scarcely distinguishable because there was no concentration of settlement; from the air it looked like a cluster of villages with wide areas of field between.

But it may be for this, for its spaciousness, that in all Africa there is no lovelier capital city, with its shady corridors of eucalyptus trees, its curving walls of stone, its cobbled streets that make a few practice turns in the valleys of Addis itself, then go plunging into the fields. The hundred acres of my Free French Delegation, the gift of great King Menelik, lay shining upon the hill, the leaves of its gum trees twinkling like aluminum in the thin morning air that had me short of breath. All is spacious but your lungs in this high place; for the first two weeks in Addis at nine thousand feet you pant into your breakfast, drowse over lunch, and sleep at night in lumps of an hour at a time.

But the Ethiopians made me famously comfortable in token of their regard for both France and the United States, for I was an American in the Free French forces, doubly an ally. At times their hospitality was embarrassing, as on the morning when I realized that all about me was the parade ground and that I, second lieutenant, was invited to review His Majesty's troops. I sought frantically to remember how I myself had been reviewed, how reviews had appeared in newsreels, and stepped out smartly to do my bewildered best for America and Ethiopia and Fighting France. The troops took it well.

A morning finally came when Mr. Tassfi Tagani, Minister of the Pen, brought me His Majesty's summons. It would be a social interview, he said; no need to submit written questions. His Majesty was eager for news of the Fighting French.

The great car was sent for me. We sped up the hill and swung past the guards and the gate, and drew up at the gleaming palace of the Emperor Haile Selassie I, Conquering Lion of the Tribe of Judah, Elect of God, whose family name is Ras Tafari, He Who Is Feared. I was passed from hand to hand down corridors and up flights of marble stairs. The secretary, Tassawork, met me, slid an eye along my uniform, and bowed me through several rooms furnished in elegant English taste.

We came to the door. Tassawork opened it slowly. He whispered to me, "His Majesty is on your right." I entered the long, simple room, sidestepped the great Dane, turned right, and clicked to a stop before the Emperor, who was rising from an ebony armchair. He came part way to meet me, and as he took my hand and looked me straight in the eyes, not imperiously but searchingly, seeking to know a friend, I had an impression of strength and warmth, of instant cordiality such as I have rarely experienced with great men. There was no professional charm and no patronage.

"Soyez le bienvenu," he said. His voice was soft but sonorous. He talked with me in French, for although he speaks English excellently he prefers the fluent French he learned from his childhood tutors. He leaned forward in the armchair, intent, eager, military in khaki uniform and three rows of decorations. I spoke of my amazement at Ethiopia's resurrection.

"I should be very happy," he said, "if you could have seen my country five years ago, so you could judge the progress we have made, lacking the help of nearly all our superior men who were assassinated in the war. You must not forget that my people have had less than forty years of contact with Western civilization." His great dark eyes shone, and he knit his fingers tightly.

I spoke of the interest and sympathy which America has always had for his people. He knew that; he believed in the duration of that friendship. "If you like," he said, "I will write you a little paper for the Americans. I want them to know of my feeling for them."

This was more than I had hoped for. The Emperor clasped both knees, lifted his bearded chin, and asked, "When will we end this butchery?" I hazarded the guess that it would be in the first six months of 1944, and he nodded. "Not later," he said. "The patriots of Ethiopia, like your Fighting French, have never given in. And they have fought for us and died for us on our own soil. I have the deepest

189

regard for your General Koenig of Bir Hakim and General Leclerc of the Tchad. I think," he said, and looked out the window toward a little bird, which was singing more sweetly than any canary, upon an amaryllis branch, "perhaps I can write you a little paper for your troops of Fighting France."

"We should be grateful, Your Majesty," I said, as a knot in my chest uncoiled. I stood up then, eager to hurry this promise home, and the Emperor took my hand. He held it longer than strangers do, and again looked me square in the eyes with a fierce sort of friendliness.

Turning, I reached impulsively to pat the immense great Dane. There was cataclysm. He heaved up thundering, landed with a roar on my shoulder, and attempted to lick off my ear. His Majesty smiled sweetly. I made an awkward obeisance around the dog, and went for the door, forgetting that I should back out.

My little papers came at last, with a note from that canny Minister of the Pen. They were magnificent, a long message to the people of the United States, lauding their liberty and soliciting not their financial aid but their moral support. And the second lengthy document was to the troops of Fighting France, praising their courage, tenacity, and "the beauty of their pride."

Suddenly there was a flare of lavender across the documents on my knee, and I looked up to see lightning in an ominous sky. There was the tinkle of rain in the wattle trees, then a roar of thunder. Even the elements, I thought, delighted in Ethiopia as a battlefield, Ethiopia that has asked only peace and the way to wisdom since the lovely Sheba's day.

Hell on wheels was that train across the desert from Diredawa in Ethiopia to Djibouti in French Somaliland. The hot season had not yet begun, but the heat of winter blew through the carriage in gusts that stopped our breath and clogged our pores. I held on my lap the fishwife's naked baby, massaging it from time to time with the bottom of my cold glass of gin. The fishwife sang. Her little husband beat time on the thermos jar, and on his shirt pocket danced the biggest Lorraine Cross that I had ever seen.

The old train wheezed, "A-tachatcha-a, a-tchatcha-a. . . ." The air solidified like a junket, darkened, heaved in upon us thick with rain.

190

The desert grew gray. It was a ragged waste, a dirty desert unlike the clean desolation of the Sahara. Frowzy bushes clung to it. Its occasional camels were shedding, their hair peeling loose in great scabrous patches. I had another gin to lift the gloom.

"Voilà!" cried the fishwife. "Djibouti!" I sighted along her arm. In the foreground was a snarl of barbed wire, relic of the Italians' defense, and a little farther were the relics of their defeat, a dozen camions mangled and burned by the British artillery. Far to the east was a golden tube of sunlight where the rain had ceased, and within it lay a little city as white as chalk. Djibouti. The sea behind it was almost black.

The train lurched into the station at last, and suddenly I saw the group of French officers, neatly tailored in shorts and shirts, awaiting me. It is not easy to be casual in getting rid of a hot, naked, and slippery baby with one hand while you buckle on a revolver with the other, but I managed it finally and joined the officers on the platform. I was doubly embarrassed, for as one of the first of the Fighting French to come to Djibouti from the front I knew it must disappoint these men to discover that I was actually an American.

In the Cercle des Officiers, fronting the sea, we looked across that arid town, flat as a blistered pancake, and ate the monstrous, marvelous crabs that are the one staple of Djibouti. As I dripped in a dinner climate of 110 degrees, I dreamed of Maine and the sharp surf beating on iron rocks, and the smoke of clambakes whipping cold and harsh against my eyes, and Lucille, my mother, with her blond hair whipped to leeward, smiling her white teeth at the cold surf.

"You know, we did have even meat," said Captain Simon, who would die a few months from now in Tunisia beside us, "the greatest variety of meat you can imagine, when Vichy walled us on one side and the British walled us, because of Vichy, on the other. We had donkey meat, camel cutlets about a yard long, boiled dog, and jugged cat. Perhaps you have noticed that there is scarcely an animal in Djibouti even now. I ate hyena once, and that must be a record for any carnivore."

The doctor got up to close two of the broad windows against the northeast monsoon which was whirling dust across our table. "Beriberi and scurvy were terrible," he said, "because of the lack of fresh food. Our gums shrank and all of us except the administrators had long teeth like horses. You could tell Pétainists and De Gaullists at a glance. We made salads and soups of grass, when we could find it."

"I remember," said a second lieutenant with a small faun's face, "that our pathetic little brothel just managed to survive. Our money was useless to the girls, for there was nothing in town to buy, but the Vichy chaps paid them in tinned food which they alone could get."

Fanny Marcelle, a Stygian Somali woman who admitted that she was of a certain age, mended my clothes and gentled my ignorance, snapping my neck violently betweenwhiles when I got a crick in it from the punkha. The punkha must be understood to be a sort of fan, a flap of weighted cloth suspended from the ceiling and activated by a little boy sitting on the floor. He pulls a cord which makes the flap flop back and forth, flicking air at his employer. I had two flap-floppers at night, the little boy and his tough elder brother who sat behind the younger, whacking him to keep him awake and occasionally dousing the flap with water which would give a sort of coolness to my dreams and give me cricks in the neck.

Fanny Marcelle would pounce on me and wring my neck with Somali osteopathy when she saw me looking one-eyed at the typewriter. Then, as amends, she would mix me a Madagascar rum with the saline water from the tap, and tell me the native's tale of Djibouti: of his confusion when his masters, who had counseled him to emulate them, fought among themselves, of his splintered faith when the omniscient French colonists who had always told him that the English were good people and the Germans bad, now said—because they were Vichyist—just the opposite. And it was exasperating first to be ordered to dig a slit trench as protection from aircraft, then to plant vegetables in it—for they won't grow in Djibouti's sandy topsoil—then to jump into one's own garden and ruin one's beans when the British reconnaissance planes, quite harmless, came over. The shrapnel of Djibouti's own anti-aircraft was the greater danger.

"Crack!" would go my neck as Fanny Marcelle gave it a wrench again, and my lungs panted "a-tchatcha-a" like the tired train, when the shutters burst open and the thick wind engulfed me.

In Somaliland the governor put every resource at my disposal, including a continual and abhorrent Tripes à la Mode de Caen. I collected a treasure in Vichy documentary film and a mass of correspondence, actually tied with pink ribbon, between several colonial Vichy governors. These I sent to De Gaulle's Comité Nationale in London, and fine sport they made of them.

I cabled in code to the French Delegation in Cairo. "CONTINUE MADAGASCAR REPORT GAULLISM THEN SOUTH AFRICA SEE SMUTS," came the reply. Over British Somaliland we flew, and Kenya and Tanganyika, and I was nostalgic for the days when we hunted lion and black rhinoceros, and down the coast of Africa to refuel at Lindi, a land filled with sisal and the loud ventriloquist's laugh of the gnome who ran the resthouse. Stumbling on one wing, we curved over the Mozambique Channel toward Madagascar. The Comoro Islands lay peacefully to the left of us, faithfully French. They had refused to traffic with Vichy politics and Japanese submarines that had crazily come this far.

We crossed the coast of Madagascar, not very far from the Antarctic now, and flew low over opulent, uninhabited hills, then red rivers that seemed to be carved of Chinese cinnabar. The hills as we approached Tananarive were nicely terraced, the houses set in compounds shaped like frying pans, and these were walled against the bandits who still were active in the provinces.

The capital town of Tananarive was very Swiss and lovely. On the outskirts of the city the houses were like those in fairy tales, tall and narrow and thatched and blind, their tiny windows placed haphazardly. You followed the cobbled streets and the houses became higher and leaner still, with roofs of tile gracefully curved at the eaves. And above them towered the massive palaces of the last great queen and the prime minister, who was her husband. Some of the surrounding hills had curious gashes in them, for there was once a king who had claustrophobia and disliked hills; he spent his and his people's substance in trying to hack them down, and the remnants of his Caligulan folly lie raw in the cool sunlight of Tananarive.

An American in French uniform, I was suspect here. I, on the other hand, suspected the so-called Free French Information Service, which smacked of Vichy to me, but over its dead body I managed a broadcast to tell the isolated Malgache of what De Gaulle's loyal

193

army was doing in Tchad and the Western Desert. This didn't go down at all well; I found myself without a room and sleeping without a mattress in the corridor of a minor hotel.

But from General Legentilhomme, the High Commissioner, and the British General Smallwood, I received hospitality and intelligence of Vichy's savage undermining of this innocent island. Gaullists were hurled into jail and their property was confiscated. The children who had put up the signs, "Death to the Traitors of Vichy," were mercilessly beaten and dragged through the streets in chains, moaning, "Mooramoor . . . mooramoor," which means "Gently . . . Gently." Madagascar, at the end of the world, was a child dragged in chains behind Germany's Juggernaut.

On my last rainy night I came down alone and afoot from a high suburb of Tananarive where an old professor had shown me the last treasure he owned in the world, for his sons had died in the fighting and he had sold his possessions to aid Free France. He had shown me an egg fourteen inches in diameter, of the terrible prehistoric bird named Aepyornis Maximus. Filled with dreams of the past when birds must have been as frightful to lesser life as our planes now, I skidded down the wet cobblestoned street that curved suddenly left and right, following the brink of the precipice. The lights of the shops beside me were few, but the moon made a quicksilver puddle of Lake d'Anocy far below. The little shops still open were reminiscent of France. There was a Tabac, which had no tobacco in it, and a Café des Chauffeurs, which lacked coffee and had no chauffeurs. I had a hot grog there, although the proprietor would lose his license if caught at this hour selling liquor to the military. He was a gentle old Malgache with cheeks like russet apples, and he wore a sort of pullover of raffia which must have scratched him well.

"Scratch? *Mais oui, mon lieutenant.* But the mosquitoes are so bad in this season that it saves you trouble really. But we must have warmer clothes than this, and there is no cloth to be bought. Crocodile skins, yes, but I would be even more unseemly in a crocodile skin, would I not? And the peasants, *mon lieutenant,* they who tend the sugar cane that permits me to give you illegitimate grog, they must

194

have cloth for warmth before the cold season comes in May. There will be tuberculosis everywhere if this inconsiderate war isn't finished soon."

"*Je vous remercie, monsieur le patron.*"

"*Au plaisir, mon lieutenant.*"

Soaking wet and thinking fondly of the raffia shirt, I hurried down the cobbled hill and lost my way through a street glistening in the moon reflected from the eastern windowpanes. I came then to a fairy-tale house, small and narrow between its blowzy neighbors. Its front wall was the color of sand and its crooked doors and shutters were painted blue. And beneath the eaves was one window lighted, with two children leaning from it, like the children of Maeterlinck's *Bluebird,* framed by softly lighted rafters beyond them. They were only shadows and their voices were shadowy as I hurried home. They whispered, "Mooramoor . . . mooramoor. . . ."

Out of the last lovely sleep of that morning came a dream of Richard de Roussy de Sales, propagandist, parachutist, and monitor of his fellowmen. The goblin grin of him reeked of wine and garlic and somebody's perfume which I had smelled much of the night before. He chided me. He leaned halfway into the dream, and spoke poorly of me. He praised my publishers' patience; he appraised Matilda; and he took a dim view of everything other than the war which was still to be won, and the brilliant news of it which he, at least, was writing.

Then he faded somewhat, and the light flicked against my eyes, and Matilda was sitting bright and upright upon the pillow. I sat up, too, to get my back to Richard.

Matilda said, rubbing the cold cream from her face and putting on her eyebrows, "Beel, you are going to begin the book today. Have you got any grog . . . for me?" Richard hadn't quite gone yet, and I was too sleepy and too much in love with Matilda—as one may be in the early morning—and much too cautious to talk. "Beel," she said, "Beel, my cabbage, this is B-Day when you begin the book. . . ."

And I said finally, being an old Frenchman now, "Yes, my cabbage, yes, my little rabbit, yes, my old branch," and went to sleep again.

It was glacial on the airdrome. I sought my plane sleepily, as I had sought so many others, feeling that this must be the last farewell to the Richards and the Matildas I had loved.

I knew too well about The Door, and I thought of it in capital letters now. I knew that door of peace which all planes have, painted a comforting green like the doors of hospitals, locked by three simple catches—the emergency door. It led nowhere but to peace. Slowly you would walk down between the aluminum seats, blithely eating pistachios, and twitch the catches until the door fell out. Then you would follow it into the wind.

And no one would be embarrassed or troubled at all, and you would be rested in one of the wastelands between the Cape and Cairo.

This wasn't melodrama. It was sheer fatigue, the fatigue of the Fighting French during the years I had been with them. It was the fatigue of too much war and frustration, of too much writing on a vaporous wall in the lulls of action, of too many Matildas, who were warm and useful spies, of too many memories, indigestible together, vomiting up in you.

Madagascar was well behind us now, and our plane, a Lodestar, flew high over the sea and then the fertile ranges to Johannesburg, and I held my head, thinking of Matilda, who wanted merely a lot of information about our troops, and affection, and our joint security in my writing a book and marrying her, so that I wouldn't be returning to any silly war and she would remain unhanged.

We touched down at Johannesburg, and I saw already at the hangars the good companions who were helping me on this mission, which was to get some sort of amplification or moderation of Field Marshal Smuts's recent statement that France as a nation was finished. The war artist, Geoff Long, whom I had known first at Tobruk and Alamein, had arranged this, the South African Information Bureau had sponsored it, the French Military Mission in Cairo had approved it, and here I was in Capetown, the length of a continent, where I missed Smuts by half the length of his departing plane.

Geoff was there to meet me, a long, blond lad, pulled thin like taffy, and so were Joan and Claude Cansou, who directed the French Information Bureau. Claude had done half of his excellent work, not only for the French, but their allies generally, from the bed where he lay ill during most of the war. He was a navy lieutenant with a record to envy, and he champed like a sea horse as he banged out his articles in bed. My failure to see Smuts probably made me look rather desolate, so Claude said, "Don't you mind, old Beel; we've got broadcasts for you, and you're going to make a film, and Mother Smuts will see you herself."

Propaganda is no fun, even at Johannesburg, which is a smaller and kindlier New York, compact of tall buildings, opulent with food and friendliness. Propaganda is as obvious a commodity as a vacuum cleaner under the arm of a traveling salesman; you knock at the door and say, Look, here it is, all wrapped in cellophane, a precious thing. But no matter how cunningly packed, its wrappings are transparent. I was a pretty good propagandist, I think, but it was a thankless job. I loved my orphan French so much, and I was so proud of them, that my spiels by print and radio probably sounded as though I were boasting of a people I had invented myself.

I had been on the receiving end of cameras for many years, and that had been embarrassing enough, spying at natives with light meters, and flashing mirrors on their breasts, and tugging them like puppets here and there. They deserved to see me that morning, quavering as I forgot my lines. The great square yawn of light burst at me and burned to a crisp the simple lines.

"Camera!"

Davis: "It has been a long war since I was last in South Africa, in 1939. I had come down from the north where—when—where . . ."

"Cut!"

"Sorry . . . where we had been shooting lion, a gentle beast in comparison with the one we are fighting today. I saw then the first great impulse of South Africa at war, and I saw the momentum of it later when I met again my South African friends in the Western Desert, during the Allied offensive which—which—"

"Cut! It's perfectly natural, Mr. Davis. Would you join me in a glass of rum?"

I damn well would. I was shaking.

"Camera!"

". . . which cleared this continent finally of the Axis hordes.

We, the Fighting French, have fought beside your Desert Rats and
we know their caliber. The men of both our armies have fought as
volunteers for the common cause. . . ."

"It's just thirst, old boy, dehydration. . . . Camera!"

". . . we need the shoulders of the free men of France and of South
Africa behind the Allied Juggernaut which is roaring into Europe to
crush this tyranny of our time. . . . The penguins of South Africa just
don't seem to care . . . but I should hate to have my children remember me as a . . . penguin in this global . . . this global . . ."

"Give him another rum."

". . . war . . . !"

The South Africans are a vital race, a race that works in the
morning as youth should do, and they seemed intent on rebuking
my sloth by getting me up in the morning, too. So it was no surprise
to have Joan call me at 8:00 A.M.

"Damn it, child, I've just gone to bed."

"Then you'll just get out of it! Mother Smuts is seeing us at her
farm at nine. I'll pick you up in seven minutes."

She made it in six, for my sins, and we drove away with nothing
but the taste of toothpaste in me. Joan sat straight before her wheel,
an amber lass and freckled, and as we raced up the rolling road
I marveled again at the strange content that came to me in the
company of Joan and Claude. Perhaps because they both had been
so desperately ill, and were undefeated, they emitted warmth to the
chilblained spirits of the rest of us. Strangely, though they were
"intellectuals," they had the great and most rare old-fashioned quality
of goodness. Intellectuals are easy to come by, a dime a dozen, but
the people who are wisely good are obsolescent. These two were
more devout and good than either France or I deserved.

We went humbly and angrily to see Mother Smuts, like children
whose family decency had been impugned, hoping that we had misunderstood and reluctant to badger an honest wife behind her husband's back. Mother Smuts in her farmhouse was, in the nicest sense
of the term, a character. Her gray hair was touseled, her glasses hung
askew, her stockings had slid halfway down her calves. I wasn't

sure that her black-and-white printed cotton dress wasn't put on backward.

We had tea and Greek shortbread on the veranda, with books and dried or pickled entomological specimens piled insecurely around us. Joan and I sat tight together, tense, for this was an important interview for France, and there seemed no conversational gambit toward what we wished: to ask why South Africa's great Field Marshal Smuts had maligned our France. I noticed a bottle of clear fluid which seemed teetering to fall on my head, and "Ouma" explained that it was sea water from the Cape, which she had gotten and brought home to her natives who believed it was good for rheumatism. That was the spirit of her.

She dropped the sock she was knitting and leaned forward to take the hands of Joan and me. "Children," said Ouma Smuts, "what the Oubas said was that France would not rise in his lifetime. But the Oubas," she added quietly, "is a very old man."

18 ~~~~~~~~~~~~~~~~~~~~

The eager death of John—grass is
good for you—Bill sees the moon

IN KHARTOUM on the way back to Cairo I picked up Carel Birkby, that tough gargoyle of an explorer turned editor, and went off to Asmara with him and an inebriated pilot type. I had serious work to do there, but Carel kept it floating pleasantly in the iced buckets of Italian champagne. The pilot type grew happier and happier, too, with the result that on the way back to Khartoum the plane crash-landed at Kasala and, though none of us was hurt, all but one of our champagnes exploded.

The rescue plane got us back ten minutes before my broadcast was due. We rushed to the studio with the uncut script. I had had no time to work it down from an hour's lecture to the specified five-minute talk. So we sat securely on the floor with it, our backs against the wall, the microphone upon my knees, and the champagne on Carel's. We still were pretty rocky from the accident, and my voice shook annoyingly until the produce of our enemies calmed it.

The prim English spinster who was running the show began making frantic gestures at the end of four minutes, for I was in full voice at last, chanting of Liberty and Equality and Fraternity, of Glory and Justice, of France which had lost a battle but not the war, of De Gaulle and the Free French, of the battles I had seen them win.

Carel silenced the lady with a gesture and wrote on the champagne label, "This is genius! For God's sake, don't stop him!" Nothing could have stopped me. The singer, who was next on the program, began fidgeting, but such was the power of that champagne as Carel fed it to me from an aspirin bottle that I enraptured her. By the end of the first half-hour both our ladies were seated on the floor with us, eagerly scanning the script ahead of my lines and by turn accepting the aspirin bottle. I talked for an hour, mounting to the tremendous climax of a company of Maoris on a bayonet charge, shouting their fearsome battle songs, and I tapered away—for the champagne was exhausted—to my French on a night patrol humming the melody, *"Avec Mes Sabots."*

"Magnificent!" said everyone, and the telephones began ringing, for all Khartoum agreed. I went swaggering away triumphantly, a man in liquor, you might have said, and Carel said, titubating, too, "It *was* genius, old boy—for me to mix the vodka with that champagne."

Cairo, to which I returned with a bump, had been the nearest there was of home for me during the last four years. I kept Room 38 at the Continental-Savoy and returned to it after every campaign, and I grew to cherish Cairo. I was never well in it. My skin rotted. My viscera fumed. I had troubles with both my French and my Americans. But I loved the ready humor of the Arabs, and the morning mist across the Nile, and the great ibis which would come sweeping in at dusk to adorn the trees like folded buds. I got to love, when I was not there, the meaningless wrangling of Arabs at night, and my friends were amusing and curiously good, most with the same blend of blood in them, Arab, French, and Jew.

I was spoiled at the Continental, probably because I was the only one awake at 4:00 A.M. when the servants had time to talk. I slept during the day and worked in the cooler hours. The charwoman and chambermaids and Gamil, my floor boy, would stop at my open door to explain to me the world which I hoped never to understand. Gamil, taking my phone calls, introduced himself as my secretary.

The chambermaids of the first and second floors, led by Mademoiselle Elice, aged seventy-two, would drop in alone or in delegations to have a drink of the vodka we brewed in chamber pots, over the little electric stove that cracked one pot after another and seared my tables.

It was Easter in Egypt as elsewhere, and I wakened with a dozen tinted Easter eggs, a personal cable from General de Larminat in Algiers, and an order from the French Military Mission to join my Spahis somewhere in Tunisia. The quick ecstasy in the dark, the half shave, the nibbled toast, the ritual embrace beneath a glaring bare bulb were like a thousand others at this moment in this war.

There had been four of us the night before on my balcony eating an oyster stew, including Lenore, and Tania whom I truly loved fraternally. She was tall and Polish with desperate eyes and long black hair and a lisp. We didn't know until after the war, when she was knifed on the stairway of a London hotel, that she worked for British Intelligence in Cairo.

I had loved Tania non-fraternally and wholly once, when we had walked beneath the trees of the Ezbekiah Gardens, stopping beneath a tolerant tree to shout, like idiots, the great thing of our love, and rush home to my room at the Continental-Savoy, the fireplace blazing and Tania's tears sparkling as she made the ritual gestures and pretended she loved me. She didn't. She was as lonely as I was and sincerely in love with one John Jorochs, a rare Irishman in this war, who had been sent by British Intelligence behind the lines of beleaguered Greece.

And more wonderfully than I knew of my love for her, I knew of her love for him, which was a hungry and an aching one, and our assembled tensions tapered, or perhaps grew, to a friendship which is unusual as a requiem to physical love. We would dine together or dance snugly together at the Champagne Club, and talk of John Jorochs who soon should be coming to Cairo from behind the Axis lines in Greece. John Jorochs had become my brother or my son, so there was no incest now. It was a strange and hearty sublimation.

And on the night before I was to leave to rejoin my troops, Tania came bursting through my door. "Bill, John's here! He's called from downstairs! He's on the stairs! Bill, oh, Bill, there's my John!"

Feeling a bit like a tough old clam in my oyster stew of love, I continued brewing it until John came in quietly, and there was, quick as a handshake, that immediate understanding which is a treasure. It was so good that neither of us was embarrassed by Tania's searing presence between us. We ate on the balcony and talked quietly for hours of war and poetry, but there was a tension in John which I knew had nothing to do with me or Tania whom he loved as much as she did him. It was a joy to watch the concern for him in her tremendous eyes, and see the response to it on that hard and tender and funny face of his.

As a good officer he controlled his tension until about fifteen minutes before midnight, when he stood up suddenly. "Tania, darling, I've got to go . . ."

"John, tonight?"

"To my room upstairs, darling. I've an appointment at midnight with a—with a Greek."

"God, John, not tonight!"

"Bring him here," I said.

"No . . . no. Tania, what's the number of your room? I'll come back later if I can—if it's not too late. I can't tell you now what luck it is to be able to see this man whom I've looked for all over Greece. He may make all the difference in our action there." By now John was at the door and his face was in the darkness of the hall, but I could see his eyes looking at me, not at Tania. "Bill," he said, "take good care of Tania," and he was gone.

"John! John!" Tania called, but he was gone in the shadows of the blue black-out bulbs. Tania ran to her room to wait.

I was awakened in the morning by footsteps running toward me down the corridor, though they should have made no sound as Tania

202

was barefooted when she burst through my door. I jerked up in bed. "John's dead," she said. "John's been murdered!"

And so he had. Old Mademoiselle Alice had brought him breakfast and found him dead at his table, and the British Military Police had already reported that one of the two glasses of whisky and soda in his room had been poisoned.

Nourished on Easter eggs and vomiting the tragedy of John's death, I left the plane at Kairouan in Tunisia, borrowed a jeep, and drove toward Mount Zagouan in search of my troops. Zagouan was surrounded by a range of mountains from one horizon to the other and inhabited by the last desperate men of Rommel's retreat to the sea. It was evening, and the enemy guns burst orange, flickering from spot to spot along the purple walls. The bark of one of our own seventy-fives crashed by my ear, and in the blaze of it I saw the red forage caps of the Spahis and realized that, for the duration, I was home.

We were now under the command of Leclerc, who had completed his fabulous march from Tchad to Tunisia, harassing the enemy's rear. His headquarters, when I found it that night, was a stark truck dug into a pit. I lifted the flap of canvas and climbed into candlelight which showed Leclerc taut behind a box table, cadaverous in his hooded Arab cloak. Although he was ill, his ardors were undiminished. We were back to our own land again, he said, to the border of France, and the Métropole was not far beyond those narrow mountains and the narrow sea.

Not far, no, but the night around us was tumid with the explosions of our own and the enemy's guns. There was that to go through still. Leclerc's blue eyes were cold in the candlelight that reached deep into them beneath the hood, and his deep voice rose a pitch: "Listen, Hassoldt Davis, I want it known to all that we are the undefeated, we, the Fighting French. We have never capitulated; we have signed no armistice; the Hun has never beaten us; we have made no compromise; our children cannot reproach us when we return."

The patient, arrogant "wheer" of a shell went over our heads and burst in the enemy's mountains, while I was thinking of Leclerc's six children, somewhere, lost to him, in France.

Our Senegalese were entrenched in the flat land between Djebel and the Jerries. Patrols of them went out continually, mainly to snare the enemy patrols and bring 'em back alive so that we could question them. Those Senegalese were terrifying men, as black and shiny as a typewriter, with the same sort of wide-spaced teeth. Huge they were, powerful as gorillas, but their sight and touch along an ack-ack gun were as delicate as a chemist's upon his microscope. It was a strange thing, such precision in great hands which could tear a raw goat apart. They came hulking from trench to trench, bringing their fat fleas with them and the curious odor of their bodies, which was like cinnamon in hot oil.

It was said that, although they were no longer head-hunters, they had asked politely at Bir Hakim if they might remove the heads of their enemies. They would be good companions for the little Gurkhas who, with their kukris, were geniuses at decapitation. The Gurkhas, however, removed the ears, too, and when they returned from patrols their pockets were always searched, in the interest of hygiene, for the salad of ears which was usually in them.

The Senegalese admired the Gurkha and thought that the funniest story in the world was the one about the tiny Gurkha scout who met an immense German and removed his gun by cutting off the hands that held it. The German just laughed at the little man, squaring off to punch him with his stubs. "Hah! Hah! Hah! *Heil! Heil! Heil!*" he laughed, which annoyed the Gurkha so that he sliced his razor-edged kukri through the German's neck. And the German laughed again, in his arrogant, semi-Aryan superiority, and said, "Ach! You never touched me!" And the Gurkha, walking away and splitting moonbeams with his kukri, said, "Just wait till you shake your head!"

In my transient cavern, halfway across no-man's land, was a telephone, and its discreet tinkle was friendly but odd to hear amid the other noises, the blast of a shell before or behind us, the quiet but crisp commands to the men, the panting of an old Senegalese who had taken refuge with us, the dainty click of fingernails as someone caught bugs and split them. A Jerry plane came over and dropped three bombs just for the hell of it. We huddled tight, waiting, talk and thought in suspension for a moment, until the planes passed.

Tinkle went the telephone, and a message came to Captain Gilman asking whether he had any men acquainted with transport mules. This didn't interest me much, for it seemed to me that the planes were coming back. Gilman relighted the last half inch of the communal cigarette. "Precision bombing," said he, "must be a job of conscience, and it can't be much fun."

"Wham!" said a bomb, precisely enough for me.

There were those, and I was one of them, who held that the Western Desert flies were worse than the fleas of Tunisia, but there were the flea partisans, too, and there was much to be said for their argument. The fleas were bad, even in those open fields beneath the sun. A former Italian slit trench was a proper booby trap, and the abandoned native huts of mud, so cool in appearance, were simmering hives. You had merely to put your foot inside the door and there was an instant explosion of fleas which covered your leg black halfway to the hip. There is no incubator of fleas comparable to that of an Arab hut which has been used by soldiers.

So I rolled out my blankets beneath an isolated twenty-foot cactus, which gave me a prickly shade. The grass grew tall around me, and it, too, gave a sort of shade at night, when the sky was ripped and brilliant with cannon fire. It was somehow protective and comforting, that tall grass.

I got to like grass. We ran short of cigarettes and couldn't remember the colors of drink, and because the whole Eighth Army was moving so rapidly forward, we were, for a time, short of food. I used to wander through the native barley when my stomach ached for nourishment, and pull the long stems and eat the tender part. There were usually two telescopic joints in a stem, and each, when slid forth, would reveal a slim, succulent inch which was better than celery. By two-handed picking I usually could garner and eat fifty or so in about five minutes, and be full of vitamins, too.

I came tearing along the road on the back of a motorcycle, clutching the slippery ribs of the insouciant Calmet. I had known young Dr. Calmet for more than a year; I had been bombed with him, shelled with him, machine-gunned with him, and always he had stared death down, without turning his small impertinent smile from the face of it;

but now I saw, as I had seen curiously before, that if a brave and intelligent soldier is in continuous action, he doesn't always become inured to danger; he may remain as brave as always, intellectually, but his physical reflexes may twitch beyond control.

For now, with each explosion from the hills, Calmet ducked, and though he grinned over his shoulder at me, his grin twitched. He was unaware of it, and I hadn't noticed the development of it because I had not been in progressive actions which he had seen. I don't believe I ducked or that I was afraid, for I still hadn't been hurt more than by the wounds of athlete's foot and a torn knee cartilage. And I remembered subconsciously that I had decided long ago not to care very much whether I personally was continued or killed. Consciously now, I cared a great deal; I wanted to go into Tunis and into France; and I wanted to write again, and eat Brie cheese, and go to the Tien Shan Mountains and the Baboon Pass. I wanted a morning drink of champagne with a good companion who had a hangover, too, and to shape things with the neat small tools I loved, and to be loved by the people I had loved when all this started. I also wanted to make my bed and lie in it, for a long time, alone.

I turned cautiously in my saddle to see if Bill the dog was following. He was, with his seeing nose so close to the tire, to keep our smell, that I was afraid he'd scorch it. Calmet turned, too, because I had swerved the motorcycle. "That sacred Bill!" he said. "Sainted Virgin, but I'll fix his bloody eyes!"

The camp of the Spahis was packed up and waiting. We sat in the twilight for a while, behind the comfortable cactus which hid us from the enemy guns. As the dark deepened the flashes of artillery quickened on both sides and the noise of it became as steady as a snore. There was no moon, but in the light of that reciprocal barrage I was able to make out the white stars on the blue background of my astronomy book. Our old pasture was a muddy green, and the enemy mountains, as we saw through the cactus spines, were edged with gold by the burst of the guns behind them. We'd be moving up, in a little while, to the mountains and to Tunis at last.

Calmet was sitting quietly in his ambulance, and Bill lay sleepily across his knees. I felt slowly that something wasn't normal with Bill, and moved with my tin of beef to the opposite bench of the ambulance.

206

Calmet spoke in the drowsy voice of surgeons. "I gave him a shot of morphia, two grains, about an hour ago. Dogs tolerate much larger doses than men, you know."

I was worried and confused. "But art thou really going to operate on his eyes, now? We're supposed to move at half-past . . ."

"There's plenty of time. And I want old Bill to see when we come into Tunis. Give me a hand, young Bill. And thee, Quinat, and you, Acobas."

We had just dropped the curtains of the back of the truck when the loudest and most unhappy sigh in the world went past us. It passed, and then the father and mother of all explosions went off about half a mile away. I could feel it tear the earth to tripe with a roar of concussion that nearly ripped my heart from its hinges. It was the multiple, simultaneous blast of six rockets from the German nebelwerfer.

Bill, doped though he was, shuddered. Calmet picked him up and laid him across two camp stools. He said, "Hold this flashlight, Acobas, straight into his eyes." Calmet's long nose cast a scalpel-shaped shadow upon the wall. "Bill, when I clip these retractors to his lids, thou wilt hold them back, and steadily."

Bill the dog winced then, but he was too sleepy to mind very much. Another shell, a common one, went over us and he didn't move. Calmet washed out his eyes with a boracic solution poured from an Egyptian beer bottle, then dripped in cocaine.

My hands on the retractors were shaking a little, and so Quinat said, "Did I tell thee, Beel, about the pigeon? About Montgomery's pigeon which turned cowardly and abandoned us because of the hospitality of the Fighting French?" Calmet was bent over Bill's head now, and with a Graefe knife, a delicate blade about an inch and a half long and the breadth of a fingernail paring, made an incision into his right eyeball just where the white of the eye met the iris. "It was at the first battle for Tunisia when the general gave pigeons to the commanders of the various forces involved, with orders to send them back to him as their objectives were taken. . . ."

Calmet took his objective skillfully, his thin hands never hesitating. He slid the blade through the clear chamber in front of the iris, then with a swift sawing movement enlarged the incision until the blade emerged at the top. This shook me a bit. I managed to hold the retractors with one hand and with the other to stroke the warm and quivering leg of Bill. Quinat continued his story.

"One of these pigeons, a brawny bird, was given to the Fighting French, and such a favorite was he that he was petted and spoiled by all the cooks of our regiment. He grew fat on the Legion's soups and the Spahis' wines, and slept off his hangover indigestions on a nest of hand grenades. . . ."

Calmet said, "Those forceps, Acobas. No, the little ones." He inserted them gently into the wound, grasped the iris close to the margin of the pupil and drew it part way out. Neatly he snipped off a portion of it.

All hell broke loose in the mountains then, and the ambulance rocked with the detonations.

"*Couillons!*" exclaimed Calmet in fine argot. I relaxed the retractors a little, so that I shouldn't rip Bill's eyelids. Calmet waited a moment. "Give me that cystotome, the instrument with the small hooked point."

Quinat said, "Montgomery flung the Eighth Army forward, and we took our objectives, and all but one of the pigeons flew back to him with the good news. That was Popo, of course, the pet of the Spahis and the Legion. . . ."

"Acobas, my old one," said Calmet, "hold the light straight on the eye, will you? I don't want to puncture it. Good." Deftly he introduced the cystotome through the wound he had made and scratched the capsule of the lens. A little gelatinous material, part of the cataract, issued from it, but as that wasn't enough he pressed gently on the lower part of the eyeball with a tool like a minute spoon and the chamber suddenly filled with the grayish-white jelly.

Said Quinat, "A week or so later, someone remembered that Popo had his mission to do, too. He was taken from his hand grenades and the message was attached to his leg. He was half asleep and didn't care. . . ."

Calmet carefully probed his little spoon through the slit and spooned out most of the substance of the cataract. "That's all," he said.

"But not at all!" said Quinat, irrepressible. "The chief cook . . ."

"Quinat, wilt thou shut thy maw and give me the atropine?"

Calmet put a few drops into the eye to dilate the pupil, then gently

208

closed the lids, laid a pad of gauze upon them and held it in place with a jaunty bandage.

"The chief cook," said Quinat quickly, "lifted Popo toward the north where Montgomery was still advancing, and tossed him sadly into the air. 'Go, little pigeon, and tell of our triumph!' he said. The pigeon rose like a brick for a couple of yards, and fell in a fat lump to the sand. The cook stared at him severely, but still Popo didn't care, for there was much too much good food and wine in him. Without a flutter of a wing he rolled to his feet and started walking, staggering, toward the German lines, his tail feathers between his legs. . . ."

"Quinat, son of a pigeon and a bat," yelled Calmet, for the racket had increased again, "couldst thou hold puckered for a little while that orifice which thou callest thy mouth, and let the poor pup rest?" He turned his head and its sharp shadow toward me. "He'll be all right. I'll do the other eye in a week or so."

"Thanks, old Calmet."

Calmet shooed us from his ambulance, and I carried Bill to my bedroll beneath the cactus tree. I sat down on it with him and washed his muzzle with the rusty juice from my canteen. The firing was only intermittent now; the day's war was dimming; and at one o'clock precisely, as if by arrangement, it stopped. I sat thoughtfully with Bill in my arms, bathing his dry nose, until he squirmed awake and sat up with a shake beside me.

To my left the moon was rising, bronzing a marabou, the tomb of an Arab saint, upon the hill. The Germans in it would be our prisoners tomorrow. The moon rose clear over a tortured land which for the moment had accepted the armistice of sleep. Bill sniffed; it was as if he had smelled that fine fruity moon, and I lifted his bandage tenderly, wondering if he could see it now. He saw it, for the first time in years. He lunged from beneath my arm and bayed with such gusto that I quickly bandaged him up again for fear he would give our position away to the Germans in the tomb.

He was trembling when he sat down in the crook of my arm again. Slowly the moon moved toward Tunis and toward our Fighting France, and Bill and I stayed wide awake all that night long.

The moon went down over Rommel and the Italian general, Bastico, and into the sea they went and we, the Fighting French, were left gaping at the void where our war had been, our hands empty of anything immediate to do. There would be a rest for us, said Leclerc, and we would go to Morocco to be re-equipped with American uniforms and guns and tanks, and then to England to await invasion of the continent.

I wasn't waiting. I wasn't dead yet. "The best I can do," said General Leclerc, "is detach you and send you to the army of General Juin in Italy."

This was a shocking notion, that an old Free Frenchman like me, lease-lend though I might be, should join the North African forces we had deplored, the great army of 350,000 men which had refused to fight in 1940 on the African soil that still was France. But it was better than waiting.

"Bien, mon général," I said, and saluted with a shaky hand.

Two nights later I was back in Cairo at the Hôtel Continental, to get a plane to Italy. There would be one at 4:00 A.M. and I was up at three, sitting on the terrace with my feet over the balustrade to cool them in the stinking wind of Cairo. The odd infection had eaten my toenails off by now. What would they think of me, the old companions of Tchad and Libya and Tunisia, leaving the Free French to join the now regular French army which had not fought until America entered the war? I pulled the military map of Italy loose from its thumbtacks. The bulge north in the Allied advance across it was still the bulge of the French of General Juin, far ahead of the Americans and the British to the east. These, too, were Fighting Frenchmen, and they, too, were mine.

19 ∾∾∾∾∾∾∾∾∾∾∾∾∾∾∾∾

Italy—my eunuch poet—the
town of the hush—the four
spinsters of San Gimignano

I WAS FASCINATED now by the manner in which
you get anywhere or nowhere in a war, without directions to tell you
where a hulking great regiment is, or a comrade is, or a piece of
cheese on the shelf of a bombed-out shop. But I got to Rome and
made a broadcast for the French, and to Siena which General Juin
had just taken, thumbing my way, but, as an American in French
uniform, a suspect always.

Juin sent me north again toward the concealed and rather dainty
burps of cannon. I had an orderly now named Mekki, a Moroccan
eunuch, once chief of his sultan's harem. He was a proud man. His
great teeth returned the glint of the tiny stars; he ignored the road and
drove straight at forty miles an hour, watching the stars as I would
watch insects; he was the only man I ever knew who could drive with
his stomach. His hands rarely touched the wheel. He smoked or
scratched his secret head beneath the turban, and manipulated the
steering wheel with casual twitches of his enormous paunch.

Around the breadth of Mekki's belt were seven revolvers—seven
being lucky—and he had seven daggers, mostly in his boots, which
made him limp. He talked incessantly in a voice an octave or two
above a jeep's, and my first chill of this Italian campaign came when
I realized that he was a proper poet.

He had no hesitancy at all before me, his new master. He yawned,
his arms spread out, and steered the car with his navel, and he said,
in excellent French, "I have composed various songs of love and
death. They may bore you, *mon lieutenant,* but for me it will pass the
time to hear them."

Switch went his belly as we rounded a bend.

"Here," said Mekki, "here is our falcon, this heart on my sleeve, on my wrist, on the twisting good fist which could cripple a moon, if the bird were not on it—"

This brought me up smartly on the jeep's hard seat. Mekki leered at a star. "The flight of our love must be crippled at noon, and no later nor earlier—"

We were going faster now, and I was holding the brake handle. "Justly," said Mekki, "the twins of the night, the cold Gemini, might, in their search and despair of a bed, take a bright bird to lead them—"

The road wound through splendid hills, dark green and soft as velours, and herds of prisoners in dingy gray came marching past us, but I saw little of this, for Mekki's poem was enchanting me, coming from such a pumpkin of a man and the commonest of orderlies.

"Here's a fine comet," he said, "and most modest. Hold to me now, to my heart and my wrist, lest our falcon, our proudest beaked anguish, should plummet upon the warm womb of the comet, the tomb of us. . . ."

We passed General Gouillaume's Goumiers, the terrible Arabs who were slicing great chunks off the German rear. In their hoods and hand-woven cloaks reaching to their knees, carrying loads of more than seventy pounds, they trudged up the green mountain road, jerking their fringes of foul beard from left to right, looking for anyone to murder or rape. And they were so good at both that they must have been poets.

They had, at least, the old, romantic conception of war in regard to camp followers. Their whores followed them almost to the front lines. They took pride in their trade. Their clothes were voluminous and colorful, and as we passed them in their special camions they danced gaily upon their heaps of mattresses. And I thought seriously that the hard-fighting soldier, the effective soldier such as the Goumier, does damn well deserve his love.

Morale is a fancy word, to describe all that our soldiers need—as the men they must be—and are not permitted. Morale was created by Marie Stopes of the other war, when she organized the brothels of France and saw to it that their liquors were good. Morale was not encouraged by our dry ships plying through frigid gales, nor by nostalgic telegrams—at reduced rates—nor by paper pin-up girls.

Morale, in our war, was rightly enjoyed by the Goumier who could spend fifty Italian lire to go to bed with his whore, and a hundred lire to talk to her only, by the campfire, drinking tea, as the Goumier values conversation at twice the price of love. He would clean his carbine carefully, warming his oil by the flame, and smack his wench a good one, and cherish her dear insults as he went over the hill to another man's war.

I had been detached from my First Regiment of Moroccan Spahis "to"—as the French have it—the Fourth Moroccan Mountain Division, and now I was arriving dizzily to be redetached "to" the First Regiment of Moroccan Riflemen for the sake of a patrol action into San Gimignano, where the Germans might or might not still be.

Once upon a hilltop there lived four old ladies, and their names were Mrs. North, Mrs. East, Mrs. South, and Mrs. West, or so they called themselves, for they had been so long away from England, and the war had beaten so at their little old skulls, that it was simpler that way. They played bridge, and when a shell plunged shivering upon the town of San Gimignano, it made a noise like "Trrrump!" and the one who first shouted "Trrrump!" in echo could have the choice backmeat of what sometimes was rabbit, but usually cat, for dinner.

They had been bombed from one inn to another in the ancient towered town; the Germans had interned them and finally released them when they needed further jail space, as we, the French, approached. They waited for us confidently, shuffling cards and crying "Trrump!" with each shellburst that powdered their hair in plaster even whiter than it was. Then they sat listening, deaf as posts, to the hush that meant life for a few minutes more.

We waited, too, but with little patience. We didn't want to waste either men or matériel, but neither did we want to miss this show. Our armor had already fought half the length of Italy, with inadequate replacements. This terrain might be superb for the tourist and a joy to the infantry, but it was hell on metal.

Our plan was to send the Americans, rich in tanks, to establish a base at 0430 hours to the left of us, then pump in our infantry at 0630 hours toward the tiny town of San Donato, which would give us a springboard for assaulting San Gimignano on the hill.

Now it was night at the command post of my borrowed regiment, and around us were a dozen French and American radio cars, isolated from the rest of the camp by a white tape barrier, reporting quietly the messages from our forward troops. Our 105s, just behind us, shot deafeningly over our heads, but there was no voice raised in the operations tent, where we stood, following the troop movements on our charts. Nine officers stood around the long table while Colonel Brissaud-Desmaillet gave his orders and explained just how it was that the battle was to be joined. You would have said that this was a company of surgeons coldly planning a vivisection; and that is what it was.

The stars were hard as steel, and the mountainous horizon shimmered with the soft glow of enemy guns. The woods around us were full of fireflies, making fun of us with their minute explosions. The earth crackled beneath our boots, for we were treading, oddly, upon oyster shells which had no business there.

I ate my K rations with War Correspondent Eve Curie, that fabulous woman who had journeyed among warriors around the globe, and now was writing of them. She stood tall and thin in the starlight, her head regal, her eyes sharp with humor which had no place now, her bruised lower lip a little heavier than it should have been. A few weeks ago her jeep had rounded a curve and been trampled by a Sherman tank, an insect beneath a mastodon, and she had been in hospital until a few days back.

My section began its work from the hilltop village of Cinciano. There was a tall house there, ruined, and in the attic, littered with debris, we watched the enemy a couple of hundred yards away in San Donato, bringing water from a well, sloping a mortar directly toward my nose at the binoculars. One of the Americans asked Eve for an autograph, and the other asked me, the lesser author, for a cigarette and the time.

It was 0630 hours, and our artillery erupted, their flashes dimmed by daylight. At 0430 the tanks should have reached the base of departure, but they had been impeded by the wooded and hilly terrain and the resistance there, so we were trying to smash that now. The Germans and their Italian Fascists knew every chestnut tree, every

214

plum tree and olive tree before us, whereas we were advancing into unknown terrain.

It was time for us to go. I thought I had never been so comfortable in an attic. San Donato was a blur of walls and steeples and windows the color of lead. The two hundred yards were a very long way. From a haystack to our right came the stern stutter of machine-gun fire; some of our men went down with their bellies ripped, but Sergeant Abdullah rushed forward crouching and grenaded the haystack from behind.

From beyond a modest crest we were belabored with mortar fire, and we plunged from tree to tree as the ground gaped and the sky speckled ahead of us, until we got beneath the walls of San Donato. From the first casualties that fell to us we realized that we were confronting the 29th Panzer Grenadiers. They were young, clean-shaven, and arrogant as they rolled beneath our guns. Up and down the field we stalked them, and our grenades tore through their windows, and we drove them out to stumble beside the cattle they had slain. Our Moroccans ran with a sort of loping stride, regardless of their heavy packs and everywhere the mines. They burst in spumes of gray smoke and dirt, but other whole men replaced them inexorably.

We took San Donato, but there was no respite. At our new observation post we munched a butterlike cheese and drank harsh red wine. The chapel gaped open beside us, ten feet deep in rubble; a Christ, thin and thirsting, looked down on our thirst and approved.

"Ambulances," said old Sergeant Mallin, beneath his binoculars. "There's a dozen Red Cross hearses moving up past point 264." His red beard waggled happily. "So we must have laid that bunch out, too!" Mallin is dead now, and we buried him as he wished, erect like Clemenceau, his beard combed and tilted toward Mars.

You could feel that the Germans were retreating; death draws a vacuum behind it. We were up next day at 0430 hours, grimy, still tired, and San Gimignano on the hill looked like a pleasant postcard as we approached its skyscraping towers. We sent two battalions forking round the town. Four tirailleurs preceded our section of thirty men who were to take the highway into it, while our sappers cleared the road of mines ahead of us and directed our armored traffic around the burst bridges. We, the PBI, as the British call it, the Poor Bloody

Infantry, slid down the burst bridges and toiled up again, going fast.

In the front of the section Mallin was on my left and Eve on my right. She limped on the leg the Sherman had crushed, but she kept going at the pace set by those champion mountain men, and she justly got a Croix de Guerre for it. "I'd hate to have them think me a nuisance," she said, as we scrambled down and up a demolished bridge.

They didn't think so. It was her affair. They had Germans to worry about, for though San Gimignano was probably evacuated, probably there were snipers left behind. And, despite the care of our sappers, there were surely mines and booby traps along our road between the olive trees. We came upon slips of paper. *"Achtung! Minen!"* The German rear guard had fled us too fast to remove the notices.

Steadily we moved up the hill. A machine gun, far in the woods to our left, spat forth six shots. Black above our heads were the towers. The tirailleurs advanced and spread out on each side of the road, contracting to the fighting Moroccan crouch, their guns stiff in their hands. We followed with the foolish pistols that become the dignity of officers, held tight, pointing uselessly toward the gaping windows. I felt like an extra in a melodramatic film. We were clearly in view; we had no cover even in the fields by the road. This was so silly an advance that Mallin and I, like villains, held our pistols high and squinted our eyes and laughed.

San Gimignano was now close above us, dark and backlighted from the East. We crawled through the debris of more broken bridges, wondering if our tanks could somehow by-pass them, and suddenly, on a rise of ground before the city, there was a child running away from us, and hot on its heels were what looked like civilians, who might conceivably be rushing to warn the enemy. We hurried now, out of the cinema of black-and-white illusion, into reality that was red and warm beneath the early sun. I think that most of us were not afraid, but very angry. We pressed close to the wall on our right, and passed the first houses safely. There was no one behind their shattered windows. There was still not a sound from the city; there was a terrible hush as of a city with its breath held in. And the child still ran ahead of us.

We came to the crossroads before the walls and edged around it,

216

careful of mines, and crawled into the shadow of the arched Porta San Mateo. Then the ghosts appeared, the pallid Italians who had hidden in the catacombs these past several months. There were not many of them, six or seven here, and four or five peering at us from the corner ahead. Then they saw that we weren't Germans. Some of them cried like cats and fell upon us; they tried to shake our hands which held our guns, and covered us with slippery kisses. We couldn't stop; we had to distrust them; very thin was the consciousness that we actually were the liberators of this town.

The high gray walls would be ideal for snipers, their guns targeted to the civilians as well as ourselves. Mallin strode along fiercely behind his jutting beard, brushing aside his admirers to right and left. I walked in space beside him, exalted, hoping that someone, for Christ's sake, even the enemy, would do something to relieve this tension, and Eve seemed to be jotting down that a rabbit was dead and looking at us with pale pink eyes.

We split into three groups and moved carefully through the town along three parallel streets. Like all war, it seemed bad cinema: the hush, the ragged soldiers, the guns expectant, the empty windows, the thirteen towers colossal against the dawn. And what was most terrible was the hush.

We were aware of possible danger, but we knew, too, that we were walking above the fearful hearts of a city in the ancient catacombs and dungeons beneath the street. The bolder citizens, the more naïve and the opportunists, darted out to greet us. They were certain now that we were friends. I fended them off as well as I could, until we came to the so-called partisans.

We saw them at the end of the street, and the hush was upon us again; we passed between the cathedral of San Augustine and the blasted shops. We moved toward each other deliberately like partners in a country dance. And there was Roberto in a toy tin helmet you could smash with a marble, the young and the eloquent and the pretty Roberto whom we soon should hang for his perfidy. And the doctor was there, and someone who called himself the President of the Committee of Liberation, and the round Dutch priest, who wanted both information and tobacco quick. Too heartily and too quick. There was also a thin man who kept shouting that he would have no pillage here. He orated alone by the fountain while we moved steadily from door to door.

Mallin was climbing with a couple of his men up the principal tower; his corporal was placing a machine gun on the steps of the church.

The partisans were mighty proud; they seemed almost to be liberating us. They crowded upon us, fumbling us, as they struggled in front of us to look straight into our eyes, and suddenly a hysteric frenzy seized them, and they wrestled like children in their happiness.

"But you are French! You are French!" they cried.

"Listen," I demanded of the crowd, "are you *sure* that *all* the Germans are gone?"

"Sure! Sure!" they shouted. "They've gone north to Casale!" And someone added, from the side of his mouth, "Except, perhaps, there might be a few of them in that tower."

That was a chilling thought, as we were trapped by the crowd in an open square. I sent a couple of Moroccans to spread a path ahead of us. The Dutch priest babbled of the hero he had been, and I looked up at the still, square tower, one of the thirteen for which San Gimignano is renowned. Little blue flowers miraculously blazed in it, for this was Santa Fina's birthday. But affixed to the roof of it now was a ragged cloth which I was certain I had not seen before.

I had forgotten Mekki, who came padding behind me. "I believe it is the moment," he said, "for Master to have a drink."

"Shut up, Mekki," I said.

"I shut up," he replied, "but the great bottle is open."

There was a whinny in the sky and a blast that shook the world as the first shell struck the little town. Stones from the tower fell around us. A pigeon plummeted. And there came the hush again as we stood stiff against the wall, until Eve said quietly, "That's just to get our range. We're for it now." Then Master, and many others, had a drink, and Mekki became the most popular eunuch in San Gimignano.

Men came running. Others slouched past with a stretcher on which lay a second lieutenant, his foot split like the bloody hoof of a goat. We got him into the cellar of a hotel, and I fed him my drink and tortured his foot beneath the sluice which an old coifed woman was

218

pumping. I bound the foot and shot morphine into him, while some-one passed slices of mortadella sausage, which we ate greedily.

I was looking, sick, at my hands, and the blood on the mortadella, when a voice behind me asked, in genteel English, "Would you mind terribly if we took just a slice for the four of us?" I was half-turned, and the next shell crashed. A wall fell and blocked the cellar door. I continued turning, dazed, to see the four old English ladies quaking at their table. There were pots full of thin soup on a wood stove behind them. The gray steam went through their hair in the candle-light.

One of them said "Trrump!" and delicately resumed her embroidery of a quaint panel on which was stitched "God Bless Our Ho . . ." "They call us Mrs. North, Mrs. East, Mrs. South, and Mrs. West," said Mrs. South, whose hair still had traces of red in it. "We are English, you know, and we are so glad to see you. We seem to be the lost battalion, don't we?"

They did. But my attention was only half on them because of the shelling which had opened up in earnest now. Quick, there would be the whine as of a giant hungry, then the thunderous bite and the gobbling of the town outside.

Mallin shot a hairy forearm toward me with a bottle of grappa. I drank it to his health, which would be blood and dust a few days from now. Chin back, the fine red beard would push up prettily among the green grasses. And there would be another friend gone, as almost all of them went, the good ones. You began to wonder what was wrong with you, that dear God, who permitted war, wouldn't let you die.

I turned to my four old ladies. "What the devil are you doing here?" I asked, without much concern. "Trrrump!" came the shell, and a scarlet, dripping man fell down the cellar stairs into the arms of the doctor. He screamed, *"C'était bête! C'était bête! Quatre ans de guerre et je suis blessé bêtement! Merde!"*

We carried him down the tunnel of the cellar. I had never carried a man before, and I was amazed at how heavy he was, bent in the middle and twisting. There was the sound of something dropping by my feet. I kicked it aside, not knowing it was his arm. His voice said, *"Merde!"* and then he died.

When we returned, my four old ladies, interrupting each other because they all were deaf, explained that they had been schoolgirl chums and then emancipated ladies of means, and the war had caught them as tourists in San Gimignano. "We are quite used to it actually, although the Germans cut off our water when they left last night. And there isn't a great deal to eat. Some of the boys found six bombed cows the other day, but five of them were already rotten. We've had some fine plump pussies though. They do well on the rats."

A shell slammed through the hotel above us; they were coming at the rate of one every two or three minutes now. This was different from the bombing of Berlin or London. This was personal. It was meant for Mallin and thirty-three men, and Eve and me. (Where was Eve? Where was that notebook meandering now?)

There was another shell, and a crackle of stone walls splintering, like old dry bones. San Gimignano was a distinct and tiny target, black and sharply edged against a lavender sunrise. I got my first Croix de Guerre for being the calmest man, they said, in San Gimignano. I was exhausted and since, for the moment, there was no work to do and I had to stay in the town anyway, I saw no reason why I shouldn't have the siesta I had earned.

There was a row of artillery outside my requisitioned hotel room, but it didn't bother me. I slept well, blind and calm and courageous, for I was snug in my pit beneath the war which was tattering life around me. You forget your medals almost always for the things which you don't do.

I wakened strangled by my helmet strap, and the shock of a shell exploded, a wave of light flooding my eyes as the wall fell gradually between my room and the captain's office. I was covered with plaster. I shook my head and saw only the bright sky through the hole where my captain had been. Kneeling on the foot of the bed, the brass rail in my hands, I leaned like a gargoyle over the street. It was true: I had lost half a hotel.

The captain was intact, however, and Mallin, with an elbow on a mule, was simply discussing the weather with him. "Ah, Beel," he greeted me as I emerged. "We've got to see the shelters and the cellars here. There may be people hurt in them. And there may be Jerries, too."

220

We sent three men up the tower where the white cloth was, and seven of us, led by the pretty Roberto, hurried through the tunnels where the citizens of San Gimignano stood, for they were so many that they had no room to lie down. This was a medieval hell, the hundreds of pallid faces retching hope at us, the hands tentative, the occasional candlelight. There was no water here, and sanitation was impossible.

A fat old woman hunched shaking in a corner; I drew my hand across her forehead and suddenly she went to sleep; or she may have died. We hurried on, through half a mile of catacombs, through the hands that clutched at us, caressing erotically—so great and strange was their love of us—our rigid pistols. A neurotic girl of about twenty fainted with the barrel of my pistol in her hand. Love and peril, or love and the orgasmic release from peril to peace, are much alike.

We hurried from the mouths that chanted, "They are French! The French!" Two of our men lay dead there. Ten others were wounded. "Trrrump! Trrrump! Trrrump!" crashed the shells, much faster now, and rubbish fell out of windows. I heard the sheep bleat of a shell approaching, and plunged into the gaping hotel, just in time to miss a ton of friezework. "God damn it!" Mallin yelled. "We can't do anything till this lets up! I'm going back to sleep."

That was an odd and inexplicable experience. Seven of us just sat down and went to sleep again. We sat, knees bent, leaning against the wall of the cellar, our shut eyes facing the shattered doorway, and waited in the hush of sleep for six hours more. There was nothing else to do. We had only simple guns as tools against the Germans who were pounding us from many miles away. We had done our best for the wounded. Evidently the bulldozers and the engineers hadn't yet repaired the road, with three bridges lacking, that should take our tired bodies home—home to the lullaby of our 75s in the hole beneath the hill.

The shelling was continuous, the worst any town in Italy had suffered from the Germans, and each shell landed within a few hundred feet of us. But we slept. And our four old ladies placidly played cards, or embroidered "God Bless Our Ho . . .," regarding us as small boys who had played too hard that day.

Mallin and I got up occasionally, to rinse our mouths with wine and dutifully make the round of the town. The wounded, military and civilian, were being evacuated on the lee side of the town by jeep, their stretchers strapped down to the hood. "Trrrump!" said the bomb, and a mattress, like a flying carpet, sailed over our heads. We ducked smartly, and I got my head beneath an iron chair, which was difficult to get off again. We sidled back along the walls to the dungeon of our old ladies. They were waiting for us, pert as birds, and still playing bridge.

"Now look here, young man, did you really kill them?" demanded Mrs. East, trailing her fingers languidly, like a canoeist, across her soup, to see if it was hot enough. The others smiled at the shadows tossed by the candle, and the rectangle of daylight in the door was dimmed by the passage of a man and an animal, perhaps a mule.

I heard the metallic whine again, and the immediate "Trrrump!" of the shell that fell square upon us, and the avalanche of rock. I saw the cards hover for a long time in the air, while the blood and the guts of the mule floated slowly toward us and enwrapped the faces of me and Mallin and our four old girls. Someone, probably the mule's driver, was moaning crazily, "Jesus Mother of God! Mother Jesus of God!"

And Mrs. South, wiping a white swathe across her bloody face, said, "Trrrump!" and Mrs. West, in the hush, said, "Trrrump . . . Poo! . . ."

20 ∿∿∿∿∿∿∿∿∿∿∿∿∿

The man who couldn't take off his halo—return to France—war is a bore

WE RETURNED TO MY new regiment of the Fourth Moroccan Spahis, to Colonel Loth who had requisitioned most of a château in the hills, feudal and Fascist and lovely. Without a compunction we moved the family into the better rooms and occupied those the Germans had most hospitably had a few days ago.

The family, comprising a marquis, a marquise, and their daughter who everyone thought should be his booty and due, were very nice to us of the colonel's staff. They loaned us their own dining room, and it was embarrassing to offer them the rations we could no longer eat, without remembering that these people had responsibly been denounced as Fascists and that we were flinging them bones. They were too well bred to intrude on us at table, and too discreet. We ate in the corner and talked of our new orders for France, and of the moons we had admired from Morocco to Tahiti, and particularly, one night, of the halo of Pierre. . . .

It was a hell of a halo, said Captain Morette. It looked more like brass than gold, and usually it was lopsided. It was a jaunty, rakish, and devil-may-care sort of halo that was a disgrace to the French army and to Pierre who wore the thing. It shone at night, so you never were safe on patrol with Pierre; and how he could sleep in it God only knew.

But he did sleep in it, or it was said he did, for apparently he couldn't get it off, though this was questionable, too, because no one we knew had ever met young Pierre. No one doubted, of course, that he was a hard-fighting corporal, but he was always being sent on secret missions and changing his name, so it was not remarkable that we hadn't actually seen the man. He had been with the first troops of De Gaulle, it was said, in Africa; the Foreign Legion had seen him glowing at Bir Hakim; and now he was supposed to be somewhere among us in Italy.

Dr. Marchaud took a poor view of him. He had just received his first penicillin from the States, and he wasn't going to let us forget it. He jerked up his head in the candlelit darkness of the dining room and said, "In the first place I don't believe these stories about Pierre. In the second I'd prescribe a very dry diet for those who do. In the third, I'll bet anyone a number of francs that penicillin will cure whatever kind of excrescence the boy may have around his head."

Colonel Loth slid up from his seat. He was a triangular man. His body was triangular, his head, his mouth, the cut of his eyes. He went to the window and asked the driver of the scout car to turn on its

223

radio. The voice came through, the BBC program of "Les Français Parlent Aux Français," and it was so intimate in that great room that we had to listen. It was almost a whisper, and what it said was scrambled lunacy, but we touched and rubbed each word of it like men telling their beads, seeking the beads of sense.

"The baby," it said gently, "has been glued to the ceiling. . . . The sausage breathes. . . ." The eight officers of our mess sat very still around the long black refectory table, while the clandestine messages came through from the families of France, messages which had been agreed upon before men left France to fight in Africa or Italy. Each was a cipher smuggled to the BBC in London. Many of them were heard, if at all, a year late, but they were sweet as a caress in the dark of the war. We all were leaning slightly toward the window and the radio outside.

"The dentist," said the whisper, "is enraged. . . ." Then the static thickened, and we could make out nothing for a while. The younger major turned his head that was round and wrinkled like a walnut, and remarked, as though it was of no importance, "I don't think I am going to enjoy coming home among the last of the French. How many days now before we embark?"

The younger lieutenant, Guiringaud, said loudly, "Five, *mon commandant!*" The older lieutenant, our Count de Breteuil, said apologetically, as he always said, "Hmmm, *c'est la guerre!*" The older major, whom we called Monseigneur, turned slowly his pale gray face that had hardened over a rubbery humor, and stared at the open door. "Monsieur le marquis," he announced, "your partisans are here."

A ragged band of men of all ages filled the door, most of them draped with ancient guns and pinkish shirts, for now that Fascism was ended they were Communists. Like Stalin and Chiang Kai-chek and Churchill and Roosevelt. The marquis, graduate of Princeton, said from the shelter of his bookshelves, "You want the horses, of course. Take them. And you may sell one for each German you catch. This is blackmail, of course." Then he returned to his Plato in vellum.

And from the chimney corner, inset in a sort of cave of stone, I heard a soft "No! No!" The marquise was there with her little sergeant, an American, and they both were very drunk on the eau-de-vie which was distilled on this feudal estate, as religion was privately distilled in the family chapel beyond the low arched door. The flames of the fireplace showed us the silhouette of the marquise and the sergeant struggling over a crucifix which the sergeant, understanding little Italian, had thought was his souvenir.

"Red wine," said the radio clearly again, "should be sliced very thin. . . ." The colonel was telling a story in his strange and charming manner, with a few words, then a gesture, a few words more, a wink, a pout, a whistle; a great deal of whatever he said was pantomime.

Deep in the chimney corner the marquise, pale and drunk, her lipstick smeared, wept into the crisp blond hair of the sergeant, and their hands were linked around the crucifix. Monsieur le marquis continued Plato by candlelight. This was a frustrate house: the marquis couldn't quite understand Plato, the marquise couldn't quite touch the core of her sergeant's youth, the partisans in the stable had no one to fight with any more, and we, the old Spahis, couldn't yet return to France.

The radio said: "The leviathan has torn his tail. . . ." We sat staring into our purple wine. The younger major's lips drew back in a snarl, and closed again. The colonel said: "One day, if the war is still on, one of those messages will be for me. For four years I have waited for the words, 'God is my fleece,' which my wife was to send to let me know that my boy was on the way to join me. Surely he can't still be in France. He must be fighting somewhere, and trying to find me, but I have changed my name, too, of course."

I moved restlessly to the window and looked out at the windy night, remembering the deserts of Tchad and Libya, the Tunisian fields, the peaks of Italy over which we had fought on the long way home. We were still exiled, awaiting orders to embark for France. A starlit path led up the mountainside in front of me, winding between the fires where our Goumiers crouched with their campfire girls.

Morette was speaking sleepily, and his lean musician's fingers moved in and out of the shade which his heavy shoulders cast. "To come back to Pierre and his fabulous halo. Psychologically, the story is very odd, for Pierre appears to be the toughest fighting man of this or any war. He loves to fight, and when he isn't fighting he's drinking like a whale and making love like an octopus to eight women at a

225

time. He seems to want to be the baddest man alive, but his tough luck is that he is always doing good."

Captain Morette looked around guiltily, as if he had said a naughty word. There was no place for goodness in our war, and just as he had clipped his hair to the skull and concealed his musical genius, he who had fought the war early and hard and urgently was embarrassed because he had begun an explanation of the extraordinary Pierre which applied, as he realized in the course of it, to himself. And he had to continue.

"Pierre fights goodness," he said, looking down his nose at a small piece of Spam on his plate, "as the rest of us are supposed to fight sin, but every once in a while he suddenly finds that he is helping someone, or just making people and animals happy, and then he gets roaring drunk again and knocks his friends about the ears and goes a-wenching crazily and tears off to the front lines again to kill another batch of Huns. And all the time his cursed halo is shining round his head."

There was a storm brewing. The roof tiles creaked and crept a little closer, like crabs. The radio crackled through the message from France. "The . . . bristles . . . are . . . turning . . . in. . . ."

"They say," said Guiringaud, "that his commander once caught him barefooted, and a dirty Algerian was lacing up the boots Pierre had given him. This was just before Christmas, and Pierre was so angry at being caught in his good deed that he told the major what he had always thought of him, and added, quite irrelevantly, that he was going to get a German that night and serve his head with a sour apple in its mouth for a Christmas feast. Then before anyone could stop him he scrambled off toward the enemy lines, his halo glowing and bobbing about his head."

The marquis by the bookshelves pondered Plato, the candlelight wavering over his ascetic face. His wife, the marquise, was trembling and saying "No! No!" to her little sergeant. We were too tired to go to our bedrolls on the cold tiled floors upstairs—most of the antique furniture of the château was still stored in the cellars, away from the bombings. These Fascist folk would destroy their country with their lusts, but their fine furniture must at all costs be saved. And I forgave them much for this. Their race was old and selfish and querulous, but it clung to the beauty of its once-great past.

Distraitly we roasted chestnuts over the candle flames, turning them on the points of our knives. Their aroma was rich and sweet, a little, said our mess boy, like that of opium. He had come from Indo-China, an *évadé* and volunteer.

"I've heard tell," said Morette, "that Pierre has fits over that halo of his at times. For one thing, it's hot as hell in summer, and it can't ever be very comfortable. They say he'll clutch it in his immense fists and shake it till his teeth rattle, trying to get it off, but then it constricts tighter and tighter around his head till he has to let it go. He jumps around like a madman, roaring, but strangely enough he never swears. That seems to be the only vice he lacks."

I was consolidating a button with a piece of wire, for lack of thread; it held well, but it scratched if you didn't carefully turn the ends. The colonel was looking glumly across the somber horizons he had traveled since he was last with his family in France. He was still trying to make sense out of the radio, probing at the static-crusted words. "Button up the blackbird, Daddy." This was not for him.

"Poor Pierre," said Guiringaud, "it seems he couldn't find a helmet large enough to fit over his halo, and though the halo was reputedly bulletproof, it protected only part of his head, and anyway it had to be covered because it shone at night. The engineers finally made a sort of helmet for him out of a Jerry can. It was a terrific helmet, at least a foot and a half in diameter, and he looked like a colossal mushroom with it on."

The doctor said, "Bah!" and returned to his dreams of penicillin. The older major—Monseigneur—cleared his throat and spoke pontifically. "Whether or not you believe these stories about this—this phenomenon—you must admit that there is a great deal of evidence in support of them. I myself"—he paused—"I myself have talked with an officer who claims to have seen Pierre when he first got that hen of his."

"Hen? What hen?"

The major looked at me severely. "It is commonly known that Pierre is followed everywhere by a hen. My informant maintains that one night during the battle of Castelforte he saw the enormous figure of Pierre lunge up from a ditch, howling at his men to follow him. His huge helmet had tipped sidewise, and his halo shone like gold. He was gesturing wildly with his pistol in one hand and the hen in the other. The hen, too, had sheltered in that ditch. Pierre had saved it, knowing the ditch would be blasted at any moment, and since then the hen has followed him everywhere. It was a nuisance at first on night patrols, because it cackled so, but Pierre made a sort of muzzle for it.

"I, myself," the major went on, and he told of how he himself had met another officer who claimed to have seen Pierre striding down the road carrying an Italian youngster of about fourteen upon his back. In each of the youngster's hands was a whopping big revolver, pointing straight ahead over Pierre's shoulders, for he wanted to be a partisan, too. When the major's informant saw them, the halo had slipped partly out from beneath Pierre's helmet, and the boy was squinting around the thing. Then Pierre saw the officer, and his face turned black with fury at being caught in kindliness, and he let out a yowl like a banshee and went loping down the road toward the nearest bar. The boy on his back got so excited that he began shooting off his two big pistols, to left and right of the halo, scaring the wits out of the poor townsfolk. Pierre was drunk for a week after that.

The younger major grunted and rubbed the soot from his chestnut. "Tell me a tale of France," he said, "of a landing in France, and I shall listen acutely." Even above the wind came the sound of a jeep approaching along the mountain road. The Moroccan women whinnied, and suddenly the racket of the radio burst through the window like a flock of squealing bats. "For the love of God, turn that down!" the colonel cried. There was a moment of silence while the scout-car driver dialed out the static and we listened to the jeep approaching the château.

The voice from London came through again, clear as bells. "God . . . is my fleece. . . ." My skin went cold. The colonel jerked in his chair and sat stiff. "That's it!" he said. "If my boy—"

The jeep slid to a stop on the gravel drive, and we turned toward the door. It opened with a crash and we saw in it a huge young man, swaying, with a pretty girl on either arm. He was wearing a helmet so large that it reached almost to the tips of his shoulders, and from

228

one of his jacket pockets protruded the inquisitive head of a hen. He shook the women from him, clicked his heels, and saluted.

"Mes respects, mon colonel!"

The colonel remained staring through those hard, triangular eyes. "It is you, Pierre?"

"I . . . Pierre."

Then he lurched across the room to the chimney corner and gently took the crucifix from the marquise and her lad. He folded their four hands together, and returned to his women at the door. It might have been the firelight that glinted gold on the inside of his huge helmet.

"Father, within an hour I start back to France. I shall see you there. God bless you." No one, not even the colonel, moved. The marquis held his Plato like a shield across his heart. Both the marquise and her lad were whimpering. I remembered a beggar cremated at Calcutta with a halo of flame around his head. The officers at that long black table were bent forward, taut.

The corporal in the big hat saluted. *"Au revoir, mon colonel. Au revoir, mon père. . . ."*

War is a bore. War is mostly waiting. The Americans, the British, the troops of Leclerc were invading France while we beat our heels in the mountainous bombed rubble of Italian towns, waiting for transport to Marseilles, for our war in Italy was done. Orders came at last, and overnight we were embarked on American ships, heading home.

The shore of France seemed thin and transparent as we approached it in the evening, and it was hard for many of us to believe that this really was France again. There were young men who had evaded the Germans at sixteen and seventeen to join us. And there were graying men who had left their families and had no word from them this long while. The maws of our ships opened out and lipped at last the shore of France, and we rushed through them to touch the soil of France and lick its rain. A couple of the youngsters flung sand at each other, laughing crazily.

This was at Istaque, to the west of Marseilles, and we were to be quartered at La Valentine to the east of it, which meant a march of about twenty miles, for our vehicles were behind us on other boats.

Up the long gray street we went, marching as proud as we could on the cobbles, singing, and grinning stiffly at the crowd which was there to welcome us. They plunged into our ranks with bottles of beer, and our Moroccans reciprocated generously with crackers, chocolate, cigarettes, and, their best gesture of all, the Italian cologne they rubbed into the hair of the girls in passing.

The rain, like wires, drew a blanket of night upon us, and we marched past windows where people jammed to see our chanting shadows in the dark. These were our own people, even mine, but in their narrow little theaters they still seemed not quite real. Although one of my heels was already worn raw, I had that strange lift of ecstasy around the diaphragm which you get only when you are in love and know you are loved.

The road led over the hills to the château which had been requisitioned for us. The Germans had been there and not long before us; there was almost no furniture left in that lovely old house. We dropped on the floor to sleep until another chanting came up the road. It was a band of so-called partisans, chanting the "Internationale" of Russia; although they were Communists they still didn't know that their Communist hymn had been replaced. They were a lousy bunch of bandits, bedecked with antique arms and the loot they had pillaged from other châteaux. Colonel Loth gave them the ground floor, and established a sentry with a sub-machine gun at the top of our stairs.

This was no homecoming, yet. The old quarter of Marseilles, west of the Vieux Port, was a mountain of dirt and stones and nothing useful. The Germans had blown it apart for two reasons: the true, the effective, FFI, had refuged there, and it might have been eventually useful as a submarine base adjacent to the port. So some forty thousand tenants were dispossessed and their homes blown to bits; forty thousand men, women, and children fled to the mountains or plodded like zombies into Germany to work in the munitions mills.

Marseilles, liberated, was still grim. The flux of winter washed it with a bitter rain. I requisitioned a third-class hotel room for my trips to town. It must have been dandy for the Germans who pre-

ceded me, for they were ardent sun-bathers and there wasn't a pane
in its windows.

There was nothing for us to do but wait impatiently for the action
that must soon be ours a few hundred miles to the north. Even
Marseilles was better than the barren château of La Valentine. We
resented childishly the constant sight of German prisoners, thin and
gray, like herring with hats, erecting barbed wire around our landing
craft, or unsnarling the hundreds of miles of it which they had coiled
along the shore front. We wanted some of those robots, too. I passed
the time in trying to pick up a Marseilles accent, rich with "ong"s
and "ang"s, to disguise the Boston one which I still had.

Now to encourage us, we supposed, we were ordered every few
days to march a little farther north, from one great estate to another.
We were invariably welcomed as a buffer to the bandits who pretended
to be FFI. At the château de Rozy we swept these people from the
yard. There were Italians with them, and Corsicans and bastard
Basques, not a Frenchman in the group.

Had we known then of the world ahead of us we should have
been less eager to rush into battle again. We should have been content with the company of those towns convalescent upon the hills,
with all that was quiet around us, with the whittling of swagger sticks
from old trees which were peeling in curious blotches, green and
yellow, as though they were camouflaged. But we grew mean and
querulous in that delay, nostalgic for the fighting which took on the
false aspect of sport; we had forgotten the hurt of it.

We had left good friends behind us, dead, and lively friends in
Italy. We were alone here, a thousand men, sitting fallow as the
woods around us, and I fell in love with a serene and gracious tree.
Her branches were sleeping now, and the twigs on them; and the
foetal buds were sealed against the winter cold. I thought, watching
her, my tree, how content she must be with her many memories of
birth. Drowsily she would recall her decision to bear a grand branch
just here, a responsible branch, and she would dream the joy again
and the pain of its pushing through her bark. And in time and remotely
the branch would bear a granddaughter of a twig, and the buds would

burgeon almost secretly, independently of the gods who should keep their minds on poems and not fuss with trees.

Still there was no front for us. We were lost men looking for a war, the remnants of which now, since the liberation of Paris, were in Alsace. And to Paris we were now directed to await new orders. The troops were lodged in Luna Park which, next to Coney Island, was the greatest amusement center in the world. They pitched tents beneath the roller coasters and bedded down in the Tunnel of Love. I was assigned a luxurious hotel room; one wall of it was riddled with bullets where the Germans had shot the patriots of the underground.

All the good nations of the world were milling here, some of them despising France for her capitulation in 1940, but all of them newly invigorated by the nearly mystic maternal balm which Paris dispensed. The boulevards were jammed with soldiers, mostly American; the civilians cowered, for even the German occupation, though less kindly, was less awesome than this.

There was an advantage in the red cap of our Moroccan Spahis in that friends could recognize us, as our enemies had, at a distance, but it was a nuisance, too, for we were stopped constantly by women with pitiful eyes, demanding importunately and yet very humbly if by any chance we knew their sons who might be with us. "Surely you knew him, my little Gabin; he was only a corporal, but he was always quoting Péguy, and he was a great raconteur of the stories of Marius and Olive." Gently I shook them off in the crowd, explaining that the war was bigger than I or young Gabin, bigger than a regiment with its old red hats, bigger than all the lost youngsters of our world. And they followed me, saying, "My son ... my son ..."

I went down the Métro, the subway, gloomily, and was waved through the ticket barrier with a smile and no fee. In that long, sanitary tube where thousands had sheltered from our bombing the same thousands bustled courteously. This was the true France again, decolonized. The lovers stood face to face dangerously near the edge of the platform as if to challenge the contradiction of death, and with their arms on each other's elbows would with dignity approach and kiss each other soberly, little birdlike peckings, then withdraw to study each other's eyes, then continue their solemn, serial, deciduous kiss again.

232

Again I was detached from my regiment to do my extracurricular broadcasting while Colonel Loth and the regiment were ordered into Alsace—"somewhere in Alsace"; they would get specific directions on the way. "You'll catch up with us, Davis," said Loth, "as soon as you can. You're an explorer, you know."

But when I had finished my work in Paris the war was rolling so fast toward Germany that the bureaus in Paris were unable to tell me where my regiment had moved. It should be somewhere near Mulhouse, they said. That was enough. I piled on my kit again, the two haversacks, and started out.

21 〜〜〜〜〜〜〜〜〜〜

*Alsace—man nude—Marius and
the golden wall—Mekki sings*

IT WAS AS simple as this: GHQ put me in a truck headed in the general direction of Alsace, and away we bumped eastward, along a road pearled with frost.

At last we could hear the guns; the war was somewhere near. Gradually, as we met French troops, we tapered the distance to my Spahis, until I found them at Flaxlanden in Alsace. It was good to see the first of them with the red patch and star on the sleeve. They wore that curious expression which with the soldier is one of content and business combined; they were tense as women giving birth; they didn't talk loudly. We would be in action soon. The labor pains of battle are unmistakable.

I arrived almost in time for dinner and so was fined three cigarettes, German ones which had been given me as my accumulated ration. Colonel Loth finished deliberately his conversation while I stood stiff beside him. His elbows were on the swastika of a German flag.

"Beel," said the colonel, "you will sit down there." It was at the

233

end of the class, because I was inferior in rank to all of them, but it meant that I belonged with them at last. As a foreign volunteer and probably a suspect character I had had the place on the colonel's right before. Now I cherished this humble place. De Dibadère poured me a glass of schnapps and Captain de Chevrautel said through his twisted mouth, "Would you like some boots, my son? They belong to the Germans right now, but you will meet us at my mess tomorrow morning at five-fifteen, and we may find some boots and a little fun."

The city of Mulhouse was half ours and half the Germans', and we had, too, recently arrived to determine which streets belonged to whom. There was one chimney taller than the others, and smokeless, with a sort of scaffolding around its top. Our destination, the railway yards, lay in the center.

De Chevrautel pressed his foot down, and when the snipers sniped we went smartly around a corner, and around another corner whose shops bulged from the bomb blast of a few days ago, until we reached the railway yards. There was our treasure, a line of freight cars in no-man's land.

A mortar shell landed just beside us, spurting mud at us, "Whoosh-whoomp!" and we jumped from the jeeps and crawled fast to the lee of the freight cars. There was heavy machine-gun fire on the other side, but none of it came near us. I looked, on my belly, from side to side and saw our Moroccans lying flat at the corners of red-roofed houses.

"Burglar, have you got your tools?" said De Chevrautel, and my eunuch Mekki tossed his head. Mekki made a spongy jump to the sill of the first freight-car door and in a moment had it opened. Individual rifle shots were cracking at us now, but we rushed into the train, to that mountain of black gold that was built of knee-high German leather boots. And then we saw the food, which we flung out first to our Moroccans who had come erect and laid down their arms in their eagerness. There were tins of butter from Denmark, tins of cheese, the wines of France, and cases of Cointreau. And after them, we delved like rats into the pile of boots, flinging them out of the car against the hail of bullets which enveloped us.

After the next shell had rocked the car, and we had jumped and

234

run for the jeeps and zigzagged out of there, bumping high over the ruts of ice, away from the chimney and the "Ps-ee-uh!" of bullets, I realized how cold my feet were in their low Egyptian shoes, and held up my new boots, one on each hand plunged warmly into it. Every one of the boots was for the left foot. Where the right ones were we didn't know. Unquestionably the Germans had won this round.

The high priest of Flaxlanden was a grand old man who distilled the best schnapps of the region and was loved by all of us. His bread was brown and sticky and excellent with Münster cheese, and although he would teach me nothing of either baking or distilling he did point out that the hilltop air was here so pure that I had merely to follow my nose down the street to find roasting bread or schnapps in the brewing. My nose supplied the officers' mess, and my nose was highly thought of; never could I leave our billet without someone, even the colonel, most solicitously ascertaining that my throat was well covered by the scarf and my jacket was buttoned to the chin; the shells of the enemy were disagreeable, but microbes in my nose would have been calamitous.

We moved on to Morschwiller, which was the opposite side of the bridge from Lutterbach where the Germans were busy shelling us while their commandos lay low around two thirds of our perimeter. It was an unpleasant house that we of headquarters had chosen. The shells from Lutterbach slid too close by us, and between their whinnyings we could hear the screams of the children in the cellar being beaten for having "fraternized" with us.

That was a decayed house, a house of groping hate, this great château whose attic was thick with straw for the German troops which had left it yesterday. We seldom saw the family. They lived like troglodytes, fat, soft, the color of worms, stinking with the hate they had for us because we were fighting to recover Alsace for France. They were loyal German Alsatians, but there was no need to arrest them; we let them simmer in their hate and cautioned our sentinels to let them pass from one house to another and to watch them as they sneaked across the bridge.

I lay in the dark one night, cold and thinking thin, cold, tenuous thoughts. Half of our men were in the holes on the edge of the village, bluffing the Germans who were in holes, too, about three hundred yards away. They were fairly well protected against patrols by a netting of booby traps. One of them would have my room tomorrow night, for it would be my turn then, if we got through this night intact. I was too tired and too cold to form the memory of instructions round and whole. Sleep bulged slowly toward me, and thinned, and retracted again. And I thought—keeping myself awake with fear and thinking—if I can have two hours' sleep, or one hour even, I'll be faithful to this job. I'll serve it.

Beyond my window the Moroccan sentry cried, *"Halte là!"* and someone said a word, and I waited, tense, while the sentry fumbled for the correct reply. He wouldn't be very helpful if the German paratroops should try to take the village tonight. Our heavy artillery, mostly 75s, barked like sleepy dogs, "Roomp! Roomp!" and the reciprocal shells of the enemy passed close above our roofs with a high, falsetto stammering before they crashed.

I lay in that dirty bed, smoking, turning my head from left to right, following the trajectories of shells, toward the Vosges Mountains of France or the deep forests of Germany, beyond the Rhine a few miles away, thinking that my Spahis, cavaliers, should have their steaming horses for comfort here. But we were motorized, and a tank is cold beneath the hand. And even our tanks were now far from us, in Flaxlanden, while we waited as infantry in the trenches by the bridge. The river beneath it was flooded with rain and snow. Mekki had grumbled, "In the harem, it was never so." Mekki had never seen France before, but now he was fighting for the ideal of it; and like an animal scenting pain, he didn't like the bridge.

It was a common railway bridge, distinctive only by the corpse of a Sherman tank, one of ours, wrecked in the middle of it. The Germans held Lutterbach and were waiting complacently for our next attempt to cross. I was tired and sick of war, and my lean thoughts straggled to why I had been so foolish as to give Mekki my only pair of pants to mend tonight.

The reply to this came suddenly. There was a blast like all hell exploding, and half of my room with half the house crumbled into blazing dust. In that first moment of panic I heard my sentry's voice rise to a scream and again order, *"Halte là!"* There was no reply, and I knew then that the German paratroops were in the village and outside my window, too. They couldn't get up my stairs, for I hadn't any stairs any more; there was a cataract of fire where they once had been. I snapped on my flashlight, wet a towel, tied it over my nose, and staggered around the room looking for my pants. There weren't any pants, of course. I swung a shirt and raincoat over my shoulders, and shoved my feet into the German boots, thinking idiotically that two lefts still didn't make a comfortable right. I heard German voices, shrill and arrogant, in the courtyard, as I jumped through the fiery cataract, holding my shaky pistol tight.

I fell into black night, into a void of cold, and I could feel my buttocks tighten, shrink with gooseflesh. *"Halte là!"* said an uncertain voice in the dark, a German voice, but I slid around the blazing wall and ran like hell down the street toward the colonel's headquarters. And once I shot off my gun at a shadow that challenged me. The colonel wasn't there, so I ran on toward the bridge. There was only one retreat and that was forward, into the enemy's camp, across the bridge. I heard the crackle of tommy guns behind me; my Spahis must have left the town. They were retreating toward the enemy, too. There was no question of my taking command of anyone, even of Mekki, for there was no one to take command of except the Germans.

I was cold to the marrow of my bones. All my worries of the past and all the war diminished, contracted, to the elemental pain of cold. The rain slapped at me like nettles and I cursed it. I yelled at it stupidly and stumbled through a garden which was sown with our own mines. That didn't bother me, for with the flash of cannon in Lutterbach I saw haven, a little hut at our end of the bridge which should be our advance command post. I approached it respectfully, calling out the password, and found one of our captains and a Moroccan rifleman there.

"You, Lieutenant," said Captain de Breteuil severely, "are a pretty sight indeed. What kind of a strip tease do you think you are doing?"

There was a round red stove, and I burned my bottom on it. The Moroccan averted his modest eyes. "Look," I said, "if you've got a pair of pants—"

"I've got a pair of pants. I wear them. Regulations, you know. I've also got to cross that damned bridge before the Germans discover we're still here. The squadron has gone over and we are attacking, strange though it may seem. Tie this scarf around your tail and we'll see what we can do."

The Moroccan snuffed the candle and we returned to the night. It was snowing softly, a caressing snow against the skin and treacherous with cold. The three of us held hands like children as the Moroccan led us onto the bridge, and behind us I heard the sound of German small arms, and behind that the "Roomp! Roomp!" of our artillery two villages back. It was so dark on the bridge that it hurt my eyes, and we stumbled continually, trying to walk the railway ties.

"Hole," said the Moroccan, and we stepped far around it. Ahead was a small sound as of someone pecking at metal. "The wreckers," said the Moroccan. "They're trying to dislodge the tank. No good," he added. The jacks were creaking. I forgot my coldness before this horror, the tank, the destroyed machine of destruction, the dead, deliberate great engine of death.

I was being pulled down the embankment. "Careful, mines!" said the Moroccan. We fumbled our way into the pit and along a sodden path, and the snow fell on us and I slid in its slush, and I remembered the clean campaigns of Africa, of Tchad, Libya, Tunisia. That was a good war, with no civilians to clutter it or starve in it, a war of mighty distances, not this obscene and intimate fumbling in the mud and the dark. Somewhere ahead of us the river whimpered, and we stopped, feeling along the embankment until we reached the burlap bags and the entrance to the tunnel we had made. We crawled like moles, headfirst, around and over the barrier, replied to the challenge, and walked across the bellies of sleeping men toward a tiny glow of coals.

Before we could speak to the lieutenant in command we heard the German shell explode outside, then the clicking of dirt as it fell around us. I squatted over the coals to warm my bare backside again. "They know we're here?" I asked.

"They damn well do. We've had this for twenty-four hours. But I don't think they really want to destroy the bridge. You have seen that they haven't damaged Alsace very much, for they hope to come back. They still think Alsace is Germany."

Our Moroccan, impatient as a dog, led us through a twisted tunnel and onto the bridge again. It was a very long bridge and very cold. De Breteuil ahead of me was breathing hard, but he said, with his usual calm, "This war, *mon lieutenant,* displeases me." We stepped high like circus horses over the uneven railway ties. De Breteuil said, "If the bastards haven't sent out patrols to support their paratroops and stop the likes of you and me, I shall esteem them less. And if there is not a patrol around this bridge, I shall buy you three, even four, of your sacred Camemberts when we get to Paris."

My teeth were chattering too fast to reply, and I held to my small, wet, comfortable pistol like a swimmer to a straw. I thought, I don't mind dying, but let me have my last agonies warm. The wind, wet with snow, slashed at my thighs, and I thought: I'm all the men nude of this war; I'm the men denuded of decency, of shame, of warmth, of tenderness, of all but faith. I'm the faithful thug in the night.

We stumbled on, and I thought irrelevantly of warm sunlight, and of my Armenian elephant which had earned me a strange repute throughout the armies of France. I had never really known an Armenian elephant—I don't think it even exists—but the rumor from Congo to Alsace was that I had a marvelous story about one. It was a weird and disquieting experience to be challenged at the popotte, the officers' mess, by some newcomer who would ask, "Is this the Davis, that son of an American, who married an Armenian elephant?" I always disappointed everyone, not knowing my own tale, but nonetheless the report of it grew.

Now to keep my mind from shivering as my body was, I tried to compose a story about an Armenian elephant. "He was actually my stepson," I said, "twice removed, and his red corpuscles were insignificant, for he had lived twenty years in the tropics, like me. But he was braver than lions when his pants were on. . . ."

"Shut up!" said De Breteuil. Ahead, over Lutterbach, red and green Very lights were going up, eerie balls of fire, like the toys of a witch. Something was happening, or was about to happen, there. The Moroccan tugged De Breteuil, who tugged me, and we went down the embankment to the first houses on the edge of the river. Our Spahis had held three of these for several days, but we approached them warily in the utter dark, feeling our way along a barn, a pigsty,

239

stopping to listen, palping a sandbag, inching through some cavernous place which was full of invisible men. I got an elbow in the eye.

"Listen," said the Moroccan, "someone coming." I heard the faint squish of boots in the mud, and felt colder than ever.

The dark laughed quietly. "That's only Abdulla here beside you. He's just learning to chew chewing gum."

But it wasn't. I blinked a flashlight to see two Moroccans with a stretcher with what remained of the carcass of a man. Someone explained, "Poor Ali. We've been looking for him since yesterday, when we tried to reach the church."

Then he added, as if it were a casual afterthought, "I got back, the only one of the wounded who did; we lost sixty men. Half of us were simply wounded, shot down through the stained-glass windows. We rolled over and over in the square, trying to roll away. Then the Germans came out. They didn't want any prisoners. They were shooting the wounded through the nape of the neck as I crawled off on my knees and elbows; they'd got me in the hands."

The voice was extinguished as if the night had gulped it, and then I heard it again, a sleepy drone, "A company is going back tonight. . . . You want to see the captain? . . . He's in the cellar. Merde." There was a machine gun making a noise like someone spitting teeth on a hardwood floor.

Down the black stairs we went and turned into what looked like a photographer's darkroom, lighted only by a red-hot stove. The captain and three native lieutenants were squatting close around it, studying the map of the village we were to attack. Captain Pouilly was unshaved. He was slow and determined, a stolid hero, and as I excused my lack of pants he excused his beard. He panted; his voice was like some wood-wind instrument, like an oboe muted. "We have been in line now for twenty-seven days," he said, "and for ten days in this abyss." He wasn't complaining. He was proud of this.

The field telephone jangled softly on the dirt floor beside him, and I heard the crackle of straw beds as men in the dark were wakened. Pouilly spoke over the phone to our artillery, gave them their directions of fire, while with his right hand he poured us wine. (". . . ten days in this abyss . . .") The men here were volunteers for the second attack upon the church, and I said, "Look, if I could have a pair

240

of pants—" But I was ignored. I didn't like running naked, even alone and in the dark, and I asked them again.

I was still ignored. The captain's hands swam like fish across the chart, pushing the enemy to the east, drawing our troops to shelter along the river front. They were long hands and clean, the hands of a French aristocrat doing a dirty job. I thought of the thousands of French hands I had seen like this, moving over a chart, cherishing a gun, typing orders with two fingers, digging at the earth with fingernails . . . the laying on of hands which would heal France again. And I thought: Old Father, Father called Mars, will there be no peace ever? Is there no home for us, your bastards, for the nude and hollow men who keep your house?

De Breteuil shouldered past me. "It is 13:33," he said, and though his voice was a whisper the Moroccans on their heaps of straw began to stir, to arrange their long scarves, to find their guns.

Captain Pouilly picked up his telephone. "Mortar fire at 13:35. I'll signal."

"Christ," I said, "can I have a pair of pants?"

The Moroccans were slipping up the stairs. Pouilly held his telephone with his left hand while with his right he moved his glass of red wine back and forth so that the light of the glowing stove shone through it in a purple shadow upon the chart.

Now I was scared. I was short of breath. I heard the "whanh-whanh-whanh" of a German shell approaching, and the "troomp!" as it landed very near us. The native lieutenants had left the fire and were quietly herding their men up the stairs. I caught one of them and gestured to my naked thighs.

As he moved away quickly, I flicked my flashlight on him and saw him strip the pants from the dead Moroccan, whose stomach, as the French say, was *"en confiture."*

"Fire!" said Pouilly to his telephone. The vomit rose up in me as I put on the pants, and the fine false courage of war rose with it, and I went up the stairs then, the faithful thug in the night.

There was a little man, and his name was Marius, and he lived in a fine trench in a valley of Alsace. I loved the Captain Marius as all of us did. He was of the old Free French who refused the capitula-

241

tion and the armistice, and fought with us at Alamein, which made a particular bond between us. He fought through Tunisia, too, collecting snails and flowers and the fish of swamps, tending them gently as he tended his friends, for he loved all good things alive.

War was a bad thing, said my Captain Marius.

He was the purest of aristocrats, swearing by profit through labor, although he had little money of his own. He hadn't labored hard in civilian life, and didn't ever want to. But laboriously he killed Germans, because they were bad. He collected snails, and when they died, he ate them quickly, with magnificent garlic sauce to honor them. We understood that he had eaten also, in wine which gagged him, his father's ashes, for he believed in the simple things, in the absorption of the virtues of the dead.

I would see him in the trench, smiling, tiny, broad-shouldered, bespectacled, directing his post with authority, and my heart would wallop as I went away, carefully crawling over the trip wires of his mines, for I knew that our gentle Marius would not live long now in the midst of this evil war. He was too gentle, and he fought too hard.

The snow was melting in Alsace. The sun came out, and a new war with it, a war of slush and mud, a slobbering war. We moved toward the Rhine from ditch to ditch, racing for the advance ditches of Captain Marius, not only because they were the cleanest, but because he deliberately left small surprises in them, a rare egg, a five-franc note, a torn page with the address of someone he loved, somewhere.

All the woods were shattered here, the branches frayed by shrapnel, the twigs dangling, the pale pink roots bared and upright like so many human limbs the war had left. Captain Marius looked at them with pity through his thick glasses, for to him the death of the woods was nearly as sad as the death of men.

"It's worse," he said, "perhaps for the trees. They've got to stand and take it, like the solid little peoples. There is no defense for them. Their green honesty isn't any good. There aren't any trenches for the trees." We were lying flat in the mud, which was oyster-white with thin snow. Marius flicked his glasses up his forehead, and lifted his binoculars carefully, then slammed them down again and buried his face in the mud, as I did, too, for a smatter of fire burst from the trench we had been looking at. It was only sub-machine guns, and that was encouraging, but it shook us to have them know that we were here.

We spun on our middles and started crawling toward another tree, a fat one with its old heart splintered. There was blood around the eyes of Marius, where his glasses had been, before he smashed them in the mud. "Hell," said Marius. "I don't like to complain, but that caps it! Doesn't it, Beel? I'm so farsighted that I can hardly see even your dirty face now."

"Shut up, *mon capitaine*," I said.

"But damn it," said he, *"mon lieutenant,"* he added, "there are limits to what common sense can stand. Meanwhile, will you give the order to remove that pest of a trench ahead of us?"

We got back to our Spahis and sent a platoon forward, and saw our men rushing, staggering, lower and lower as the bullets ripped into them, until they all lay in a new barricade before the trench. I banged my cheek against the cheek of Marius as I took his binoculars; I twisted them to normal vision, and I said, "Jesus, the corporal got it, too, but I think he's pretending dead."

Then no one moved for ten minutes or so, until three Germans came out of the trench, and their shadows reached far toward us, as if even they, shadows, were seeking us behind our tree. And the silhouettes of the Germans seemed huge in the sunset against the golden little village behind. "Don't shoot. We'll get them," said Marius, with the binoculars to his eyes again. He began to run his thumb and forefinger rapidly over the extra clip of his pistol, to count the bullets in it, and said, "In a moment we'll take them, Beel." There was the creaking of one of our tanks to the right of us.

I looked through the binoculars again and saw the Germans, the black silhouettes of men, stepping over our dead, slashing at them with sticks and rifle butts to make sure they were really dead.

And one discovered the corporal and struck him so hard across the nose that I could see the blood gush from his nostrils. He didn't move, although he was alive and they knew it, and the butcher who led them plunged and twisted his stick into one of the man's eyes. He heaved in agony, and the German, taking him by the hair and leaving the stick in the eye socket, shot him neatly through the nape of the neck.

243

Marius said pensively, "France and Germany are like Siamese twins, united by hate. Come on." We started forward with the first, rather disdainful, blast of our tank toward the trench. We held grenades and pistols only, counting on the tank to defend us. The Germans kept firing stupidly at it with their inadequate guns and when Marius and I arrived above them they flung their thick hands up and screamed for our protection.

They were eight, three Germans, the three who had wounded and beaten and killed our corporal, now wanting to surrender casually, and five slave combatants, a Czech, a Russian, an Austrian, and two Mongols. The three Germans smiled and shrugged and tossed away their guns, as if they were tennis rackets, after a good game lost. The Austrian twitched like a marionette.

A mortar had got our range and was geysering earth around us. Marius could see nothing near him without his glasses, so as we marched our prisoners forward to the golden village, he asked, "Was that close, Beel? Are they trying to get us or our squadron in the woods?"

And I said, "Yes, *mon capitaine,* that was damn close. Do you mind if I encourage these bastards to run?"

"Oh, no," said Captain Marius, "you mustn't do that. The village looks quiet, but our tanks are just entering it, and there may still be snipers there. Let us walk slowly." He reached out his hand and took that of the superior German officer whose hands had been clasped firmly above his head. "Lead me to that wall over there," he said. "You made me break my glasses, so now I can't see very well, and I can't ask the Lieutenant Beel because he has to keep you covered. You understand?"

The giant German led Marius like a child, and I followed, wincing as the shells came out of the sunset to our right. I thought I saw movement in one of the windows of the wall ahead.

"Here we are. Here's a good wall," said Marius.

"Mon capitaine," I said, "there's a sniper up there, I think."

"Hah! Then get these five foreigners to shelter, and leave me the three Germans. And quick!"

Just beside us was a high heap of rubble, and I herded my prisoners behind it. It was between us and that black window in the golden

244

wall. I moved out again and squatted at an angle from which I could cover my docile charges and also the three arrogant Nazis with Marius.

Marius, pistol in hand, poked his three gently in their bellies and forced them against the wall. Their fists were still clenched above their heads. Their eyes stared hard as the eyes of hobbyhorses; their lips were thin. Marius walked before them, looking with his half-blind eyes at each one carefully, and said, "You *are* the three Germans who beat our corporal with the stick, aren't you?"

"Yah!" said one of them, and tried to spit, but it was scarcely a mist that came from his mouth.

"So," said Marius, "I've got to shoot you. I'm sorry for myself, too, because I hate it. But you're bad men of a troublesome people whom I don't like, though I've tried to, really. You wouldn't know, of course, that some little man of you, in occupied France, tied a burning fuse to my pet tortoise's tail, or that another little man of you practiced goose steps across my crocuses, or that another little Nazi superman nearly convinced my wife, while I was fighting you in Africa, of the lies you published in our country journal." The German spat mist again, and Marius offered him his flask. He refused. "And look," said Marius, "you're really not good Nordics enough to be good sportsmen, for we saw you beat our wounded corporal with the stick, and you ... or you"—Marius stood back to see the shape of them— "pushed the stick down into his eye—"

I was watching the black window in the golden wall, and I yelled to Marius as the thin snout of a gun came out. I fired up at it, but thirty yards with a pistol is hard. As I dodged back to my prisoners I heard our tanks again. Marius was saying, "Look, forgive me for this. I'm all for charity, but you're bad and bestial men, and I've got to shoot you now. It might comfort you to know that I'm fed up with this war, too. I don't at all mind dying, and I probably will before the end of it.... Are you ready now?"

The black snout of the machine gun in the window protruded a little more, pointing almost straight down. I cried out to Marius again, but my voice was shattered by the gun in the black window above. The three Germans crumpled first, and then my Marius. And before I could move I realized that the creaking of our tanks had ceased, and I waited for the shelling by them which that must mean.

245

I watched the dead, waiting. The three Germans lay in patterns, rigid, mechanic. Marius lay limp and at peace with his pistol in his arms, like a child with a Teddy bear. Then I heard the great shell coming, and drove my head into the rubble. The explosion smashed me senseless. I became aware at last of the smell of burned earth, harsh, acrid, of the dribble of earth upon my back, and of the shimmering space where men had been and once there was a wall.

Colonel Loth had munificently given to Mekki and me the kitchen of a house abandoned by the Germans that afternoon. There was little to confirm their reputation for tidiness, except that they had left a number of their lice behind. I spread by bedroll on the table, and Mekki laid his on the floor before the fireplace. A pot of soup was suspended there, and we had some of it. I rolled over to sleep as Mekki, indefatigable, built up the fire and rustled his papers in the important way which meant that the muse had come to him and he was about to write a poem which would ruin my sleep.

I was too tired for even dreams. Nothing had ever been so good as the stroke of heat across my shoulders, nothing so safe, in an uncertain war, as the solidity of the old pine table, nothing so savory as the odors of garlic and thyme and such which rose from its scored planks.

"Cry in the night," said Mekki, his voice as soft as the coals just now igniting. I drowsed again.

"Cry in the night to your sons. Cry them home, from the cells of the Huns and the stuttering stone of the mills where they grind into guns the good body of France.

"Cry havoc. Cry hope. And they'll hear in the dark of our coming. They'll know the thick drumming of cannon, the strumming of wings over death . . . and the bells in old steeples.

"We, the faithful of France, have held France in the Tchad. We, the people, have fought in the flux of the sand and the great Sheba's hills.

"Bir Hakim weaned us. The hagard Tibestis determined our drive to the sea.

"Qatarra, Himeimet, the vale of Zagouan, with all its fine poppies and burgeoning dead, led us surely toward home. We laughed on

Mount Maio and shuddered in Rome; for the boon of our anguish was not death but living, the giving of Huns to our sons in the night.

"We, the people, cry in the night to our sons, cry them home as we now stagger home. . . .

"Paul of Gaul, are you there? Are your scythes fit for reaping? Is the gray grain dry?

"Michel, lad, where are the wolves of your keeping?

"Old Pierre of the rocks, is your fruit piled high?

"Young Jeanne of my heart, shepherdess, mother, have you tended your flocks?

"Ah, let no horn be broken!

"This is the token: the cry in the night and the chanting of wings over France. Cry Christ in the night to the high hills of France where the free men have gathered and fathered their arms.

"In the pulse of our sons, in the blood of the bled, is the echo of France again.

"Christ, son Christ, cry France. . . ."

22

The cheery asylum for the insane
—the man who killed everyone

THE GRAY NEXT DAY began with the sourest telegrams as we moved forward. There was resistance at Soultzmatt, tank destroyers and bazookas, and somehow the Germans were slipping through us to the Rhine, which they crossed by cables, hand over hand. The Americans were shooting them like laundry pins into the water, but they still kept getting across.

We established and abandoned three headquarters that day, for our few troops were spooning up the Germans and either taking them prisoner or tossing them into the laps of the American XXI

247

Corps. I became useful because, being of the First Moroccan Spahis which wore red hats and the only one of my new regiment that did, we discovered that our prisoners thought I was a Russian. I would stand, grim as a Cossack, just in front of the prisoners to be interrogated, and there was never any need of a third degree.

All that day we had heard talk of resistance in the "asylum," which sounded odd, but we entered Rouffach and found the asylum for the insane with no trouble at all because there were so many bullets coming out of all its many windows. There weren't any lunatics, perhaps. There were Germans. The place had been long ago taken over for an officers' training school, and we found it had been an efficient one as we thrust our tanks between the dozen buildings of it and finally chased the Germans out.

It was paradise. We were cold and hungry. We were dirty and tired. The Germans semicircled us in the hills, but we sank into the womb of this superior Insane Asylum and forgot them for a little while. We explored the cellars to find stocks of loot from Denmark, butter, cheese, flour, sugar in great sacks, mustard, sauerkraut, candy, clothes. And best of all was the apple juice, which we guzzled with schnapps.

Then we came back to our fine rooms with sheeted beds and central heating, and took hot baths, the first in months; but we couldn't yet relax. The Germans were much more numerous around us than we were in the asylum's hundred and twenty-two hot baths, and they had to come through, tonight, through the slot in the hills which we were blocking.

Being nimble with schnapps, I had secured an excellent room, and locked the door and pretended it wasn't there, and shot three German mules, towing Germans, from my window, before the colonel and his staff arrived. I conducted them cunningly through this lunatic museum, offering a fine coat to one, a swastika to another, a toy to a third. Bathed, and clean as death for death which wasn't particularly probable, but which one couldn't ignore, I returned to my good room. On the desk lay a poem, half-finished, in German. There was a child's Nazi chariot in a corner of the room, and the bookshelves so quietly whispering to me were mostly filled with such fairy tales as adults read. Gnomes and trolls and the good small folk were in them; war would have been preposterous among them. And beside the soft pillow of my bed stood three German bazookas.

Never in the war had I been so happy as I was in that small room which should have stunk of my enemy. His men now would be coming from the hills, two thousand of them creeping in the night down the valley of the river Ohmbach, south of Westhalten, in a desperate attempt to reach the Rhine. I turned off the light and opened the window. Against the gray sky, lighted by a moon from behind us, was a little house, so close I thought I could put my hand upon it. I did. It was a birdhouse, and there was suet on its veranda and straw between the banisters. The German who had had this room had loved birds as he had loved poetry and fairy tales and bazookas.

I was still in the dark when there was a knock at my door, and it was pushed open to frame the large silhouette of Mekki. *"Mon lieutenant,"* he said, "my respects, *mon lieutenant.* A terrible thing has happened."

I kept looking past the birdhouse to the valley from which the Germans would shortly come. Mekki knew that I was annoyed with him. He knew I had seen him in the cellars lugging away sacks of sugar which he would sell to the people of Rouffach who clustered around the door, Francophiles suddenly, demanding their ration of German loot. "Where have you been, Mekki?"

"I excuse myself, *mon lieutenant,* but I have only been making poems." He knew me well, this eunuch and poet and very casual valet. "Poems," he said, aligning my boots, "about women, and thou won't approve of them, for thou wilt tell me that the North American Institute of Fiction Writing or the Pelham Institute or something discourages the embryo writer from writing about what he doesn't know. Ah, yes, *mon lieutenant,* thou hast chided me, a poor eunuch, because I sing songs of love. But the life of the mind, *mon lieutenant,* the lonely dream, is that not valid?"

"Clean those shoes, Mekki, and clean your own. We may need them in a hurry." I closed the window and turned on a little light. Mekki scrubbed my unease away as he worked on the shoes. He was curiously consoling, this big blob of a man who was a better fighter and better poet than I should ever be.

"Thou hast not asked me about the terrible thing," he said. I was

249

looking at the photograph of the thin and aesthetic and thoroughly decent-looking criminal who had had this room, and the books of poems in it.

"What was it, Mekki?"

"The poem, *mon lieutenant,* the penultimate poem. I had once a title for it, a thin one, about middle-sized, which fitted nicely in Arabic script, and suddenly, 'Whoosh!' it went away." He paused, on his knees, brush in air. "It was a title, when written in our flowing script, about the width of a hand to look at, and as wide as the world. And I have never recaptured it. I am such a stupid one."

"How did it go, Mekki, underneath the title?"

Mekki leaned back, his pudgy palms on the floor behind him. He nodded his own approval, as Arabs do:

"Count them, the fingers of my gray heart, and the fingers of yours which are four.

"Hold them and turn them and twist them apart, till the four of yours meet with the four of mine, wonderfully.

"Tip unto tip of our hearts' pulses, lift them to each of your eyes, to anoint them.

"I have no fifth to rejoin the blind sentinel, staggering, lost, at your door.

"Ours are old hearts, and lopped and delinquent, stopped by the love which we scarcely have known.

"Ours are the lingering fingertips, cold at our hearts, which would tear them.

"These two, this fifth of a phantom, and this of your own, shall retreat like thin urchins from terror and love."

We were too tired to worry about the door in front of us which led to the subterranean passages connecting the buildings of this immense asylum. Colonel Loth and Dodelier and Dépenoux sat grimly thinking of the trouble we would surely have tonight. The door of the tunnel opened slowly. A little man came out of it, leaning like a beggar toward us, and looking like a clown. His face was white and bruised as marble, his knees knocked, then spread and trembled. And he whimpered terribly upon the long road from his tunnel's mouth to us.

250

We watched him across the table. There were six of us eating cold rations, and Mekki as a sentry at the tunnel's door. His pistol lurched with the lurching of the little man approaching us, then jerked suddenly as another man came up behind the first one. The colonel squinted. "There's Death," he said. And it was nearly that. The creature who had once been a man caught up with the little clown and linked arms with him, for he, too, was falling, and the little clown hadn't the strength to shake him off, though he was obviously terrified.

One after another our wineglasses clinked down upon the table. There was not a murmur but that of the artillery to the west. The colonel said, "Sit down," when those two frightful Frenchmen clawed over our shoulders at the wine. They took my place and Morette's, and we stood close behind them, our hands on the backs of their chairs, so that we could watch the tunnel's mouth.

The glass of the little man rattled against his teeth, and he said, "I, sir, have been called a poltroon, a coward. I, sir, am proud to be an atrocity, alive."

Some of us lifted our glasses, and none of us said a word. Colonel Loth leaned forward finally. He asked, "You were taken as hostages?"

The lean old man who looked like Death spat his wine upon the floor and vomited and wiped his gray beard nicely. "Hostages," he said, expunging the vomit with his bare feet.

The shell then came out of the hills and moaned past us and made a soft and liquid explosion, probably in the Rhine, a few miles to the east. The colonel spoke to his adjutant. "Call Fabritius, and tell him he has to do better than that. We're not shelling Germany yet."

Old man Death managed to keep a gulp of wine in him, and said, "Look, take your guns out. Put a machine gun here. For they'll be coming up, vomiting out of the tunnel like me."

I leaned forward and put my hands on both of his, to steady him. "Who will be coming up?"

"The Huns. The bloody Huns. The bastards, the Huns. The Huns who call me Papa Death because they made me the executioner of my own people in this hole. They gave me a gun, and they gave me suggestions daily, but I really was free to kill whomever I wished." His hands shook beneath mine. They needed wine. I gave him wine again, and even at the sight of it his twitching stopped.

251

Our light burned out suddenly. It was a tiny bulb, attached to an automobile battery, for the wires of the hospital had been cut. While the Commandant Dépenoux was replacing it, the voice of Papa Death, fluid with drink, said, "They told me that if I was a good boy," and I remembered him in the dark as a corpse of sixty, "my wife Elice, and my two daughters Claire and Lolette, and my son Guy, wouldn't have to do it any more."

The little voice of the poltroon scratched across the dark. "Let me tell you. He didn't collaborate. We feared this man whose name I still don't know. But he got our messages, because the Germans trusted him, and helped many of us to escape, and shot some of us when he was obliged to, but without warning and always when we were asleep."

I lit the candle. There was a rumble in the tunnel beneath us, and the poltroon and Papa Death leaned back taut against the table facing it. Their glasses had spilled and their fingers were in the wine. Colonel Loth got up quietly and opened wide the half-opened tunnel door, and laid his pistol conveniently across his tin of Pork with Egg Yolk (Ration C).

"You shot them?" he asked.

Papa Death said, "Mother of God, I had to do it, for the people I love, and also for him. . . ."

We heard it coming, the Germans' shell, and before we could be amazed that they still had artillery in the Colmar pocket, we heard the crash of it and the stutter of earth against the walls of the house. Colonel Loth spoke curtly to Fabritius on the portable telephone.

Papa Death was calm as death by now, with that wine in him, and he watched the poltroon narrowly. But the tiny man was feeling better, too, and he walked up to Papa Death and talked right under his nose. "You came limping from bunk to bunk last night, and we could hear you coming by the slap of your hand against the posts. Most of us didn't know whom you were looking for. You came— slap, slap—along the passage between our beds, and most of us lay there shaking, and some of us crawled away beneath the beds like moles in the dark."

The cat sound from the tunnel became shriller as it approached us. Part of it reached in to us as a thin, chill quaver, like a fingernail

252

scratching a blackboard, and part of it was a sleepy moan. Papa Death drank half the wine in his glass, quickly, his Adam's apple bobbing, and flung the rest of it into the face of the poltroon.

The poltroon didn't flinch. "Slap-slap," he continued, without even drying himself, "until you reached our bunk, and I felt your hands counting me among the others until you came to the middle one who was asleep. You leaned down to him slowly. I could smell your breath, and it had the stink of fear. And suddenly your gun went off. When I stopped trying to beat you away, because you had gone, I reached out to the man in the middle and felt the blood upon his chest. He tried to say, I suppose, *'Vive la France!'* before he should die, but all that came from him was a shivering whimper like *'Vi-vi-vi-vi-vi . . .'*"

Out of the mountains then came the terrible rod of sound, the terrible tube with death in it, the thin terror, and the explosion close to us sucked our breaths away. The air was torn from the room and the steel shutter bent, and the tunnel spewed a blast of wind with the stench of death.

And then the men with cats' voices came reeling out, their arms locked about each other in a hideous ballet; little men, tall men, Frenchmen, and all of them emaciated. They wove up from the tunnel, locked by each others' arms, staggering three steps to the right, two to the left, and moaning and mewing at us without the strength to lift a smile at their liberation.

Papa Death jerked his hands from the wine puddle and held them, palms forward, dripping purple, beside his hips. His voice was clear but tremulous when he said, "I killed that man!" and he pointed with his finger dripping wine at one of the crowd, and his lips began to twitter before he could say, "And I killed that one!" and his voice twittered up an octave. "Mother of God!" he screamed, "didn't I murder this one, too, this very day?"

The poltroon had his arm about him, to help him face that tortured ballet. The colonel's quiet, triangular eyes were on the tunnel still. Morette's cigarette was dead between his lips. I pulled deeply on mine as another gust of decay and death spread from the tunnel over us.

The poltroon said, "We cut your bullets, Papa Death. We cut their noses off, so you had just the thinnest film of lead to make a wound convincing to the Germans. They were almost blank cartridges you thought you killed us with. And we drugged those men you meant to kill. And we buried them alive in the cellar's loose and shallow earth, so we could dig them up when the inspectors had passed. You've killed no one, Papa Death. God help you. . . ."

I went back to my room and bed, and took my boots off only, for the Germans were still coming from the hills, and we might need to meet them quickly. Mekki knocked and came in, and took the boots out. He stood in the door, dark and solid and whimsical. The artillery in the hills began again, and Mekki said, "There are the trolls again, beating and beating upon the drums that are their hearts. . . ."

23 ∿∿∿∿∿∿∿∿∿∿

Hennessey with Hemingway— *"Chicken doesn't go with my hat"*

SUDDENLY THE END of the war came, and I was lost in a world without a roof. Time had stopped around me. I could go home to 226 Fifth Avenue with the sporadic shakes I had developed out of simple war tension, but wasn't there anything bigger than me to fight for any more? There was. There was Indo-China fighting against the Communist-inspired Vietminh, and some of my own Spahis were already there. Look, old Bill, I said, do you fancy yourself as a soldier of fortune? And I said, No, am I not still giving half my earnings to the Free French? And I said, Look, are you still trying to get killed? Stop this nonsense, said I. Like Bill the dog, I've got one seeing eye at last; I want to see a roof on the world.

By now my book on the Free French in Africa had been published in Paris as *Feu d'Afrique,* so I hitch-hiked to Paris with my second Croix de Guerre, feeling a little more confident in what I secretly knew were my good intentions. Sometimes I had suspected that I really liked war—except for the noise and the people hurt in it—but more deeply I knew that what I preferred was a butterfly ranch.

Colonel Loth sent me to Paris to try to get a movement order as volunteer for the Indo-China campaign. There weren't nearly enough of such idiots, so I got it easily, but transportation was another thing. The Americans were flying east regularly, but they would have no part of me unless I should join them. They denied me—an American since 1620, by God—the advantages of the post exchange and the army post office.

Leper that I was, though fighting on the same side as my Americans, I went truculently into the bar of the Hotel Scribe one morning. The Scribe had been taken over by American Public Relations and, as I was not accredited by the State Department, I had no right to it. Ernest Hemingway with a glass stood at one end of the bar and I at the other. We hadn't seen each other in about ten years.

"Good morning, Ernest," I said.

"Good morning, Bill."

We got our glasses emptied.

"You've seen Waldo Peirce? He should be here."

"No."

We had moved a little closer now, and we felt better, but not very much. "Brandy and soda," said Hemingway. "Two."

We had that one and moved toward each other and the focal barman. We had another one, and stuck out our damp and cold right hands which wiggled but met. I said, "Let's sit down."

We did, and we talked until it was time for lunch, when we were steady as judges, and Hemingway was saying, "Bill, a man should stand proud at a bar. A drinking man is straight and vertical, with a mirror before him to judge the state of his poisoning." And occasionally he got up to look at himself carefully in the mirror, as though his reflection was one in a book he might do, and say, "Perhaps seven more, or eight—"

Ronald Mathews, a good correspondent, came in from Russia then, and without any pretentiousness took a tube of toothpaste from his pocket and squirted it into his mouth. This was a little surprising, for Ron was a sober and sensible man, a minor gourmet. He explained

255

to us that in Russia, while there was a lack of sugar, there was plenty of toothpaste from the United States, and that his lusts had grown through terrible ones to this.

Rupert Downing joined us, neat as a pin, exhausted, and opined that work was the ruin of the drinking classes. Hemingway took a look at the mirror again. "Five," said he, "a sad and a four-letter word."

I asked Hemingway, "What are you writing now, apart from the articles for *Collier's?*" He fidgeted, moved his chair, and replaced it. I looked into his empty glass darkly and ordered another round. "Book," he said, "but I'm not sure of it. Damn it, I don't know what to write." The prodigious Ernest didn't know what to write.

Brashly I said, "Stick those articles of yours together, and you'll have a book." He was fiercely diffident.

Cliff Webb of the *Daily Herald* came in and yawned and sat down and yawned again. Cliff was large and genial. He had a double gin. He leaned toward me and said in a whisper, confidentially, "Bill, I had a dream last night, or was it this morning? But anyway it should make a magnificent cartoon. Imagine a couple of characters at a bar, their feet on the rail and their elbows on the counter. One is a man and the other is a polar bear, and the man is saying to the barkeep, 'Two whisky sodas—one with ice.'"

Hemingway got up to look in the mirror again. "Three," he said.

Our table talk had turned to women, and someone maintained that the women of Tahiti were exceptional and that the musky Jewish girls were the dearest of all. And another held out for the small and proper Somali women. I protested that one of them had stolen my alarm clock.

A covey of American war correspondents came into the bar about then, and we turned our faces graciously away from them as Hemingway said, "These laddies should have the rules of the Geneva convention tattooed in reverse upon their backsides, so that they could read them, standing, before a mirror."

Mekki, my good eunuch orderly, brought the tickets to me: Paris to Saigon. "I shall follow you, *mon lieutenant.*" Somehow we were off at last, the bad elves behind us, the clouds beneath us. The modest farms of the Midi slid past us, with their fringes of golden trees. The cliffs bore lonely houses on them, and there were huts between the mountains. And there was the blue shield of the Mediterranean. If, I thought, you could open the green Door of the plane, and ski on the wind, sound asleep, if you could sleep—

Must I forever return to Cairo? I wondered. Where I was as unwanted as every European? But, unlike Paris, in Cairo there were taxicabs and someone to carry my baggage cheaply and fairy-tale shops full of wonderful things, eggs in mounds, and cheeses, and whole horizons of steaks across the windows. There were gladiolas and perky roses which smiled at you, and I felt like a yokel, so happy was I. Through the years I had somehow managed to maintain my requisitioned room with terrace at the Hotel Continental-Savoy, just in case of such a contingency as this.

In Room 38 lived Senubis, her tresses flaming like her love for Eustace, who also lived mostly there. Senubis was part Arab and part French and very beautiful and, next to me, the best cook in Cairo. Eustace was a war correspondent whom I had run into that night as he came hobbling from the Birka, that sector, Out Of Bounds to troops, where the naughty girls lived. He was holding one hand over his groin, the other behind.

"Eustace," I said severely, "how many times have I told you . . .?"

"My dear old Bill, I was there about an honest business, getting local color, giving tit for tat as an honest tradesman would, and I had duly removed my pants as one would remove his hat elsewhere. Etiquette, you know. I was spang in the midst of my research when the door opened slightly and a brown hand got a grip on my pants. The hand grabbed one leg of them, I grabbed the other. I was in no position to move just then, so we tugged back and forth until there was a rip, and fortunately I got a two-handed grip on the other leg and managed to escape with this divided whole. You talk of wounds!" he scoffed, looking to right and left through the taxi windows, for we had just drawn up before the portals of our hotel.

Slowly and with dignity we went through that swank, well-populated corridor, Eustace holding his pants together before and behind. "Poor devil," said someone on my left. "There are lots of them who return from the war like that."

In Room 38 at last, with little Eustace wrapped in a blanket,

Senubis looked up from her stove and glared at me. "You, Beel," she said, "are a mischiefer! And you!" she said to Eustace, "are the most egotesticle man I ever knew!"

The English of Senubis always humbled us professional writers. We saw that she was expecting the party which we both had forgotten and had prepared a magnificent soup. Eustace, too, was a cook and, when he wasn't writing of blood and guts, sent back exotic menus to his paper. He sniffed. "I'll have that recipe," he said.

Senubis kissed him and forgave him. "Boil and eat your artichokes, my little dove, but spare their hearts for another day—as you don't do with mine. Then you will put them into a chicken consommé, and add to them the rumps of celery, cut fine as wire. Boil it slowly while waiting for Eustace to come home from his whoredom, and serve with a dash of butter and some grated cheese."

My respect for Senubis went up smartly after that strange soup, and I saw her frequently at the Champagne Club. Once, studying the menu, she pondered and deliberated, while the waiter nudged suggestions at her, and finally she said, "Dearling" (her English was mixed), "dearling, I just can't eat chicken tonight, it doesn't go with my hat!"

Her tantrums were atomic. She couldn't sleep in Eustace's bed, because he snored. He would anchor himself on his stomach with arms and legs outspread, a pillow on his head to keep him down; and still, she said, he snored. We consulted Freddie and Gutka, and one or the other asserted that if your companion snored, all you had to do was whistle and the snoring ceased. So Senubis and Eustace and I spent hours sitting beneath the trees of Zamalek with their savage flowers, while we tried to teach her to whistle; never could she learn to whistle, or Eustace not to snore, so they parted again bitterly, and forever, until Senubis had cultivated sufficient insomnia to ask him home, and he came with a peace offering of three white mice.

I knew them well enough to drop in on them of a morning when Eustace, his eyes haggard, had come through the night snoreless, and of course without sleep, Senubis snuggled discreetly beneath the sheet beside the wasting frame of him. "Good lovers," she said complacently, "are not born but made. Is it not true, my little one?" Eustace snored at last in the assurance of my protection. "Listen,"

said Senubis, "his snore says No. No-no-no-no. . . ." She turned the
bump of her back to Eustace and me, and I sat apart and sipped my
tea fraternally. "Now he does not even know," said Senubis, "what
a cool oasis I am in this damned hot bed!"

Across the window flew an ibis, his thin legs behind him like chop-
sticks clutching prawns. Senubis, I noticed, was rubbing her back
against her pile of pillows, and Eustace, snoring wonderfully, was
also scratching his back. And some bird was chirping, "Quizzical,
quizzical, quizzical!" Senubis sat straight up in bed, throwing her
wonders to the wind and scratching, too.

"There are buggers in this place!" she said. I put down my cup.
Eustace sat up suddenly and glared Senubis down into the pillows
again. "I do not speak well your English," she said through the sheet
in her teeth. "But this place is full of buggers. Do you not say, one
bug, two buggers? I have buggers on all my back."

"Damn it," said Eustace, assertive at last, "now you're scratching
me!"

Senubis was furious. "Beel, you old satire, you, you won't protect
me against this satire in his own bed?" Eustace snored. Senubis was
serious now. She leaned over him. "Idiot! Sleepy one! If you want to
argue, let me get my clothes on first, so I can argue with dignity.
Also I can go out quickly and slam the door!"

I sneaked to the door and closed it quietly. They were inseparable.
They had permanently the best table at the Champagne Club. They
danced there, and argued nonsense. "Your ears," said Senubis, "are
like adjectives around your silly face."

"Have I told you of my Uncle Kate?" said Eustace, his large lower
lip protruding. He put the cage of three white mice upon the table.
The orchestra played tangoes; the mice slept; the dancers passed
inverted across the green mirror on our ceiling; Eustace sat still,
contemplative.

"All right, my lover," said Senubis, preening, "go and browse in
your sleep. Do you sleep, dear, with that lower lip inside the bedclothes or out?"

The music tapered off, and one little man with long hands began
to beat a drum gently with them, and I began to shake. "Sorry," I

said. "This embarrasses you more than it does me. It goes away in a minute or two."

"I am so cozy with men who shake," said Senubis, "but best of all when I am dancing or making lof. Eustace does not shake well. Will I dance with you, Beel?"

We danced, in my fashion, to the thick rumble of the drum and now a thin plaint from a violin, and while I was remembering that this lean and lovely Senubis, her red hair flicking the faces of passers-by, had spent the last four years as an ambulance driver with Leclerc and the Free French, she began to shake. She held tight to my clavicle, and I thought we did a fine rumba with both our shakes. Senubis put her cheekbone to my throat, and shook, and said, to my illusions, "You are embarrassed more than I that I shake. There are so many of us. It is silly, but we shake." She drew away from me, tossing her hips to disguise her real tremor, flaunting her rumba more courageously than I.

"Let's go back to the table," I said.

We sat down, with our chins on our fists to keep our elbows solid. An old friend, Captain now, Dupont, followed us in a pretzel path through the dancers. "Don't stop," he said. "I'll be shaking with you if they play that drum again." We got him a soup to match ours, and all of us, even Eustace, left our spoons alone. The drum beat on, irregularly. The violin twined a whine into a braid that held your heart, so all you could do was shake away from it.

At the next table to ours was a magnificent orchid surrounded by American officers and WACs. Their colonel, who was poorly digesting cigars and chewing gum and whisky neat, got up at last and leaned over us. "Pardon me," he said, "but are all you really shaking, or am I still seeing things in a blur?"

24 ∿∿∿∿∿∿∿∿∿∿∿∿∿∿

Volunteer to Indo-China—the rebels,
the Vietminh—I become a sorcerer

THIS WAS OCTOBER AGAIN, a yellow month in a dark brown war. The sands blew at us, and up went my plane at last toward Baghdad, a leg on the route to Indo-China. Mekki looked down through the sweat of his brow on the windowpane and leaned forward to say to me in the seat ahead, *"Mon lieutenant,* it is through saintliness that evil triumphs." I pondered this for a bit, and ate the dried lunch from the carton.

"Yes, Mekki?"

"This desert, *mon lieutenant,* was the Garden of Eden once." I looked out the window at the tremendous emptiness of it. "That was in the days of Adam and Eve; my ancestors," he nodded, "yours, too. It was when God used to go walking down there, and the viper also, and Isaac, the wandering Jew."

"Be quiet, Mekki, I want to dream and digest all this."

We flew over the Dead Sea, 1,292 feet below sea level, and touched down at Lake Hammaniya for refueling from pumps which shimmered in that hot sand. The next hop was to Basra outside Baghdad where we spent the night at the gigantic and lost Hotel Shatt-el-Arab. This seemed a homecoming, for I had passed here in 1939 with the Denis-Roosevelt Expedition on the way to Burma and Nepal. M. Golvin was still managing it expertly, and Pedros, the barman, was tending with fingers as delicate as a coiffeur's the thin glasses with his elixir, his balm of martini.

The little things impinged their memories, the frogs by the swimming pool, the curious obsession of the native servants, in long nightshirts, to walk barefoot upon them. Mekki lay down upon his elaborately embroidered bedroll before my open bedroom door, and I went slowly to sleep, watching the pulse of his cigarette in the dark.

Our pilots had us up at 2:45 A.M. for a breakfast of sausage and

261

tea. Dimly we moved to the plane in the dark, sucking the last puffs from our cigarettes, tamping them into the sand, talking more easily than in daylight before we should enter and be clamped into that Iron Maiden. We slid shut the curtains against the dark which would soon be brightening, and went to sleep again, our hands holding a magazine, smoother than usual in the dark, or a bunch of keys with their little metal faces. We went down the Persian Gulf and across the sinister great promontory called Trucial Oman, and stopped at Dubai for an accessory breakfast. This was a forsaken place, with one sheep and four Englishmen on it.

Persian Djask was as hot and flyblown as I remembered it; I was unsure of my neighbors because of their masks of flies. And Karachi simmered around the nude Indian tailor, sitting cross-legged in the middle of its busiest street, sewing buttons on a customer's soaked shirt. I found a mistake in my movement order, which ordered me to report to the French military authorities in Ceylon before going to Calcutta and Saigon, and this I did, flying half the length of India to that exquisite island where I had just time to see Buddha's tooth reposing in a gay gilt shrine, and make a Free French broadcast in my sort of French.

The colonel had just returned from Indo-China. "You'll like it there," he said, fishing for a lizard which had dropped plunk from the ceiling into his glass. "After the first ten opium pipes you'll ride winsomely, a volunteer, into all the excitement you could wish. And they'll shoot at you from ambush and slice your living eyeball like a hard-boiled egg."

Up I went again, against the sun, holding my living eyeballs and trying to catch up with the vagrant sleep of years. Calcutta was a worse military hash than Cairo, with the English, American, French, Gurkha, and Sikh troops swarming through it, and nowhere but the barracks to lay my head for days until the French Military Mission uncovered some letters which General Leclerc had written about me. Then I was given a magnificent apartment with garden and servants in a pleasant neighborhood frequented by the socially elite and the sacred cows.

It was my fifth November seventeenth of the war when I at last got a movement order for Bangkok and Saigon, Indo-China. Saigon was

beleaguered. A few miles away were the Vietminh and their vagabonds who were doing their utmost to ruin the country for their brief
picnic of pillage. It was imbecile. Long ago the French had found
the lonely and pleasant house that was Indo-China, inhabited by
children who hated one another and fought among themselves for
the kernels of rice and culture which they were too young to grow
efficiently. To the benefit equally of the French and the natives the
French counseled the tending of crops, the structure of roads, schools,
hospitals, that the natives might live more pleasantly and more profitably than before. Foreign trade, which had been negligible, increased,
to the advantage of both the colonists and the people of Indo-China.

Exploitation is a word used only by the children of such a house
who won't heed their elders' advice. You could say that we, the
Americans, exploit Hawaii, Puerto Rico, the Virgin Islands, but no
one who has crossed salt water would assume that these children of
far lost houses could patch their roofs against the world's awful sky
alone. Humanely, there were only two courses for the foster parents
of Indo-China: to abandon the country until, out of its havoc, social
and economic, the people asked for guidance again, or to police it
justly. The native was too young to realize that his parents, too, were
struggling, in this world without a roof, to defend him against the
harm which he or a neighbor might do to himself. Exploitation in
Indo-China was simply the intelligent business of setting the child to
selling newspapers, mostly bought by the parents and resold to keep
the parents healthy and buy the eventual education of the child.

My old Spahis were here, and the great men I had known in Tchad
four years ago, De Guillbon and Philippe and Jacques and Massu—
colonel now—and General Leclerc. It was always wise to ask Jacques
Langlois, aide-de-camp to Leclerc, whether the "Chef" was in good
humor before you had an audience with him. It was wise to ask
Philippe also whether Langlois was cheerful. Good humor was not
common in Saigon at this time when the French Communist newspapers were writing of us as "the assassins of Leclerc" and "the
butchers of Massu," and our old companions, who had survived five
years of war, were being ambushed in the jungle not by enemies but
by the snotty little urchins whom Leclerc and Massu were trying

to protect from the naïve ideology inspired by the Japanese and the Communists.

The Japs had gone to the villages, and one of their barkers, sitting high above the crowd on the limb of a tree, would crack an egg and pour it from one half shell to the other, with the white dribbling out, until finally the yolk was left, round and golden and alone. "Look," the barker would say, "here is the white race dribbling out, and what is left? The rising sun of Japan!" He would then display the yolk, and toss it as high as he could.

General Leclerc received me genially. He was the Leclerc of Tchad again, not of Paris at its liberation, when his drive had worn thin. He was still thin and assured, but a little gentler now; he wasn't fighting an enemy. He was so simply tolerant that he didn't even remark that I wore my proud new cord of the Croix de Guerre on the wrong shoulder.

"You are of the commandos, the Ninth RIC," he said. "Your old Spahis are here. You had better rejoin them. There is Bergamin of the Western Desert campaign, and Major Divry of the tanks at Himeimet, and Connus of Alamein."

"Merci, mon général."

"Bergamin will take you to the lines, and Major Fonde will give you your orders. Or Colonel Massu." We stood up, and I made a clack of the heels, which is not always successful, least of all in sandals. "You will leave at 5:00 A.M. Try to hurt no one. Good luck."

Slowly, as a convoy goes, we went north to a spot called the Three Frontiers, the junction of Cambodia, Cochin China, and Annam, bumping and siphoning the wine from our barrels into our dusty mouths. Very gay we were on the way to war. We stopped at stockaded fortresses and watched in the distance the smoke of rubber plantations set afire by the Annamites. We should be in them soon. The French had grown them to the profit of this colony, and now the insurgent idiots were burning their fortune down. It was logical enough that any people—the American Indians, for example—should want their independence, but that they should destroy their own property was absurd. We had adopted a race, and we had loved it.

264

We had set it honestly upon the foundations of France's commerce and her culture. And here in the jungles were the plantations burning.

Our outposts had been burned by the pseudo-Vietminh, and beneath the cold rain of the hills we crouched with our prisoners and only triangles of corrugated iron to cover us. We took their arms away, arms parachuted a short while ago by the Allies for use against the Japanese, and we fed them, as Leclerc had ordered, with our own rations, and interrogated them to learn how many cartridges they had been given and how many expended, and who were their chiefs. Their chiefs were usually the rogues we knew—not nationalist at all —or some of the thousands of Japanese who were still at large. The incitement of the true Vietminh was clear to the British, the American, or the French military observers: it was purely Communist.

A curious thing was that we were now employing Japanese mercenaries, and flying round the country in Jap planes flown by the Jap suicide pilots of the Kamikaze. My first flight with them left fingerprints on my parachute and others on my pistol and my brandy flask. In our chase of the insurgents in the jungle, we took no Japanese but dead ones. The natives we interrogated as gently as was wise. War correspondents, urbane ones, have written of French interrogation by third degree. This does exist in every army; it is often a necessary cruelty for the saving of thousands of lives, but I lived with the angriest men of all the war and, among the many prisoners I saw interrogated, I witnessed nothing worse than a kick in the pants when a prisoner was arrogant. I saw prisoners shot in Indo-China as in Africa and Europe, shot out of hand and illegally according to the arbitrary rules of war, but one was shot by a man whose wife had been raped and knifed by his prisoner, and another by an American kid whose bowels had been broken, systematically, day after day, in the prison camp where his warder had kicked him until we freed him and put the warder in his charge.

The French Moroccan Spahis, who were my people, and none too genial after five campaigns, did persuade these recalcitrant bandits to talk, but mostly we accomplished it with promises they knew were clean. Indo-China, we said, would be free in the French Federation, and we and they would punish those whose cupidity was against our

265

common interests, and this land would prosper again, and we both would be free.

Colonel Massu, whom I had not seen since years before at a place called Faya, in the African sands between Fort Lamy and the Tibesti Mountains, was heartening to meet again. When I first met Captain Massu, my colonel now, it had been in a sort of adobe hut at Faya, in a room shaded from the heat, lighted by the bright skins of animals on the floor, the shiny tongues of panting dogs—their ears lopped close for fighting—and the glistening of camel saddles which you held to, with one arm, while you lifted Massu's fine food with the other. This had been the semester before the final hook to Tripoli of General Leclerc.

Massu, a desert fighter, had somehow converted his men to snow troops in France and recently to jungle people here where we had this dirty business. We were sniped at and killed in ambush, and it was impossible to catch all the snipers because they could slip through the tangled liana vines, and chasing them we would usually fall on our faces within the first ten yards.

The war which the French paradoxically but justly called a war of pacification swept smoothly as a flame under the direction of General Leclerc, Admiral d'Argenlieu, and Colonel Massu, behind the flame the Vietminh were fanning in their retreat to the north, burning their country to spite the French who alone had made it prosper since the decline of the Khmers.

"This war," said Mekki beside me in the back of the truck, "this war is the vomit of peace." It was that revolting, but it was good again to taste the dust and laugh at our smeared and yellow faces, remembering Alamein, to bounce hard among the wine kegs in the camion—it hurt and it was good—to give or obey an order fraternally, to swap the old banter of companions reunited at the end of a world in war. But Victor had died just yesterday, on this road, when his armored car plunged into a sort of elephant trap prepared by the Annamites. Victor had been sliced in two by his steering wheel.

We drove through the towns of Massu's conquest, Mytho and Tay Ninh and Ben Keo, where very accurate archers attacked us with poisoned arrows which did us little harm. Mekki, who got one in the

266

back, said it made him thirstier. At Budop we encountered the strangest little soldiers in the world, the men of Moi, a timid tribe who wore long hair wrapped up in buns. They seemed soft as women and fought like ferrets when Massu enlisted them and turned them into combatant guides who understood at last that the structure of French Indo-China was a securer shelter than their huts of leaves. These primitives worked faithfully for us, despite the Vietminh's offer of one thousand piastres to anyone who would join them.

Shivering and full of fever from the lower lands, we squatted beneath corrugated iron tepees. The posts of the French stockade were still smoking around us, for the Vietminh had pillaged and fled about an hour ago. I looked glumly into the cold rain of this plateau, frustrate, wishing I could shoot anybody, even me, holding to the odd and actual souvenirs of memory which malaria affords you.

I remembered the bat, three feet wide from the tip of one wing to the other and balder than I, which had fallen before our refuge, and was still there, sodden, because we were too tired to pick it up. And I remembered the advertisement in a Cambodian paper for "Hair Manure." The rain came down like marbles on our tin roof, and with hands bandaged in gauze mittens I got a cigarette between my teeth, and thought of the children singing the sale of their meat scraps in the relatively peaceful cities. In my misery I mentioned to my captain what a pity it was that we couldn't enjoy the beneficent opium. He smoothed the dirt which was his bed, and said thoughtfully, "Opium is a climate." I got my back against that wall of tin and shook as hard as I could, for the real fun of it; my hands hurt, and my bones were grating. I remembered what Dr. Marchaud had told me once, in the snows of Alsace, about Galen's four cardinal signs of inflammation—Galen lived 1,900 years ago—Rubor, redness; Calor, heat; Tumor, swelling; and Dolor, pain. I was inflamed, and thoroughly, and I stuck out my tongue for a couple of raindrops, as the Mois and Radets, the most timid and the most savage people of Indo-China, came up the path to offer their allegiance to us.

I didn't want any kind of allegiance just now but the allegiance of my marrow to my malarial bones, and my bones to my skin which had been burned and infected and had disappeared from parts of me.

All I wanted was my own misery, neat. But they came in with obeisances, the Mois, the chiefs of our neighboring tribes, so we sat up in our blankets, dim-eyed, as Mekki put it, and damn near dead. They put down in a circle their enormous crocks of thin rice wine. In them, propped by the floor of rice at their bottoms, were straws from which we sucked in turn as much as champions should, while one of the chiefs replenished the crocks simultaneously from his stock of honest water, so that the level should remain the same. I was a champion sucker, because all the world did hurt me so.

Our interpreter told us at last that among our guests was a sorcerer, who had three times fought against the French. I had seen this old sorcerer's blue eyes behind the gold of the candlelight. They were good eyes, and his mouth moved sternly as he spoke for his fellow chieftains, telling us of his children who had fled his house of leaves to the school of the French, of the paddy fields where white men had made water grow.

Three times, he admitted, three times he had fought against the French, and cursed them expertly, and conjured demons to beset them. And what did the French do? They nourished his crops, with tricky tubes, and did I know any tricks which he could take back to his tribe, to convince them that the French were not merely good but artful? The French sorcery was good, he said—he took a suck at the tube—and the profit of this, as in any enterprise, should be divided between its agents.

I knew a trick or two, and produced them. My jumping coin jumped as it had in the Times Square magic shop for ten cents, and my sorcerer was so impressed that he gave me his own brass bracelet out of respect for the superior French sorcery. This was pretty good propaganda, so we both took a swizzle of the wine, watching each other cautiously, and then I showed him the shilling gadget I had bought in London many years ago. All the brown, earnest heads were bent across the jars toward the flame where my mechanism severed the steel throat of an image with a steel sword. All the heads returned quick to their wine, when they saw that the steel throat and the steel sword were both intact. Better propaganda than that for a shilling was not to be had. The sorcerer gave me his blanket, too.

268

25

The burning hands of jungle war—marriage again—French Guiana—Devil's Island

I DIDN'T KILL anybody in Indo-China, nor did I save the life of an enemy Vietminh soldier as he lay writhing with one of my companion's bullets through his guts, in a burning rubber plantation. Through the smoke and the flames I came howling to know where the companions were, and someone howled louder than I, this Vietminh shot below the belt. He was a little fellow, lying in a downy quilt of smoke. The rubber trees crackled with the bursting sap, and flames lashed above us like light in an opal. I leaned down to succor him or put a bullet through his head as might seem humanely best, when there was a gush of wind along the grass between the trees, and boiling liquid latex spurted across his face and my hands. We both screamed. I got my finger through the hole of the pistol trigger, but I couldn't pull it with the pain. The latex stuck like glue burning. Choking with smoke, I rubbed my hands on my pants and saw great patches of skin come off the raw meat which had barely recovered from the tropical infection.

That was the end of my war, with hospitalization and a new movement order from General Leclerc to the effect that I should be carried by plane across the world again, an *évacué sanitaire* to New York. Leclerc poked me in the stomach when he saw my bandaged hands and said, *"Bonjour, boxeur.* You've boxed enough. You're going home."

"But, *mon général,* I can't go home. I have no passport. The Americans tore it up."

"You are going home not as an American but as a French officer *en mission* to talk about the part of the Free French in this war. They can't refuse you. Bless you. Beat it."

So to Cairo I went again with those damned hands which the

269

French and the British had been able to do nothing to cure. Desperately I let a Greek doctor transfer blood from my arm to my bottom, and it did no good. My fingernails had sloughed off by now. I tried the Egyptian sorcerers, who treated my raw meat successively with tar, my own urine, and finally the night-long lapping of a dog. The sorcerer's assistant rubbed beefsteak on my raw meat and the dog licked it off as I dozed on a Cairo roof. It was no good. I was falling apart.

I had never thought of asking help from the Americans, but by chance I found the warm friendship of Colonel Patrick Welch, the very Irish chief of American Public Relations. He was a grand poet, and what bothered him most was not that my hands were painful but that they were useless on the typewriter. "Ye're a woeful sight to see, man," he said, when I'd read him the new poem written clumsily in pencil. "It drives me crazy with thirst to see you trying to get a glass to your lips, and smoking a cigarette between those paws is ungraceful. And your love life—if ye have the strength for it—must suffer. But your poetry must go on, b'Jasus. Ye're for the garbage can, unless I can get the American witch doctors to help ye."

He could and they did, with their antibiotics, and my skin came back like a rose petal, and in a month I was fit to fly again on my odd mission to America, a Free French officer of *Mayflower* vintage.

It was to Paris then that I went again, and on to New York by Air France, proud and virginal in my new skin. I got off the plane at LaGuardia Airport to find my mother awaiting me, chic and lithe and handsome as be-damned after these five years. And there was a girl with a Rolleiflex, obviously a professional, alternating her snaps between the French cabinet minister and me, of all people. She was pretty and blond, I noticed, but I was too much excited to see a dozen of my faithful correspondents to pay her attention.

It was next morning when I reported at the Free French Delegation that I ran into her again. She had a little swagger as she approached me, but her lips quivered and she was not at ease. Boldness and timidity were knotted within her. "I'm Ruth Staudinger," she said, in a voice slightly husky, and a timbre which made my dainty new skin crawl. "I work here, and we need a photograph of you." I had a date for lunch and I was late.

"Can't we do it another day?"

"We need it now," she said firmly. So she took it and I rushed away, puzzled because my skin was still creeping as I remembered her. This was inexplicable, because I couldn't bear blondes and had gone so far as to make myself unpopular with them by stating in print that they smelled like boiled milk.

I understand less of the matter now than I thought I did then. Sometime after her champion good photos were finished, and I had seen her frequently, I took a good sniff at her and she smelled like caramel and hot rum, and I began to realize at a pace that was vertiginous that this Ruth had everything I might want in a wife, not that I wanted a wife at all. She had beauty and culture and courage. She was orderly as I was not. Unlike me, she knew how much money she had in the bank. She was a superb photographer who could accompany me in the jungles. And she smelled like caramel and hot rum.

So I married her, to the surprise of both of us, and we sat wide-eyed across the table, wondering what the devil we were going to do now, particularly in regard to money. I leaned forward in my great book-lined room. "Could you learn to use a moving-picture camera?"

Gravely she nodded. "I've had a notion simmering," I said, "of an expedition to French Guiana for a book and a film. No one yet has gone from the coast to the Tumuc-Humac Mountains on the border of Brazil. It's rotten country, bad climate, bugs, disease, Indians who have never submitted to the French."

"I'm for it," said Ruth tranquilly. "Money?"

I was halfway up my dreams of the expedition by now. "A bagatelle! In a few weeks I'll have more royalties on *Half Past When* and I'll return to Paris to get demobilized, collect my pay, and the royalties on *Feu d'Afrique*. But first things first. I must finish these Free French lectures."

Never in my life had I been so happy. It was as though I was discovering not Ruth but myself. I moved in an electric trance, writing well, broadcasting with a verve I hadn't known for years. Ruth quietly

271

vitalized everything I did. I rushed to Washington to see Ambassador Bonnet and the French general for expedition permits in Guiana, freedom of customs, armed guard if need be.

Now love is a wondrous thing, but very confusing; it breeds love at a shocking rate. I loved all the world and laughed at that old jerk Death whom I had chased over dale and desert during the last five years. I loved every one of the five flights of steps which led to my farmhouse of an apartment at 226 Fifth Avenue. I loved the skylights enough to wash them at risk of life and limb. I loved the tropical fish in their tanks amid thousands of books; even the eel was dear to me, and the dogs, of course. I loved carpentry and cooking, of which I wrote articles for the gastronomic magazines.

Filled now with the power to work miracles, I flew to Paris for demobilization, but obtained permission from General Leclerc to wear my uniform with a captain's stripes—for prestige—among the Indians of South America. The Ministries of Health, Information, and Colonies gave me letters of recommendation to the Guianese authorities, as did UNESCO above the signature of Julian Huxley. I collected my army pay and the royalties on *Feu d'Afrique* and flew to New York and Ruth triumphantly.

We had dinner by candlelight, holding hands so hard it disturbed eating. The giant dog Snoozer, furthermore, was mostly on my lap. Ruth took a sip of Chianti, purple-gold with the candles' flame. "How did you do with money?"

"Fine, oh, just fine. I brought back over five hundred dollars!"

"Ouch," said Ruth. "I certainly married no businessman. Do you realize we'll need more than that for film alone? Darling, you don't belong in this world. How many francs did you get?"

Contritely, I told her. Ruth choked on a popover. "Divine idiot," she sputtered, "do you not realize that that makes five *thousand,* not five hundred, dollars? We're in business!"

The Explorers Club honored me with permission to carry the club's flag on the expedition. The New York Botanical Gardens and the Caribbean Commission backed us cordially. Pan American World Airways offered us free flight to Cayenne. The Quartermaster Corps

272

of the United States Army gave us a ton of equipment to test for jungle fighting. My mother's dear new husband gave us two Bell and Howell 16-mm. movie cameras. And too many companies to enumerate supplied us with more provisions than we could use, in exchange for eventual publicity—should we come back alive. I had not told them that the expedition previous to ours had consisted of fifty Frenchmen, of whom forty-nine were massacred by the Indians. But the insurance companies have their wily ways of information, and only one would take us—at 25 per cent more than the householder, whose life was more hazardous than ours.

We flew down in darkness to the only airport in French Guiana, and got a lift along a jungly road to Cayenne. At 10:15 P.M. there wasn't a light anywhere, not even in our Hôtel des Palmistes. Ruth, who sees in the dark, found a door, and we knocked up, as the British say, the ebon proprietor and walked upstairs with him over a number of ancient dogs.

The room, the ghost of mosquito netting, the moon through a latticed window, the mildew, the frowsty candle, the twitter of bats echoing through the roof of corrugated iron, the sweat in the eyes smarting, and the taste of it were curiously good again. The colonies I had lived in were blended of these. I was home again, in the dank discomfort which I loved.

It was my hope to pole and portage up the Maroni River, which separates French from British Guiana, into the territory of Inini, continuing along the Awa River into the Itany River and finally branching into one of the creeks, still going south, until we reached the fabulous Tumuc-Humac Mountains on the border of Brazil.

This long, low range, almost entirely unexplored, was once thought to be El Dorado, the legendary lost land of the golden cities and the lake called Parimé, where the Incan kings, fleeing from the brothers Pizarro, had built a tiny state. So very wealthy were they that each morning they dusted themselves with gold, and each evening washed it off in Lake Parimé. Sir Walter Raleigh, who had soiled his cloak and literally lost his head before the queen, was one of the earliest explorers in search of Manoa, El Dorado, the golden city.

My intentions were more modest. I merely wanted to study and record the customs of the Indians and the bush Negroes transplanted here. Lover of the world's fleshpots that I was, gourmand, miser, I should shy from Lake Parimé if ever I should see it blazing in the sun—said I to Ruth. We waited interminably in the flat, hot, jerry-built town of Cayenne, for our provisions were held up by a dock strike in Martinique.

As a further road block the territory of French Guiana was being converted to a department of France, the old governor leaving and the new prefect coming in. So also would an even greater upheaval, from our point of view, be coming in a few months from now, the torrential rainy season. We passed our time in gathering information about French Guiana's greatest claim to fame, Devil's Island, which is a misnomer for the bagne, the penal colony as a whole, consisting of Devil's Island, Royal Island, Saint Joseph Island, and four settlements on the mainland. Many stories have been written about Devil's Island, but none of the authors is on record as ever having put foot on the island itself.

Devil's Island never had a murderer, a guillotine, or more than twelve men on it. It was an island of the elite, a soft asylum for political prisoners such as Ullmo and Dreyfus, where they lived in quiet freedom. The island group is properly named Les Isles du Salut, the Islands of Health, in the days before the convicts came, when they were a place of repose for convalescents. Only because the entire penal colony was being closed were Ruth and I permitted as the first non-officials ever to visit Devil's Island itself.

Fifty-two thousand criminals in clown's clothing, striped pink and white, had passed through the bagne since its inauguration in 1854. Their paths were various; most of them died prematurely. Eighteen hundred libérés, freed prisoners, were still staggering around French Guiana as clerks and houseboys, and the wise ones knew they never would go home again. They hadn't the fare, and the physicians counseled them to stay in French Guiana with their thinned blood and to count their corpuscles like pearls.

Ruth and I were permitted three trips to Devil's Island, to film it, to prove to the world that it was abandoned now. Slowly and as on a

274

rocking horse we teetered over the waves which separated Cayenne from its dependencies fifty miles away.

We hove into port beneath the dark green hills of Royal Island. We backed and filled and came rushing giddily back to the quay of granite blocks at the foot of the terrible little hills where the prisoners had lived. No one was here now but the wardens and a few incorrigible murderers, who tended the lighthouse and the boats arriving. They waited for us at the quay, three lean men looking like all their fellows, with thin lips, high cheekbones, sunken eyes, and that glance over the shoulder. They helped us ashore without a smile.

Devil's Island lay before us across a strait about two hundred feet wide. It was very small, an oval island packed with palm trees.

"What's that thing there?" said I. Beside us on the rocky shore was an iron edifice of wheels and cogs. Directly opposite on the shore of Devil's Island was a similar structure.

"There used to be a cable running between the two to take provisions across and sometimes a man who was sick. It's a hell of a piece of water for a boat. Current for one thing, and sharks if you tip over," said Gouleau, our dark escort.

The job of greasing the cable, he said, was so dangerous that the convicts who volunteered to straddle it and slide back and forth along it with an oily rag were rewarded, when they didn't fall among the sharks, with two bottles of wine and three ounces of tobacco each.

"Here's our ship," said Gouleau. A heavy-timbered whaleboat came around the tip of Royal Island, sucked quietly and rapidly toward us by the current. Six men in striped uniforms were resting on their oars. Ruth and I got aboard gingerly with our camera wrapped in Pliofilm. The men grinned, spun us in a semicircle for the take-off, then bucked the current for half an hour until we came almost within grappling distance of Devil's Island, where the current outmaneuvered us and sent us slithering toward Trinidad. It was a straight pull now. The water gargled like a demon against our bow as we inched, millimetered, toward the platform of stones which was the dock.

"That, I think, is a shark," said Ruth.

It was; a dark blue sickle slipping effortlessly upcurrent. As plain as teeth and tide was the fact that escape from Devil's Island was nearly impossible.

275

Devil's Island was pretty close to the dream of that lush, green, outlandish island you had in childhood. We climbed the casual, gently winding road the convicts had built to the central ridge of the island, perhaps fifty feet above sea level, and looked the length of it across two rows of little stone prisons. They seemed more like country cottages now, with vines dangling before their open doors and the gardens of the former inmates still blooming unattended. It was a peaceful scene but for the square watchtower with its gun slots.

"That's Dreyfus's house behind you." Gouleau pointed.

"In its day," said Ruth, putting a filter on her lens, "it must have been a handsome villa." House hunters in Westchester, I thought, would pay a fortune for that snug little estate if it could be transplanted. A stone wall surrounded it, and within was a generous house of two rooms, one for Dreyfus and one for his personal military guardian, who amicably philosophized with him on the trials of being outcast, played chess with him, and took him on walks to the other end of the island, to sit respectfully beside him while he cut images in the rock to baffle scientists of a hundred years from now.

26 ~~~~~~~~~~~~~~~~~~

Haircut by a murderer
—leprosy is in flower

I REMINDED THE prefect that the rainy season would be on us in several months, and that our food from the good sponsors in America must come soon to be of use to us. We should have to leave without it otherwise, without any stocks at all except rice and beans, since Cayenne had nothing to furnish us.

The prefect yawned, slapped a hand on my pile of credentials, glanced at their signatures, and passed them to me with a sigh. "You have my permission to leave." The busy man stood up, obviously in dismissal of me.

"But look," I said, "doesn't it interest you that—" The letters which the French ministers had written had impressed me, and their interest in my examining their wilderness had made me hopeful of enthusiasm here, for there are three Guianas, the French, the Dutch, and the British side by side, nearly identical in resources. French Guiana lagged far behind the other two and was desperately in need of colonists and development, a situation which I could help with book and film. But the impression growing on us was that we were interlopers, that we were suspect here, maybe spies.

The next Tuesday was an exciting day, what with the bad butterflies swarming. The bad butterflies gave us the itch as swarms of them flew over Cayenne, dropping the barbed fuzz of their wings into our every pore. In the harbor lay a cocky contrived sort of vessel which would take us, deck passage, to Saint-Laurent. Saint-Laurent was on the Maroni River, the frontier between French and Dutch Guiana, our base for the long journey upriver by canoe to the mountains.

The mountains were terribly far away, we thought that afternoon as we repacked our baggage, stiffly, keeping a balance with the dysentery which beset us, and walking sedately, mincing, to the hospital for our shots of emetine and opium. Dysentery is too long a word to be chalked on public walls, but it is meaner than many another.

Next day we chugged into the Maroni River and limped ashore at Saint-Laurent, another penal settlement where we were imprisoned for weeks, while we tried to get paddlers for the expedition upriver.

Saint-Laurent was a shabby colonial town whose businesses were two: the gold which came from the territory of Inini and the convicts in the Camp de la Transportation. It was beaded with the most hopeful and most empty shops in the world, their shelves laden with vacuum and a little rum distilled by the industrious Sisters of the Order of Saint Joseph de Cluny. It was called by the natives "pee-pee ma soeur," but it had kept this benevolent mission living. As we had been obliged to start without our American provisions, we bought rice, flour, beans whenever we could. Fortunately the Pall Mall people had got a crate of cigarettes to us, for there were none to be bought in Saint-Laurent.

In vain I searched for a haircut until one day the director of prisons

277

took me into the prison itself and put me into the large hands of a convict barber who was eager to tell me the story of his innocence.

"Monsieur," said he, "it was no more than you would have done, if you had been a good husband and a professional barber." Snip-snip went his shears. "Caught the man *flagrante delicta,* as we say, with my old woman. He had the nerve to ask me for a haircut next day. Nobody but him and me in the shop, you see."

Snip-snip went the shears by my ears.

"So first I clopped him on the head with a bottle of lotion, just to make him sleepy, see? Then I gave him a harelip with the scissors, then I pulled his top eyelids out and snipped half-moons in them, then I notched his ears and made an ornament of his ugly nose. Then I hove him into the street, but how could I know that he was a bleeder? The cops jumped me just as I was applying the alum to save his life. . . ."

At last we had good news that some distance up the river there were canoes approaching—Boni canoes with paddlers, who, mysteriously, by the rumors of the river, had learned that we needed them. And on the same day we received our provisions from Borden's Milk Products and Dorset Foods, destined for jungle testing but wonderfully acceptable now. We drank cold milk made of Klim, and iced Borden's Instant Coffee with a dash of rum, and treated the more deserving of our friends, including lepers, to Dorset's meat stews.

Our spirits were so lifted again, with the assumption that we should soon be leaving Saint-Laurent, that we found quaint now many of its customs that had been abhorrent and downright diabolical before. Now we only smiled when we were awakened by the frantic church at the corner, knocking us out of bed with its insistent bells from five-thirty to six in the morning. It was no invitation to worship. It was furious, commanding, threatening hell to the sluggard—me—in bed. It was like a Chinese water torture, but these bell notes were of molten brass. And when the energetic padre next door marched his Boy Scouts back and forth before our house during our siesta, instructing them in the bitterer uses of the bugle, we just said philosophically, "Ah, but we'll be up the river soon. . . ."

Maurice Demougeot managed a profitable wood industry in a country where, literally, other colonists had been unable to see the wood for the trees. Intelligent, tolerant, he represented the perfect colonist. Gently he pulled the mosquito net from around us one sleepy morning and tickled us awake with a blade of grass.

"I was just dreaming," I yawned, "that you had sold two tons of the violet wood to the cabinetmakers in America."

"Sacred Beel!" he roared. "You are telepathic! I have within this hour sold twenty tons of *le bois violet* to your sacred country, and I am leaving immediately to make a small grateful gift to the leprosarium of Acarouany. Will you two sluggards get up and accompany me? Here is champagne, iced, and you will have to subsist on it till the journey's end."

His launch moved us slowly upriver, and the champagne bubbles in crystal glasses sparkled against the dark jungle trees which overhung us. Pink flamingos flew in wedges above our heads. Parrots yapped at us. Alligators splashed from the swampy banks. It was too good to be true; it was just like the films, I thought, although film could never have this blend of odors, the musk of the jungle, the electric ozone smell of rushing water, the scent of champagne, and your own good sweat. This was where I, once a little boy swinging on magnolia trees, belonged.

Suddenly there was a hush as the motor was turned off and we moved in under a canopy of foliage and a great cliff where a lost world might be. The water eddied around us and made no sound. It held its breath and slunk past the leprosarium of Acarouany, the lost world.

We climbed the many clay steps to the plateau, following an aged convict leper who bore a yoke on his back from which hung two five-gallon petrol tins of river water. We passed beneath the black arms of a wooden cross to enter an immaculate village where at first nothing seemed to move, although we could see figures standing, lying, sitting, in the blistering shade. Then they moved, as in slow-motion photography, around us. They were terrible cartoons of men and women, for some had no noses and some no ears. One Annamite boy danced crazily ahead of us, striking the stylized boxing postures which his Khmer ancestors had commemorated on the walls of Angkor Wat.

279

Like most of the others he had been sent as a convict to French Guiana, and had paid for his crime doubly by contracting leprosy here, but his spirit was unbroken; he punched fists without fingers at the bare sky and pranced on feet without toes. An old, old man crawled on his elbows and knees from his hut's doorway and spoke in thick words like bubbling porridge to the missionary, Father Izart. When he had had enough fingers to carve with, he had whittled a sign for his dwelling: 1916—*Pour La Vie.*

Ruth walked with Mother Geneviève and three of the extraordinary young nuns who were devoting their lives to the lepers here. There had been a fourth, but she had recently contracted the disease and lived in a leper hut like her charges.

The obstinacy of the human spirit, I had thought, was imbecile. The attitude of never admitting unquestionable defeat was a burden greater to those who served the hopelessly afflicted than their suffering was to themselves. But humbly I recanted at Acarouany, seeing the individual gardens behind the huts, hearing a phonograph, visiting the barbershop run by a fairly whole leper, who encouraged a healthy vanity among his clientele. And there was a multiple murderer returning from the hunt with a deer which he would share with all the village. The cornea of his eye was like a tiny cesspool leaking from a rotted brain, and his nostrils were like a baboon's, uptilted, one of the most evident signs of leprosy, which is now politely called Hansen's disease. And there was the gay old lady with cheeks rouged by some vegetable dye, but without hands, who graciously shook her head in refusal of the flowers I picked for her, saying cryptically, "Thank you, monsieur, but I am still in flower."

27

Jungle honeymoon—"territoire inconnu"—the matriarchs of Apatou—Raphael, our convict cook

I WAS RATHER embarrassed before Ruth because I hadn't yet produced a going expedition to confirm my bold talk of a venturesome past. The explorer discovers a great deal to be lived up to on his honeymoon. Here were the great cases packed high on the veranda beside us. The shotgun—the pistol—the Holderness Underwater Aqua-Gun—all were clean and oiled, though probably disappointing as armament to one accustomed to movie expeditions. Nor were there pith helmets or high boots, those encumbrances to exploration in the last century.

It was like the war. We had remained packed and ready for the alert, as though we were in trench holes, waiting for the arrival of the Bonis and their canoes, which had last been seen near Portal Island. On the night of our liberation from the penal colony, dogs howled at the moon, arbitrary cocks began crowing at 3:00 A.M., and the alarm of the church bells exploded while we still lay wet and dreamless and panting in the dark.

Mohammed, our Algerian former convict cook, wandered around our mosquito netting till he found one of my toes which he jerked with his strangler's hand. "The Bonis have come," he said in his deep zombie voice, "and I have started the porters with the baggage to the river."

On this sweltering morning the three of us marched somewhat grumpily ahead of our column of convict-drawn carts, lent by the administration and laden with mountains of equipment for the five and a half months we were to spend in the bush. Three months of these were to be without contact even with the upriver traders, since there was a huge gap between the last Boni village and the true wilderness where the nomadic Indians might or might not be. We should have and send no mail. We should have to keep our film with us, preserved as well as we could against one of the world's worst climates. We would have no radio, as ours hadn't arrived in time. The world couldn't reach us, nor could we reach it as we plugged up the river which had killed at least one man of every expedition which had gone even two thirds of the way toward our goal, the Tumuc-Humac Mountains.

I could scarcely believe it, but we were off, "into the unknown" as the "intrepid" say, each of us—Ruth, I, and the cook Mohammed—in his twenty-seven-foot dugout canoe with a thatched shack at the stern. There was barely room to turn around in this pomekari, but it was a cordial home beneath the sun. Suspended handily from leather thongs were my cameras, notebooks, cigarettes, charts, and my miniature armament.

The black Bonis who paddled us would become as interesting to me as the Indians we should meet later, for they were unadulterated African Negroes, descendants of the thirty thousand or so slaves dragged to the New World. Many escaped from the plantations of the three Guianas and the Caribbean Islands. At home in the bush, which was almost identical with their African homeland, they waged war successfully against the Dutch, freeing their fellow slaves and exhorting others to join them, until in the latter part of the eighteenth century the white men sued for peace. The treaty, which is still effective, was dictated by the blacks—or Djukas, as they called themselves—giving them freedom from all colonial laws, a sovereign country of their own in the forest, and a substantial annual monetary tribute from the Dutch forever after. Dr. Morton Kahn has pointed out that this reversal of white exploitation is probably unique in the world today.

Our Bonis of the French Guiana were almost exclusively rivermen, and sociologically inferior to their Djuka cousins across the river in Dutch Guiana. There was little heart in them, and no ambition. Their art was narrowed to the intricate braiding of hair, the exterior decoration of their huts, and the fine phallic engraving on the interior of their womblike calabashes. Their music was paltry tom-tom, too tired even for the discipline of rhythm.

282

During that afternoon I had felt that there was something wrong with Eimo, Ruth's bow paddler. There was a certain look in his eye and he was sweating more than normally and brandishing his long pole rather than swinging it. And from time to time he had thrown out his chest, bared his teeth to the sun, and chattered, "Zig-azig-azig! Zig-azig-azig! Zig-azig-azig!" a tuning up of his one-man orchestra for a feat of song which should have made the baboon quail. We could understand enough of the Boni language by now to know that his lyric was not complimentary to the black man's burden—which was Ruth and I.

Now at the landing of Apatou he bared his white teeth and screamed, "Eiiiiiiiiiii-mo!" announcing his male presence, and we drew into the clay steps of the riverbank and climbed them, ducking beneath the fringe of palm fronds, called azang pau, which was suspended over the path to brush the demons from us. We looked boldly up the long wooden nose and into the eyes of the Aflamu idol, which was there to intimidate the likes of just such as us—and these were the same eyes, undercut, cavernous, that I had seen in many West African fetishes.

It was pure Africa we were entering in South America, even purer than the Africa of today, which has changed in many ways under Arab and European influences. The decadent Bonis, never refreshed by evolving cultures outside their inbred group, still built huts which were duplicates of those of their ancestors on the Ivory Coast. The amulets, or grigris, hung in little sacks from their necks, were straight survivals, and the tattooing by irritated cicatrization, particularly the nubile tattooing on the belly, was the same as that affected by the Gold Coast slaves who were once called Coromantis. "Coromanti" is still in use as the name of a ghost which is seen in the forest, among the flange-like roots of the fromager trees. It resembles a bubble about three feet across, and explodes around anyone who touches it, driving him mad.

Moima, the matriarch or woman chief of Apatou, greeted Ruth warmly and was rather cool to me and the mere Boni males. She was a champion old suffragette with close-cropped gray hair. As in other matriarchal villages, we noticed that hers was remarkable for its

283

cleanliness, its gardens or abbatis, and the architecture of its thatched wooden huts which were invariably of two windowless rooms sealed by hand-sawn boards against the demons.

In such a matriarchate the women usually rule better than the men in the patriarchal villages. The woman chief has her corps of female councilors, and matters of general policy are decided by them. Men serve as functionaries in the production of children and crops. Warriors have not been needed for many years.

As among other members of the race generically called Djuka, descent is traced through the female line, not through the husband, the nominal father of the mother's children. Inheritance is matrilinear, through the mother's oldest male relative.

Mohammed, our cook, became the meagerest of us males when he had finished a bottle of my rum and had started testing the demon bottles around the matriarchs' doorsteps. The goblins would get him, these wise women said. They had done so already and long ago.

On one side of us the women were pressing out the poison of manioc, pure prussic acid, by squeezing it through wicker tubes, then soaking the pulp and drying it to make cassava, cuac, and tapioca. Youngsters were carrying younger youngsters on their backs, in the African way, not on their hips as the Indians do. Old men were thinking together and snuffing a liquid snuff brewed of rum, tobacco, and pepper. Young men stood upon a rock patient as a frieze, their bows and arrows poised over the dark river where the coumalu swam.

An old woman was bent far down to the little broom with which she swept the village immaculate, and another matriarch, in a slot of the jungle behind our hut, in a mottled shaft of sunset, was putting clay heads upon the bamboo platform of an altar beside a pot of ruddy liquid fenced with blood-red spears. This boded no good for her enemies, probably male. But there was a third woman following her, black and beautiful, not a matriarch yet, still wearing her nakedness haughtily beyond the deadline where a G-string, the calambé, should cover her maturity; she had come to the sacred grove to suspend her dream boats, hollow crescents of clay wherein her dreams might voyage to the dreams of her beloved.

Ruth and I sat quietly before the hut and made friends with the children, and talked as well as we could with their very self-sufficient mothers. They brought gifts to us, pot stirrers of wood called kabu, and the lavender necklaces called nyoké, to ward off illness, which surely were strung with the same seeds as those of the Middle East.

We sprayed the little heads with Aerosol and became magicians immediately. For Ruth, whom they called "Papa," as they called the queen matriarch "Granman," the mothers danced a gentlewomen's dance, sitting on their tiny individual stools, flicking palm to elbow and elbow to palm rhythmically with rich clopping sounds, tossing for inflection their bakelite bosoms and chanting.

The song stopped short, truncated. We could hear the insects metallically singing like music boxes. The red howler monkeys broke that pause in a rising roar across the horizon.

Eimo, slung in his hammock beside our hut, came awake. His voice rose, steaming and jerking, as though his river, the male Maroni, were tumbling backward up the falls. The matriarchs of Apatou picked up their stools, slung their babies, and walked sedately away, with merely a nod to Papa Ruth, while Eimo howled like an ape at God. Eimo's was the last word, a noise in the night with no love in it, and his echo suddenly was a whisper of hammocks swinging empty in a rainy wind.

For days now we poled along stretches of the river which were thorny with rapids, walled with immaculate timber, but quasi-civilized. Canoes spurted past us and the naked Bonis or Boschs in them would salute us with tremendous cardboard helmets which they had painted and silvered in the same deviously phallic designs which made all their woodcarving remarkable. And women and children alone would scoot suddenly over a wave and past us, in minute canoes, steering with token paddles.

In the morning we perceived that nothing on this river ever changed, neither life nor death; it was a fusion of them. The hush of its pools and the roar of its rapids mingled together, as sleep and waking did. You could neither hear nor ignore the yawn of it: not quite sound, not quite silence. The butterflies flew uncertainly. At night the old monkeys howled. The sun was never hot enough to make you sweat

285

with gusto. The bugs were languid. Nothing was absolute in French Guiana.

This was bad river, the boys said, but they said it on shore, with their backs to it, lest the water-god, the serpent, should hear them. "And farther along?" I asked, as the canoes edged into the white waves.

"*Anaboon!*" they said cheerfully. That was "bad," too. My rough map of the country confirmed it; there was a saut, or rapids, every quarter inch for the next two feet of map.

Slowly the long poles of the bowmen led us through secret paths of foam. The sound of a Pan American plane, so high as to be invisible, shuddered in the sky. The passengers were probably being served their prefabricated luncheons now, by natty little hostesses in high-heeled shoes. And I leaned back contentedly, for a moment between rapids, and blessed my great uncomfortable world.

We rounded the bend before the Saut Singa Teté, a brute of a falls, unloaded the canoes, and hauled them by immense vines across the spurting rocks. We moved into a bistouri, a by-pass, arcaded and curtained with vines and vegetable parasites. The sunlight caught us like a golden fist again and tore us from our smooth water to the rapids above the falls, where we saw what is called a mountain in those parts, Mount Lebidoti, about a thousand feet high. The Bonis cheered, for this was true Boni country at last, no matriarchs in it.

You could feel, at this hour, the tiring of the boys, and knew it to be almost exactly four o'clock, whether or not the day's march had been harder than usual. In their business of transporting traders along the river, particularly the Dutch, they were accustomed to business hours, from six to four, and we were therefore unsettling in that we liked to work later than four to get the opaline twilight shots; to sit up late at night, reading or discussing what a fine thing anything was; and to get up only when there was no more sleep in us at all.

Afokati would sigh a sigh to produce an echo and gently urge his companions to bear with the bakra, the white man, until we found a village toward the setting of the sun. He was a patrician with a finer tolerance of other people's caprices or convictions than any of the bakra he bore to their destinations. He was a sterling gentleman, and I was often ashamed before him.

286

Ruth called across the space separating our canoes, in her rich voice, *"Zumba-zumba,* Afokati," asking him to go slowly here, for she had her camera against her cheek.

"Pardonnez-moi! Madame! Excusez-moi!" It was continually startling to discover that the choice of French phrases he had learned had been those of courtesy and gallantry, among perhaps a hundred words which were his entire vocabulary.

We came to Wacapou, which was to be our last village where people wore clothes, on a rainy evening, approaching it where the river widened and pressed its currents taut against the shores.

Ruth, in her canoe just beside me, shook her golden hair and the dark curls of sleep from her eyes. "I am not," said she, "speaking to anyone this afternoon. Or only in baby talk. Soul's gone. Up toward the bow, I think. Waddles like a duck."

"Hey? Hey?" I asked solicitously.

Wacapou was a single line of huts along the riverbank, and the only available lodging space was occupied by two gendarmes and their convict cook, but as their quarters were more than large enough we accepted their invitation and moved into a part of the house which had once been a store. From the doorway of it that evening we were filming the Tululu festival of masked dancers when a heavy hand was laid on my shoulder with the sort of touch which even the innocent can recognize as the hand of the law. It was Ferdinand, a square spare lad, one of the gendarmes, our hosts, clad in khaki shorts, muscle-fitting shirt, and pith helmet pulled low over the brows.

"Quick!" said he. "You have quinine, yes?"

I moved him politely out of the way of Ruth's camera, saying, "Yes."

"It is Jacques, my companion, the other gendarme. Malaria, and I think blackwater fever now. The black bloody urine is all over his bed."

In the brown darkness of one of the inner rooms of our rambling shack lay the captain who had led young Ferdinand upriver in search of escaped convicts. He was emaciated. His bed was drenched with red-black fluid. We turned him over, shot him full of quinine, and stumbled over the legs of the moaning figure on the floor.

287

This was Raphael, their faithful servitor of the moment, escaped convict and cook, whom they had brought back with them from the village of Mademoiselle Victoire, a little farther south, where he had been preparing escape to the Dutch shore. When the sick gendarme groaned, he groaned, too, and Ruth and I were touched by his sympathy. We looked at each other and understood each other without words: could we induce the gendarmes to take Mohammed back to the prisons, exchanging him for Raphael, who should cook for us and be sympathetic and devoted to us?

"Hah!" said Ferdinand, as we sat at the raw wood table outside the sick man's door. "It is agreed. You may have him. You may bring him back alive, or shoot the pig." We had a drink out of dirty tumblers.

Our gendarmes really didn't care whom they brought back alive, so they took our quite incompetent Mohammed with them to Saint-Laurent, leaving Raphael to replace him. It was a bad gamble; as a cook he was as hopeless as Mohammed and, being brighter than Mohammed, he was more dangerous. As an officer I could of course shoot him.

28

We learn of the fearsome Oyaricou-
lets and meet the Roucouyennes—
love with five feet—father has a child

ON THE MORNING OF departure an old missionary arrived from a year's labor upriver, and squinted at Raphael with an appraising eye. "Wasn't it you," he asked, "who kicked the cat at Toto village?" He asked us of our journey, and we asked him of the Indians whom he had not noticeably converted. He sighed, standing by our canoes, eating sardines from a tin. One of them escaped to lodge shimmering in his beard.

288

"My children, I bless you," he said, raising his hand above the canoes. "You are going to a land which I want never to visit again. Though the Roucouyennes are gentle people, you must distrust them; they are covetous. If you meet a band of them who perhaps have not seen me or other whites before, it is possible that they might not prevent your receiving an injury, an upset in the rapids, perhaps, so that they might get your goods without actually attacking you."

He leaned back against a short crucifix on the bank. It was not a Christian but a Boni device, with rags of someone's ancestor moldering on it. "If you go far enough you will witness disturbing things. There are men among them who are telepathic. A few years ago I met an Indian who was fishing far down-river from his village. He couldn't possibly have known that I would be there. We exchanged presents of food, and as his canoe drew away he said, 'My daughter will be waiting for you on the sandspit.' And three weeks later, there she was, waiting at twilight on the only sandspit for miles around."

The padre took off his helmet and rivers of sweat ran into his beard, washing out the sardine.

"It will be cool in the creeks," he said, "beneath the great trees which are God's, and there you will hear voices, I think, but they will not be God's voices. They will be the evil tongues of Indians you will never see; at least I hope you may never see them."

"Oh?" said Raphael, blinking.

"What's the name of this tribe, Father?" I asked, also blinking.

"They are the Oyaricoulets. Coudreau has mentioned them, and one other man. You have heard of him. It was he who came back, the only one of the party of fifty who had gone to survey the western Tumuc-Humacs. He had slept in a tree because he was afraid of snakes. So the Indians missed him. He wrote in his report to the governor that for weeks his party had heard the voices in the bush around them, and from time to time they had found a white ball of kapok on a stick, which is a peaceful sign. It was the night after they saw the red ball, and ignored it, that the massacre occurred."

"Oh?" said Ruth.

"Oh!" said Raphael firmly. I judged that he had some antipathy to the Oyaricoulets.

One of the virtues of this expedition was that there was little time

289

on it either for regret or anticipation, and it became increasingly evident that we must distract Raphael from both. That, for the most part, we succeeded in doing. With ruse and shock we learned to shadow these two thirds of his life, but the present, the current third, was a bitch in the manger to us. I think we managed to ease the pain of his memories and his prospects, and in effect he said to hell with them, but it was his sharp, aching, actual every moment that tortured him.

By the end of the first day with Raphael on the river we knew we had with us a complex of prima donna and problem child. Somehow we were never very much aware of the tried and true assassin in him, and this was fortunate for us who came to doubt the loyalty of our paddlers, distrust our Indian guides, and suspect the twisted shadows behind the trees which were God's.

We paddle-slugged out of the Maroni River and into the Awa, which was a bit narrower with the divergences, called bistouris, forking around little islands lashed one to another by tree creepers, vines which couldn't possibly cross the water, but did. Amphibious serpents pulled them, said our Bonis, and attached them to the opposite trees so they could cross without getting wet.

Suddenly this was the jungle of the old books which teased my childhood, those quartos full of rich engravings showing men no bigger than insects against torrential cataract and towering forest. And here really was the toy canoe awaiting us beneath a bow that arched like a plume; and it held live Indians.

I was nearly as happy as when reading about them long ago. I looked back at Ruth, but her emotions were as usual tied to the practical business of photography; as I made a gesture without words to Afokati to move our canoe slowly toward the Indians, I saw that Ruth had maneuvered hers so that the light fell on a good angle shot of our meeting.

The Indians were blasé about it. They were painted a brilliant vermilion, and upon the long black hair which hung to their shoulders they wore red and orange coronets of woven feathers, placed squarely, as serious Caucasians wear their hats. I made an adjustment to mine. The bow Indian said a guttural, "Haliki!" which meant "Come here and listen," so I was later to learn, and Afokati said "Yepeh!" which meant "Friend." I reached out my hand and my fingertips were taken by the rear Indian, who seemed to know something of what a handshake was. Afokati introduced him.

His name was Malfatti, a Roucouyenne; he had been the guide of the geographer, Richard. The other Indians had not seen white men before, but were not hesitant in accepting the half calabash of taffia I offered them, while by the magician's art of misdirection I managed to pour Three Star Hennessey into my own.

Malfatti fished around in the bilge water of his canoe and presented me with a half-drowned bird, its legs tied together, which I couldn't imagine what to do with, as it seemed neither nutritive nor decorative; and I gave him a sort of chauffeur's cap, which he dropped carelessly into the bilge. We were beginning to understand each other already.

They took the lead with their fine canoe of overlapping, two-colored woods, and we wove through the spatter of islands at the juncture of the Aoua, the Itany, and the Marouini rivers. Among these islands, slipping from one to another and back again, they had for generations fought off the enemy tribes of Jamares, Oyampis, and the blond and long-eared Oyaricoulets.

Just beyond, on the French bank, we came to the nomad village which for a week or a month or a year was Malfatti's, depending upon the pressure of other migratory Roucouyennes from the jungle behind. It was because these people were migratory and "changed waters" often that few had chanced to meet the very rare white travelers.

Negroes and Mongols react in quite different ways to the first appearance of a European. The Negroes either flee their villages or go into ecstasies of welcome or both, whereas Indians of our hemisphere and Asiatic Mongols show no slightest sign either of fear or wonder. I had visited small villages in Nepal, deep in the Himalayas, where the likes of me had not only never been seen but not even heard of in legend, and the realistic Newars had simply accepted me, somewhat to my disappointment, as they would the arrival of an albino in fancy dress. I was just a blemished and benighted person whose ways weren't theirs, that was all, and so I was best ignored.

This was our experience among the Roucouyennes. We were

classically welcomed by a troupe of braves rushing out and shooting enormous arrows straight into the sky, and so straight they flew that the Indians had to step aside when they returned to earth. This gesture of welcome, common among Indians, has been interpreted as an offer to shoot even the sun for the visitors' delectation.

We then were led to the largest of the conical thatched huts and left to our own devices. It probably was the explorer Patrice, he who left his dactylo or stenographer with the Indians, who first saw the Roucouyennes. Crevaux points out that their own name for themselves was Ouayanes, from which perhaps the word Guiana is derived, to which was added the prefix Roucou, the name of the berry they used to stain their bodies red. That custom, they were to explain to me, served three purposes: it made them beautiful, it protected them from insect bites, and it prevented sunstroke, which was rather doubtful considering the brilliance of the red dye.

The early explorers of the nineteenth century, Crevaux and Coudreau, reported the presence or the alleged presence of other Indian tribes on the upper Awa and Itany rivers, but they were neither seen by us nor by that infinitely more capable observer, Captain Richard. On the French side were the Emerillons, the Jamares of the long ears, and the Oyampis, who at one time nearly decimated the Roucouyennes. On the Dutch shore were Yapocoyes, Comayanas, and the fabulous race of white Indians with blue eyes and blond beards called Oyaricoulets—descendants, perhaps, of the diligent dactylo.

These, with the Galibis of the coast, the few Arawaks and lesser tribes, Coudreau estimated to number fifty thousand in 1877. Coeval estimates pare this down to twenty thousand, and I doubt that now, judging by the reports of gold seekers in the bush, there are more than two thousand Indians in all French and Dutch Guiana, unless there should be a secret city of them, maybe El Dorado, somewhere in the uncharted wilderness west of the upper Oyapock River.

The younger folk turned in early as we did. The elders sat around the embers, drew doodles in the sand, and talked. Almost nothing ever happened. Many a traveler would have been impatient with such a placid life; he would have organized a dance and paid for it. It was the way of those Roucouyennes, their normal way of living, which

292

I found of interest. We were to see a dance, in their own good time, when we came down-river, but it was nothing specially done for us.

The bed manners of savages, or hammock manners, were a matter of intense concern to us as we slept amid them or tried to sleep while the invisible orgy pulsed around and above us. Wearing exotic pajamas Ruth had whipped up on a Chinese sewing machine, and tossing on the striped sheets she had confected brilliantly with elastic loops to hold them on the cots, we looked up at the dozen Indian hammocks slung variously from the cross timbers of our hut. All were hooded with a homespun material, barely porous, to keep out the mosquitoes as well as the gaze of earnest students like ourselves. Roughly they were of three sorts: the double hammock in which older husbands and wives slept crosswise; the single hammock in which children slept, sometimes three together, diagonally, their pert faces defying the mosquitoes outside and their long hair streaming down; and the hammocks of the young mixed couples and the homosexuals.

None of them were ever still. Through the cloth we would see the quick movement of Mama's fist as she scratched her old man's back, or the sly movements of fiancés. It was as good as counting sheep to count the imprints of feet in the hammocks, then close our eyes to sleepily review them; then, if that didn't work, to look up again and count them again in their changed positions. We would lie peacefully, sucking the little breeze through our nylon net, listening to the teo birds. Raphael, drowsing drunk at the foot of our cots to guard our privacy, started up once and shook us, "Capitaine, do you see what I see? In the hammock over there? *Five feet!* Count them!"

"Now! Now!" said Ruth, lighting a cigarette. There were five feet, all right, only one of them upside down, and whenever we wakened that night there were still five feet, although in different positions; and thereafter none of us drank cachiri wine.

Thus we slept, or tried to, on the hot nights among the Roucouyennes, during the pregnancy of the rains. I would waken panting, my arms spread wide against an air that was almost palpable, confining an urgent rain. And I would sit up in terror of the knowledge

293

that our work was far from finished, that the Tumuc-Humacs were far away, that the great rains were soon to burst upon us, that our film was perhaps half done, and whether this was good or bad we still didn't know, for there it was beneath our cots, dried in the desiccant silica gel and cooled by damp cloths around its airtight tins. There was no way to send it back for development; we had to keep it with us all these months and trust that it would come out well.

Knowing Ruth's quiet competence to deal with anything photographic, or anything at all, I could say blindly, Yes, it will be all right, unless a canoe capsizes or the film is carelessly left in the sun. And I would turn, assured, to watch her sleep and look above her at the little gray bodies suspended like moldy cheeses from the thatch: the vampire bats churning their courage to brave the light of the India oil lamp and descend upon us. One would let go, drop, straighten, veer toward a hammock, and flip back to the thatch again, a test flight. Before dawn they would be whirling around us on wings of stinking velours, and if your toe or hand should touch the mosquito netting, and you asleep, you would waken to the "pit-pit-pit" upon the ground of your own blood.

The noise of what Ruth thought was labor pains came from the hut of an old Indian who was rolling in his hammock with a raw baby clutched to his sinewy breast. This was the odd custom known as couvade, which was common in Pharaonic Egypt and is practiced by many Indian tribes in South America. The mother bears the baby right enough, but it is the father who takes to his hammock and groans as if the pangs of birth were his, and must convalesce, furthermore, for a month after his baby is born, abstaining from wine and intercourse, and eating lightly.

The mother rests for a little while in her hammock, too. She is comforted by a steam bath. A fire is built under her hammock, a pot of water is put on it, and the steam rises directly to her loins. There is not much time for such self-indulgence, however. Someone must chop the wood and do the gardening and prepare the little dishes that Father likes. He meanwhile lies languid, the baby cuddled to him, and receives visits of congratulation on the fine job he has done.

There is always a scene when Mother takes the baby from the dry breast to nurse it at her own. You can see the worry in Father's face, his concern that Mother, in her well-meaning but clumsy way, might not hold the darling right, or might drop it on its head. If it is a boy child, Father makes a game of bellowing for meat, and when his warrior friends bring it to him, he pretends to stuff it down the throat of his heir, until Mother takes it away again.

Being a father among the Roucouyennes is quite a trial.

29 ~~~~~~~~~~~~~~~~~~~

Mutiny begins—we reach El Dorado—the sinister white balls —and the red one—revolt

OCTOBER WAS HERE AGAIN, October lay again on the river, a yellow effluence, a golden pounding sunlight which you knew anywhere in this latitude to be the precursor of the rains. The trees were quiet and you saw scintillations around them that were heat and the souls of trees escaping to the river again. Parched and sober as October were the trees. As were we, paddling, portaging, hauling, day after day with both the Bonis and the Indians I had employed as guides, stupidly having paid them in advance with cloth, cutlery, sandpaper, mirrors.

Camped beneath a roof of thatch, Ruth would check her cameras and curl in her cot exhausted, and I would sit up for a while with my notes, but mainly to watch Ruth with the wonderful ache in me that was my love for her, and sometimes I would hear the incredible but actual singing serpent, the anaconda. It was a whooing, whiffling sound which the natives maintained was the voice of their snake-god. It was a high, sweet voice with such an urgency of desire as Adam must have heard in a world scarcely more primeval than this. It was evil. The red howler monkey which usually lulled us with his chanting would quieten before the voice of the "boa" and be small in his top leaves.

It was in approaching the Alama River, a confluent of the Itany, that the first signs of mutiny became known to us. I had started some time ago to prepare our rivermen for the work they would have to do when we came to the end of water, the end of the creek which we would take through the mountains to the Brazilian frontier, when they would have to walk on their feet and carry baggage. This lacked appeal to both Indians and Bonis. Afokati made me a life-sized drawing in the sand of the little load which he, a riverman, could carry on his back when obliged to use feet for transport, and Malfatti, our Indian chief, gave us an example of how he was going to run ahead of us when we should take to the woods. Like this, he yelled, and we looked up to see him running in the strange way that these Indians have, erect, head high, crooked elbows moving like pistons by his ribs.

We were very firm. We explained again that we didn't run like that and that also we couldn't see much if we did. We had to see much, we said. I was opening the jerry can beneath me when I saw behind us, in our hut of palm fronds, another sign of dissidence: the occupation of Raphael.

"What is that thing?" I asked Raphael, pointing to the stick in his hands. He had wound on it what at first I had thought was our nylon cord, a ball a foot thick. I went over to him and he smirked at me. It wasn't cord; it was spaghetti, cooked, wound round and round the stock like a fisherman's line.

Ruth admired the pattern of its winding. "But what is it for?" she asked amiably.

"For the escape," he replied as to a child. "I've had enough of it, both the prison and this river where we'll get our heads cut off. You can come with me if you want. I've made enough spaghetti for three."

We had taken no tents with us. A tent in the jungle is as silly as a sun helmet. The slight air is baffled by it; insects seek its refuge; and in the Bad Lands such as ours, in these Tumac-Humacs of glamorous and evil legend, the tent was a trap. So each night the Bonis built

296

for us a house of fronds, and after dinner we received. The Bonis came first for their shot of taffia, then the Indians joined them to watch me practice my legerdemain, a form of solitaire which improves with audience participation even if it goes wrong.

The soft, grinning sausages of Malfatti's lips should have warned me one night when out of the dark he, in turn, produced egg after egg, iguana eggs, a rarity, and a fine gesture for a recent mutineer. We went to sleep talking of the good, the reformed Malfatti, and in the morning sat around the breakfast fire eagerly while Raphael broke egg after egg into the skillet, and flung each one over his shoulder at the rising sun, until I stopped him at the ninth. That egg like the others contained a baby iguana which had been on the verge of birth and was warmed to wiggling life in our frying pan.

"I would take a dim view of that so-called gesture," I said to Ruth, "and I will reproach Malfatti for it, if I wanted to spoil the joy of the morning."

"What joy?" she asked.

"The joy, darling, of seeing my first Tumuc-Humac. Look. That." A few miles up the river and seeming to block it was a gray-and-green rounded mountain, the Knopoyamoye, said our guides. In the Andes it would have been called a hill, but it had dignity here, though without much allure. It was like a hunchbacked footman before the estate of El Dorado where lived the noble peaks of Timotakem and Temomairem. Narrowly we saw before us our El Dorado, and the legend's end.

Once we camped above the river, on a bank of clay. The Indians at their fire were whispering among themselves, and the Bonis at their fire were whispering also. Our Raphael was no whisperer, thief and murderer though he might be, so Raphael said aloud, "Those parts-of-female-genitalia who are traveling with us and watching us from the shore seem particularly cheerful tonight."

We listened. Surely not more than thirty feet away from us in the dark there were men talking, but I had tried before to rush them, and tripped on roots, as I fell with their laughter gurgling another thirty feet away.

By morning we had still not slept very much. When the sleep was shaken from us we still heard voices, still gay. We took to the canoes, rounded an amphibious tree which held beans three feet long above our heads, and with a twist of canoes to left, then to right, went straight into the woods, into the thin vein which was our creek, the Ouaremapan. We insinuated ourselves another hundred feet and stopped in a clear space of water. The gushing of red sunlit water still came from the paddles which had abruptly arrested us. No one spoke, or looked from left to right, or made any gesture. There was suddenly not a sound from our neighbors in the woods, while I, also quietly, was looking around for the reason for this strange stop.

Nobody but I looked at it, when I found it at last. I whistled to Ruth, and she and Raphael did look. It was a ball of white kapok, about six inches in diameter, on the end of a four-foot stick planted in the southern bank of the stream. The glaring white of it was shocking against the green. It hurt the eyes. It was as flagrant as a scream in the dark.

And yet I was relieved to come upon it at last, as evidence of the intentions of our invisible hosts, and confirmation of the honesty reported by Coudreau. There should be, from time to time, a white ball as signal that strangers might continue in the country of the Oyaricoulets. Whereas a red ball, such as the one which had caused the massacre of the party of forty-nine Frenchmen, meant distinctly that one should go no farther.

"That's clear enough for my taste," said Ruth, as we backed up our canoes to film the Indian sign. "But why do they leave a white ball permitting you to go on, if they won't even talk to you, or come out to trade?"

"Name of God!" said Raphael, closing one eye, grinning, nodding knowingly. "Madame cannot be so naïve. They will lead us up the garden path with their damned white balls, like they did the other party, to murder us when they're tired of your pretty face." He doffed his straw hat gallantly. "That should take some time, madame."

The only answer that I could guess at was a village somewhere farther along this creek Ouaremapan, which might be interested in trading with us, or at least in regarding us as a diversion. According

298

to the tales we had heard there should be several white balls after the first one.

Now because we were far away in a land that wanted none of us, and because no one—neither among our Bonis nor our Roucouyennes —was on our side now, we took some pains to make Raphael understand that he was our friend, that I should do my best to get him pardoned when we returned to Saint-Laurent. But it was no use. When I offered him one of the rare sausages from my own plate he had fits again: we treated him like a dog, flinging our ordure at him. It became plain that, should we have active trouble with Indians, Raphael would take to the woods.

What he would do there was beyond my imagining, for the woods were cavernous and hostile. Even our creek was a tunnel lighted by speckles through the filigree of branches and leaves. Unseamed huge rocks rose in a wall to form the fundament of the mountain on our right; on our left was impenetrable liana; beneath us was a maculate water of black and gold where long-legged insects floated; in front of us there was always a log.

The log would be a tree from thirty to fifty feet long, fallen athwart the stream, and impossible to move. The Indians would throw up their hands; but the Bonis would chop valiantly and in an hour or so we would have a tunnel made which permitted the passage of our canoes for another few yards, to another barrier, two feet thick, of fine hardwood, much prized by cabinetmakers. Sometimes we made a distance of half a mile a day, hacking and hauling, sliding under snarls of branches as we lay flat with our dear cameras in the wet bottoms of the canoes, or seesawing them over half-sunken logs which were impossible to cut.

"Good going," Ruth said often, with complete sincerity, to cheer my morale, while we lay on our backs in the cool stream at night.

"Brazil," said I, "can't be more than three hundred logs away."

We could hear the angry jabber of our Indians, and when they quieted we could hear the equally ugly mutter of the Bonis, and when they, too, were silent we could listen to the soft voices of the invisible Oyaricoulets in the forest.

There was a mountain on our right, to the west. I learned that it was Mount Ga Mongo, unlisted on my maps. We should go up it, said Malfatti, and look into Brazil. While I was considering this, I was also covering the soles of my bare feet and the bottoms of my toes with adhesive tape. This I did craftily and unseen by the boys. I sprang ashore in a sprightly fashion and went up the hill like an antelope, barefooted to all appearances. Ruth, who walks on air anyway, sprang along even more nimbly than I, while the boys lost time in wonderment.

We knew we were at the top only when we started to go downhill again. I was content to learn that only a few yards from the river, where there was less moisture in the soil, the forest, the jungle of the books, became clean as the woods of a park, with no undergrowth because the majestic pillars of trees, which propped the "jungle cathedral" of the books, impeded the sunlight.

From the top of Mount Ga Mongo we saw practically nothing, because of the speckling of the leaves before us on every side, and as it would be the work of hours to clear a passage for a view I agreed with Malfatti that there was Brazil just yonder, sure enough. So far as we could see through the speckling leaves, there were blue hummocks to the south with yellow-white cubes like old teeth rising among them: the great, the legendary, the sinister Tumuc-Humacs, where Lake Parimé and its golden cities shone in the dreams of the old adventurers, and would always shine for me.

So we went down through that docile jungle to the boats again, and as we continued up the creek, hacking our way every thirty feet or so, I kept thinking of the jungle and how like a lion it was, superficially ferocious when you met it at the water's edge and timid in the darkness beyond. On the high ground above the creek you could stroll anywhere. It was only the swamplands you had to fear.

All afternoon the clouds were curdling gray. They began to rain toward evening, and in our naked canoes we sat despondently beneath plastic ponchos, knowing that the rains had beaten us. We felt no cheerier when we came to another white ball of kapok on a stick, indicating that we might go on. The Oyaricoulets, walking invisible beside us, were talking louder now. They laughed. They no longer seemed to care whether we heard their machetes cutting the undergrowth. At sunset, or about the time of it, for we couldn't see it

300

through the rain, we still had found no possible camp site. The creek had become a canyon with granite walls.

"We'll sleep in the canoes," I said to Malfatti. He turned in his canoe, which seemed inextricably entangled in lianas, and, without focusing his eyes on me, said that soon we would come to a hut, a carbet, which he had built as a base for his dog raiding in Brazil.

"Soon" was amazingly sooner than I expected. We cut through a tangle and found a clearing in the creek, where it was three or four yards across. There were two tiny carbets on the sloping bank, simple roofs perched close to the ground. We took one, the Bonis the other, and the Indians, grunting in the rain, quickly constructed for themselves a splendid house of thatch. I protested that ours was not large enough for us and our baggage, and where was Raphael with his kitchen to go?

I saw then that we were in the midst of pure revolt. Neither Indians nor Bonis would budge to extend our roof or patch the holes through which the rain jetted as from a dozen faucets. There was no use arguing now. In a few minutes it would be too dark to see. While Ruth arranged baggage, storing film and cameras cautiously, Raphael and I hacked a short, twisting path to serve as lavatory—the woods were so thick that there was scarcely standing room outside the hut —and made props for the tarpaulins to cover and extend the roof.

"Toma!" I yelled. "Where the hell's our wood and water?" It was his job to supply these to Raphael every evening.

"Wood and water? Wood and water?" echoed Toma from his hut. "The water is all around you, and the wood is wet!" Neither they nor the Indians had a fire. At that moment of misery Raphael became heroic. Swearing like the apache he was, he waded into the creek and hauled out logs from beneath the surface. Carefully he chose certain ones and ripped off the soaking bark of them as though to make a fire. The Bonis were laughing and describing him vividly.

But there was a super Boy Scout in Raphael, and with the initial aid of a little kerosene he soon had a blaze as high as the hut and the logs themselves were burning. "Oil in them," he explained with a snarl.

Raphael wakened me in the morning and I parted the thatch to look at the creek where he was pointing. The canoe with our good Indians was drifting by; they were gesturing to us dispiritedly, to say that there was nothing they could do. We ate breakfast without much conversation, watching our journey fray before our eyes. There were no more Indian canoes along the shore, only our three long ones. All the Indians but Malfatti had gone, and his canoe with them. The Bonis sat in their hut saying nothing. Malfatti, who usually was sociable with them, sat alone in his, with his longbow and arrows on his knees.

When Ruth and I went over to them we were greeted with grunts from the Bonis, and Malfatti simply turned his head to stare into the woods. He stared so long that finally I went to the spot where he seemed to be looking. I found what I suspected, the red ball of kapok on a spear.

We returned to camp, told Raphael, and spent that day in cleaning guns. Here, in the midst of the mountains, with Brazil close enough to shoot a bullet into, it seemed disgraceful to be forced to return, and if we should do so there was every likelihood—as we were to confirm later—of our being ambushed by Malfatti's men. If we pushed on, we had the Oyaricoulets to worry about, and they had now given us notice.

I called to Afokati and Malfatti to come over and discuss this, and they called back, "Later on." At last, later on, I had to go to them. Malfatti, never looking at me, said straight that he must return to his village. He fiddled with his long, poisoned arrows.

I was at a total loss as to what to do. I thought of trying to force Malfatti at pistol point to guide us, but there were too many dangerous intangibles. As we ourselves were being threatened with war by the Oyaricoulets, it would be imprudent to declare war against my own men. Ruth could help me somewhat, and courageously, but I couldn't count on Raphael, and it looked like an insuperable ordeal to struggle up the creek with a camera in one hand and a pistol in the other, to guard my guides by night and day. We were so deep in the forest by now—much farther than any white man had ever been—that with the slightest lack of vigilance on our part we could be knocked on our heads by our guides, and forgotten about. The authorities could never prove that it was not the Oyaricoulets who had done us in.

It was five in the morning when Raphael wakened us. The rain was tickling our tarpaulined roof, and the sky was the color of an unwashed zinc sink.

"Look," said Raphael. "Get the pistol." I got the pistol first and leaned on an elbow to peer through the thatch. In the creek a few feet below us was an Indian canoe I had never seen before, and standing in the stern of it was the thick statue of Malfatti, cautiously paddling away.

I couldn't imagine what Raphael wanted me to do with the pistol: shoot the Indian, hold him up, bring him back alive? And to what good end? Ruth had slipped from her cot to mine and was leaning painfully across my ribs, watching Malfatti. "That's the shot I've been waiting for," she said, referring to photography, not ballistics, "but let it go."

We watched it go around the bend, ate breakfast thoughtfully, prepared cameras and knapsacks, and went to say a few curt words to the Bonis. These were elaborated on by Raphael at the top of his voice as we hacked our way for fifty feet or so up the creek. He then had no more breath, and I was able to remind him of the red ball of kapok on the spear, and Ruth to remind me that since we had seen it we had not heard a sound from the Oyaricoulets who had accompanied us for so long. That did not, as the saying goes, put stomach in me.

There was another thing I had been wondering about. Where could Malfatti have gotten that canoe? He had none last night.

We were emptying our rubber boots of water and scraping black mud from our legs. Raphael turned his leer upon me. "I asked my friends, the Bonis. Malfatti told them that not far up the creek was the Indian path to Brazil, and a little beyond it was a place where the Roucouyennes sank their canoes, to hide them from the Oyaricoulets while raiding in Brazil. He borrowed one of them. The next man returning will borrow someone else's, and so on until someone gets stuck."

"That's encouraging, because he got the canoe sometime last night, which means that the entrance to the path can't be too far away. If we miss it, we'll probably stub our toes on the canoes."

"Or on an Oyaricoulet," said Ruth.

"Father God," I thought aloud to Ruth, "guide me through the torrents of my folly. My Indians have deserted. My Bonis are petrified. Brazil may be over there, or we may even be in it, but at least we know that we are in the Tumuc-Humac Mountains, our goal. We never contracted to go to Buenos Aires. It's raining too hard to make film. Nobody wants us here. Nobody loves us. Would you hold it against us, Father God, if we just went home?"

Under the lash of the rain the branches were nodding, as was the red ball on the spear. God, Massa Gaddu, had said yes.

30 ~~~~~~~~~~~~~~~~~~~

Ambushed by Malfatti—
test of a traitor by wasps

OUR BONIS, who had decided to go home anyway, were putting the last thatch to the pomekaris when we announced that we would accompany them. Our employees accepted us graciously, for they would have worried about us eternally, alone in the bush with the Oyaricoulets whom they swore they had seen making faces at them. The only evidence that they had actually seen these Indians was that they described them as the "long-eared ones," the same phrase used by Coudreau when he had met them years ago. They also agreed that the ears were stretched by tubes of bamboo in the lobes.

Despite the work of clearing we had done, we made scarcely better time on the way out than on the way in. With the rains, the waters had swollen tremendously; there was a rise of eighteen inches, and the bridging logs we had slipped under before now had to be cut through at water level. This, with the hot breath of the Indians on our necks, was not much fun. The Bonis swung their axes with enthusiasm, which was doubled when once we saw a string of pink flaming feathers swinging from a limb. Afokati opined that pink was still red, though less violently, and that perhaps, Massa Gaddu be praised, we would come to white feathers if we worked fast, and then to none.

The river beneath the rain was like a rough gray worsted stretched tight from shore to shore. There was no sign on the surface of the mighty current that hauled us away and flung us off downstream. In this area which had been strewn with visible sharp rocks on our way up there were now none above the surface, but they couldn't be far down. We traveled like torpedoes, and nearly as fast, before a seething wake. The paddlers didn't paddle; fore and aft they steered adroitly.

Slipping from side to side in the current, quivering like compass needles, our three long canoes raced down the river. The river was rising several inches a day.

Suddenly we came upon a bend in the river at a saut called Doichine, and a group of rocks in the middle of it with a huddle of Indian women and children on them. When we came closer I saw that these were the families of the Roucouyenne guides who had abandoned us. The queasy, irrational feeling that tells you something is wrong walked with cold, sharp claws along my spine. I yelled to Afokati to stop, but the current pulled us forward toward the bank, and we had nearly reached it when I saw the Indian Malfatti half hidden by a tree, with a shining machete swinging from his hand. Behind him, against the green, were other patches of red roucou-dyed Indian bodies.

This is the sort of moment which should make you feel like a dyed-in-the-wool old-time explorer, but actually leaves you with bile in the esophagus. I stood up in my canoe, making an excellent target, and poured half a bottle of good cognac into the water. This alone astonished the Indians and Ruth—and me. I cut a notch in the side of the cork and without too much fumbling found the can of carbide,

305

pried it open, poured half of it into the bottle, stoppered it, and flung it overboard in the direction of Malfatti.

Time stood still as death while I examined the cartridge clip of my pistol. Ruth, standing up, was doing the same, and Raphael was whetting his machete on the sole of his sandal. I was considering how thoughtful it was of the Indians to put their children and womenfolk on a rock, out of the way of war, when there came a deep submarine "boom" as the water, seeping into my bottle, formed gas with the carbide and exploded.

Bubbles burst at the surface. There was a stink of brimstone. Great fish and little fish heaved up, stunned. I took a pot shot at one of them and hit it. I think our paddlers were as scared as the Indians, for they shouted angrily. With a howl Malfatti realized which side his war was buttered on. He jumped into his canoe, followed by four so-called braves, whipped to the rocky island, collected the non-belligerents, and shot down-river before I could even ask Ruth if there wasn't another bottle of cognac somewhere.

I began to shake when I saw Afokati shaking and the hands of the wrestler Abbibal trembling on his pole.

"Downgo!" said Afokati, meaning, "Now we go down the river," and we pushed into muddy waters, the drainage of the swamps and the glutinous shores. For a while there was an oval of blue sky between the clouds, and across it, like sparks, came a flight of parrots, green and red and gray. We veered and twisted, spun halfway round, straightened with a jerk, and slid silently through the Mama Saut, a bitch.

A hideous laughter came from the canoe behind me. It was Raphael's, and he was dipping up the river in his straw hat and putting the hat on his head. "I can't help it," he howled, drunk as a coot. "They were so funny, the wild Indians, when your fizz poop went off. Much may be said against you, Capitaine, but no one can say that you are not a great fizz pooper!"

We passed Malfatti's village, and there was no one visible, not even a dog, but the shelter it offered to our fatigue looked rather like a trap to me.

"We had better camp on the other shore," said Afokati, "on

Yana Mali's land. He's a Roucouyenne like Malfatti, but no friend of his." I transmitted this to Ruth, and our three canoes slipped through the twilight to the riverbank. No one came to greet us from the huts on the slope above. We made camp, ate cold, putrid, dried fish, and turned in exhausted.

The head of Chief Yana Mali, blurred through the mosquito net as we wakened in the morning, was not prepossessing. It was more Mongoloid than the others, with higher cheekbones and heavier hair. He brought us gifts of dozens of eggs all rotten, and a piece of smoked cayman tail. He obviously knew a good deal about us, and probably had heard from Malfatti himself. He and his villages accorded us their greatest compliment: they neither bothered nor bothered about us during the few days we rested there.

It was in this spirit of pleasant relationship that one afternoon Yana Mali, holding the hands of Ruth and me as we walked through the village, said, "That smoke over there may change the whole life of a man." We took the outer path around the thatched huts and went through a tunnel in the forest. Half-a-dozen Indians were holding torches beneath a large wasp's nest. When most of the wasps were drugged with smoke, the Indians cut the nest down and returned to the village with it.

We squatted in a circle around Yana Mali as he dug the doped wasps from the nest. They wiggled a little. His very red-painted son had woven a mat of green-and-yellow rattan, and into the interstices of this Yana Mali put the wasps. He would slip their fat tails into feather quills, push the quills through the holes in the mat, carrying the tails through, then remove the quills, leaving the wasps caught, alive, by their slender waists. They were huge beasts, an inch and a half long.

When hundreds had been trapped in the mat like this and I was wondering if ever I had seen a more useless-looking machine, Yana Mali said, "This is to test the courage of a man."

"How?" I asked politely.

He explained that every boy of the Roucouyennes at the age of puberty must undergo the test of manhood before he could be accepted as a warrior. This consisted of a torture by wasps or ants, whichever was the handier. Trapped in the mat, they were placed upon his chest by the oldest woman of the tribe, first the side they stung with, and then the biting side, and then alternately for hours until the youngster fell with fever and pain. If he had not cried out, he was accepted as one fit to fight for dogs in Brazil.

"But now," said the chief, "now we prepare the wasps for a different matter, which is very much the same." And he went on to talk of warriors who sometimes were thought craven by their fellows. These were few, he said proudly, but when the case was proved, they were forced to submit again to the test, to prove them men and warriors. There was such a person among them now. Malfatti was his name.

"Eh? Our, so to speak, Malfatti?"

Everyone talked at once, which made it even harder for me to grasp, but finally it came out that the village of Yana Mali was noted for a number of things: its courage in battle, its low incidence of homosexuality, and its fealty to the French administration. The renegade Malfatti, in his relations with my expedition, had breached Roucouyenne honor. It was regrettable, and Yana Mali apologized in the name of his people. By now all the interstices of the mat were filled with live and kicking wasps. It itched and ached me to look at it.

Ruth said, "But we don't want Malfatti punished. . . ."

I added, "All I insisted on, and what I shall advise the préfet at Cayenne, is that Malfatti shall not guide another expedition."

While we were walking to the center of the village, it was pointed out to me that the wasp test was not punishment at all. It was simply necessary that Malfatti prove, by courage, his right to reinstatement in the tribe, for he had been, in his time, a respectable warrior and a fine bush citizen. Such a man should not be lost. He should endure a little salutary pain and prove to the world of the Roucouyennes that his peccadilloes upriver with us were temporary aberrations. Such was the law of Yolok, their one god.

In the center of the village the tethered dogs were howling. The sun had a whole clean heaven to itself at last and was scorching the earth so fast that you could see cracks form in the clay. No one was about but an old woman. From some sort of special hut came strange, monotonous sounds of fluting, followed by two drunken Indians who spilled through the door, arm in arm, tootling on three-note flutes made from the tibias of jaguar. One of them was Malfatti. No one but ourselves and the squatted hag stood there in the sun to watch the antics of their preparation for the trial. They danced forward and back together, approaching and recoiling from the hag, tootling on their flutes, taking a nip occasionally from their gourds of cachiri, the raw corn wine.

Malfatti may have recognized us, but he gave no sign of it. Up and down he went with his partner, up to the hut where the old woman was standing now, holding the wasp mat which Yana Mali had given her, and down to the river and more slowly back again.

Then the ceremony of Malfatti's trial, in a terrible silence, began. He was leaning against the thatch of an empty house, his arms spread out like a man to be crucified. The old woman was slowly and gently touching his arms and his face with the mat, the stinger side, and as the wasps felt flesh behind them their whole bodies writhed.

Malfatti trembled. At least half the wasps, perhaps a hundred, had stung him, and he knew that the wasp, unlike the bee, does not lose its stinging needle in the wound. The old torturing woman, who had probably been doing this for many years, now turned the mat against his nipples and applied the other side. His face had twisted, green-blue veins had swollen at his temples, but he had not yet cried out.

The torturing hag continued her work. Flick . . . flick. She pressed the mat, one side then the other, against the blood-flecked chest. Malfatti's arms were spread against the roof and his blunt fingers were tearing thatch from it. Sweat poured slowly, because of its oiliness, over the wrinkled flesh where his eyebrows had been shaven, over the lashless eyelids, and down his cheeks to follow their furrows to his twitching upper lip and drip upon the limp lower one.

Yana Mali, holding my cigarette awkwardly as a schoolgirl between forefinger and thumb, remarked that it might be hours yet before Malfatti fell. It was more than three hours now since the trial had begun; the sun was setting, bronzing Malfatti's black hair, brazening the palm thatch behind it. All around the oval huts the dogs were howling, not for Malfatti but because their dinner was late. It was the prelude to a symphony of hysteria.

Ruth's hand was shaking as I took it from her camera; she was more tired than the man writhing beneath the wasps. She had been at this for four hours now, moving forward and back and in semicircles, on her bare feet which were surer than shoes. She sat on the ground quietly, with her camera and tripod folded against her chest like some great dead bug.

Dragging our shadows behind us, we went to our own hut. We had better be leaving Yana Mali's village. The moon, as if pulled on a cord around the earth, ascended as the sun went down. There was darkness suddenly, sprinkled by the lights of fireflies. We put our baggage together, listening. We stopped often, waiting for Malfatti, whose twisted silhouette we still could see, to scream or collapse upon his bloody shadows. But the hag kept on. Malfatti held to the fraying thatch, drooping a little.

Yana Mali may have felt that we suspected him. He went around our hut collecting the junk we had thrown out and the occasional surprise of a useful thing with which I had hoped to hold his vague allegiance for half an hour more.

He sat on the ground squarely between Ruth and me and the heaving, drooping silhouette of Malfatti, and told us in detail, slowly, of how the wasp mat was used.

When a Roucouyenne couple wished to marry, he said, they were placed in a hammock together, nude, without even a calambé; and the top cover of the hammock, which served to keep out rain and mosquitoes, was sewn down tightly all around except for one small opening. Into this was pushed a basketful of live wasps and ants. Then the opening was sewn shut with some fine sadistic petit point, and the loving couple was left for the night. The elders sat around them or slung hammocks nearby, watching the vibration of love inspirited by wasps and ants.

Yana Mali smiled. *"Hipok?"* he asked. "Good?"

"Hipokedah," I answered fluently. "No good."

He turned his head, listening. "Then," he said, "if in the morning the two young people still love each other they are married. If they don't . . ."

On the river edge by the canoes the Bonis were chanting as they had not done before during all this expedition. It was a good sound;

310

we would record it later; not tonight. The only disturbing element of it was Eimo's shrilling voice.

Ruth told Raphael to pack up his kitchen fast. I prodded my six men to the hut and the baggage so fast that they had no time for thinking.

When I was bending to pick up a film dropped from my pocket, I saw the red apparition of Yana Mali, who must have sluiced himself with roucou only a few minutes ago. Now that we were going away, said he with a grimace such as Malfatti had not yet shown, now that we were returning to Cayenne and would see the préfet, didn't I think that I might suggest to the préfet that he, Yana Mali, should be considered chief of Malfatti's village as well as his own? Malfatti, he said, could not last much longer beneath the test. He had once cried out as a warrior never should.

The three of us were walking toward the canoes, Yana Mali between us. He stopped once, and I listened, too, to a low keening, a terrifying woman's song. The rain came down. Ruth climbed into her canoe. The dirge of the woman stopped; there was silence; and when my ears became accustomed to sound again, as one's eyes become pitched to perceive grayness in the dark, I could dimly hear a concerted mumbling from the hut where Malfatti had prepared for his ordeal. It was mean and fierce as small thundering.

I stepped into my canoe and stayed standing. The Bonis pushed off. The rapids were silver ahead of us, with rain and a strangely piercing moonlight. My canoe, Ruth's, and Raphael's were abreast. Eimo's song had depth in it, a healthy baritone. Raphael was talking fondly to his stove.

31 ∿∿∿∿∿∿∿∿∿∿∿∿

Film in New York—the
Ivory Coast—cannibal justice

QUAINTLY CLOTHED IN tropical khaki, we re-
turned to New York in a blizzard and holed into my apartment at
226 Fifth Avenue. The friends who had kept our tropical fish returned their progeny to us. The gourmet-explorer who had promised
to maintain my perpetual soup—now two years old and the pot never
emptied—returned it in the copper pot proudly. He had kept it on
the back of his stove, adding the spare vegetable waters, meats, and
bones to it occasionally, clarifying it faithfully once a week with
cheesecloth and a beaten egg, never letting the pot be empty, but he
had been on a binge the night before, and to celebrate our arrival had
added bananas and red wine to it. I promptly clarified it, too, and as
a cold soup in a cold winter it was mighty fine until I had integrated
my colleague's caprices sufficiently with beef stock to make it potable
hot.

New York was wonderful, but we didn't have much money again
and so gave gigantic parties to cheer us up, and worked maniacally on
articles and the editing of our French Guiana film, which miraculously
had turned out well. Hollywood supposedly throws out one foot in
ten; we left about one foot in three on the cutting-room floor and
sold the rest to Warner Brothers who distributed it under the title—
by no means of my choosing—of *Jungle Terror* in America and
France. It didn't pay for the expedition but it did incite Warners' to
lend us film for a new one.

Many people would like to be explorers, and for every trip of mine
which the newspapers have mentioned I have received hundreds of
requests to join it, some of them from women who would pay their
own way. What they don't realize, as Ruth will attest, is that although
danger may be appealing, and tigers and cannibals nice to recall,
there is a long space of moral and physical decay between excitements.

This space is filled with bugs and malaria and dysentery and jungle rot and thirst for unpolluted water and the ennui of living in an isolated unit with no news of the day and all personal past histories expended.

I computed that, if one is lucky, an expedition takes about three years. The first year is devoted to planning the thing, getting the money, personnel, and material, obtaining the backing (usually moral and not monetary) of scientific and cultural institutions, and finally the approval and aid of the government controlling the territory you are to explore. The second year is the journey itself, when you may or may not have fun. I believe that no serious exploratory expedition, even to the Bronx, New York, can bring back a useful study of the mores of the inhabitants unless it has spent at least a year among them. The third year is sheer drudgery, for explorers are usually broke by then and have to capitalize on the work done, to write the book, to cut and edit the film and screen it from here to Hollywood for producers, at great cost in whisky, until finally someone buys it. Then the cycle spins over again.

Our film was sold to Warners', and that was a good thing, and the book found an American publisher and six European publishers after that. Lord Calvert honored me with its distinctive advertisement. I became Mary Margaret McBride for a week of radio when she was on vacation. Lectures and television programs, which once I would have dreaded, became meat and drink to me.

But the members of the Explorers Club said, "Good show, old boy. Quite a trip. When are you off again?" The huge animal heads all around the club looked down at me accusingly as though to say that, as I didn't shoot them, I was their delegate to relatives at home. I began to feel unwanted and searched for a new goal which had not been tramped before. In this shriveling world it was hard to find.

Ruth and I sat before the great globe by candlelight, for our movie projector had blown the fuse. I spun the globe slowly. "There's Borneo," I said, "but the Indonesians have it and they won't let you film the primitive peoples." I spun the globe again, my finger pushing the dust off it. Ruth put down a pair of vodkas over Asia. "There are the Tien Shan Mountains, mostly unknown, but they are in the Russian domain. Not a chance." The spark of my cigarette moved up

313

and down Africa, most of which I knew, till it stopped over Mauretania. "That's it! And old De Mauduit, who was in the Free French with me, is governor!"

We wired him and learned in reply that he was now governor of Tchad, which no one in his right mind would want to revisit. He was sending us a friend from the Ivory Coast, he cabled. The friend arrived, a leprechaun type, a wood merchant, and sat seriously at our long refectory table, talking of the Ivory Coast. This was a duty dinner for De Mauduit, with long pauses in the desultory conversation which was in French. To fill these I talked of our Bonis in French Guiana, the descendants of African slaves. He lighted a cigarette over his scallops and wild rice, and turned again to the pile of French Guiana photos beside him. "It's the same African type," he said, "with even the same sunburst tattooing around the navel. Would it not be interesting to you to compare them to their relatives in their original homeland?"

Oho! thought I. This notion is not bad at all! He kindled under my interest. "Somewhere," he said, "there is supposed to be a sorcerers' village, where young people are trained as sorcerers, fetishers, and witches. It is said to be a true school of magic, and no European has been there, not even a tax collector, because no one knows where it is. The sorcerers who graduate from the school are frequently employed by the African Communist agents who abound in French and British West Africa."

"Oho!" said Ruth aloud, and meant it. The radio was playing the "Danse Macabre" of Saint-Saëns, which seemed to depress our leprechaun, although it brought back to me fond memories of my early writing days in Paris.

"It is said," he sighed, "that in this village there is elected a King of the Golden Wood, a King of the Dance, who holds his appointment for exactly one year and whose stipends include the village virgins, the best food and palm wines—everything he wishes—until that year's end when he must dance alone at full moon and be killed by a golden arrow. . . ."

"O-bloody-ho!" I shouted, making the man jump. Ruth nodded wisely.

A few months later we landed with sixty-three pieces of equipment at Abidjan, capital of the Ivory Coast. The governor looked appreciatively at the letters of recommendation I carried, from UNESCO, the French Embassy in Washington, the American Geographical Society, the American Museum of Natural History, the Institute of Fine Arts, and the Institute of World Affairs. It occurred to him that we were neither spies nor adventurers, that our interest in French territories might conceivably do them some good in the way of publicity. Here was one official who understood that, although we were interested in stamping out the calumny of "exploitation" and promoting the development of the Ivory Coast for both the whites' and the natives' profit, our equally justifiable objective was to record the rapidly changing native customs before they should be entirely lost. He gave us freedom of the port for our equipment, guns, cameras, two Lambretta motor scooters, and the enormous rest of it. He lent us a Renault truck and a soldier-interpreter, N'dri, who spoke six dialects of the fifty-three on the Ivory Coast, plus Djula, the lingua franca of the markets. And he lodged us in the Institut Française de l'Afrique Noir, a most attractive museum which encouraged native artists by employing them to copy or evolve the woodcarving of their ancestors.

"We do our best," said the governor, a blunt, bronzed man who preferred his inspections in the bush to office paperwork. "Look out there." We went to the window of his magnificent marble palace. "Right down there is the market. One of our native sanitary inspectors, in disguise, bought a human hand in it a little while ago. You see the lagoon over there?" He pointed over the roofs of moderately modern houses. "Somewhere in the lagoon is the head of a man. We found his body last week. Sacrifice to the fish-gods."

"Good!" I said thoughtlessly. "That's just what we—"

The governor waggled an ivory paper knife at me. "I know. That's just what you're after." He smiled, this extraordinarily comprehensive man, thinking probably that any other explorer would announce officially that his major interest was the civilized progress of the country, while I was thinking that any other governor would send me packing to Harlem to get my native rites.

"I have an idea," the governor added. "Though I can't give you an inkling as to where your Sorcerers' Village may be, or your golden-

arrow dancer, it might be very helpful as a start if you went to Abengourou a few days from now to see the coronation of a native king,
Essey Bonzou. It will coincide with the Sweet Potato Festival, which
occurs only once every seven years, so you're in luck. You'll find
gory customs there, hideous ones, animal sacrifices, and maybe a clue
to those other things you're after."

The town of Abidjan ran up and down a hill and slithered off into
the jungles squeezing it. With the opening of Port Bouet it was soon
to become one of France's most important colonial cities. But I didn't
want to wait for that. Like every other tropical town it had its castes,
which were five: the political folk, the military, the wealthy industrial-
ists, the merchants, and the natives. Social as well as racial miscegena-
tion was practically unknown.

Ruth and I went somewhat divergent ways. Hers led to the Cercle
Sportif where the wealthy assembled. Mine led to the Cercle Militaire,
which was stuck off in the bush, halfway to the cannibal clubs. But
at the Militaire you could get your teeth into the drinks. The food
had, as the French say, authority, with garlic and pepper and curry.

The driver of our truck, named Quodio, was expert, but I was
afraid we should have trouble with him, for he was a great lover. He
was bullet-headed, purple-black, and his color seemed to grow even
denser when the sorrows got him. His maleness, he said, was on the
wane, so he was constantly trying it out. We were within a week of
starting for the bush when Quodio complained that something was
wrong. Maybe, he thought, staring at a cloud, it was due to his having ridden the bicycle without any pants. "I am being destroyed by
the bicycle. I shall divorce the bicycle," he said.

Quodio had a fine bicycle, and he had four wives, who I assembled
and cured with my wonder drug. I even put a pill in the bicycle bell.
That was dandy. I was a sorcerer.

"Tomorrow morning we are off," I said, feeding Quodio pills.
"And we are leaving your bicycle behind."

Bounding away from Abidjan toward Abengourou, Ruth and I
sprawled exhausted amid our great baggage, the provisions, the out-
board motors, the rubber and plastic boats, inflated now to ease the
jounce on the cameras and tape recorders, the two motor scooters

316

suspended from the ceiling, the dog called Zobi, and more useless personnel than I can now remember. There were N'dri, who was interpreter, and M'blah, who was cook, and various relatives coming along for the ride.

Now I had the woods to myself at last. These trees were my family. We might argue and I might have to push them aside a little, but I'd hurt them as little as I could. The trees everywhere had been hospitable to me. Here I was among friends, among my trees, my quiet cannibals, my birds and beasts and bugs and serpents. They had coursing blood or sap in them; they were neither ambitious nor defeatist; they were hot with life and they minded their own businesses even when they must kill their neighbors.

Ruth, exhausted from packing, never flinched as a native-driven camion came hurtling at us around a bend. We knew by now that Quodio did as well on two wheels as four. A great deal of our mobile viewing of the Ivory Coast was done on the slant.

Ruth pointed out a blur of a woman with a basket on her head and I swung to see the glistening back covered by a spiderweb of blouse. "They are undressing a little," Ruth said. It wouldn't be long before we were to find them dressed in their tattooing only.

I was interested to note, through N'dri's instruction, that the tribes of the Ivory Coast still kept pretty much to themselves, unlike those of East Africa, where you would find Masai, Kikuyu, Ingoma mixing at the market place. Intertribal fear was still strong here. The village on the other side of your plantation might gobble you up as they would your crops. Except at Abidjan we rarely saw natives with radically different tattooing along the road of any particular section.

The woods were still with us. Their leaves, like hands, caressed our brutal male truck. The arm of an old dowager tree was politely raised to let us through. Liana vines swung in festoons from a hundred feet above us, and occasionally a troop of monkeys came swinging along them. But they fled as we went hurtling by.

Ripping through the dust, unconsciously ducking our heads when it seemed that a vine drooping from a hundred feet up might lasso our truck, trying to keep an eye on the bouncing baggage, counting heads occasionally and shoving the sack of cool squashed bananas

317

more comfortably under my coccyx again, I listened attentively to the young French circuit judge we had picked up. His words flashed by me like bits of torn cloth. His nose was marvelous, so turned up at the end that his sunglasses, always slipping from his small sweaty ears, could be caught with a little upward jerk of it.

The judge was saying, "... *bouillon de onze heurs,* the eleven o'clock broth, we call it, a poison made of the bark of the Tali tree ... or the *bois rouge,* painless, leaves no trace for autopsy.... In native courts beneath the central tree the suspect must drink a liquor composed of Tali wood which has been steeped in gin and the justice-fetish which has been steeped in the same gin. The suspect drinks it and does not die if innocent.... I, a judge, have had to try native judges who sometimes force the accused to plunge his hand into a calabash of hot oil to take out a metal ring. If he is innocent, he should not be burned. But because I have been long in the colonies, I have made many innocent men legally, publicly, obviously innocent by letting it be known that if one soaks the hands in the sirups of certain plants one may plunge them with impunity into the hottest fluids."

Ahead of us in the night were still the trees like witches, slapping claws at us across the road. Only one headlight would light, so we were going slowly enough to hear the first of the rumbles.

"That does it. That's the piston again. Stop, Quodio." We stopped and listened. "Turn off the motor." The rumbling continued, but it wasn't ours. Far away in the forest before us were the drums.

"Agni drums," N'dri said quietly. "Agni tribe near Abengourou." It was there we were going, for the coronation and the bloody rites. Our boys muttered rapidly, all together. N'dri seemed to be trying to calm the others. An owl said "Who?" and some thick-headed drum said "Whom!"

My skin crept a little and I thought, "This is my world, dark and spiced and frightening, accented by a little golden moon. This is the woman I entirely love." For I had had but one repetitive dream in all my life, and probably more than anything else it had formed me as an explorer. I had dreamed the world unlike our pictures of it in the geography books: that brilliant globe surrounded by darkling space,

318

that neat, geometrical conceit, confined by margins to restrict infinity. In my dreams the sky was luminous and my world was a woman caught in mid-stride across the sky as she came toward me. And she was a dark woman of a scintillant blue-black and her features were not Negroid but sharply Caucasian. Her hair fell long and smooth to her shoulders and was golden in wonderful contrast to her blue-black skin. And glowing from the pits of her arms and her groin were curled crescents of gold.

There's one for the analysts, I would think in the morning, and forget it, which is probably why the analysts have so far been deprived of it and me. But on nights like this in the jungle I was physically close to my dark, glowing, bewitching world.

N'dri said, "Quodio says—that Tiemoko says—that Moussa, who is an Agni, says—that the drums are at Adao, the sacred stream where all the old kings are buried with their thrones. The fetishers are digging up the thrones. And the sorcerers are eating men. In the town of Abengourou tomorrow we will see the sacrifices of cattle and chickens and goats, but we will not see, I hope"—and N'dri looked into a black place where the owl was asking "Who?"—"the men, always strangers, who are taken to be secretly sacrificed. You and Madame are perfectly safe because you are white, but we others, with the exception of Moussa, are strangers they would desire."

32 ∼∼∼∼∼∼∼∼∼∼∼∼∼∼

Coronation of a king—the thrones
are blooded—a curse is put upon me

ON THE GREAT DAY of the Festival of the Sweet Potatoes and the coronation of King Essey Bonzou, we drove down a little road bordered with flowering trees and came to the dusty town of Abengourou. The harsh wind called hamadan swept down from the deserts, through the southern Sahara and the sere lands of the Mossi in High Volta. It parched our lips and cracked them and curled our leather. We installed ourselves in an empty government resthouse above the town, and were squatting for breakfast over the gasoline stove when a cry of great fear came from somewhere among the golden-thatched little houses below.

"They've caught someone," said Moussa. "They'll eat him." I fried my bacon on the other side. Our boys were all uneasy as we looked down upon the thousands, literally thousands, of dark pilgrims who had come from hundreds of miles away for the festivities. They were dressed in their gayest pagnes, draped over the left shoulder and exposing the right breast.

The bacon eaten, we shouldered our way through the hot mass of the slowly lilting crowd. N'dri did his best to catch up with the news. Essey Bonzou, approved by the governor, would be the successor to the puppet king of a previous administration. Bonzou was legitimate, being the nephew of the last legitimate king. I was interested to find that here was another enduring similarity to the customs of my Bonis in French Guiana: descent was matrilinear in a matriarchal society.

"Three days ago they buried him, the last king, the usurper," N'dri said.

"But didn't he die some time ago?"

"He did. They buried him as is customary in a shed attached to his own family house, not the palace, and let the offerings of fruit rot on him until the new king was to be crowned. Then they dug him up secretly at night, and carried him to the mountain, and buried him beneath the river Adao. It is said that ten men were sacrificed that night."

An old woman, with a green ribbon around her head to cure the headache, bumped into me. I bowed, apologizing, and she made the mistake of bowing, too, and howling with pain and holding her head put a curse upon me. More cautiously we moved forward through the crowd of celebrants. Faces came at us, enlarging suddenly as though blown through a funnel. They were so near they were enormous, sweated and scarred and out of focus, bouncing, swirling, their sharp teeth flashing close under my nose. It was like trying to shake hands —without your glasses on—with a multitude.

320

"So they buried him beneath the river Adao," I repeated to N'dri. "Can we not go there?"

"Capitaine, you ask of me always the impossible." Governor Péchoux had already told me that the river Adao was so revered that he would suggest we stay away from it. N'dri said, shouldering a way for us through the crowd, "There are guards around the river Adao, because the tribes which are hostile to the Agni would surely steal the gold which is buried with the kings. And there is a woman"—he hesitated, his round face twitching—"an albino, a sorceress, who kisses you in the night and afflicts you with the worms." The albino Negro, here as everywhere in Africa, was an accursed being.

N'dri said, in as loud a whisper as you can make in a crowd, "For a fete like this, the river Adao is deflected from its course, the last dead king is buried with the ancient ones, and the thrones—which are really stools—of the ancients are dug up to be anointed anew, secretly with the blood of captives, and publicly with the blood of beasts, as we may see tomorrow, when Essey Bonzou, King of the Agnis of Indénié, will be enthroned."

Everywhere around us were the musicians blowing out of harmony upon their oxen horns. They were individualists, and each had three notes only—inhale, exhale, and poop, but they so conceived their symphony that their melodies didn't overlap. It was a doleful music, a soughing of anguish, and nobody, nobody, smiled in that crowd of thousands who had come to celebrate.

Essey Bonzou came at last, surrounded by his courtiers in their finest raiment, pacing beneath a huge green parasol which was constantly whirled by the slave behind him. By the thousands the crowd surged around their king, spinning, cavorting, tossing vegetables like jugglers into the air. I saw six white men, no woman but Ruth.

The next day was a heller. Everything happened. There was the fete. There was a man who was said to know the way to the Sorcerers' Village. There was a pox put upon me.

Inhale, exhale, poop went the ox horns at daybreak. We sat on boxes in our baggage-littered cell and drank our coffee fast. A slight green lizard let go from the ceiling and landed precisely in my cup. I salvaged him and his tail came off in my hand. The day was beginning inauspiciously.

I called the boys and allotted cameras, film cans, tripods, reflector. They got a ten-minute start and we followed them on the scooters to the cubic whitewashed palace, where the crowd received us, as usual, with the applause due to dignitaries, because of those thundering little scooting machines. Nothing can compare with them for the promotion of prestige among primitives.

The square before the palace was jammed with celebrants, and we nearly ran down the virgins dancing. The whole land of the Agnis had been combed for virgins, nubile, pure, and yet adult enough to transport the stools of the nine dead kings. These girls danced madly up and down the dusty streets between the huts of mud, clad in white to affirm their virtue, each carrying a white-wrapped packet upon her head, the gore-stained stool of a king. They scarcely knew what they were doing, for they were in an authentic state of trance. Hypnosis and self-hypnosis are common in Africa. Clasping the cloaked stools as if their very virtue was in them, they pranced through the lanes always opened ahead of them by the crowd, serpentining toward King Essey Bonzou, who was becoming restive.

Out of every street, from every court and doorway, came the milling, roistering mob. Princes were borne above the heads of us in elaborate litters or palanquins draped with brilliantly colored cloths, while beside them danced their servants carrying parasols twenty feet high to shield the royal complexions from the sun. The courtiers flourished golden cutlasses; old women flourished bottles of cheap trade gin, cavorting nimbly. Ahead of each litter swooped the dancing griots, howling the praises of their chiefs.

"O-o-o-o-o-o-o-o! My master has ninety wives and he disposes of nine wives nightly!" one would sing. Another, capering like a goat, would answer, "My master is Lord of the Elephants! With the spear which none but he can hurl he transfixes them two at a time, by their trunks, to a tree, and leads them home for the pleasure of his one hundred and ninety wives!" "Eh-eh-eh-eh-eh-eh!" bawls a third, turning somersaults in his gilded robes. "My Lord Chief Sorcerer has a thousand and ninety enemies, but they are small, only nine feet tall, so he blows his fierce breath into them, *against* the wind, blowing

322

them up to a size worthy of his combat with them. Then, with an eyelash, he pricks them, and 'whoof!' they're gone!"

The glorious litter of Essey Bonzou came titivating past us, casting a great sunset shadow as it was held at full arm's length above the shoulders of his porters. King though he might be, he had only six wives. Behind him came his Chief Lord Sorcerer, also sky-borne, in a hammock made of leopard skins stretched over long ivory tusks; he was a gaunt, haughty old man, aware of evil and the dangers which, but for his surveillance, might beset the king.

Our boys couldn't tell us why the fool king always was carried close behind the sorcerer, jiggling and grimacing, making swipes at the air with his golden scimitar. You could surmise that he was a scapegoat, that the sorcerer passed on to him whatever injurious charms or spirits he had diverted from the king. This one looked like a Christian martyr, obliged to play the clown, and the sorcerer glared at him from time to time.

Bedlam was a whisper in comparison with our king's courtyard when we had fought our way to it and finally up a rickety flight of stairs to a balcony from which we might film the sacrifices. The balcony sagged slowly, loosing a plank or two on the heads below. Ruth didn't turn a golden hair as she set up the camera at a spot where three planks looked friendly. There was a window sill within reach in case the whole balcony should let go. Gingerly we looked over the edge, and into inferno. The nightgowned virgins had reached a frenzy. The crowd parted before them, closed behind them as they curvetted with the stools on their heads, now swinging in a circle around the three enormous parasols sheltering a row of multicolored priests. The girls sank to a crouch together. The priests took the stools and reverently undid their white wrappings. The ox horns bellowed as these thrones of the great ancient kings were at last revealed.

They were crescent-shaped, carved in one piece, black and silken with the blood of old sacrifices. The priests arranged them solicitously beneath the parasols. Essey Bonzou, sitting on a true throne now, studded with brass nails, gave a rather timid command for the slaughter to begin. Everyone howled his praises. The courtiers beside him brandished their long golden staves. I was fascinated by these for they were amusingly carved, one in particular which had a little platform on its top with two golden sculptured men apparently eating at table.

A cow had been haled before the stools and the priests, while the priest-butcher, clad in white with white turban, circled it admiringly. Then everything stopped as a griot's stentorian howling came from the courtyard gate. And there was the genial, spike-toothed Prince Adingra making his dramatic entrance. I would have thought it impossible to wedge a weasel into that mob, but the prince, standing above it in his litter, directed his court like a traffic cop.

He grinned at us as he passed on the level of our balcony. "You must come to see me," he yelled in his excellent French. "I'll give you a real party!"

Then the sacrifices began with a rush. They were not nice sacrifices. Cattle, goats, chickens were flung to the ground and their throats sawed open. There was silence now. Thump, went the cow, and you could hear the priest's panting as he hacked at the throat. The surgeon-priest knew when to stop. Adroitly and suddenly he jerked up the cow's muzzle, and the blood gushed forth in an arc as thick as your arm. The priests pushed their stools at it, each of the nine elbowing his way to be sure his stool was anointed. The drips were caught in a basin by a fanatic whitewashed witch, crawling on all fours, mooing like a cow, slavering, caressing herself with the blood.

Now the priests were rubbing the blood into the stools to re-sanctify them. They massaged them with love, holding their art work at arm's length and squinting at it to be sure the holy paint was evenly spread. Their glorious costumes were stained, their faces smirched. Here was ecstasy.

It was during one of these frenzied days that there occurred a contretemps which should be of interest to the sincere souls who ask if I ever had personally witnessed primitive magic. There was a witch dancing round us, her bare breasts flapping, her sweat streaming through the white paint with which she had daubed herself. The dust raised by her cavorting added to the mess of her, and she drew new patterns on it like a nasty, lunatic little hoyden drawing on a wall. Up she'd pop and run in a furious circle, dipping to the ground,

324

flinging back her arms and head, then suddenly stop, shimmying, while some poor benighted god, with no place to go, possessed her body.

"Now there's a holy one!" said Quodio, the chauffeur, who was very much for another tribe. "Axle grease wouldn't melt in her mouth."

Moussa, our Agni porter, leaped for Quodio and was about to clobber him with the Leica when I intervened. I needed both the chauffeur and the Leica. Moussa glowered at both of us and walked off, leaving the Leica in the dust. I yelled at him; he kept on.

"Heh, what's this?" I asked Quodio.

Quodio spat. "Ask him where are half our cartridges, and the blow-up pillow, and the jumping-out knife?"

"Oho?" said I. You become miserly with words in this hot land. I hesitated to fire Moussa for theft, but it had to be done. Theft on an expedition, where everything is precious, is bad enough, but Moussa's surliness and antagonism could be dangerous. We weren't wanted in this country. We were interlopers, and so we must choose the most tolerant company always. Although our motives were, God knows, benign, I could take no chance on having anyone with us whom I could not implicitly trust.

We searched Moussa's slight baggage for the cartridges, the blow-up pillow, and the jumping-out knife, and found nothing. In the morning a number of the cartridges had been replaced carelessly in their boxes, and I fired Moussa. This disagreeable business gave me pause whenever I was on the point of hiring or firing an inhabitant of the witching woods. Moussa disappeared as if by magic, and as I squirted lime juice onto my papaya at breakfast, I became accursed.

"What's happened?" Ruth asked, without too much concern. "One of your eyes is glassy."

"The right one?"

"Definitely. Wink."

I could barely get the eyelid to close.

"This, darling, is damned odd. I'm like that all the way down. From the top of my head on the right side, straight through the middle of my nose, chin, navel, et cetera, I'm half-paralyzed, and the whole right side of me is beginning to ache like hell!"

"Weird," said Ruth, wrestling with a mantis in her hair. "Try the

325

aureomycin." I did, with hot milk as instructed, and found that my right teeth hurt. The faithful N'dri was looking at me oddly and trembling.

"Fever?" I asked.

N'dri's mouth twisted before it spoke. "No, no, Capitaine, no, no. It is you who frightened me. The pain goes down one side of you only? Through you? Dividing you, no? So that one part is good and one is awful, maybe?"

"Precisely!" said I, trying it through the left cuspids this time, because I needed the labial P.

N'dri continued trembling, and to cover his embarrassment helped himself to the mantis in Ruth's hair. He bit off its head, spat on it, and trampled it underfoot. Zobi, the pup, tossed the carcass around. "The mantis," said N'dri, "eats the eyes of dogs." His eyes were fixed on me. *"Mon capitaine,* see the missionary doctor first. There is time."

"There isn't. Get the stuff into the truck."

For three days I stubbornly refused to visit Father Zenzadrine about my affliction, convinced that I, big medicine man, with the multifarious pharmaceutical products given me by Lederle and Schenley Laboratories, with all those wonder pills, could cure anything organic. But as I hobbled around, or drove the scooter with one arm and one leg, or typed and photographed unilaterally, painfully, I began to wonder whether the trouble was organic, after all. I didn't like the boys' looking at me as if I were without hope.

And I was concerned by N'dri's accurate description of my et cetera being divided, one good and one awful. On the fourth morning, nearly rigid and thoroughly aching from head to toe on my right side, I rode resolutely off to visit Father Zenzadrine.

"Father," I said, "could they cut off my right side and leave me without paralysis and pain? I have not had a chance to tell you—"

"Ah-*ah?*" he said, his eyes popping like blueberries in a custard. The younger missionary dropped his bread. "The right side?" Father Zenzadrine took hold of me, hiking his cassock between his legs for better effort, and shook me till I yelled. "He has it," my two Fathers said together.

326

"Has what, God in heaven?"

"The curse. But the ancient curse, my son. Banal, unpleasant, harmless in the end, when you reach the end."

"Yes? This is a curse made by men, not by microbes, Father?"

"Have you had any difficulties with the people here, the Agnis? Have you struck anyone?"

"No, I mean yes, I did discharge one of my boys for stealing, but I didn't touch him."

"He had money?"

"His wages, yes."

Father Zenzadrine sighed. "Please don't think of mumbo jumbo, son. This is a factual job, and there's not an old-timer on the coast who can't recognize it. Put simply: your boy went to a witch doctor, a sorcerer, and paid him to do this thing to you in revenge for your having fired him. You will tell me"—and I did—"that no one but your own faithful cook had a chance to poison your food, and that Mrs. Davis ate from the same pot, and you will say nonsense."

"And if it wasn't poisoning that Moussa paid for," I said, "the only alternative is hypnosis, suggestion, which is absurd. I've been too busy even to think of Moussa."

Father Zenzadrine sighed. "I know. I'm a God-fearing man and shouldn't have anything to do with such matters, but I advise you to send your boys around Abengourou, to try to find where Moussa went on the day you fired him, where he spent money. If he went to a sorcerer, you'll have three choices: wait for your troubles to wear off (and maybe they won't), depending on how much Moussa paid the man; pay him yourself to have the curse taken off you; or go to a fetisher for a counter-charm. I, personally, recommend prayer also, twice a day, before meals."

N'dri returned in the late afternoon to find me sitting on the window sill, where I could stretch out my leg without touching anything. "Tiemoko found the sorcerer," he said gravely, "but he won't accept our business for at least a few days more, until the value of Moussa's payment has run out, even though Moussa has gone back to Abidjan."

"Uh!" I said, flinching at the pain.

327

"So I have ordered a fetisher," said N'dri. "The king's own. He drinks."

"This one?" I pointed, furious. "He's the old—old man who sneered at me yesterday, and thumbed his nose at me, by—by the wayside," I ended lamely. "Where's he going?"

The tall gray-haired dark man flowed in his robes around the corner of the house, where the outdoor kitchen was. He was flexing his knuckly fists. I got to the back window just in time to see him take a sock at the nose of our cook, who began listening immediately to what he had to say.

"When he has finished," said I to Ruth, "invite him inside, and serve him a crème de menthe." I struggled into shoes and the special-occasion shirt with the war ribbons on it. The fetisher spoke very good French. Framed by the window, his hair was platinum, his pagne of gold, and his crème de menthe like an archbishop's emerald upon his hand. He was, said he, the Chief Aka Comoé of the Betti tribe—which was far away, near Liberia.

He said categorically that all our information about the Agnis was wrong, that his "children" had told lies to us, that it was he in the good old days who had the right to cut off their jaws or gouge out their little eyes. For lies. He drank a great deal of crème de menthe, "Pippermint" brand.

N'dri, Quodio, and Tiemoko sat on their heels, their hands clasped respectfully before them. The old man beamed at me, and I saw his hand coming, slowly but straight, toward my poor right shoulder. Palm open, it advanced inexorably like a hooded cobra. I was fascinated, petrified.

"No! No!" I hollered.

"I shall hold you," he said. "I shall hold you." He did, with a grip of which a gorilla might be proud.

"If you want it again," he said, over my dead body, "it will be one thousand francs. If you don't, two thousand."

What I needed was a good medium to get my voice up for me. My ghost turned to Ruth and whispered, "Give him the two thous... Two, see?"

"You will be all right in the morning," said Aka Comoé, departing, kicking the cook as he passed. Almost immediately he thought better of this action, returned, raised his pagne above his knee, and kicked the cook again, but good.

"*A Dieu!*" he added.

In the morning I was quite cured, from here to et cetera.

33

The old slave trail—the great gentleman with three mustaches—north to Tehini

SORCERERS' VILLAGE? we asked, to the left and right of us. The white administrators laughed it off; we would have to be better detectives than they to find that school of evil. Evil because the sorcerers of the Ivory Coast were invariably mixed up in politics. Native agitators, trained at Dakar, went from village to village stirring up the people against the administration, against the Europeans generally. The movement for independence was growing throughout all French and British West Africa.

"The chief of the agitators," said the French commandant of the district, "is named Gogro. You've probably seen his little Russian-red car." We had, and had wondered about it. "Well, he is touring the land to stir up the sorcerers, and if he doesn't reach the Sorcerers' Village eventually, I'll eat his greasy hat. You might do worse than follow him."

It was late in that afternoon, with a sky glowering and the motor rattling in a sinister way, that we took off. Sensible people would have spent the night in Abengourou and taken part of the next morning to have the motor checked. But not I. We heard that Gogro was already on his way north along the lesser of the two roads—which sensible people rarely took—the old caravan route which led to Bondoukou and across Africa and Asia to faraway Cathay.

"I may be wrong," said I to Ruth, "but I'm not far from it."

"Say that again," said Ruth, as the engine turned over bumpily.

"This Gogro may be heading for some sort of sorcerers' village, but he is taking this degenerate road to throw us off the track, and is heading for Lobi country. The Lobis are the plate-lipped people, like the Ubangis, very naked. I'd like to meet them anyway, as they have a terrible reputation. True primitives worth cultivating, at least by you and me."

Night came to us quickly; there was still a sulphurous light above the tall trees, and a gunmetal, blue-gray cloud in the middle of it. This grew larger and thinner rapidly. You could see sulphur through it now, and when it expanded to reach the filigreed horizon of the trees, we got the first clicking of rain on the roof of the truck.

Quodio turned on the headlights at last just as we bounced over a fairly soft log. The lights flickered, but the rain was beautiful when they chose to illumine it, like golden grain flung at the windshield. Ruth sat ahead of me, next to Quodio, and the golden grain of rain seemed to come slanting through her golden hair, against the night's shadows. Skip it, I thought; it is just love; keep your eye on the road.

But there was no road to see. We were hurtling through blank darkness, through the tunnels of a dream. I reached for Quodio's bare shoulder, gently, so as not to alarm him, and said, "Quodio, my old one, slow up and then stop, for I think our lights are out."

Gradually we picked up speed again as our eyes became adjusted to the lavender blaze of our lamps. The jungle did really smell of spinach. The rain's hot fingers caressed my back, and I took off my shirt and tossed it to Ruth and leaned to the wind, saying, but to myself in loneliness: whatever this is, I am more than married to it; my love of this night and its hot rain is deep and awful as the rain of my own blood through my heart.

We passed through Agnibilekrou on the old slave trail, and met the wonderfully hospitable bushcombers there: Vezoiz the merchant, who gave us his "standard peek-neek dinnair" of soufflé and champagne; Father Favier, who divined water by swinging a flask of holy water over the dry earth—sometimes he swung gin; Monsieur Vet-

330

tiner, artist and linguist, who painted himself black and joined the native councils when agitators like Gogro, who had just been through here, tried to foment trouble.

And we came to Gombelé where the forest was abruptly replaced by plains, leading into the desert and Timbuctoo. And gasping with dust we came to Bondoukou where we were given a cube of concrete structure to live in while the boys worked on our limping truck. Gogro had eluded us here but we were eager to get on to Tehini of the plate-lipped Lobi folk, and passed our time blessedly with the great, the incomparable Abraham Hallage, one of the Most Unforgettable Characters I ever knew.

Monsieur Hallage, born in Lebanon, had come early to these distant plains and had become a mighty merchant. He had married a native girl, and while his wife now took care of most of his business he caught up with the social life which his years of industry had denied him. Social life was sparse in Bondoukou, practically limited to the company of Monsieur Anglade, who was a commercial crony, a couple of white officials, and ourselves, none of us averse to Abraham's early-morning hospitality. A drink with laughter at 10:00 A.M. is not considered a misdemeanor in the tropics. Abraham never wanted to, or needed to, drink alone.

You went through a mud-baked alley to find him, and up a rickety flight of outdoor stairs to a balcony that drooped considerably over the panorama of Bondoukou. You kept a hand on the window sill while looking down on those flat brown adobe houses and the blue smoke of their fires half veiling them. From the mosques all over the town would come the call of the muezzin, the marabout, a haunting call. We could see the devout below us washing their faces, hands, and feet at the blue teapots before entering the narrow gate of the mosque. No other worship has such a narrow gate as theirs. And no other gate was so wide as that of Abraham Hallage.

We would hear him suddenly, and cling tighter to the window sill as the blast shook the balcony. *"Punaises!"* he would bawl. This meant "Bedbugs!" and applied to nothing, as though one should cry "Zowie!" It was said that he used to yell *"Putains!"* until that got him into trouble with his lady guests.

"Punaises! my old Bill and my beautiful little Ruth! You have

come to see me. Bless you! It is nine o'clock. It is approaching luncheon, eh? I must celebrate your coming! We will have a cock-a-tail! I feel in mid-festival today. Careful, the balcony . . . there . . . there."

And we would sit cozily inside, surrounded by board walls and children, and have a drink. Through the window a snow was falling peacefully, the fluff of the kapok, the cotton tree, speckling the brown roofs. *"Punaises!"* yelled Abraham Hallage, fishing the stuff from his cognac, glowering at it—a dark Lebanese glower which used to make the Crusaders tremble.

"Maria!" We leaned with Abraham through the window and peered across the balcony and down to the courtyard where Maria was cooking epicurean delights. She was a bronzed matron, with a swish in her still. "Maria, I love you!" bawled Abraham Hallage. She tossed two hard-boiled eggs into the foutou, and smiled and nodded.

"The trouble with other people's wives," said Abraham as we sat down again with new cognac, "begging your pardon, Madame Davis, is that they are perfidious. Sometimes you can count on the fingers of one hand how often they are perfidious before you catch on to them. I was thinking of poor old N'goon, who had a trying experience only a few months ago. He was one of my darker and nicer friends, a great hunter but a faithful husband, just like me—"

"Abraham!" There came Maria's voice from the courtyard. We leaped to the window. "I love you!" shouted Maria, tossing two more eggs into the stew.

"Compris!" yelled Abraham. "Will you shut up? You are interrupting again!"

Abraham sat down grumbling. "Damned woman," he said. "And as for my old friend N'goon, poor fellow, he had started counting his wife's perfidies from his thumb and got almost as far as his pinkie when he said, like you and me, '------ -------------.' Forgive me, Madame Davis, but I must make this clear. That he *did* say in his distress to one of his faithful slaves, who admitted that he would have made the same remark under the circumstances."

"Slavery exists still?" I asked.

"Slavery exists, though of course it is forbidden. *Punaises!* Where was I? You are as bad as my wife! Had I reached the pinkie?"

332

"You had told us what N'goon had said."

"Right," said Abraham. "So N'goon took the faithful slave into the forest and whispered to him, saying that it was usually on nights when he went hunting gazelle with his head torch that his wife's lover came to the hut. He knew who the man was because there was always a strong smell of garlic when he had been around. Now he, N'goon, planned to go hunting this very night, and surely the lover would come. So the slave was to wait, then *wham!* and *whisht!*—with first the back and then the front of the machete, he was to stun the lover, rendering him docile, and slice off his you-know-what."

Abraham Hallage leaned back and sighed, expelling smoke through his nose. The blue smoke tangled with his mustache, twined through his eyebrows. He looked like a forest fire.

"But that night it rained, so N'goon did not go hunting. He stayed at home with his wife and drank bangi, and ate a foutou full of garlic, while his wife smiled in the old way at him. And they went to bed on their cow skin together, lying on their backs together, each of them dreaming; she, perhaps, of how nice it would be to have a husband who was a slave, and he of the gazelles, the leopards, the antelopes. And he dreamed of her, his wife, at last, till that dream wakened him, and he reached to embrace her in the dark, as a shadow even darker bent over him. . . ."

"What happened then?" Ruth asked.

"Aw, madame, you know what."

Skirting the edge of the Gold Coast we made pretty good bush time in the borrowed pickup; our truck needed major repairs. But what once had been a caravan route was furrowed and pitted now, with wild trees growing in it, and bushes uprooted across it where the elephants had passed. We came to Laoudi, which was a village of four huts and one well, and to Bouna, a Moslem town with a fortified mosque in its middle.

From Bouna we rushed northwest along a sandy road toward Tehini of the Lobis, our boys drying up behind us on our mountain of luggage. From time to time we would hear N'dri's shrill, crack-lipped, city-slicker laugh when we passed a Lobi woman. I would turn to chide him, for she might be a zoological specimen to him, but

333

to me she was precious, a woman neglected, of a tribe which had been studied at book length by only one ethnologist, so far as I knew. N'dri, black Baloé, thought it amusing that a Lobi girl should wear bone discs in her lips but almost no clothes.

The eye of the casual observer noticed the discs first, then traveled rapidly down over firm, rounded breasts, which gave the acute observer pause, for African breasts, when young, are usually pointed, pear-shaped; when old (at the age of maternity, about sixteen), are drooping, flat, pendulous. The African wife is proud to be a mother and display the well-used dugs her children have tugged at, very often to the age of five. So far as I know, the Lobi matrons are the only Negro women of Africa to have the globular bosom and be proud of it.

As the car sped on toward the heart of the Lobi country, Tehini, we passed one and another of these tribeswomen.

"N'dri!" I would yell. "You'll never become an ethnologist. You are a carnal man."

"*Oui! Oui, mon capitaine!* But is it not scientific to wonder about these strings suspended from the belt in front of the green leaves *derrière?*"

It wasn't much of a costume or cause for wonderment. The strings of bark hung from a thin girdle in front, and heart-shaped leaves, usually wilted, pouted impudently behind, waggling as the maiden walked.

"I couldn't make love to one of these, *mon capitaine*, I would laugh too much!" The other boys, too, were howling with laughter. I was becoming indignant and protective, very much like a guide for tourists who didn't appreciate the rarities he was showing them. Worse, I was paying my saucy tourists to visit their own cousins and become friendly with them. They owed me a certain collaboration, without public hilarity. People, like chimpanzees, become hostile when not taken seriously.

"N'dri! Quodio! And you, Tiemoko! I'll have no more of this!" I said severely. "You may laugh at this country and its thin trees, but the people in it must become our people for a month. *Compris?*"

We traveled soberly along that dusty road until at last we judged we were in Tehini, for there was a large, thatched administrative sort

334

of structure on a little knoll. There was no concentrated village, no market place. A group of huts with a wall around them was a sleeping-sickness compound, according to a sand-blasted sign.

Ours was a dream house, as they say, a long house of whitewashed mud walls and neatly thatched roof, a semicircular veranda looking over the barren world of Tehini, toward Timbuctoo on one side and the far, rollicking wet sea on the other. If it hadn't been so big I would have put my arms around it. I loved it.

34

A very naked people—how to become a power in a Lobi home—disgraceful adventure among the Hippotragus Equinus

IT WAS GOOD THERE, in that ex-military post, dating from the days when the French and the Lobis didn't know each other. It was good to waken with the pure crystal smell of the morning and stretch on the hard bed and trace the fan-shaped mats of the ceiling, lazily, and duck as the bats and swallows swirled above us between the eaves. We could smell lime trees and mangoes in our silver-brown dusk. We would hear the cackling of the pintards, the guinea hens, like the voice of breaking glass.

We became fond of the Lobis because of their honesty, their impeccable cleanliness, their joie de vivre. Of all the peoples of Africa, I found the Lobi the most congenial, the closest in spirit to me. They were not black but just the color of polished kitchen copper, possibly from some distant blending with Arab blood. Like most of the other races, they had come from the East, and crossed the Volta River around 1770. It seems that they settled on the lands of the Pygmies and killed them off or absorbed them. When the French arrived in the nineteenth century the Lobis were so busy battling among themselves that they scarcely noticed the presence of these white intruders. When they did, they turned gleefully upon the French, fought them lustily until 1913, and were definitely pacified only in 1925. It was a great sorrow to them, for the French didn't want them to fight anyone any more, and what were they to do with their spare time?

Even a Lobi must be prudent in his research among the Lobi belles. Oddly for Africa, adultery scarcely exists in this happy tribe. If a wife commits it, is found out, and still wants to return to her husband, she must wait outside the door of their soukhala until he shall have sacrificed a chicken to the fetish, *and* a dog. Otherwise he will die the moment she touches the family grain, which apparently is symbolic of insemination, as is our wedding rice.

There is no punishment for murder among the Lobis, except the reciprocity of it; it is an honorable occupation like the head-hunting of other tribes, and indeed it has been brought right into the home. No boy is considered a man until he has killed either his father or his mother. This should be done as early as possible, at the first reproach which the boy interprets as an affront to his manhood. The deceased father's brother, incidentally, inherits everything, including wives and assassin children.

When the boy has committed his murder, he is highly esteemed by everyone, including his fiancée, who has awaited just this to become his bride. His friends bring him gifts of chickens, and for three days there are dances and the drinking of dolo, or palm wine. Then a sheep is killed, and its blood drained into a calabash for anointing the warrior's hair.

A funeral, for a Lobi, is almost as much fun as a marriage, like a rollicking Irish wake. The corpse is tied securely, sitting up, to the fetish tree. It is left there for three days or so while the neighbors, men and women, dance around it, tossing dolo into its gaping mouth as though to say, "You're still with us, old fellow, and you must share in this frolic for which we really have you to thank." The corpse has had enough of it when it makes a public spectacle of its hangover by decomposing.

It was Tuesday afternoon in Tehini. We could tell a Tuesday blindfold because we had arrived on one, and counted seven and seven and seven of the days we were marooned in Lobi land, waiting for our truck to come and fetch us. There was, of course, no telephone here, no bus service, no post, for there was nobody here but us Lobis, growing a great deal older from one Tuesday to the next.

But this Tuesday was a famous one. It started with a bang as our phantom, the little red car with Gogro, the Communist bloke, came charging down the road and past our veranda, never pausing. N'dri's pretty washerwoman reported that Mr. Gogro in the red car had told the Lobis we were up to capitalist mischief, and that the banker of the village, a tall blue boy in rags, had given that car such a kick in the *derrière* as to toss it nearly into the *hypnoserie*.

The next news of interest was that a cousin Lobi a few villages away had run amok and murdered forty people. Forty! Did I understand? They counted it on their fingers and toes. There was a man! We should have a dance this night. But meanwhile (this was still Tuesday) perhaps I would do my friends a favor. There was a troop of *antelope cheval* (roan antelope, *Hippotragus equinus*) which had come out of the game reserve to the south, cocky as be-damned, thinking they were still under the white man's protection and chomping away at the Lobi crops. Gogro, lecturing from his red car, had already made certain reflections on the matter, to the effect that the white man had formed the animal reserve to deprive the dark citizen of his provender. Would I go out and scare these ravening beasts away, or at least shoot a few of them in revenge for the havoc to the crops?

Apart from the fact that I have always been hesitant to kill anything but man, my armament was of the rudest, a slingshot, an old army pistol, a shotgun, an underwater spear, and brass knuckles. None of these seemed quite the thing with which to cow the horse antelope. Our hunt was not successful. Ruth with Quodio, I with N'dri, on our scooters went weaving across the savannah. N'dri carried what he called generously my "boom-boom" charged with sparrow shot, but I had estimated my chances: the scooter should be able to outrun the herd over a long stretch, and if we could ride straight into it and come up beside the giant stallion, like a cowboy

337

racing an express train, N'dri could push the muzzle of the "boom-boom" against its heart and probably tickle it to death with the sparrow shot.

Ruth let out a whoop as we rounded the corner of a termite hill twelve feet high, for there were the horse antelope come to meet us. Towering high above our little scooters, brandishing horns like stalagmites, their shoulder muscles knotting right up to their baleful eyes, they coughed and came in a mass of hundreds at us.

The scooters went out from under us, wheels spinning in the air, motors roaring still, and we backed against the termite hill as the charge came and divided around us. There was a pretty moment when one of them impaled my hat which I was brandishing like a bull-fighter's cape, and went off with it triumphantly on the tip of his horn. Then, suddenly, they were gone. The motors choked and lay limp. Our pale black boys snuggled up to us, just as the assault from the rear began: the termites. We went home, mighty hunters, dispirited.

It was quite a day, our final Tuesday. We were changing into clean khaki in preparation for the dance to celebrate the murder of the forty neighbors, and behind the house marched a file of Lobi ladies glistening from the bath and wearing fresh leaves. N'dri, valeting me with my four articles of clothing—shirt, pants, sandals—stood suddenly still and said, "Feel?"

"Feel what?"

"The truck!"

"Your head is out of order, my boy," I said.

"No, no, Capitaine. Just stand still, loose like this, and you will feel it. You can't hear it yet. . . ."

I stood so loose that I had to lean against the wall, and then I felt the truck. It was a thin vibration growing quickly stronger until it was blent with sound, and there, down the long road coming from Bouna, was the truck bolting toward us merrily. When it reached the terrace, it was piled with black heads like grapes; the Lobis had hopped it to bid us hurry to the dance; we could ride back to the festival place.

Away we went, sitting on people's heads, banging the Djula driver on the back, so happy we were. In a square of adobe sakhoulas surrounding a fetish tree, the dance, so-called, was well begun. There were immense jars of dolo against every wall. You took a ladle made of half a calabash and helped yourself to it, flies and dust and all, and with a quick gulp it was down. A flask of brandy helped this considerably.

The orchestra sat in the shade of the fetish tree for inspiration. The instrument called the balofon was about the size of a master xylophone, but resembled more the Balinese gamelan with resonating gourds beneath the keys. It was played at a terrific pace and its notes were clear as the ringing of crystal glasses; its tone was almost visually silver.

We with the chiefs were surrounded by bouncing bodies. They swirled, ducked, feinted, coiled their line and snapped it loose in individual frenzies. It was a woman's dance, this first one, and was called Kena Sabena, and the purpose of it was to fling the knees, spread wide, as high as possible, synchronously flapping up and down the breasts. Oop, oop, oop they went, faster than the eye could follow, as if to tear themselves away from the bronzed and glittering chests.

Mixed with the bright ringing of the balofon music there occasionally came the shock of the drums. They would start with a little muttering among themselves, then one of their voices would explode. It shook you with its violence. The young men shot arrows to the sky, like graphic grace notes, and the dancers chanted something of which I could only distinguish the repeated word "Yho!"

This interested me, for I had heard it in other villages, usually when I was querying the people about magic. "Yho!" in Liberia, which wasn't far away, meant simply "Hello," but when used in several quite different dialects of the Ivory Coast, my boys could only assume that "Yho" was a place, and one obviously of importance to all these various tribes. Could it mean heaven or hell? Could it possibly be the name of the place we sought, a mountain or a valley where the seminary of sorcerers would be?

I put my cameras aside and collected around me N'dri, Quodio, and several Lobis who spoke a modicum of the market language, Djula, waiting for the outburst of the drums and the chant again. It came suddenly. My avid interpreters, every one an ethnologist now,

339

bent their ears to it, and agreed as to its context which was filtered through N'dri and reached me in French. It was good poetry and great news:

> Come swing to the drums and encircle the seeds
> Of your love with a dance. Let the pounding
> Of grain and the flashing of arrows be fertile.
> Slash your love, pound it and mold it again,
> And fling it this night to the wizards of Yho. . . .

"The wizards of Yho?" Were they sure, my interpreters? They were sure. Their heads bobbed. And where was Yho? Ah, that. . . . Was it a real place with earth beneath it and a forest and huts? Ah, it was thought to be, but no Lobi knew. Ah, no. . . .

Never, except at sea, had I been so aware of so much night around me. From the veranda where we were drowsing on our canvas cots the hill sloped away beyond the small shadow mountains made by our feet, and Ruth's face next to me might have been very close or infinitely distant, lightly clouded by the soft night blue of her hair. I felt like St. Exupéry's Little Prince, knowing that he must leave this good place and go to the real world far away.

We must leave Tehini and return to our jungles which now seemed gross in comparison with this lean nude land, as the jungle people seemed heavier, coarser. Against the light sky I saw a black star now, a spider in a web which he had attached on one side to the eaves, and on the other side mysteriously, for its supporting strands went up and up and they could only be attached to stars. Benignly weary I followed them, sliding smoothly at first, floating from one to another, then bumping over knots where the spider star had become confused.

I sat up in bed, awake. The sky was paling.

340

35 〰〰〰〰〰〰〰〰〰〰

The elephants' mountain—
the wood of the sacred apes
—the monstrous termite queen

LATER THERE WOULD be a wind in the woods, a wind in the grasses, which would mean the death of a man. It may have been, I later thought, this same wind that followed us as we came down, through Bondoukou and Abengourou again, to Abidjan where I was to meet Khalil Sabeh, whom I was to kill because of my friendship for him. I do not mean this to sound melodramatic. There were other deaths on the expedition, concrete and abstract, but the death, probably murder, of this sterling man might never have occurred had we not found that we shared uncommonly a lust for mystery and danger.

Khalil Sabeh stood straight, bronzed, huge beside a window framing trees. He was the greatest ivory hunter on the Ivory Coast. He was Persian, I believe, and what I liked first about him was that he kept drawing farther and farther away from the window until he was able to frame the red-and-green flamboyant tree with a silver monkey on the highest branch, like a Persian miniature.

Here was the odd thing, that there should have been spontaneously and immediately a hearty warmth of understanding between us, the solid meshing of the good gears of friendship. I could work with this man.

"Come and see me at Gagnoa," he said. "You can help me."

I could not have guessed how I would help him down the last of his jungle paths.

We rolled out of Abidjan toward the setting sun. We were away to the woods again with a new truck, new provisions, fresh film, and the confidence that in the western mountains were hidden the old customs we sought.

"Anh . . ." said N'dri cheerily.

"Anh . . . anh," replied Quodio pointedly, twisting the truck on two wheels around an outward-tilted curve.

"Anh!" contradicted the apprentice, banging his head on the roof.

I had long ago given up trying to learn any of the fifty-three native dialects. The monosyllabic conversation of my boys, subtly expressing their profoundest thoughts with a simple "Anh," decided me to let semantics alone.

"Anh!" I said loudly, and everybody jumped. The truck swerved. Quodio slowed it, looking nervously over his shoulder at me.

"Did you mean that, Capitaine?"

"Carry on," I said. "I was only joking." Judging by the expressions of everyone, including Ruth, it was a pretty poor joke, which might have been fatal on a curve.

We drove to N'douci, a fork of roads crotching some of the more evolved but less courteous cannibals; it was said that they didn't even take off their felt hats while they ate you. We turned to the west, to Tiassale and Divo and Latoka, along a road of marine twilight, and then to the considerable town of Gagnoa, where we burned out a couple of bearings and cracked a couple of springs, opportunely near a mechanic whose rum was excellent.

We went on the Lambretta scooters to see Khalil Sabeh in the neatest and most enormous plantation I had ever seen, with a trimmed hedge around it and a graveled driveway leading through great flower gardens to a spacious house. Sabeh served us champagne; it was a hot afternoon. And as we lolled on the leather cushions Sabeh said, as though talking to himself, "You know . . ."

"Yes?" I knew that this was the important thing he must tell me, that I had waited for.

"There is a mountain," he said, "which I must climb. Do you like mountains?"

"Yes."

"This is a peculiar one. You must take me seriously when I tell you that I believe it to be the elephants' graveyard of these parts. Of course we've all read the stories of elephants going to a certain place to die, and we've read, too, that this is nonsense, that fossil ivory is picked up anywhere where elephants live and die. Still we

342

haven't explained why there are so many elephants alive and so few skeletons of them found."

This was true, according to all professional hunters I had known. And the Ivory Coast was named for its ivory, of course. I said, "Yes."

"I had better talk a preface to this," said Khalil Sabeh. "I own a plantation, which is a successful one. But I hunt elephants for some reason which is not clear to me. I respect elephants, but they damage my crops. They are bad neighbors, and I kill them. I *enjoy* hunting elephants, which is what I don't understand, for I have no feeling of vengeance toward them. Is it, do you think, that one kills what one loves?"

"Yes," I said. "Yes, and one's self, too. . . ."

"That has nearly happened to me. I'm an old-timer here and I know my native boys, who are more of the family than servants, but once they burned down my house, and once, when I had captured a baby elephant and was raising it on powdered milk, someone let the baby, a fetish elephant, of course, loose in the night, probably to die before it could even reach the mountain. I had a lightning rod on my house, and there I found, next morning, impaled upon it, the arm of my little elephant's keeper. The man died, of course. Loss of blood and the planting of certain herbs in him, like cloves on a ham."

"Champagne?" The servant was blue-black, broad of shoulder, unfriendly. I wondered how much French he had understood. Khalil Sabeh leaned forward like a mountain and fixed me straight with his long blue eyes. He raised his glass and set it down again.

"I must go to the mountain," he said. "I have asked a dozen Europeans to come with me during the years I have wanted to go. I told them frankly the strange beliefs about it. Sure, they would go, the great hunters; but they didn't. No. Most of them had been here long enough to believe a little as the natives believe. And as I do."

The eyes of Khalil Sabeh were lonely and fanatic and fierce upon me. There was no need for them to be—and this is hard to write about—for the pulse you know as the one which makes you lust, often futilely, for women or clean air or a horizon to dent, had begun at my temples. This I must do, I knew. This I must do. I must go to the elephants' mountain.

"What are these beliefs?" I asked.

"Don't do this," said Madame Sabeh.

"I think you and I could do this," said Sabeh. "The beliefs are these, and my boys will confirm them. The mountain—it's a hill really —is not far from here, and rises quite straight from the little village at its base. It's a quiet village. I have never heard laughter nor a drum in it. The guardian of the mountain, an ancient man, lives there, and for years was the only man permitted on the mountain, though now it seems his son goes with him, being trained to take over whatever priestly service the old man performs way up there, at the cemetery of the elephants."

I was interested to see the red end of my cigarette trembling. Was I afraid, I wondered, or was this the ecstatic trembling I had once known when halfway up a cliff at night, during the war, a plain assassin?

Khalil Sabeh spun a wand of useless very old veined ivory between his fingers, and called to his head boy. "Bring the other boys to me," he said.

A dozen of them came, in shorts, some with shirts, some without. They seemed uneasy, and I assumed that the waiter had been reporting what he understood of our talk. I remember a little fellow with ears which flared like an elephant's. He didn't like me, I knew, for the pulsing at my temples had stopped as it does when danger becomes certain. One should never be frightened of danger, of an elephant's charge, of the dark path, of a lover's packed baggage; mercifully the fear goes at this last moment.

Sabeh said to the boys, with a casual nod at me, "Here is a friend who loves Africa as we do, and he is a little afraid of the mountain as I am, but he will go with me to bring back to you the truth as to what is there. It is your mountain and you are frightened of it. We are, too. Perhaps the elephants die there. Perhaps there are demons. Perhaps it is a very old mountain, and harmless and no good. You could still grow crops on it. My friend and I will climb it alone, unless some of you . . ."

Quietly the boys went away, without a sound, on their bare feet, their knees spread so that their starched shorts shouldn't touch. When they should have reached the kitchen, one of them whinnied like an elephant, but louder than any elephant I had ever heard.

344

N'dri was seated at the doorway, a faithful sentinel. I asked him to bring Quodio and Tiemoko to us. They came at last, reluctantly. N'dri didn't look at me. Obviously they had heard the kitchen talk. I said to them quietly, "You will come with us to the mountain. You are Catholics, not animists, and you are the governor's boys."

They shook their heads, and considered their toes. No-no, no-no. They went sadly away again. Khalil Sabeh's long hands opened in a shaft of the evening sunlight. "It seems we must go alone," he said. "I could never force these boys to come. Nor can women go to a sacred thing in Africa. We must go alone without arms or cameras, honestly."

I said, "We'll go to this mountain, Khalil Sabeh. We'll go. . . ."

So it was understood that when I had finished my mission to the west I would send word to Sabeh, saying approximately when I should return to Gagnoa, and we would plan the mountain trip for a few days later.

"Keep an eye out for the Pygmies," he laughed as we took off in the truck. *"They* might come with us!" I saw that two of the kitchen boys were at the window listening. They didn't respond when Quodio waved.

We were still in well-forested country, but the road was flattish and we made good time toward Issia. The woods were rich with life, and I said to Ruth that here was the affirmation of living, a vital world that breathed, lusted, fought, died in knots. Sit with your back against a tree, quietly, and even before the ants discover you, you will hear the crepitation of a leaf and see it move with a giant Goliath beetle under it, white and black. What may seem the bark of the tree before you will become detached and turn into one of the poisonous spiders called gofa in the Beti tongue. Looking up through the lace of ferns twelve feet tall, you may see the green monkey called yurba playing trapeze games for none but himself, or the white-nosed monkey called lokpoua, who has discovered you and is making wry faces.

Sometimes in the truck, more often preceding it like a motorcycle escort on our scooters, startling beast and man alike, we went through Issia toward a wood called Beti Tapia, of sacred monkeys. We were

345

encouraged, for the more the country became primitive westward, the more we heard of "sacred" and magical things. And indeed the wood of the monkeys was magical with the amity of a dozen simian tribes living abnormally together, the little green monkeys, the white-nosed lokpoua, the savage baboons. They had the run of the village at the edge of the trees and could pillage the huts or tickle the babies as they pleased.

Once a day they were ritually fed by their priest, a black giant named Alfé Bogué, who would be brought to the edge of their wood in a gorgeous palanquin borne on the shoulders of minor priests wearing robes of purple and orange, slashing at the wind with golden hatchets. Bogué rang a great bell and instantly the woods boiled with monkeys. They came galloping along the paths, springing over each other. The leanest top branches of the trees bent down, and the monkeys swung, as I once did on birches, to the ground. The little green monkeys in their gaiety came leaping from bough to bough, tossing the flowers of the flame tree and the hibiscus before them. The baboons, big as bantamweight boxers, broad-shouldered, walking on their knuckles, came lumbering forth, wrinkling their black corrugated noses, scratching their pink behinds.

Savage though Bogué might be, he was a forthright and progressive man. He stood beside me, tossing his largesse to his sacred beasts. "Do you have," said he in the Beti tongue to N'dri, "any penicillin?" which he pronounced in perfect English.

"Do you have," I replied quickly, "any knowledge of where is the Sorcerers' Village?"

"Yho!" he gasped, and seemed to be trying to gulp the syllable back again. There it was again, Yho.

The cook M'blah suddenly appeared with a bottle containing one hundred penicillin tablets. "There were no love diseases among us," the priest said, "until the oracle determined that we should be the guardians of this sacred wood of apes. The apes rape our wives, our wives tell us, and give them these objectionable maladies, but me, I think it's the Baboon Men."

Ruth paused in winding her camera. "Who are they?" she asked me.

"The Baboon Men resemble the Leopard Men, and they act in the same way for the same cultist principle."

346

"Ah, yes, you did tell me. Claws of iron—heart-eating—Sunday supplements?"

"Yes, but let's not be flippant about it. The Leopard Society makes news because it damn well exists from Senegal down to the Belgian Congo. The French and British and Belgian administrators will show you members of it in jail, and the iron claws they attach to their wrists for tearing out the hearts of women and children, who are easiest. But it seems to be only the Baboon Society that rapes."

The priest, Alfé Bogué, was evidently balancing his conscience against the fortune in medical magic we had given him. He made certain there was no one but ourselves and the monkeys listening before he said, with a lift of his little beard toward the west, "Yho. Go to the town of Man. Seek a cleft peak."

It became increasingly clear that our boys were increasingly unenthusiastic about this Sorcerers' Village. Every native, cannibal though he might be, felt that two—always two—villages away from his home were savages who would gobble him up, and a whole village of sorcerers, a very school of them, might do even worse. I wasn't at all sure that at the last minute, as in French Guiana, when I was almost within reach of my goal, our boys would not mutiny.

We spent the night with Commandant Van of this district. "Cleft peak? That could be the Mountain of Man, about ninety kilometers from the Liberian border. Man is one of the most beautiful places in Africa, and it lies between two fascinating tribes, the Guéré and the Yakouba."

It was evening, and we were walking between the rosebushes, which were scintillating with fireflies. Van caught one and gently put it in his wife's hair, as native lovers do in Tahiti—dozens of them, until in the dark of night you can see your beloved's face.

"One of my colleagues divorced a Yakouba couple the other day," said Van. "Forced to it. The husband and wife had been sparring for many years, and their rows were a public nuisance. The climax came when the wife deliberately and in the presence of witnesses made water on a firefly. Her man dragged her to court and they were divorced promptly. The firefly was his totem, never to be harmed."

347

We lumbered through the bush to the great Sassandra River, which we crossed by one of those infernal machines, the bac, which is a sort of scow attached to an overhead cable so the current wouldn't drag it, and poled by two iron men. And we came to Guiglo where the amateur black Communists had threatened the life of the commandant a few days ago. It was the silence of the village of Guiglo which was ominous. There wasn't even a drum, but you could feel drums. There was no overt menace, but you could feel tension in the village like a nerve about to snap.

Thirty kilometers to the south was Tulepleu and the vast plantation of Alfred Leroy, who welcomed us but was very busy just now demolishing termite hills. These were structures ten feet in diameter and a dozen feet high, made of earth and termite spittle into a nearly concrete mass.

"Easy! Easy!" Leroy ordered. "We mustn't destroy the queen."

The men chopped gently, for they wanted the queen to eat raw. They picked delicately at the half castle of the queen, approaching her bedchamber, which might be a little to the right or the left. And the termite lovers and workers swarmed out in thousands, in hundreds of thousands, probably; they were difficult to count.

"Give that ax to me," said Leroy, and he picked at the core of the castle delicately, like a dentist, excising it from a two-foot lump resembling a fritter, which was the royal bedchamber. Round brown termites came from it, angrily.

"Those are the nurses."

We cut the clay in two carefully, so as not to wound the queen. We would surprise her. We leaned over her sanctum as the two halves of it came open, and she was lying there, pulsing, ten inches long, the wife of thousands of quarter-inch black termites, a blob of a queen, nasty white with a few brown spots. She was like a quilted balloon filled with milk. She throbbed. She undulated from the little black speck which was her mouth to the opposite orifice from which emerged the eggs. This was invisible because of the swarming, battling nurse termites desperately snatching at the eggs and galloping off with them to deposit them in the nursery cells—which were not there. Looking close, I was certain I could see the anxiety in the seeking movement of their heads. It was catastrophe, and there was fear in

348

me as I realized that this was the end of a world as authentic as our own, that we were the evil men from another planet who had brought this devastation.

36 ∿∿∿∿∿∿∿∿∿∿∿∿∿

The duckling dancers—we seek a
cleft peak—the fairytale house
—the hermit beneath the waterfall

A NOTABLE DATE was the eighteenth of May when we arrived in Danané, the land of the Yakoubas and the dancing kings. The Cuobés and the Guérés, competent cannibals, lived around here, too. Commandant Ottavi took us to tea with two of them in prison, which was a scarcely guarded hut. There they were, the two old women cannibals, confined for life for having eaten some of their young and sold the rest. Their garden was a neat patch behind the bamboo fence, thrusting up vegetables. They had been here for fifteen years, they said, because of an indiscretion.

There are lands you belong to, that belong to you, though they may be at the ends of the earth, and Danané was one of mine. It was rolling wooded country with branches of the Cavally River refreshing it, and there was purity here. The air was good, the road— due to Ottavi—honest, the natives impeccable, though attired mostly in their skins.

"Camembert?" suggested our gourmet commandant, as we concluded a meal of toasted giant snails on his thatched veranda. The joy of Camembert in the jungle is an exquisite experience. The cheese is flown to Abidjan from France, but only by the most perfectly joined relays can it reach the outposts in good shape. We attacked it with dispatch, for there was a chimpanzee named Ernest whose table manners were execrable.

349

"One village you might investigate," said the commandant, "is Roussi Salés, where the people are so unworldly it is said they subsist on palm wine alone."

There was only one way to the village, and that was across the river and for a long way up it by tipoye; this thatched box on poles dips and swings with the movement of the boys carrying it. It was very seasick-making. Up we would go over the huge rocks, and down with a bump into the blue swirling water. Not only did I have Ernest with me but one of the recorders, on which I was trying to get the porters' songs. These, had we understood them at the moment, would have been disquieting:

> Swing them and sway them and drown them, my sons.
> Hour upon hour we have carried the freight of them
> Over the swamps and the bush where the vipers
> Are not friendly to us. . . .
> Hush, my sons, hush, don't you sing,
> Lest the elephants, too, come to ask to be carried
> Upon our poor backs.

It was a handsome river with flamboyant trees and luminous red-and-white tick birds flying against them, and a golden mango, and here and there, placed as in a deliberate composition, the Liberian ducks. They seemed more like herons, standing tall on their legs, spreading their wings to dry them, blue-black, the color of sequins. There could be no question of our coming into sorcerous country. Even the cool air of the hills around us had the electric smell of wizards.

We reached the shore at last and continued more happily on foot to a Yakouba village of pointed roofs. It was a miniature place but with an enormous noise in it, of drums and horns and the honking sounds that geese make, and little bells. We walked quietly into it, to an excellent dance of four full-bosomed beauties who were trying to bring on the rains because their crops were dry. They represented ducklings, I was told, as ducklings love the rain. Long, curved feathers adorned their hair, their faces were striped with red dye, and to

350

their backsides were attached little platforms with the jingling rain
bells on them.

Haughtily, never smiling, they held their heads high and swung
their scarves back and forth across their breasts. They went tripping
to the west, where the rains might live, and back to the east, for you
never could tell. They did a bump and a grind which no god of rain
could resist. From somewhere in the crowd of pulsing people came
a single voice raised in the chant of this dance, a woman's or a
duckling's.

> Mother of rain, will you come to us now,
> Quicken our fields and hasten the plow
> On its journeys to nourish the young men of Yho . . . ?
> Ah, it's a Sorcerers' Village, my mother.
>
> Great mother, great mother of rain,
> Oh, bless our thin pastures and succor the grain
> That we may rejoice in your beauty again.

"Did you hear, Bill? Did you hear?" said Ruth as N'dri translated.
"Yho, a Sorcerers' Village?"

"Darling, I did. We are almost there now."

And we moved on. We must get to Man for provisions. We must
get to Touba. We must go to the west for our cleft mountain, I was
sure now, even if that meant Liberia or French Guinea. And it must
be fast if we were to film before the rains. I had some faith in those
duckling dancers.

We came up the hill at last to the important town of Man. Two
thirds of the horizon was visible to the west of us, and along it lay
the loveliest scenery this side of the Ethiopian plateaus. The Dent
(the Tooth) of Man, hulked up in a green triangle, graying to rock
at the top, and all around it were lesser hills of green, yellow, blue,
purple, depending on the clouds and the light. Far below us were
the fields with long-horned cattle grazing in them, and above us to
the north was a solemn lump of hill, once some governor's summer
playground and now known as La Bombe, for a group of young

Frenchmen lived there in isolation, devoting themselves to atomic mysteries. Here was the new and most terrible magic of the Ivory Coast.

I was prepared for neither the form nor the qualities of Paul Abel, to whom we had been directed on the chance that he might put us up. I had not expected the neatly khaki-clad gentleman he was, nor the rambling, spacious, spotless house which he had designed, being an architect as well as gold miner, brickmaker, and scholar.

"Put you up? My dear fellow, and madame, I *want* you here! Why, dammit, I like the looks of you, and the intelligent sounds you make! How rare they are, here in the woods. Look, that half of this needlessly large house is yours. Now get along and wash your faces and we'll have a drink. I'll take care of your boys."

It was one of the few houses both practical and attractive that I had seen in the tropics, with long verandas on each side connected by a high living room. At each end were sleeping quarters with bath, and the whole was covered with thatch. Beneath the eaves of it there was an encircling vent to permit the heat to go out, and the wind, but not the rain, to enter.

We went to Upper Zangué village in search of masks for the American Museum, and to Lower Zangué where a parade of girls wearing sacks came from the wood like zombies, walked without a word among the people, and returned to their sacred solitude. They had just been through the ritual of excision.

The old chief with a feather stuck in his beard and a pointed leather hat covered with gri-gri charms left us in the sun to be entertained by a ten-year-old hoyden who danced indefatigably before a dozen sweating drummers. Tomorrow she, too, would be summoned to do her stint in the wood, not to emerge for several years until she had been erotically instructed and mutilated and could proudly wear the sack of the initiate.

We filmed her through the morning as she danced her final dance, with close-ups of her tongue protruding and waggling lasciviously.

She chanted as she danced:

352

"Here is my small golden heart in my hand,
Twirling to go as I cast it before me,
To seek the young wizards of Yho ...
(Yho ... Yho ...).

The drummers have loved me. The beat of my heart
Is the beat of their drums. And I shall deny them.
None but the wizards of Yho are my lovers.

Shall I bear sons, shall I bear giants,
Shall I bear gods or the ghosts of the gods?

Love me, my drummers. I'll whirl to your drums
And fling your great pulse to the witches of Yho.
(Yho ... Yho ...)."

Yho again. We were getting closer all the while, I thought, and we must get on. But we didn't immediately, for people were too nice to us and kept sending us or leading us to villages which, they felt, could do things that would be absolutely sensational on film. They never could understand that we weren't at all trying to make a sensational film.

What held me to Man, apart from the warmth and wisdom of Paul Abel, was a fairy-tale house and the people of it. It stood on a hill among great trees above the town, with a view of mountains rolling toward Liberia.

"Let's go up there, Ruth. No one could live in such a good little house and not be both fantastic and good."

"Yes," Ruth said practically, "but they probably want to be alone. That's why they are there."

It was nearly too much for our scooters along the twisting, steep, stony path. The noise of our motors went ahead of us, and as we skidded around the last corner and almost through the living-room door we were met by Didy and Paul Duran and their daughters.

It was really fairy tale. There was love here—that old thing, legendary love. The terraced and latticed little garden, the white L-shaped living room with its many windows to the west, the occasional copper

353

pieces from France, the children and the parent Durans, seemed mystically imbued with it—not contentment but happiness. The bread had life to it; it smiled because it liked to make you happy while you were eating it. The books had been read often and caressed. Plants and pets were all over the place, you were pleasantly aware of them, but they never upset the exquisite balance of this house.

The Durans were gold prospectors (as leprechauns are) and were having what anyone else would consider pretty rough going. This they talked of rarely, but we saw them often, over drinks or dinners balanced to a nicety, and we heard bits of the troubles they had. There was the sticky business of getting permits for seeking gold. And there was the hard rivalry of other prospectors who, when Paul went into the jungle, sent natives to spy on him and burn down his camps and destroy his markers. And he would start again, and again, and gradually get the permits, and mine gold at the rate of thirty grams to one hundred and fifty per ton of earth, just enough to keep his house modestly but vitally alive. And the bread smiling.

The Tooth of Man, the mountainous cleft tooth, was recurringly the backdrop of my dreams. It was a hauntingly beautiful edifice, a mountain isolated from the others and rising through the verdure of the jungle and the bluish brush farther up to its round, white, split peak. That was where the Sorcerers' Village should lie, but it didn't; Paul and Didy Duran, both prospectors, could state responsibly that no one lived on its slopes. There was the legend that it heaved and sighed at night.

But it drew me toward it whenever I walked or scootered alone on the lesser hilltops of Man. I was returning from the cinchona plantation one evening when the copper-colored sunlight struck full upon it and upon a path that led in its direction. I left my machine and climbed dreamily, peacefully, somnambulantly, content to be alone and feeling quiet and clear inside. The worries were gone, the black stains of memory. I could climb, I thought, to that golden peak forever, so long as this tranquillity, the clearness was in me.

The path smelled headily of eucalyptus. There was the crackling passage of small invisible animals around me, and dark red birds,

354

shaped like swallows, swooped to examine me and swooped up again toward a friendly cloud that matched its paces to mine.

We went west and southwest across the Bafing River, which had a strong smell of distilled cool air upon it, for it was mountain water, and as we crossed it in the bac its ripples clinked against us, hard like coins. Up we went into the mountains again, and most of them had cleft peaks. This was country unfrequented by whites or blacks; it was still too rough for cultivation. The leaves were furry and like little hands pushing at us. The bird cries were neither happy nor cordial. This was not the docile forest of the lowlands. This growth we were wading through was aggressive, vital, ambitious, and, I am sure, clean-thinking. It wanted to be left alone.

But somewhere here there was one invader, I had heard, a British white man whose true name was forgotten or never known by my informants. He called himself, as the natives did, Cobo Gilmo, which means "the Indestructible" (for Cobo), "the Unflinching" (for Gilmo). He was a peaceful scholar, it was said, living alone, doing translations from the Sanskrit, and loved by everyone.

We came to his house by hazard. We had left the truck to walk down a slim path in search of water, for our boys had smelled it as animals do. They had stopped the truck every mile or so and sniffed, while the radiator steamed and we grew drier. We poor Caucasians, benighted by our own evolution, have lost the flair for water. It has no smell for us.

"It must be over there," said N'dri, lazily sniffing. We heard it at last, and suddenly came upon the waterfall. It was wide and shallow and I was happy to find plants like daisies foiling it, springing through the hurtling water, anchored solidly to the rock.

Mr. Cobo Gilmo's house was at the foot of these enormous falls. It was walled with white lime, thatched irregularly. It had maroon-colored shutters. From the floor to the eaves the windows went up in narrow slots about two feet wide, and the house was surrounded with them.

He came out in a sarong and tucked a monocle into his eye. His appraisal of us was cursory but careful. "It is good of you to come.

355

Will you share my tea?" he asked in a golden voice through a face like a boxer's.

We sat on the terrace shaded by tremendous ferns with fuzzy stems, twenty feet high. A couple of dogs nuzzled my knee, and a chimpanzee came like a bullet out of the bush and along the path to land with a strangler's grip around my neck.

The waterfall came roaring down behind us, and we had to shout. We talked of sorcery and anthropology. "Some of my best friends are cannibals," said Cobo, "but the government keeps getting them."

The twittering of little birds was all about us, slicing through the waterfall's racket. A servant was singing. People were happy near this house.

We had the next morning's breakfast with this amiable man, and ate quantities of small but muscular fish which frequented the pools of his waterfall. It rose majestic and sparkling before us. Cobo Gilmo had the charcoal stove, made of a kerosene tin, brought to the veranda. Here in the sun he made a fritter batter, dipped the fish in it, and plunged them into boiling oil. This went very well with the bangi cooled beneath the waterfall.

He raised his glass to the waterfall, and sighted through it. He looked around to see that the servants were out of range. "Your village of Yho is not far away. You will climb up the falls to where they issue from a cave, which is full of water demons, and sedulously by-pass it without even looking in. There will be a trail to the left here and you will follow it to the summit. You will have a splendid view across the following valley to a cleft peak, not very high, where, I think, is perched the village of Yho. I can't be more precise because my boys have never been precise with me about it."

37

The mountain and the swamp—
Yho, Sorcerers' Village—the
sacred grove—the weepers—
King of the Dance—the baboon
man and a wind in the wood

THE FALLS WERE fairly easy climbing, for they
came lazily over the rocks. Dozens of butterflies fluttered around
Ruth's head, mosquitoes around mine. The boys went up like
monkeys, carrying cameras and provisions. There was the cave at
last, but so filled with rocks that we couldn't see a demon. We found
the path to the left and followed it to the summit.

Before us was a range of hills of many colors touching the clouds
which reflected their tones in terms of gray, silver, white. I had the
weird notion of standing on my head to pretend that I was of the
cloud world and that the earth was heaven, but I didn't because there
before me was a cleft peak. I kissed Ruth heartily and tried to cheer
the boys, who were even less enthusiastic now. No one who had
spoken of Yho had ever suggested that evil was there. It was, according to all accounts, a serious training school, a seminary, for apprentice sorcerers. Evil might come out of it, perhaps, but hooded. I
assumed that the village and its adjacent wood were just too busy
to bother with mischief that might disorganize it.

The peak was farther than it seemed. Down to the valley we went,
cautiously, over a pinkish crumbling rock, which set us skidding
occasionally. After one of these tobogganings Ruth sat up, looking
disturbed. "Listen." I listened, picking rock out of my shirt. "If I were
back in my Alps I would say that that was an avalanche. Listen."

I did, and the sound was fortunately not an avalanche, but very
rapid drumming. Somewhere behind us a message was being sent,
possibly to Yho, to announce us. I reviewed our recent past. What

357

impression had we left on the natives back there? Had we seemed to them as good and honest as we really were?

The following days were of the sort that explorers exploit, but which were really just dull, hard work. We met no giant anacondas as we had in French Guiana, nor lowering lamas as in Tibet, nor elephant herds, which were not far away. We plodded. We went into the papyrus swamp of the valley and plodded through it, being cut by the sharp edges of its leaves, stung by red caterpillars as big as bananas. It was dull labor, non-sensational. We pitched camp in that damned damp swamp, and moved on again, pushing papyrus plants to left and right or hacking at them, in the direction of our peak. Ruth was superb, impeccable, pretty, quick to film the insect life of the papyrus swamp. I liked her so much that I would have been glad to settle there on a raft with her and leave the Sorcerers' Village to its friends. But we came out on the other side at last, facing the cliff.

"Look," said N'dri unhappily. "There's a path up it. And look at that crowd of people sweeping it clean. Ah, to be eaten, *mon capitaine,* and I so young, and in love with both my three wives!"

We camped at the foot of the cliff, at the path's beginning, to give the people of Yho a chance to see us clearly and us to see them. They ignored us, and kept on diligently sweeping the path until they disappeared with it round a bend. It was an enormous chore, for the path went up at a precipitous angle, so steeply that steps had been cut into it. Yet they surely were doing this for us, which I pointed out to N'dri.

"Ah, yes," said he dolefully. "They want to make it easy for us. They probably want new victims to practice their tricks upon."

In the morning we went up slowly, and saw not a soul on the way nor heard a sound except the plangent cries of birds far away, the howl of a monkey far away; this path was of a sort of laterite, pink and crumbly, which skidded away in dust beneath our feet. Looking up, I saw at last the pointed roofs of huts and then the round, white-washed walls of them, painted with abstract designs.

Up we came to the rim of the cliff and then we saw the village of Yho. And it was a thing of beauty. The gray cliffs on two sides of it dropped sheer into wells of green treetops. There were trees grow-

358

ing between the huts, isolating them, which was unusual in an African village, and on a flat rock just above us there pranced a strange masked figure.

This village, to which we were committed now, apparently belonged to the Guéré tribe which lives on both sides of the Cavally River, separating Liberia and part of French Guinea from the Ivory Coast. But it was an intertribal school of sorcery. There were Tomas from Guinea in the sacred wood, Ashantis from the Gold Coast. And there was a separate group, amalgamated, though from different countries; the pitiful albinos, who were the outcasts, the spat-upon, the pariahs of Africa, had found asylum here.

By little stages, little services, we ingratiated ourselves with the people. We swabbed their sores, which were often pretty grim. Ruth dandled the babies. I sat quietly thinking together with the grandpas among the snarled, flanged, snaky roots of the tree before the portals of the sacred wood. We didn't talk. We just thought hard about each other.

As I was an amateur magician who could work wonders with mechanical tricks which really worked themselves, I had at first been viewed with suspicion by these elder wizards, fearing competition, but gradually I won their friendship by the gift of simple tricks, one each to the Chief of Yho, the Chief Sorcerer, and the Chief Fetisher. Only we, the colleagues, knew the secrets of them.

The tape recorder was for a while a baffler. At sunrise one morning, with the mists still about the treetops, when the tribesmen first heard their voices talking back to them, shouting to waken those who were still asleep, I feared for the safety of the machine, because many natives believed that even a photograph was the captured soul of its subject. N'dri got us over that hazard by explaining, as I never would have thought to do, with a mirror. Your face went in and bounced back at you, no harm done, and with the recorder your voice did the same. It was improved even. It could be made stronger. A little boy's voice could be made loud like a chief's and a chief's like a god's. Look! N'dri turned up the amplifying button to full force and put the tape to spinning.

I had forgotten that this was a used but reusable tape from which

359

I had failed to erase several recordings made in New York, party conversations, table talk, and songs taken off the radio. N'dri had not accurately found the place on the film where the chief, now of our audience, had begun to talk, so what came out was Louis Armstrong chanting like a syncopated gorilla.

The chief leaped back in alarm, but he was evidently pleased. "Is that I?"

"That is your soul's *true* voice," said N'dri, giving me a look. "You will hear your own which yesterday you put into the box. Now it will be improved and strengthened. Listen." And out of the box came a god's roaring, but it was easily recognizable as the voice of the chief.

That did it. Everyone wanted to record now. Yho became bedlam. Everyone talked loudly, fortified. The drummers and balofon players were eager to have their music improved. The noise of this supposedly secret village became unbearable.

From time to time there would be a clonking sound from the entrance to the wood where the sorcerers went to school. "Clonk! Clonk! Clonk!" It was like the belch of a crocodile behind you, and as sinister. This came from the lotus-shaped iron bell which a simple-minded dotard of a sorcerer rang whenever women came near the wood. It had a hollow, sepulchral tone which didn't cheer my work.

The bells were made in the village, an intriguing business, for in nearly every country of the world you will find that fire and iron and magic have been bound closely together. In Tibet, in Melanesia, in Africa they still are. It is strange to note that it is not our scientists who deduced first that the world was once a ball of fire; the legend is common among Indians of one side of the world and Africans of the other. As the fire of the world dwindled it sought refuge in the trees; it became a latent sap in them, a marrow dormant, so that if you rub two branches together this will awaken it and the wood will become warm with life and be fire again.

One of my gnome-like blacksmith friends named Go banged down his rock upon the fuming metal. "This bell is for you, Capitaine. Every husband needs his sacred wood." Bang went the hammer.

"Hey!" said Ruth.

The sorcerer blacksmith looked up craftily. "I'll make one for you, madame, a little one, but it won't have a knocker in it."

When I, but not Ruth, was invited at last to the sacred wood, I was asked by the chief to carry nothing with me, no cameras, nothing in my pockets, not a cigarette. Explorers tell you of weird occurrences in the secret societies of Africa, of their being Initiated into the Tribe, of Peril and Menace and Grisly Rites. But the few of us who get in do so by simple friendliness.

Ours was a nice wood, with great trees and a golden mist over the demon-haunted outcroppings of rock. Here and there were long communal dormitories for the apprentice sorcerers. We saw groups of them occasionally, cutting down trees, listening to an old man's palaver, folding their fingers this way and that to put curses or benisons on you, and I thought of how much like naked brown Boy Scouts they seemed. They were not learning magic only; they were learning to live like men, with all that that entailed, as the girls on the other side of the wood were learning the arts of womanhood along with those extra arts which would make them witches. Intermarriage, needless to say, was not common.

My visits to the sacred grove were informal. With one or two of Yho's notables I wandered back and forth through it, stopping here at a fetish tree surrounded by glé, like clay polyps, or there at a group of art-class students who were learning to carve masks out of the stolen fetish wood of other tribes. Their work could in no way compare with the wood sculpture of their ancestors. The art of the Guérés, Tomas, Yakoubas, could scarcely have been influenced by the Europeans, whom they saw rarely, very few at a time. And those few were not often artists. I think I will not be alone in stating, categorically, that West African art is decadent, degenerate, as uninspired as that of the South, Central, and North American Indians today.

There was no clean line to this sculpture. It wasn't honest. It was spectacular only.

One morning I was roused early by N'dri and some shady companion to go quick, without breakfast, to attend a lesson of the Weepers. I was quite certain at first that I misunderstood this phrase. Without disturbing Ruth, who wasn't invited anyway, I slipped beneath the mosquito netting, put on sandals, pants, and shirt, and followed the boys through the gap in the wood, where the idiot priest sat, wide awake, his hand on the gong to warn women away.

Even at six in the morning the sun beat hard on us, refracted by the shiny leaves. It seemed an odd hour to weep. We followed the stifling shade of a path I had not known before, and there beneath a deeper shade were the Weepers, weeping. They were eleven boys in a circle around the glum wizard, who just talked to them sadly while they wept.

"Your mother is dead," he said. "She was a gossip and so she must be buried upside down. Isn't that pretty sad?" Everybody wept. N'dri and our guide and I sat down silently a little way off. "You are an orphan," said the wizard, "and nobody loves you. Some people hate you, even."

Some of the boys covered their faces with their dark hands, and sobbed discreetly. N'dri blew his nose on a leaf. "Funeral practices," he whispered. "They must dance in the masks for the protection of the dead. These boys will be the fetishers, not sorcerers. And they must truly weep behind their masks. It is not easy to do. They are making me unhappy. Shall we go home for the coffee now?"

There was a shouting and a beating of the bush all around us, one day, as we approached a little hut set alone in a clearing of the wood, through which the sun slanted. My blacksmith friend Go, the one who would protect me from my wives, led me to it and with circumspection pushed open the door, jumping back and pushing me to the ground to let any demons escape.

Then we went in to this holy of holies, and there was nothing in it but a bundle of rags, lying quite still, apparently demonless, in the middle of the earthen floor.

"Nothing is so sacred as this," said Go, gazing with awe upon the bundle. "In there"—he started to point, then thought better of it—"are the stilts. The stilts of the Tall Man of the Woods."

This was interesting, for like so many African customs which were sincerely ritual, stilt dancers appeared at public festivities even in Abidjan: acrobats who commercialized their tribal customs. "May I look?" I asked.

362

My little man wasn't trying to impress me. He just said, "No," and turned quickly to the door.

The noise in the forest was louder now. It surrounded us. There were shouts and the whackings of drums.

"What is this about?" I asked my gnome.

"Snakes," he said.

"Uh-huh, snakes. What snakes? Why snakes?" Here was the barrier of communication again. Go would assume that I, being as bright as I was for a white man, knew something about the snakes.

"The snakes," he said patiently, shaking the tassels of his hat, and smiling around his fangs, "with which we will dance today. Ah, they have caught one! Come! We must go to the village. They will be dancing there."

Ruth very pointedly asked me no questions about the sacred wood to which she had not been admitted, while I fiddled around with my cameras, eager to tell her of my excitement at finding nothing sensational at all. I did remark casually that I had been informed in the wood of the possibility of a dance this afternoon, and would she get her film ready?

It has always seemed to me strange that our modern career girls, independent and so self-reliant that they never reach for the check, should resent whatever refuge of a sacred wood the male has left. Nowhere is this psychological sanctuary more clearly delineated than in Africa.

We hurried across the white soil of the village and over the one gently sloping edge of our mountaintop, following the villagers. There were women among them. About three hundred yards below was a group of huts I had not noticed before, a misplaced Yakouba village from which the drumming came. An old professor who couldn't speak without spitting informed me that the rainy season was now beginning, and so the special sorcerers called Quezza had sought snakes in the wood to dance with them and cajole them and become friendly with them, since snakes emerged from their holes in the season of the rains.

"Perhaps," he said, "you come from a country where things don't happen very much. Here only two things happen, but they are great ones. There is the dry season which is called Voo-non, and the rainy season we need which is called Goula-non. All our people are there

363

beneath the trees to pray with the serpents for the coming of Goula-non."

They were dancing, when we arrived, beneath a tree with high dark branches which could shelter a country circus. Two men were dancing with the meanest snakes they could find: the Black Cobra called G'brou, and the Serpent Minute called Dagouteme which can kill you in one minute, although he is a little fellow, tan, about eighteen inches long.

There was about five feet of the cobra coiled about the dancer's neck, its head and tail each caught securely in a hand. For these snakes had their fangs and their venom, as the object of the dance was to inspire confidence in them so they might go home and tell the snake tribe how you had feted them with dancing and music—and promised them that you wouldn't hurt them if they didn't hurt you.

The dance was frenetic. The dancers' feet, covered with monkey fur, beat a tattoo on the earth as they swung the snakes around them, sometimes holding them only by their tails and middles, but moving them constantly so that they were dizzied or just had no chance to strike. Once the Black Cobra slipped loose and scurried toward the orchestra, which took to the trees promptly, as the intrepid expedition did—but it was returned and chided a little by the sorcerer; and to further prove his good faith, he bent backward with his hands on the earth while the dancer with the Serpent Minute placed both snakes on his belly, caressing them, keeping their heads down so they couldn't strike.

Everyone sang, and the words of the chant were heard by all the listening serpents in the province of Yho:

> *Ho! You will come now, great Mother of Rain!*
> *The serpents will sing as you sing on our fields.*
> *Theirs is the kissing of night and young death.*
> *They shall be loved by us. They are our cousins.*
> *The yielding of every cold breath of them*
> *We shall acknowledge and answer in whispers,*
> *For theirs is the earth and our own.*

I was hurriedly changing film when Ruth said, "Bill!" I looked up to see the two dancing sorcerers a few feet away, to hear the orchestra roaring as the snakes were spun in a wild pirouette and their heads plunged suddenly into the dancers' mouths, the final test of reciprocal faith; neither man nor snake should bite.

And everyone was singing.

> *Great Mother, great Mother of Rain,*
> *Of Men and of Serpents,*
> *Ho! Bless our thin pastures and succor the grain*
> *That we may rejoice in your bounty again!*

One of the snake dancers had seemed to me exceptionally graceful, and rather sad, as perhaps one would be with a mouthful of snake. It was he who had the vicious little Serpent Minute, Dagouteme. The crowd watched him more carefully than they did the other man, and I had the impression that their faces, too, were saddened as he went swirling with the danger in his hand.

I said to N'dri, "He doesn't look like a Guéré. Try to find out who he is. I'd like to photograph his head without the snake."

N'dri came back promptly, bearing lady-finger bananas, plus information. He was a good forager, N'dri. "He is one of those you wanted to find," he said. "He is the King of the Golden Wood, a Yakouba. And they say he is approaching the end of his reign."

"He dies then, doesn't he?"

"He is killed. Or he was in the old time. I don't know how it is today." N'dri made a wry face. "I am proud to assert that the Yakouba is not my tribe."

From time to time I went down the slope to that little lost Yakouba village with its thatched huts rising in tiers on terraces, and I met the dancer named Dao at last, and his one wife, Ireli, who was about to have her first child. Dao was a lissom but thoroughly male young man, and Ireli a girl of some robustness, particularly with the burden she bore. They were good to me, and soon N'dri and they had become fast friends, too.

In the evening we would sit on little stools in the dust before their

365

hut, saying, "Yes, the rain must come. We cannot make false promises to the serpents." And we would talk of the young corn and of Dao's dancing, and then look at the sky again, and if it was evening Dao would be watching the moon.

N'dri and I seemed to be his only friends. He who was King of the Dance was shunned now by everyone but his wife. And when we knew each other better and were watching the moon one night, he asked me, "You know?" I said yes, and said a little impatiently that he and Ireli should come away with us. The truck was waiting down the mountain. There was a maternity clinic about fifty miles away. The roads were still dry. We could make it in time. We could come back later to Yho.

Dao lifted his proud dark head and ran a finger around the nearly full circle of the moon. When it should be full in a few days his office of King of the Dance would be consummated by his death. He was like any youngster faced with an unjust punishment, but this was ineluctable. It was custom. He could not show bad faith to his ancestors by denying it. Even though it might mean that he would not see the birth of his son; of course, his son.

Once he cried out in the night, after a long spell of sitting without a word. The King's Dance was not of his choosing, he cried. The wind in the woods, the wind in the grass had chosen him. Could I understand? I sweated with trying, without asking explicit questions. The moon rose higher and added a wrinkle toward its fullness.

Could I see? Could I remember as he did? Could I see the high rock on which he sat happily a year ago, or nearly, thinking of his marriage to Ireli?

Yes . . . I could.

Could I see the wind in the wood, at first, bending the branches in a straight line toward him, along a treetop path about as wide as his own shoulders?

"Yes," I said, dropping my cigarette, holding very still.

The wind, said Dao, had passed over the sacred wood, and was in the grasses now, the dancing wind of death. And he sat on his high rock watching it, hypnotized, watching the straight swathe of it, just as wide as his shoulders, coming toward him as though it were an invisible serpent a kilometer long slipping over the trees and

366

through the grasses toward him. But it slid past him closely, and flattened the gardens along its narrow path until it disappeared near the hut of the chief sorcerer of that Yakouba village.

Dao knew, by the old legends, that he must become King of the Dance for a year, and feted and indulged in every way, and killed by the wind with its golden arrow at the end of his term. He did not know that the custom of killing kings at the end of a fixed term had been common in years past, among societies as far apart as Africa and Melanesia.

Nothing was denied the King of the Dance. The brightest new vegetables, the best cuts of meat, the fresh bangi wines were placed in heaps at his door. No one, under pain of death, might deflower a virgin until she had been offered first to the king. All the poor man had to do in return was dance and make everyone dance gaily for a year.

Dao, although a champion dancer, was supremely a family man, and most temperate. He loved his wife Ireli and didn't want any virgins, or any other women at all. His own bangi tasted best to him, and he could not complain of his wife's own choice of viands. All he wanted was to be left alone with his wife and his coming son, and dance when he wanted to.

He made such a noise in his distress that a nasty little sorcerer, pulpy and pale, came out of the hut opposite. We never knew his name, nor wanted to; he was simply called the Sid-nai, which is Yakouba for one of the silliest of the dung beetles which spends its time collecting dung and forming it into a ball and then rolling it always, but always, uphill, and abandoning it without its doing him the least good in any way.

"Lend me your slingshot," said Dao. He got the Sid-nai in the paunch with one of my best agate marbles, striped yellow and red, which probably I should have saved for one of the Sid-nai's meaner charms. Dao could do no wrong. He was King of the Dance and could shoot a sorcerer in the paunch with impunity, or marbles. He told us of a few minor malices of the Sid-nai. First of all the Sid-nai was the one Communist disciple in these otherwise impeccable hills. Second, the Sid-nai, while Dao was busy dancing, paid objectionable attentions to Ireli. Third . . . Dao paused.

367

Dao took my cigarette, puffed on it, waved it toward the woods. Third, he said . . . and told of how, only a few months ago, a woman had come screaming through these trees to the village, and Dao and the other men had returned with her to find her young son—five or six years old, perhaps—lying dead there with a hole in his chest, and his heart gone. Beside the little body was an iron claw.

The men followed what looked like baboon tracks until it grew dark, but Dao kept on, whistling boldly to attract the Baboon Man. He heard the rustling in the branch above him too late to jump aside, and then the thing was on him, straddling him, clawing at his heart with one claw; but Dao was an agile dancer and knocked off the mask to strangle the man, the thing, the baboon, the monster. It was probably because he felt the wart on its throat that he relaxed his grip in horror and the thing got away from him. For there was a wart on the throat of the dung-beetle sorcerer, the Sid-nai.

N'dri leaned against my shoulder, like a puppy afraid. I gestured toward the hut opposite. The Sid-nai had gone in again.

"He is there, but you never see him in the village any more. I danced with the serpents, but still the rain hasn't come, and the Sid-nai should be the one to help it. We bang on his door, but he just makes awful sounds, and won't come out. One of the baboon people must bring him his food at night. You see, I cut his chest with his own iron claw which he left behind when we surprised him. And if he lives, he can't pretend that it was not he, the murderer. And even if he puts the worst of curses upon me, he probably cannot kill me before the night of the full moon, and the arrow, and the wind."

Dao was healthy, sane, and should have the sense to accept my help in getting him and his wife away before either he was killed by the illusion that he must die at the fixed time he had been dreading for nearly a year, or by an enemy in the village who might take advantage of the night of the full moon. All native peoples are susceptible to suggestion; charms and curses do, psychologically, work with them.

Remembering this, I thought of Khalil Sabeh. I must get a message to him somehow, saying I would be returning soon to Daloa, to give him time to make plans for our attempting the elephants' mountain.

There grew more and more of a moon, and I didn't like it. The

368

chief didn't like it, for to him it was not the misty moon that might mean rain, and he was quite indifferent to the fate of our friend Dao —who was a Yakouba, after all, not a Guéré.

"Can't we bring him up here at least?"

"Ah, no, ah, no."

"Then suppose I go down and stay with him, and take the gun along?" He gave me a long, hard look. He had never shown the slightest sign of animosity before, but here it was, sharp as broken glass, and I knew that I had fractured our superficial glass friendship, that I had put my foot through it. The Baboon Men would have found my heart congealed.

But I went to see young Dao openly, and to climb with him to his rock where he watched the wind.

"Ireli should have our son today," he said. "I have asked the baby men to come from Liberia."

"Baby men?"

"The sorcerers who put children to sleep and fling them back and forth to loosen Ireli's stomach while she is in labor. One of them jabs at the children with a knife as they fly to him. Sometimes they are killed."

"Listen, Dao . . ."

"Look," he said.

Above us was the sacred grove at the edge of Yho, sloping down to the fields, the lougan, of Dao's village. Our rock stood between them. Across the tops of the trees in the distance came a little wind, tickling only the topmost leaves, but coming in a straight swathe about the width of a man's shoulders toward us. Its progress was slow but continuous. I remembered how often I had sat in a forest, quite still for a long time, to listen to its tiny sounds and watch its movements when it had forgotten I was there, and suddenly noticed one leaf waving. No other moved. There seemed to be a private wind for that leaf alone.

And the private wind, which Dao believed was the wind of death for him alone, came toward us gradually, bending a neat path of leaves, descending over the edge of the grove to the grasses, and moving quietly through them, a straight and narrow path. Bracing my heels in a crack of the rock, I watched it, perplexed and fascinated.

369

I thought at first that it might have come through the cleft in the peaks, but it would have been spread or dissipated in its long journey toward us. Now let's be objective, I thought. Assume that ...

Dao's voice sounded glum as he said, "May it not touch my house, Ireli, my son!" No, it was still bending the grasses toward us, and we were a hundred yards from Dao's hut. And about thirty yards from our rock that strip of weird wind turned to the left and gently died away.

"Tonight it will be full moon," Dao said.

38 ~~~~~~~~~~~~~~~~~~~

The school of magic—the masks
dancing—"Fear has no face ..."

IN THE DOORWAY of Dao's hut sat two colossal Liberians and three little girls, aged three to nine, perhaps. They were all dressed alike, the men and the tots, with headdresses of cowrie shell and feathers, crisscross brassières, and slightly individual G-strings. As we stepped through them into the hut they smelled like something you might use to take the smell of a deodorant away.

Ireli lay on a cowhide, nude, her belly mountainous and already in labor. She smiled at us, and when Dao took her hand she cried, not because of pain, but because she knew what Dao must do tonight. It would be the full moon of his twelfth and her ninth month tonight.

I knew, too, but I could do nothing about it now. Not only the chief of Yho but Dao had made it clear that we must stay away from the village tonight. Everyone must be indoors. He would dance when the moon was at its height. He would dance alone in the central place of the village, until the wind came over the woods and through the grasses and the golden arrow struck him down. Then only might the elder men come out, to bury the body of the King of the Dance,

370

standing up, with the arrow through him, in a secret place of the sacred grove. It was never referred to, for fear of hauntings and such.

And in the morning—but not until the moon was gone—the women could come to the central place, to find only the scarves, the bangles, the cowrie crown which the King of the Dance had discarded as he danced his way to death.

I made one last attempt. I nudged N'dri, who told Dao, that we had stored quite a bit of food yesterday in that cave behind the waterfall. Dao's eyes looked hard at me, unblinking, the eyes of the dead. Ireli's eyes clenched on the tears as a spasm of childbirth seized her, and she spread her knees and dug her heels into the earth.

Like nearly every ritual supposedly secret and sacred in Africa, the Birth-Giving Dance had been seen and filmed, though far from here, before we saw it. The dancers had to make their living, whether by aiding the travail of a woman who could pay them adequately for their services, or by imitating them as public entertainment. But here before the hut of Dao they were seriously at work, trying to help and believing they could help Ireli.

We stood quietly in the silver shadow of a tree, panting with the heat. On the doorstep the little girls were put into a state of hypnotic trance quickly by the giant acrobats. There is nothing mysterious about hypnosis, as any pedigreed doctor will assure you. The men took the children's heads gently in their hands and suggested that they go to sleep, that their eyes were tired, that now they must sleep, sleep, sleep. . . . And the little girls, knowing what they must soon endure, wisely decided to go to sleep.

They were put on their feet now, and their heads wobbled back and forth, quite rhythmically. Their eyes remained wide open. They didn't blink. The men picked them up and tossed them back and forth until soon they were sailing rigid at a distance of about twenty feet through the air; and one black giant had a knife in his hand now, with which he jabbed at the flying tot, barely missing her, before catching her in the crotches of his elbows and hurtling her back to his partner again.

The knife was to symbolize the opening of Ireli's foetal sack to permit the issue of her child. And the tossing and the jabbing would go on until the first cry of the child came from the hut. The tossed babies didn't suffer; they were unconscious. The huge men sweated, urging the birth. One of them, exhausted, stumbled over a pile of old drums and almost missed the child when she was flung to him by the man with the knife.

For an hour this went on. Dao kneeled beside us, swaying as the child flew back and forth. There must be the birth of his son tonight, before the death of him. And suddenly there was the cry from the hut, and the old midwife came out holding the baby upside down and spanking it, and it was a son, no doubt. It was quite pink, as newborn Negro babies always are.

Dao stood up proudly and took the wet little thing in his hands and returned to Ireli with it. The dancers had disappeared when I turned around. And with the terrible immediacy of night in the tropics, the darkness had come. The high-pointed thatched huts were golden, then maroon, then black against a mottled black sky, before the edge of the full moon came over the edge of the mountains; and a savage wind, like a wind in a trough, as wide as a young man's shoulders, came sweeping over the sacred wood of Yho and down through the gardens and grasses to the house where Dao would live no more.

Dao had danced last night, said all my friends the sorcerers, like street urchins hawking news. They whispered it, but in headlines: DAO HAD DANCED. And, of course: DAO HAD DISAPPEARED.

Everyone, including the women, went down to the Yakouba village, and all that village was wandering around the central place, on the edge of it, for in its middle where Dao had danced was what was left of him, a heap of scarves, anklets, bracelets, gri-gris, a pagne, and an immense wrist watch which had stopped at half-past three. The drama of this was leavened by my knowing that it had stopped two weeks ago.

Everyone of both villages was there, except the baboon sorcerer, someone said. We went to his hut and made a sufficient racket. We pushed the door in. He was there, dead as a dornick, the sorcerer, the Sid-nai, with a golden arrow through one eye. The arrow was wrapped in the golden foil that Mr. Katz of Los Angeles had specially given me to enwrap his Hot-Can Beans.

It was obvious, of course, to everyone. Whatever we discarded, tin

372

cans, bacon rinds, bottles, used adhesive tape, the pretty packaging of the Hot-Cans, was avidly collected by both children and adults without shame but with reproof to us for our wastefulness. There was no question that Dao had danced before the moon and the wind, for it was the custom, wasn't it? But whether the real golden arrow, possibly launched by the dung-beetle sorcerer, had actually transfixed him, no one could affirm, for anyone watching that dance would go blind, and if an unbeliever watched and didn't go blind he would promptly be kicked out of the village. Serve him right, the heretic, the voyeur. And if the elders of the village had buried Dao, or if they hadn't, they were sworn to silence.

But who shot the phony arrow into the Sid-nai's eye? It wasn't I, said I; and that was evident, for no one, particularly the white visitor, could cross the village of Yho beneath the full moon and go to the Yakouba village without being seen by some insomniac of a sorcerer who, like every adept, was doubtless observing signs and omens just then.

The people of Yho were saying, *"Bla g'bohouin Dhi. The sheep has eaten the panther."* I didn't think I had done it, but I had an uneasy sense of guilt nonetheless, for it was my gold foil. And I, who am quite humane, a Buddhist type really, felt a little disturbed by my satisfaction with the Sid-nai's demise. I was more disturbed by the Giaconda smile of Ireli sitting in the door of her hut with a beautiful lump of a baby at her breast.

Now it was nearly the end of the school term in the sacred wood, to which I had free access so long as I looked at nothing but the trees in it. I was put on my honor, which was indeed a trial of honor. No cameras, no recording apparatus. I could do what I liked with these when the young sorcerers emerged from the wood to pass their examination in the village proper, but I was not to violate the magic of the wood.

The students of this old school were known to have qualities when they were children by such signs as warts, moles, fancy ears, veinous congeries, as the baby Dalai Lama is discovered in Tibet. A boy who liked to wander in the fearsome woods of his native village, who had visions, peculiar dreams, or a shadow which seemed not to follow

373

him at a normal angle, was marked out for a future in magic. Sometimes he was taken by the local witch doctor to the Wizards' Wood of Yho for training, but usually he was sent off alone, even as a tot, and told not to return until he had found the wood and learned to produce grown-up magic himself. If he became lost on the way, he was obviously not good sorcerer material.

If he did arrive—and I imagine it was probably quicker than our progress—he was examined to find the signs indicating which wizards' clique he belonged to, sorcerer or fetisher. It was said that a sulphurous bad breath was a sure sign of a sorcerer. So, if he was to become a sorcerer, he would study such arts as poisoning or rotting people at a distance, and if he was to become a fetisher he would learn how to poison sorcerers and dance in the terrible masks and chase demons into the tops of trees, which were cut down. Wham!

Many of the studies for both sorcerers and fetishers were funereal, and the school had nothing against their digging up the dead—after exorcising the demons, as they were duty bound to do—and eating them, and the demons, too, if they could catch them; but it must be done privately, of course; one mustn't make a spectacle of his appetites.

The apprentices lived together in what French ethnologists call a convent, a large, malodorous, windowless hut, surrounded by trees with ghouls in them. The boys were ceremonially circumcised with sharpened bamboo (as Polynesians are) or broken glass or a rusty blade, which was rare, for they believed, as the Hottentots and the Ovambos of far-off Southwest Africa do, that iron will bring death to the genital organs. In any case, mortality from blood poisoning was high.

The girls, in their own witches' wood on the opposite side of the grove, must submit to excision, the cruel counterpart of circumcision, so that the future bride should have little pleasure in love-making, and not go wandering from her spouse. Heavy brass rings were welded about her ankles to make philandering more difficult still; and for the inveterate vagrant type, there was a mighty anklet with bells on it which usually kept track of her in the dark.

374

The sky was troubled. We had a sampling of rain. People came up from the valley and said that at Tai, on the edge of the animal reserve, there was great rain with thunderbolts. Tai was about two hundred miles southeast of us, but the swoop of the rain might strike our mountain at any time now. Photography in color would be impossible. We must get out and on the way to Abidjan soon, before the minor roads would be flooded. We had gotten ourselves placed in a blank area of the Michelin map, but all roads approaching it were marked IMPASSABLE IN THE SEASON OF THE RAINS.

The Guérés, who reported these rains, came blithely up to Yho and went blithely down, which annoyed me, considering the time and trouble we had had to get here. The easiest thing in the world, they said, was to take my letter for Khalil Sabeh to the post office at Touba, and to pick up his reply when they returned a couple of weeks from now.

So, I wrote to Khalil eagerly, giving him our only address, the Touba post office, and saying that we should be back before the rains set in, that I wanted nothing more in the world—and truly I meant it—than to climb the elephants' mountain. It was odd, you know; my hands shook when I wrote of this mountain. It was a physical starving emotion, a voracious need which explorers have never explained, least of all that one, famous for a phrase, who climbed Everest "just because it was there."

You risk absurdity in trying to explain such a completely abstract lust to your wife, even to Ruth. You can't say, There's a boiling going on in me; it is fueled by a mountain which doesn't even have a name. And I must go up it, even to find that no elephants have left their bones in any absurdly secret cemetery.

The clouds fattened and we got their tentative rain from time to time. It was as if the rain were feeling the fields, running its fingers along them, to see if it should help this or that one first. There were so many fields to attend to; and, after all, the sorcerers' crops should look after themselves, and be the last to be served.

It was at half-moon, with a ring around it, that the graduation exercises began for the students in the woods. Ruth had cleverly convinced the chief that, sight unseen, she must at least be a hermaphrodite

375

because she wore trousers, carried heavy cameras on her cubist shoulders—and so might film the ceremonies unscathed.

The night before examination day all the young women were sent out of the village to another village about twenty miles away. The old ones stayed; sterility was no hazard to them any more. The girls filed past the most ancient of witches, who was shaking so hard I felt it wise to increase the speed of my camera to one hundredth of a second; she was practically a blur. But as the maidens came by, stooping to be blessed for the long journey, she managed to lay a hand on each one's head and mumble a few words to protect her from men, demons, serpents, illness, incontinent desires, and acts of God.

This was no play-acting; it was not put on for us, because for once we were filming this unperceived. The girls didn't smile as they bent their heads beneath that quaking claw. Twenty miles is a long way in the bush. Some of them were shaking, too. When you have spent several of your adolescent years in the conventlike security of the sacred wood, even though you think you are a pretty smart witch already, the harsh realities of the unknown, unmagical world can be terrifying.

As they went down the path and through Dao's village, the elders of Yho, the professors and examiners and proctors—exactly as in any college—came with slow, sedate strides, each walking with a stick as tall as he, to the rocks before the dusty plaza where the apprentices would be put through their paces. The elders spread their pagnes and neatly sat down on the rocks. They sighed. They were resigned to a boring afternoon. They, who were too old to dance, would deplore the incompetence of youth.

Then the young men came hesitantly from the wood to display the arts which they had spent from three to six years mastering. Most of them wore fancy costumes; a few were nude, but all wore masks. They were of animals and demons, and one of a crocodile. One was Janus-faced, looking forward and back. Probably none of the students knew who of his companions at school wore which mask, for the dancer must remain impersonal, anonymous. He was no longer himself; he was what his mask portrayed.

The old-timers on their rock regarded the students glumly, and didn't even have a kind word to say for the middle-aged instructors,

376

who had patiently led the halting little feet along the path of sorcery. The little feet were calloused and flat and splay-toed by now, when you could see them at all, for the pupils who had learned their lessons best knew that no vulnerable flesh should be exposed to the Adversaries.

I divined that these would soon be the old sorcerers of their home towns, whom they would have to cope with when graduated, for when a student was graduated as an adept he was sent home to his village, if he could remember where it was, or to any that would accept him, hoping to get the office of sorcerer or fetisher—whichever he had been trained for—when the old incumbent should die. Usually he died a natural death, by smartly resigning before the younger man had a chance to practice on him his modern magics.

At home, at our hut, I thumbed reminiscently through a book by Charles Morgan, seeking a sentence which had pleased me and which I couldn't recall. But that it applied to our presence here I was certain. We were the accepted intruders. We were the aliens still. It was on page four and it read: "It strikes me as mysterious and significant that, in our moments of vision, the mask and the faces should be visible at the same time ... and that when, for a little time, one is inside the room of another's life, one is still, so ridiculously, a face at the window."

For five afternoons and beyond the sunset of each the examinations went on, and we filmed what was not repetitious with what we could afford of film; new supplies were far away—where we were beginning to want to be, too. The husband-and-wife so-called teams of the movies usually have several white associates with whom to pass the time of day. Ruth and I had been playing double solitaire in a bad climate, among a non-hostile but quite non-cordial people, for a very long time. We did our best, Ruth counting the days to New York, and I to the elephants' mountain of Khalil Sabeh, and we got good film. We sat on the rocks with the elders and regarded—pretty professionally by now, I thought—the apprentice sorcerers and their antics.

They jabbed darts into wooden figures, as other descendants of their ancestors do across the world in Vaudou Haiti today. They blended the crushed tali, or tre, bark with urine and lime for the testing and tasting of innocence (everyone looked guilty after this

377

test, I thought). They put sand beneath the eyelids of possible thieves. They slit open throats of animals in such a way that the blood flowed through cabalistic designs drawn in sand. This, too, was similar to Haitian Vaudou, and of Dahoman origin. The study of these practices is perhaps useful, but it leads to vegetarianism on a mountain where few green vegetables grow.

The oldsters sat and nodded on that last afternoon of examinations, and passed all the students, but grudgingly, just to get rid of them. Let them go home now, before they started fiddling around with their accursed modern sorcery in the village of Yho. Bloa-ye-i, the chief, heaved a sigh. The orchestra of six drums and a balofon boomed on.

"Now," he said, "we will see the real old-fashioned masks dancing." And I gathered that the flash of colors at the portal of the wood was their equivalent of our postgraduate students, chaps who took their magic seriously. The other old professors sat up and took notice.

As did we. Emerging rhythmically and with long, high-kneed strides came four dancers ornately costumed and masked, though in tatters. Every color was upon them, but faded with age, and I knew there wasn't a chance of getting these trappings for our collection. These were ancestral. Never had they left the village of Yho, and never would they. They were immense, and in their fearsomeness they were beautiful.

"How much film have you, darling?" I asked.

"A few hundred feet here, a few hundred more in the cans."

"Use plenty of it. We'll never get this again, nor will anyone else, and—I think our work is nearly done on the Ivory Coast."

The dancers must have worn a dozen layers of clothing to pad them out to the proportions of the masks. They were immense, and as they came toward us the men in them—perhaps, it occurred to me, there was no one in them but form-fitting hollow ghosts—broke into a frenzy of leaps and bounds and gesticulations that should scare the devil out of anybody or anything. They charged down upon the old judges, jumped over them.

There was one called N'leo, a clownlike mask that always laughed as it spat poison on the fiends that swarm above the new graves. And one covered with cowrie shells was called Blé Gla. He ate the feet

378

off the demons that walk under the ground. I rather liked the antics of the Tié Gla, when this fantastic character with a mask of fur and feathers was not stumbling over me. He was the most expert dancer of them all, but he dissimulated this, to fool his victims, by constantly falling down. The fourth of this whirling waxworks museum was the Bayé Gla, the Mask That Sings, the mask that sings a song of death into the heart. Little bells were attached to its beard.

I think it will be understood that I was disturbed when this one came singing at me, and singing in pretty good French, "It is very hot inside here, and oh-oh-oh how it stinks!" And before I could recover from this, which might be a death song in my heart, the Tié Gla with the fur and feathers fell flat at my feet; and as I bent over him he said distinctly, "Me, I'm an old man. I think I broke something that time."

It had not occurred to me that even sorcerers may once have gone to the mission schools in the bush. Tié Gla was helped to his feet, and, supported by his grisly comrades, was given the approval of head-nodding by the examiners. The group of masks, the most powerful on the Ivory Coast, went staggering off into the trees.

"Ah, that's the end of it," said the chief with a sigh. "They will leave us in peace now." Magic was obviously exhausting to everyone.

"Not quite yet," said the dotard beside him. "The village has not been cleaned. The Man of the Woods should be coming soon." The Man of the Woods was the stilt dancer, of course, who would sweep the demons, attracted by this heyday of more wizards than they had ever seen at once, from their rooftops. His counterpart was not unknown. He had danced across the world from the mountains of Sumatra to the plains of Poland, the blind man on stilts.

And he came out of these woods of Yho in Africa, stepping alertly through the trees and up the stony path to the central place of the huts, while the drums beat their mightiest and everybody yelled, and the small boy children, the only ones left, raced for shelter.

"He is quite an impressive figure," said Ruth, filming.

"How true," said I. "As I value you, dear, will you get yourself and your camera out of the radius of those swinging stilts?"

Ruth, muttering something, stepped into the shade of a gnarled old tree, dripping with ants, and changed her lens to a two-inch longer focus.

379

The Man of the Woods walked easily on stilts about ten feet high, which were hidden by long, striped pantaloons. He wore a black mask that seemed to be crocheted of some black bark, had no eyeholes in it, and must have been opaque, or nearly so. Yet he strode along nonchalantly, surrounded by four bodyguards to catch him if he stumbled. In one invisible hand—for the black sleeve covered the fingers—he had a fly-swish made of an elephant's tail and this he flicked carelessly to chase the baby demons away.

He leaned over the rooftops and sniffed, and at last he found a foul fiend. He staggered back, snorted, and began spinning on one leg, swinging the other higher than horizontally so that the wooden foot of it swept the roofs, kicking the demons from them. Higher and higher he swung his long wooden leg, hopping on the other from roof to roof, sweeping each of them clean. It was fantastic. Hard enough it would be to walk upon ten-foot stilts, and worse to think of doing it blindly, but . . .

The drummers were chanting:

> *Fear has no face in the mountains of Yho,*
> *Fear is the Man of the Woods, without eyes.*
> *Fear is the tall man, the man made of shadow*
> *And narrow as knives, and near as the demons*
> *Which haunt our strange roofs.*

. . . but to hop upon a single stick and kick the other against the clouds blindly, or even semi-blindly, was worthy of the Court of Miracles.

Around and around the village the Tall Man went, spinning precisely above the solicitous faces of his guards. Then he would prance forward, knees bent, like a grasshopper on its hind feet, and suddenly bend to smell out a demon. By the shivering of his shoulders, the tossing up of his black mask, you could see that the Tall Man was outraged. He would back away, sight the demon on the rooftop, move up again like a football player before a kickoff, and straighten and spin like a dervish and smash away the demons into the sunset clouds.

And the Tall Man would stride on, through and around the village

380

of Yho, cleansing it, discreetly followed by the drummers who pounded and chanted more boldly than they felt about the long, vicious black shape rending the clouds.

Fear has no face in the mountains of Yho . . .

39 ~~~~~~~~~~~~~~~~~~~

Death of Khalil Sabeh—rejuvena-
tion by Phui—resurrection of Dao

I WENT DOWN the mountainside occasionally, to the village of Dao and his terrible wind in the grasses, the woods. The old mean sorcerer had been buried, standing up, with the gold-foil arrow still in him. Dao's widow Ireli was blooming, I thought, though I saw no cause for it unless it should be the little prize fighter of a son in her arms. I never saw any particular man about the place, nor did gossip mention any. She apparently lived alone, helped with her food by her parents, and sang all the time. Maybe she wasn't quite right in the head—you know, the tragedy of Dao . . .

I was eating mangoes, brought from the valley, with her one late afternoon, and we were leaning toward each other, dribbling and laughing, for our faces were smeared by that delectable fruit. Laughter was a good thing, I thought. Life was a great invention, and what a pity it wasn't here to stay.

Ireli bent to her mango, chomped upon it, and looked up with her great eyes suddenly serious. "I have heard you will be leaving soon," she said.

This is one of those weird jungle phenomena which you never can become accustomed to nor resigned to, even in a sorcerers' village— that everyone should know your plans before even you are sure of them.

"Will you promise to see me on the very day you leave?"

I stood up. "Yes, of course." I tossed the great mango seed toward the last spot where I had seen the wind in the grasses, and went up the slope a little nervously, for there was a sound of wind behind me, like something snuffling at a trail.

One of my boys had returned from Cobo Gilmo's house at the foot of the waterfall with not only fresh provisions but the boon of mail, which Gilmo had thoughtfully picked up at Touba. I ripped open the letter from Gagnoa first, sure that it was from Khalil Sabeh. It wasn't. The signature was that of one of Khalil's close friends. "It is with regret . . ." it began. And it went on, three neatly typed pages of it.

I tossed off the rest of my drink and walked quietly away from Ruth and the hut to the central tree where the old sorcerers convened when they had their troubles. No one else was about during the broiling midday. I sat down between two great flanges of roots. The branches gave me some shade, but still the sweat ran from my hand down the page as I read of Khalil Sabeh's death.

He had received my letter saying that we were returning soon, and was excited by our project of going to the elephants' mountain at last. He had again mentioned it to his boys, probably taunting them into coming with us, and they had all been terror-stricken as before, and said that Captain Davis had already done one bad thing in going to the cleft peak of Yho. Three hundred miles away they knew where we were, although I had written to Khalil in English and never mentioned Yho. To Khalil's surprise, his old cook had volunteered to accompany us.

Khalil had been impatient for my return. He had driven several times to the village at the foot of the mountain, and made friends in his warm, hearty way with many of the people there—and lost their friendship the moment he mentioned the mountain. Khalil's lust for it was as great as mine, and because he was restless while waiting, he took his wife, his cook, seven boys, and went after elephants which were marauding in the plantations a few kilometers away, in a region of valleys. His wife had testified that they had followed the herd for hours, and suddenly—because elephants move with uncanny silence—

382

found themselves in the middle of it. Khalil wounded the bull leader. The herd stampeded. His native bearers rushed forward with him, close to him as he sighted the wounded elephant on the other side of the ravine and intended to finish him. The cook and Mrs. Sabeh were a bit behind.

All she knew, she said, was that there was an explosion, the silver smoke curled up, and Khalil's body crashed into the ravine. The boys nearest him said he had slipped and his gun had gone off into his stomach. This was preposterous. Khalil Sabeh, the champion elephant hunter of the Ivory Coast, didn't, surely, carry his gun cocked, and that old jungle journeyman didn't slip. He had been damn well murdered, because the elephant was the totem to some of these boys, and because they knew that we were soon to try to find the elephants' cemetery on that accursed mountain.

Mrs. Sabeh tore off her khaki shirt and with it pushed the intestines of Khalil back inside him, and tied the shirt around him. He wouldn't die for quite a while. He grunted and smiled encouragingly to his wife who had no one but the cook to help her. The rest of the boys had disappeared up the trail.

Khalil's wife and the cook made a stretcher of branches and their clothes, and carried the two hundred dying pounds of him for about ten miles through the forest to the nearest Beti village. Their porters had been through it ahead of them with their story. Exhausted and nearly nude, because she had needed more and more bandages, she pleaded with the villagers to help her carry Khalil to a clinic which was another five miles away. The natives refused, and she and the cook continued with their huge burden. Khalil smiled and pushed back his intestines when they squirmed loose. He couldn't talk. He couldn't groan any more, but he was smiling, dead, when they reached the whitewashed little house.

That should have been the end of this terrible true tale, but it wasn't. There was a half a page for me yet to read. I put down the paper, wiped the sweat from my hands and face, cleared my eyes, and took the paper up again. The gist of what remained was that a few days after Khalil's death his wife was mysteriously taken ill, and she, too, died. And, at the time of writing, the cook was in an agony which the best doctor of Gagnoa could not diagnose.

There was a postscript saying, "P.S. 1: On your return, Captain Davis, it might be advisable for you to by-pass Gafnoa, taking the Daloa-Zagoretan-Sinfra-Oume-Toumedi road on the way down to Abidjan. It will be a bad road and the rains will be coming, but you might be expected to go through Gagnoa.

"P.S. 2: Our mutual friend, Khalil Sabeh, would be eager to have you know of a native rumor, no doubt ridiculous, that many very young elephants, without father or mother or the usual auntie helper, have now been seen coming *down* from the crater where the cemetery supposedly is. It is said that these young elephants are transparent and keep trumpeting so that most of the people near the mountain have moved away."

It is impossible, when writing in the first person, to describe the torment, the awful desolation that death leaves behind, nor would it serve any purpose at all. But the death of Khalil Sabeh, although I had known him at only two luncheons, was to me the collapse of Africa. White man though he was, he represented Africa, her plantations, her animals, her jungle cleanliness. I saw for the first time that the native who had murdered him was not merely the untutored child to be excused for wrongdoing, but as vicious as we grown-up people are.

The liberality of Khalil Sabeh with his servants was affirmed by everyone. There were a dozen families of former employees whom he continued to help with medicine and money, so my boys told me, and there were several pathetic little cocoa plantations, scarcely more than cocoa gardens, owned by aged black friends to whom Khalil had lent his own men when the crop was due for harvesting. They would miss him, his goodness, his vision and verve.

N'dri and Quodio and M'bla had all known of the tragedy before my letter arrived, or so they said. Someone had told someone who told them, but they had not mentioned it because they were hoping I would forget the elephants' mountain and not drag them to it. Was I sure now that I wouldn't be going? they asked. Yes, yes, I was sure. Then they could tell me further details of Khalil's death.

The first was that the cook was slowly dying in torture by poison administered by the murderer to do away with a possible witness.

Madame Sabeh had not been killed by him, but by Khalil's own devoted houseboys, who had been with the master innumerable years and worshiped him. They had killed her because she had the evil eye and glanced at him when he was rushing to finish off the wounded elephant.

It was a mess, frightening, revolting, and the worst of it was, for me, that I knew I was indirectly responsible. Had I not accepted his invitation to the mountain, or teased his boys and mine about it, or written the letter saying that we would be going soon, Khalil and I might have talked it over again, and given it up. And he would still be tremendously alive.

It was Chief Bloa-ye-i, bless him, who quite unintentionally made me happier with a problem of his own. He took me to the trouble tree, and I chose a couple of places between the flange roots on the opposite side from that where I had read the letter. We leaned back as in deck chairs, side by side. It was drizzling, but we were protected by the tiers of heavy foliage. He was wearing his fancy brown bonnet with the gri-gras sewn inside it next to his skull. Somehow he always seemed to be laughing, for he had only one visible tooth, a whopper, jutting up my side of his gnarled old face, and when he opened his mouth it smiled all alone, magnificently.

"This I would tell to none but you," said he, and he offered compliments on the sorcery, magical and medical, which I had done in the village of Yho.

"Nonsense," said I. "Those things work themselves."

"But no, but no," said Bloa-ye-i. "You are their medium. They are passed through you to us."

I hadn't thought of that, so I said, "Of course!" Now certain Guéré magics, said he, Beti magics, Toma magics, Yakouba magics, I of course didn't have, but I did have specialties. I had killed the demons in the outhouse tree (with D.D.T.) and cured ulcers, venereal diseases, headache, and such. Hadn't I? I nodded modestly, pretty sure of what was coming.

The chief spoke to me as man to man. He was no longer young, he said. He had six wives, and he was growing older. Did I understand what he meant?

385

"Phui!"

"Phui? I don't understand this word."

"It's a kind of medicine," I said, thinking quickly, and thinking also, a little astonished, that this was quite true. "It's kept me worrying for many a year." I tapped his old shoulder and nodded thrice.

He leaned over the root, his hand shielding his mouth, and asked hoarsely, "Have you got any?"

The menace of this challenge to my white man's magic gave me gooseflesh, for if I failed to revive him I would lose face and get no further cooperation from him. There were several small but significant scenes we wanted to film tomorrow.

I took the chance with no alternative. "Have your wives, all six, in your hut tonight, after it is dark, so no one else may know of this. Build a small fire in the middle of the hut and let it burn to embers. Put upon the embers that old skull which you never use anyway and which everybody stumbles over."

"But it's my aunt's . . ."

"The very best. You probably ate her. May she have mercy on you."

The chief smiled suddenly. "She was quite famous for love!"

"Perfect," I said. "Get her to help tonight. And come to fetch me when everything is prepared."

Perhaps you have never prepared a Phui. I hadn't. Ruth was away somewhere, probably filming the witches who welcomed no man now, so I had the problem alone. Remembering that the toughest aphrodisiac, Spanish fly, used mainly for horses, was made of the wings of the Cantharides beetle, which did not live in Africa, I sent my yeomen to the woods to collect any beetles they could find. I put them tranquilly to sleep in cognac, removed their wings, and pulverized them. The cognac-macerated and pulverized wings were now introduced into a mixture of absinthe, rum, a huge quantity of red pepper, and a soupçon of garlic (which was unknown here) for flavor. I added some black pepper, just to be sure, and shook it well.

N'dri squatted before me, his elbows on his knees, hands clasped together beneath his chin, fascinated. He never had seen magic such as this. Nor had I.

386

There was a timid tapping on the roof thatch and Chief Bloa-ye-i beckoned to me with his pink palm. I put the bottle of brew in a pocket, picked up an iron pot and my magnetic shocking machine. This tiny but quite magical device I should explain. My father had given me one, an expensive toy, when I was very young. It consisted simply of a magnet, a wire coil, and a cog-wheeled handle to spin the coil inside the magnet. And this generated electricity and shock, when the two tubular handles attached by wires were held in your opponents' hands. It was the living womb of electricity, and to me black magic.

It was an impressive little thing; you could see right through it, as through a miniature Arc de Triomphe; nothing hidden; but you could line up three or four stalwart Negro bucks, holding hands, the end men holding the tubes of this three-by-four machine, and spin the handle, and crank them right off the ground with the electric shock it generated.

Quietly we crossed the plaza in the rain and entered the old chief's hut.

Six sullen wives sat waiting in a circle around the fire in the center of the hut, sending up its smoke to a platform where I could dimly see the dangling beards of old masks. They said nothing, but they moaned from time to time, whenever Bloa-ye-i's aunt's skull made a crackling of speech from the coals. It was a handsome scene. That master of the macabre, Charles Addams, could have made linear poetry of it.

I wasn't very confident of my role as great white sorcerer, but I pushed the chief masterfully to the fire and sat him down and put him under hypnosis as easily as I had the urchins of the Harvard clinic many years ago. He must watch the fire, I said, and his old aunt's glowing skull, which had on it just that point of brilliance which would tire his eyes. His eyes were sleepy now, I added. They would close soon, and I would talk to him and help him when they were closed. The moaning of the women stopped. Hypnosis was no novelty to them, or to the chief, a willing subject. His eyes were closed.

I balanced my iron pot on the skull of his aunt, and poured my hell broth from the bottle into it. I was unhappy because this was impossible to film, and worried that it might not work. When the first

387

sizzling came from the pot, with an aroma which could easily be identified as brimstone plus Pernod, rum, beetle wings, garlic, and pepper, I poured it into a Tupperware plastic goblet, cooled it a little, and put it in his hand.

"This is for the bull," I said, "the he-goat, the elephant you are, young Bloa-ye-i. This is the Phui."

The old man's eyelids flickered, and he tossed off the drink at a gulp. (Did I have a right to do this? I thought. Was I playing God?) I motioned to the wives to come closer. "Your wives love you, my son," I said. "You can feel the warmth of them close to you now. Have another drink of Phui."

He did. "Good," he said, his eyes still closed. I put the shocking machine on the ground, and spat on it only once. The youngest wife held one tube of it on his left thigh, the oldest on his right. "Be brave, young elephant, Bloa-ye-i," I said.

He was. He was also gaily drunk. I cranked the machine, and the effect of the first charge was interesting. He relaxed and looked younger. His wives stared at us both with awe. I cranked until my wrists ached. There was no doubt of the electrical charge in him, a titillation, perhaps, but it was my hell broth which was really doing the work. The chief assumed an expression of beatitude, and wiggled.

This was enough. I stopped. Bloa-ye-i stared blithely into space, where love was, and all his wives stared with him. I slapped him hard and woke him up, and everyone, including himself, said "Ah," and I went back to the hut to bed.

When you have spent years in lonely places, jungles, deserts, mountains, you are unlikely to be aware of the changes that occur in you. They are subtle ones and usually not admirable. Among colleagues you notice them and think that you couldn't be like that, touchy, defensive, exhibitionist because you are defensive, timid in crowds though you may be the lion of the party, jealous of your fellows, cleaner than most metropolitans because to live in the bush exacts cleanliness, reserved as to the allure of white women, independent though you may be, desperately poor, as explorers usually are, impatient with abstractions such as politics, inclined to shake with the old fever at the least propitious moment, and in love with nothing,

nothing at all except the dream of returning to the desert, the jungle, the mountain where you dream, quite selfishly, alone.

But these are physical oddities that happen to you. You become intolerably tolerant of everything so long as it lets you go your own independent way. You become simple, perhaps, not in the sense of idiocy but in childlikeness, trusting people as the primitives do, and finding without surprise that those you trust, trust you. You don't lock your door or your baggage.

You have, however, because of these years of the bush, an unusual alertness to false notes and imminent alarms, a rather telepathic quality that Dr. Rhine of Duke University has had the courage to investigate. You are, for example, awake in the middle of the night, a few seconds before the telephone rings.

In the magical nice village of Yho I was suddenly awake and clear of dreams, looking up at a fuzzy moon with the rain pelting across it. There was no sound for at least a minute except Ruth's breathing in the other cot. I sat on the edge of mine and opened the green nylon mosquito net.

Chief Bloa-ye-i, drenched, drunk as a coot, came waltzing toward me. *"Capitaine,"* said he, "you have made magic for me. By tomorrow I will again be master in my own house." And he left.

The chief's hangover did not help us on the morrow, when we wanted to film the fill-in shots, people, landscape, and the glade in the sacred wood. The rain was interesting as pure line, diagonal and nearly solid, but there was no light behind it. We had no contrast, depth, shadow.

Ruth, the best of cineasts, and the most equable companion of any jungle, looked very beautifully grave. I was helping her to pack, perhaps putting things in the wrong places, but it didn't matter now. Perhaps neither of us quite realized for a while that we were packing to leave Yho and the Ivory Coast. It seemed that we were just making order in the hut, as we did daily, until we looked at each other across an army trunk and smiled, and sat on the earth at each side, looking at the ends of the unknotted cord.

And we listened. Through the tumult of the rain, from the sacred grove, came the raucous singing of the mask with the beard of bells,

389

the Bayé Glé, the mask that sings death into the heart. I was uneasy. I was certain there was no danger here, but unquestionably the chief's cure would not last another night. And no one had been very friendly today. The eggs we had bartered for had been rotten. The hen we bought had had black feathers—not very obvious, but they were black; honored guests received pure white birds only.

"Agreed?" I asked Ruth.

"Yes, definitely."

N'dri had not waited for the decision which we had just now made. I realized that for some time he had been wrapping camera lenses and accessories. "Listen to me carefully, N'dri. I want you to tell Ireli that we are leaving tonight, but I want no one else to know of it. Take the path behind the forge to Dao's village, and tell Ireli to come with her baby as soon as she can."

When he was gone, we began unpacking to find my pyrotechnical apparatus, the skyrockets, Roman candles, and Chinese firecrackers which had served me for years as an antidote to witchery. We were repacked when N'dri returned through the hot night rain with Ireli and the child in her arms and a pitifully small basket of her precious goods. Never had I seen a woman's eyes glow as Ireli's did now.

I went to the door of the hut. Quodio, M'blah, the porters, were waiting quietly. I heard the beard of bells still ringing in the wood, and now there was an inferno of clanging, unusual at night, from the roofed pit where the Blahis forged their witch gongs. N'dri opined that this was all quite normal. There could be no trouble for us. There could be no good reason for it, as we had been unobtrusive and our gifts had been generous. And I had restored the potency of the chief.

But for how long? I wondered.

True, said N'dri, and true it was that we were no longer the curiosities we once were in the village of Yho. We might be an encumbrance even, for there were things here which went on at night . . . the Baboon Men were said to be sulking, wouldn't even take off their masks to sleep . . . "And Madame Davis . . . you know," he added. He, too, wanted to go home.

I circled the hut, planting fireworks all around it. Ireli followed me,

390

took my arm. "We will go down by the path of the waterfall, and the cave of the waterfall with its demons?" she whispered.

We would, but I hesitated. "Yes," I said.

"There will be one other than the demons there," she whispered, and her breath was hot against my cheek. "My Dao will be waiting for us."

"Ireli, child, do you know this?"

"Please let us go now. I will get Madame Ruth and the boys while you do your magic thing."

I waited until the boys passed me toward the path, touching each shadow's hand to count them, and one was Ruth's, slim and good. The rain came down like bullets. I circled our hut quickly, snapping off the wax paper of the long fuses and lighting them with my cigarette.

First the cannon crackers ripped the night with noise just as we reached the path down the cliff; then the Roman candles poofed their brilliant balls of flame around the hut, where we were supposed to be sleeping; and then the skyrockets went slicing high above the village of Yho, to explode in stars. There was a tremendous wind behind us, perhaps the one which had sought out Dao, to drive him down the path to the waterfall.

Suddenly we were gone from that Sorcerers' Village, as if by magic, without a trace but for the heap of grateful presents we had left in the hut, where our bones should have been in that magnificent holocaust.

Gently, gently, we went down the blue-gold tunnel which our lights had drilled in the dark. Ruth was in front of me, trim and certain, Ireli following with her child and gently singing:

> "Old gods of the hills, will you help us tonight
> To a peace in our jungles? 'Yes,' you say, 'yes,'
> But there's no believing you. Evil you are
> And still we must pray to you.
> Never a prayer do the good gods demand. . . .
>
> We pray to you now. We beg you to grant
> That your magics be gentled, that every cold ghost
> Shall be warmed, and that we may follow the night
> To a place where love lives.

We shall hold close to it, closer than dreams,
Or gray death, or the moon, or the wind
Which has led us from Yho . . . Yho . . . Yho."

40 ~~~~~~~~~~~~~~~~~~~~~

Each one alone—"We'll see, we'll
see . . ."—Flea market—separate
darkrooms—sorry commerce in
film—zero for Moonsday—Judy
by candlelight—the witch cat

WE STOOD ON the deck of the luxury ship, taking us
to France and back to America finally, hurtling past Guinea, hot
as hell. We weren't talking, partly because we were tired after an
afternoon filming the engines of the ship, to complete a short film for
the line which was generously transporting us in exchange for whatever publicity we could give it. Half the provisions and equipment of
my expedition had been furnished free, in honest exchange for what
I might publicly and honestly say about them to an audience in seven
countries which was considerably larger than the average advertiser
could afford to reach.

Yet Ruth didn't approve of this, as she disapproved of my claim
to never having done a day's work in my life. This was, of course, quite
true, for one doesn't work at what one enjoys, at boxing in the old
days when I was very poor, or writing or exploring or making film.
Or even fighting with the Free French; one shouldn't enjoyably search
for death. Joy should be bought, paid for, by serious labor from nine
to five. Cheery spirits needed analysis more than the tormented ones,
she felt. The world was my pearled oyster and I was still in love.

As I was, standing at the rail with this wife, watching the sleek tan
beaches and the frowzy palms of Africa go by. Her skin was smooth

as silk across her high cheekbones and her slanted eyes looked at Africa, now that we had done with it, appraisingly. She was trim and pert, and her shoulders were braced squarely against the distant jungles, for she had beaten them. And gradually but terribly, with the heat around me and a wind as cold as Dao's between my shoulder blades, I saw that her content stemmed from her assumption that I considered the jungles mine. She had loved the desert places, the Lobi country, Cape Cod, which I despised because they were arid, sterile, non-vital, negative. She had never read fiction because there was life in it which she could not control. As she could not control my howling hungry love for her.

I put my arm around her waist and knew that I had been living in an arrogant dream of love. It had not occurred to me that two year-long expeditions, in French Guiana and the Ivory Coast, when Ruth and I should have none but ourselves for company, might show me up naked and unendearing. I went to the prow of the ship and watched the porpoises heaving and plunging, slithering through slick water, racing from the lunge of the world, the ship, lonely and each one alone.

There was Paris all around us now, a world of Paris, gray, gleaming, scintillant, decayed, raucous, breathless, vital as the earth and tranquil as a tomb in it, and although Ruth knew it well she was to me an intruder there. She calculated the wonders of this most wonderful of all the world's cities; I stuffed my pockets with them, I gulped them, I hugged my armfuls of them to my heart. Gayer than flowers were the pushcarts on the Rue Mouffetard, filled with vegetables smelling still of the earth, or fish with the perfume of the Breton seas. On the scooter I whistled to the least known and loveliest of Paris parks, the Buttes-Chaumont, with its precipitous hills and its lost restaurant run by a former Foreign Legionnaire, who would hurl at me the 1,000-franc lunch when I had ordered the 500-franc one. "What's good enough for the Legion is good enough for the Spahis," he would say democratically.

Ruth and I pretended there was still nothing wrong, or at least irreparable, in a joint career of exploring for documentary film which had started so auspiciously with the French Guiana expedition. Old

393

friends who had known each of us in previous marriages were embarrassingly complimentary about our partnership. I lectured in Paris with our film, *Jungle Terror,* and broadcast with Ruth in our jungle French.

Desperate to build on what we had already secured, I fostered tentatively an expedition to Tierra del Fuego, the sub-antarctic tip of South America. "No one has done a film on those dying Indians," I would say, "and this will really establish us. Cold as the devil, you know, but you wouldn't mind it, old skier."

And I shuddered at the thought, for I hated the negative wastelands. And Ruth would reply in the voice of my first wife, "We'll see, Bill, we'll see." I began to see that what I had promoted as a partnership was tipping off balance. It was inexplicable. It seemed that most of the women I had once thought I loved were in Paris, and I saw them furiously to discover that there was none I wanted but as warm friends now. Finally the old explorer was discovering that the dark terrain of his wife was inviolate. Hah, as the women's magazines would say, He Had Taken His Wife for Granted, which was precisely what I had assumed a secure love to signify. Hah, no!

"Heigh-ho!" yelled the fat old merchant at the Marché aux Puces, the Flea Market at Paris's Porte de Clignancourt. He wore the brass helmet of a French fireman and swung a silver-plated bidet in that circus of junk. Ruth with her camera caught the flash in the pan. We grinned thanks and shouldered our way through the thousands of treasure hunters, for as a sort of marital therapy we were keeping at work on the first professional film of the largest secondhand market in the world, at least a square mile of it wherein, with due searching, you could find anything your heart desired, from authentic Egyptian mummies to artificial fleas. Following its twisting one-story huts you would find a berouged and bedizened ex-actress pathetically chanting at an ex-piano. Jewels and ivory carvings from the Orient would be piled before hills of bicycle parts, bent and rusted nails, cracked chamber pots, old watches that didn't work, heaps of last century's eyeglasses held together with string.

On the sidewalks stood the poorer "brocanteurs" with their wares at their feet, a doll without a head, a live mangy dog, a tombstone

394

with its name brutally effaced. But in the interior, at twice the price, you could find the same debris presided over by the most respectable old dames many of whom had decent antique shops in the city but who came here for the excitement of the weekend. One character, elegantly attired and with the mien of a duchess, said, "Monsieur, it is an impertinent question you ask me, but I must explain that it is a social lust, as that of men who go to bars. It is stronger than we. This is our club, and there is never a dull minute in it. Now wouldn't you like to buy this slipper which might have been worn by Antoinette? There is just one, unfortunately—"

Most of these merchants were ham actors who loved being filmed and would howl greetings to us as they sat on a grimy mattress or a coffin drinking red wine in a crystal glass. Three days a week we went to them during a freezing month of August, and made friends among them whom we invited home for apéritifs. They, in turn, would bargain with us most gently when there was a bit of copper we prized. Aloyisius, tender of the outdoor lavatory, probably wealthier than I with that prosperous monopoly, would never accept a tip from me after I had bought him a wine.

These open-air merchants were as sensitive to the weather as fishermen. A good ten minutes before rain arrived you would see them glance at the sky and, with a pouncing precision, rush to cover their goods.

"Hey!" yelled Aloyisius to us. "There is sanctuary in the lavatory! Be my guests!" We waved and rushed to the only café in the Flea Market, Louisette's, a bistro on the angle of an alley three feet wide, and burst through the door smack into the bosom of Louisette herself.

"*Capitaine!* Madame! I have not seen you since yesterday!" She kissed our wet faces, and called each of us by the familiar "thou." We were *copains* by now. "There are mussels today, and the hot grog! And the music!"

Music filled the air, what there was of it amid the smoke. On a little dais beside the public washstand the two old beggar musicians played the accordion and the violin, and between the crowded marble-topped tables people danced, the bearded merchants, the panted girl merchants, the wealthy tourists, the Algerian bums. Louisette sang raucously behind her bar. The potbellied stove, warming the backsides of gypsy fortunetellers in their many gaudy skirts, spread across the room the odor of horseflesh and bargain lust.

We found a place big enough for one where we could film the frantic passers-by through the window, the rain beading it. Beside me, with her head leaned back against the crude painting that covered the wall and her fists to her eyes, was a young gypsy crying. Her pregnant stomach convulsed with sobs.

"Elena!" I shouted to be heard above the din. Her fists jerked down and her eyes like eight-balls rolled toward me.

"Ah, it's you," she said. "Will you tell my fortune for a change? He has left me."

"No, no. He'll be back. Were you naughty again?"

"No, no. It was worse than that. I permitted myself the luxury of getting used to him."

Now the one obviously great attachment remaining between Ruth and me was parental; we had conceived a film during the last year's pregnant months. Unlike babies, it had been born in bits and pieces, most of them, wrote the laboratory, good, some poor, and it would be the assembling of them which would prove whether the urchin was viable. If it was, and if it was attractive enough, we would cheerfully sell it into the white slavery of Hollywood.

We returned to the apartment at 226 Fifth Avenue. Built in 1840, it was a faithful but weary house, leaning against its modern neighbor to the north, with a slope on that side of the floor of about four inches. The ceiling was patched. Windows now opened to the wall of the building next door, six inches away. It was a farmhouse in the sky, a tremendous studio girded by some four thousand books into which were set so many tanks for tropical fish that the room could be illuminated adequately by them alone. It had the usual explorer's junk around it, masks, spears, leopard skins, prayer wheels and horns from Tibet, a tree-trunk Lobi ladder reaching high over the books to the antique clock with an etched dial showing the Somerville Insane Asylum. It frequently struck thirteen.

This place I loved, for I had made it and its furniture, mostly with my own hands, over the last twenty years, since my return from the South Seas in 1933. It was a tranquil place where no discord should be, where tensions eased, and so we worked in it quietly, Ruth in the attic darkroom to enlarge the still photos, I in the studio beribboned by film.

The film was mostly excellent, the story of our search for the Sorcerers' Village, and I was confident in the dark, with only the light of the little viewer beneath the visual memories of the Ivory Coast, that we had an honest and dramatic record of customs never filmed before. As I had felt with my previous film, *Jungle Terror* which Warners' had bought, there was something mystical, alchemical, in bringing to life with color these scenes of the expedition, and because I was first a writer I loved the building of the film into dramatic form, interjecting a face here, a landscape there, cutting in and out of a dance with the activities of the village where it took place. Mystical, too, was my relationship with Ruth during this period. We went to our separate darkrooms and each sat alone during most of the day, working on the adventures we had shared, seeing each other come alive in the past, and sharing our actual meals like ghosts. Conversation in the jungle had been facile and excited, even though we were alone; now we lived in separate darkrooms, and even at our largest cocktail parties we were each encased in shadow.

A film, like a book, is never finished; there is always a scene to be lengthened, shortened, transposed, but the time came when our *Sorcerers' Village* seemed ready to make its own way in the world. My old Tahiti friend Bob Flaherty, "the father of the documentary film," had seen it and brought a couple of dozen friends to see it at the Explorers Club, where it went over nicely. And with it we were guests of honor at the Screen Directors Guild. I lectured with it at the Harvard Club and other places and had it on television, but this wasn't enough. I had procrastinated in showing it to Warner Brothers. If it were bought by them, I would not be permitted to use it for my personal talks. I needed the several hundred dollars apiece which these brought in, for of all free lances the explorer leads perhaps the most precarious existence. We were again living mostly on the sporadic sales of articles, photos, and book reviews. It was fine to have recognition as a serious explorer, to get the French Légion d'Honneur for it, but it didn't keep us in chop suey.

We sat with Bob Flaherty in Costello's bar on Third Avenue. It was cold, but I was sweating. The usual clientele of newspapermen

397

was drunk and shouting, but I heard only the soft voice of Bob, praising the film, praising us who had attempted on a shoestring what he, as poor as we, had years ago achieved. At last I came out with it. "Bob, do we have a feature there, an hour and a half?"

Tensely as children hanging on the words of the old master, we sat before that benign white-haired genius. Unhappily he wasn't drinking; he was not well. Our drinks were untouched. Ruth and I didn't realize that for the first time in months we were holding hands hard. "Well," said Bob, "you see—" and I knew he was embarrassed. He didn't want to hurt us. "Oh, hell, Bill, I don't know! You've got a pippin of a short, that's sure. . . ." So we knew; that was it, from the grand old man of the documentary.

"Blessings on you," he said as he left us, walking toward tomorrow's drab day and his death at the end of the week. I had lost one of the dearest men I had ever known, and the hand that had guided me for many years.

Norman Moray of Warner Brothers did the kindly and exceptional thing in coming up to our studio to see the film. Film magnates don't do this; they have you to their projection room filled with sufficient secretaries, office boys, and friends so that you don't notice it when, if they are bored, they slip out in the middle of a screening. Then they are tied up when at the end of it you desperately rush to their offices. And their secretaries tie them up again when you telephone. It is standard procedure in the film industry, the toughest, the most ill-mannered in the world.

Norman Moray, bright as a pink-and-gray bird, listened first to the music we had recorded in Africa—"Good, good, good"—and leaned back on the couch with the big dog beside him when the film spangled the screen with tropic color. Ruth tended the projector and I the running commentary (dear God, don't let a splice break or a fuse blow!) and at the end of two hours of what I thought great film we turned on the lights, served a new drink, and waited.

"Pretty esoteric," said Norman, "for a travel film. I might offer you six thousand dollars to cut a short from it." There it was again. Six thousand dollars would cover about a quarter of our expenses. Night after night we screened it for the producers we could entice to the

398

studio. It cost a fortune in whisky, and took the fat off me. Before I sold this beloved albatross and got it off my neck, I screened it about two hundred times.

I flew with it to Hollywood and hawked it from studio to studio, the heavy lump of it under my arm like a vacuum cleaner. One magnate said, "Sorcerers' Village? What's a sorcerer?" Several offered to buy footage, a landscape, an animal shot, background material for their own African films made in Hollywood. It was no go. I booked a plane for New York, and picked up oddities which might serve for Ruth's Moonsday. To hell with Hollywood. If *Jungle Terror* had been such a success on two continents, *Sorcerers' Village* must do better, for I had learned more of film structure, Ruth more of moving-picture photography, and we had richer material to work with. Eagerly and confidently I looked forward to the job of re-editing, but most eagerly to Moonsday.

Ever since the days in the South Seas I had regarded Moonsday as perhaps the greatest discovery since Grandfather Davis invented the floating ball of the water closet. It might be called a marriage meter, gauging the degree of love from month to month, and is guaranteed infallible. As Ruth and I had found out that one of our tastes in common was for Christmases, anniversaries, and birthdays, in short to get and give presents, and that there weren't enough of them in a year, I revived Moonsday. The first Monday (derived from "moon's day" in the Anglo-Saxon) of every month should be dedicated by loving couples to the giving and receiving of presents. It is much more enjoyable to look forward to a lump of them on a certain day, with ceremony, than to receive them haphazardly. If one of you forgets a Moonsday you can consider it zero for love; if the presents are numerous and of particular quality and, mark you, festively wrapped, you may consider love a-boiling.

Even in Africa, in the bush, we had observed our sentimental festival, although presents were hard to find. One of mine might be a leaf of cornucopia filled with crunchy roast ants from a native market, Ruth's might be a special twig which the Africans frayed and used very effectively to brush their teeth.

Now as I came up the five flights of stairs, lugging that rejected film, I was aware of no defeat. Like France I had lost a battle but

I had not lost the war. I would start to cut the film again tonight. And there was Ruth. We would laugh at Hollywood yet, I said to the dogs which Ruth had loosed to meet me in mid-route. I rounded the last newel post to see Ruth at last, golden and trim in slacks, holding out to me a Scotch and soda.

We sat on the table with our drinks while she unwrapped the nonsense I had brought her as Moonsday presents. There were none for me.

The progress of the film was somewhat impeded by our divorce. Ruth went to Mexico and I to the darkroom, a void within a larger emotional void. I cut the film again with the dogs beside me, and made my tropical fish and the snails to spawn, and Consuela, the tortoise, would clump-clump across the house to sit ecstatically in my lap while I shined her with shoe polish. And Minou, the wildcat, the witch cat I had brought back from Africa, grew rapidly madder, racing from one end of the house to the other, a black blur sparked by her enormous golden eyes.

Adaptation to celibacy came hard and was confusing. The most poignant of pains is loneliness, and the most efficient anodynes are work, danger, women, and alcohol. Work I had plenty of, and added to it by my increasing devotion to cookery. As others would say, "Come up and see my etchings," I, since I was now contributing to cookbooks and the culinary magazines, could fairly say, "Come up and see my popovers," which were really startling eruptions defying all the arcana which women, wishing to make the cuisine a mystic art exclusively their own, had always used to beguile the male.

My cooking, however, was a dubious lure. Because it was so simply done and still so successful, it smacked of heresy. You don't get a kiss across the stove while your paramour is thinking, "This termite is undercutting the very props of our kitchen. He doesn't beat his batter till he is exhausted. He doesn't preheat his oven and popover pans until he risks conflagration. Yet there they pop, and stay popped."

And the wild rice, they'd think. Who ever heard of not actually cooking wild rice, and for a long time, too! It brought them to the shrieking point when I simply soaked the wild rice overnight in consommé and heated it for ten minutes in the oven the next day. This, indeed, was a bit akin to the etching gambit in that the more curious of them would insist on staying overnight to be certain there was no cheating.

But worst of all, heinous really, was my five-year-old perpetual soup which attracted gourmets from as far as Singapore. The very thought of it alienated conventional damsels accustomed to Campbell's cans. For it really was a perpetual soup, such as is sacred to the peasants of France who bequeath it, the pot never quite emptied— "To my son, my cow; to my daughter, my soup"—for generations until some huzzy lets it spoil or flagrantly serves the last drop. It is conceived and born of honest marrow bones and meat, to which are added all the vegetable waters, such leftover gravies as may be fitting, and such fresh vegetables and meats as a dinner may demand.

"It is microbian," snorted Judy. "It is back to the womb." She had just come from her analyst; my loved ones' analysts had for long been a curse upon me. "You have never taught it to *be itself.*" Contrary to the analysts, neither man nor soup should be itself. They should develop and evolve. Fermentation was prevented by my boiling my faithful soup twice a day, and clarifying it completely with egg once a week so that it became a crystalline consommé, when the new meats and vegetables would be added. During my long expeditions to French Guiana and the Ivory Coast a good neighbor tended my soup.

Ah, the richness, the aroma, the jewelry of dice-cut meat and vegetables I would serve to the sultry Judy who always was enraged by the state of her soul, her half-written book, by me. We would face each other between the candles while her invective diminished with the soup, and the elfin smile, which was her true insigne, appeared. Pleasantly she would talk of me now, and that I needed, and with quiet confidence she would see herself in her own just light. Thirty-three cents' worth of a soup which was at once gentle and scintillant was of more spiritual value to her than the twenty-dollars-an-hour analysis.

But no woman, no soup, could fill the gnawing hungry place where Ruth had been, and I tried by a tornado of work to forget her. This was somewhat difficult in that I was still working with material which we had produced together. I lectured constantly and couldn't deny her her just credit. I cut the film and so met her again and again. I

401

wrote the book on the Guiana expedition and adorned my pages with her, and the critics were justly generous in their praises of "this jungle wife." She haunted me properly.

I wrote poetry again, furiously at dawn, and *A Child's Book of Magic,* with the materials of its tricks glued to its pages, and became ethnological consultant to *The Snows of Kilimanjaro,* which was based on Hemingway's great tale. This was enjoyable and produced a lurid correspondence with Hemingway regarding the man traps of Hollywood. He postscripted these epistles with "Not for repetition. Repeat. Unrepeat." Promoting his film and incidentally my book by TV and radio, I made twenty broadcasts in two weeks until I got to squirm before a microphone as before a stomach pump and began to mumble in the street. Hemingway was doing fine. Africa was doing fine. I was doing fine, according to anyone's standards but mine. Leave us alone.

I had claustrophobia in New York, the greatest little city in the world, the tightest little island to squeeze the gizzard out of you, to smash you down the street like ninepins. So you became a big-shot bowler; so what? You couldn't sit back and watch the game as you could on the Île St. Louis in Paris or Telegraph Hill in San Francisco. In New York the men of good will, the men of peace, were the target, and quick as a wink you'd find yourself again a ninepin in it if you didn't keep to the upper end of the alley, among the assassins.

This wasn't for me. I needed a clean wind again, and space to fling out my arms without rasping them against the building edges which were closing in on me. I sought broader horizons through people, mostly those less fortunate than I, and found that the kindly act was not at all inspiriting; it depressed me. To be sure, I worried no longer about my own problems, but I was miserable with the miseries of those I tried to help.

There was a sweet girl I had left as a virgin before the African trip, and who now lived in poverty with an illegitimate child. There was a blind woman for whom I read, bored to death, one of my books, word by word, to a tape recorder that she might use it in her club for the blind. I had to buy glasses after that one. There was a sparkling girl, a sports writer, who hobbled up my five flights of stairs on crutches painted to match her gowns, even the polka-dot

402

number, and she brought back the limp in me caused by an indiscretion in the war. From the benches of Madison Square Park in front of my house I gathered the derelicts to serve them my perpetual soup with good French wine, and was distressed that they made off with my sixteenth-century crucifix. Although I drank hard myself, I took hopeless drunks to Alcoholics Anonymous meetings and was so bored by that truly noble organization that it was I who got the hangover. Every two months I gave blood, fanatically, to the hospitals until my great vitality was reduced to the point where I needed medical care. I was living through others, and they through me, but as a Do Gooder I was no good at all.

New York was full of parties, and I gave them and went to them, for even the least attractive lone man has an easy time of it where there is a glut of married couples and celibate women. The host will go through his phone book to find dozens of these in proportion to one fairly personable whole male.

Try though I did, I could never maintain a serene spirit at my own large parties, which usually were held after dinner, for I was of the night people and wrote best between the hours of 3:00 A.M. and seven, when gradually, in the unctuous silence of Fifth Avenue, I came alive like a bat.

We had been about twenty on the night when I concluded that, by God and by Jesus, this was false living. It was evanescent as the snow which was piling thick upon my skylights, giving a false sense of coziness and security, while down the streets came the scream of the wind that drove it. Out of the night had come these bright, smiling people, huddled together lest they disintegrate alone, and behind them you could hear the bitter wind.

The party had gone, dissipated like the pattern of raindrops on a window screen, bursting one by one into the outer vacuum that was its world. And I sat at the typewriter, not looking at it but up to the skylight where the snow was melting blue beneath the early morning sun. I couldn't write now. The ghosts of spite and persiflage and illusory drink were a stink in the house. Only the books, rising tier on tier to the ceiling, were real, and Maupi with her pups beside her. I must get the hell out of this or go crazy.

Another marriage might be a solution, but I doubted that. Judy, whom I loved tenderly, was too urbane to follow me to my far places where no paths were, and I would be the death of both of us in the constriction of New York. Nine to five, nine to five, cowering behind the bulwark of a desk.

I began to write in panic:

> *Quietly lies all our love in this hollow*
> *Which you have devised in the skull of my heart . . .*

The cuckoo, that great therapist of a bird, came out of the clock and cuckooed six times, so I tore up the verse and started again:

> *Smoothly as eels they had gathered around him,*
> *Snicking their bright little fangs as they rose . . .*

I was sitting exhausted at the typewriter now, panting at my cigarette, surrounded by the litter of my party, the butts, half-finished drinks, the gouged Camembert, the pistachio shells ground into the Persian rug, the earrings clipped to the edge of the fish tank. The cuckoo cuckooed seven times. Furiously I tore out the page and began on an old envelope:

> *You, you great swaggerer, tell us a tale*
> *Of the tumults you've lived, of your bones bursting . . .*

It was only seventeen minutes past seven now, but the cuckoo was unrestrained, and chirped out a derisory "cuck . . .," not even a "coo."

The next day was sparkling, snow-polished. The maid arrived to clean up. Judy phoned to read me a good chapter of her work-in-progress. Young Laslo, my ten-year-old chum from downstairs, brought me some handsome leaves he had picked out of a garbage can.

Maupi's pups were glugging merrily. I was not surprised at the good news that Louis Vincent, who had sponsored my publicity-paid passage to Africa, would be dropping in with an old friend for cocktails.

404

The old friend was Emil Glenat, director of the French freighter line, the CTO, whom I had heard of as a delightful, impulsive character, but never met. He sat on a stool with his Pernod and a pile of books on Toltec ruins which he had discovered in my bookshelves, and his gray, young-old face lit up with the beauty and mystery of them. He looked at me straight over his glasses.

"How would you like, monsieur, to take a trip around the world?"

Hesitantly I said, "But I've been around the world—"

"I mean on one of our freighters, as our guest."

"But, my God, I can't accept that! Could I do something for you?"

"Not a thing. It would be our pleasure. The *Tofevo* leaves next month. You will be the only passenger."

The doors of walled space were open to me again, and I could breathe again in my world without a roof.

My last night in New York was one of witchery. I had still not found a home for my cat Minou or a tenant for my apartment during the while I should be away. Minou was a black African wildcat which had made my acquaintance rather boldly on the Ivory Coast, during a night when I lay on my cot with the semi-delirium of malaria. Ruth was behind me, working over the fire, when suddenly I snapped to the consciousness that there was a weight on my chest and looked into a cat's golden eyes, reflecting the firelight. She seemed quite happy, purring and digging her claws into me. I spoke quietly to Ruth in my delirium, "Don't touch that cat. It is the black cat of death, and if you touch her I'll die." Why I should have been so solicitous for my conservation I don't know, for death would have been a relief to the gnashing of my bones and the atomic explosions in my head.

The cat spent the night on me, warming me when I had the chills, finally soothing me with her purring when I had lucid hot intervals, and in the morning she was gone, leaving a small dead mouse on my pillow. None of my natives had ever seen a mouse in those jungles.

She came back night after night—never in the daytime, for she was apparently afraid of my black boys who may have shot at her—and we fed her sardines and made her cautious friendship. Then she traveled with us through the bush, and to France and across the Jura

Mountains on the back of my motor scooter, and to New York where she lived quite happily and got her picture in the papers, a weird cat, a witch cat.

Now I am not sentimental about animals, although I love them, nor do I credit them with great intelligence, but as I sat with friends at my long table talking of plans for my coming trip around the world and what the devil should I do with Minou, as I said that I should certainly be returning to Africa, Minou leaped to the table and snarled. And when later I showed my Ivory Coast film, *Sorcerers' Village,* in color, Minou watched it as she never had before, and snarled at the natives in it, and the snakes, and whined, whimpered with nostalgia when she saw the lush scenes of jungle and the sacred catfish in their pool. I believe she missed Africa and knew I would not take her with me.

That night, for the first time in a year, she slept on my chest, and in the morning I was startled to find a small dead mouse on my pillow, in this house where no one had ever seen a mouse. And there was no Minou. The door was well locked and all the windows with the exception of a skylight inaccessible to even a cat. Minou, the witch cat, had left me as strangely as she had come, with the same gesture, the same token, and I rather expected to meet her in Africa one day.

41 ~~~~~~~~~~~~~~~~~~~~

Tramp steamer de luxe—rebellion
in Indo-China—opium for the elite
—Borneo—Australia—Chagos of
my heart—love-dove of a concierge

SLOWLY WE STEAMED to Panama in that luxurious
tramp of a *Tofevo,* and through the Gatun Lake with its hundreds of
uninhabited tropical islands. I had three cabins to myself, for bedroom, living room, workshop. We were only three at table, the
captain, a grizzled, humorous, gentle type, the chief engineer, with
whom I didn't quite see eye to eye, and I, but in four months of
travel we got on remarkably well. The captain taunted the chief with
the superiority of oriental art. The chief choked on his soup and
howled the praises of the Classical Greek. And I stuck rigidly to the
African Primitive.

At night, when the three of us had amicably worked long enough
on the thousand-piece picture puzzle, I would strip to the sarong
I had worn in Bali twenty-odd years ago, when life was truly magical,
and write the early chapters of my book on the Ivory Coast. There
would be no sound around me but the shush of the sea and the
engine's rumble when we heaved through a great wave. An occasional
blackened engineer or a tired helmsman changing shifts would appear
silently in the dining saloon where I worked and discuss the only
news of the day, which concerned the mate's tooth or the brilliance
of Orion or the flying fish which had come aboard, all phosphorescent,
and was being eaten by my pet ape. We had little news, even by
radio, of the outside world. Here was the utter peace I needed.

And the odd thing was the harmony of forty men for thirty days
at sea without women or any distraction other than the childish fetes
we organized. We egg-raced, we wrestled, we sang French ballads to
my tape recorder. There were no drunks, no pansies, no belligerents.

We were men unequal intellectually and socially, but in the great peace of the sea we were men of simple good will.

Tramp freighter travel is not to be recommended to those who must arrive at specific destinations at specific times, for one's course is likely to be changed en route according to the cargoes which the head office finds available. We were headed for Bangkok, Siam, when orders came that we should make for Saigon, then up the coast to Hanoi.

We docked in the port of Saigon, cluttered with sampans and junks swinging their frail masts across the moon. And there began a strange series of coincidences, for I met an old friend, the photographer Dixie Rees, who was shortly to be shot down over the lines of the rebel Vietminh whose troops were coming closer and closer to the city, whose partisans were in Saigon itself, boring and bombing from within. Restaurants were barricaded with barbed wire and steel grilles. During my war days a few years before the fighting had been honestly in the open. Now children of the Vietnam, the government army, were found in the capital stifled to death by green limes forced down their throats.

I was in the market, loving the nostalgic stench of it, the funereal displays of pigs' brains and rotted fish drying to make the sauce Nyock Mamm, an exquisite putrescence of a sauce which would give authority to anything it was dumped upon. Coolies jogged past in their straw umbrella hats, bearing pots of viands on each end of the bamboo poles across their shoulders. Little Annamite women, perfectly proportioned but about four feet tall, their lips stained a bloody crimson with betel nut, minced by on their wooden clogs, chanting, "Chang wha, chung tze, wing ma po woo," or sounds similar in their snub noses, leaning to spit what looked like blood between their little pajamaed legs.

The gongs of a temple seemed to be bursting all around me when a heavy hand was laid upon my shoulder. Cautiously I regarded the signet ring on its finger before spinning to grab a mighty man in uniform, the British Colonel Mike Godfrey.

"Holy Mike!"

"Holy Bill!"

He had not changed since the war days when we had accepted the

408

swords of surrendering Japanese officers. Blunt of face, blue-eyed, with the seamed ruddy skin of the Anglo-Indian soldier, he was still the dapper buccaneer I had sat beside in the courtyard of legendary Angkor Wat while the gaudy children danced by torchlight up the enormous stone steps to disappear into the life-size bas-relief of their gods dancing.

"You stink of fish," said he.

"And you of the demon rum," said I. "Have you been here ever since?"

"No, Malaya. Gurkha rifles. There are only a few thousand of the Commie rebels in the bush, but they're wrecking the rubber plantations and they're harder than the Vietminh to catch. I'm on leave. Have you had your pipe today?"

I hadn't had my pipe today. Although most of my friends, and anyone's, in Indo-China smoked opium, I had given it up after a dozen trials as not my dish. After most dinner parties in the nicest houses I had had the choice of bridge or the fumerie, a quiet, beautifully decorated den devoted to the pipe. "Ah, but you'll never have the dreams until you become a true habitué," my friends in black tie or evening dress would say, lying tranquilly beside me on the long mahogany couch that stretched from wall to wall. I had had no dreams. I had had nausea, constipation, and the sensation of lead in my extremities the morning after—all my extremities. Out of politeness I had smoked opium again and again until I concluded sensibly that a vice which you had to cultivate so hard was simply not worth it. Bostonian and conservative, I preferred nicotine and flavored alcohol.

"No," I repeated firmly, "I am abstemious. I am also romantic, when aroused. And I am now trying to find a woman named Doriel, who used to work with me here in the Information Service during the war, when, for my sins, I also met you."

The colonel shuddered, so hard that he had to sit down in the nearest chair, which was propitiously in front of the Rum Palace. "That Doriel," he said, "if I'm thinking of the one who worked with you on the radio here, was a brilliant Eurasian writer but far too beautiful, even in her forties, I guess, to be wasted on a desk job. Let's try the radio station."

The Yunnanese reception clerk slid his glasses to the end of his nose and recognized me with a smile of teeth blackened by betel chewing. "Doriel is no longer with us," he said, shaking his head. "You might try 14-on-the-Quai." This was a renowned fumerie which I had assumed to have been closed when the French outlawed opium.

Mike and I had dinner at Cholon, an outskirt of Saigon where every big restaurant was webbed by barbed wire as protection from the terrorists. This did not spoil our enjoyment of what is probably the best food in the Orient, pellucid soups, honey-sweetened pork, vegetables so sparkling that they might be faceted. With it we had the Chinese brandies Ng-Ga-Pi and Que-Wha-Lu, which have the distinction of not turning your head but merely lifting your feet and your chair somewhat off the ground.

Over to the harbor we glided and down a flight of slimy steps to a door which opened almost on the water level. Parked before it were a dozen little boats which had brought the discreeter clients. Mike and I were recognized despite the elapsed years and led down the bamboo hall past the very elegant brothel section and on tiptoe to the fumerie. Yes, Madame Doriel was here, but she was in her room with the pipe just now. She was the new owner of 14-on-the-Quai. However a heart sinks, mine sank. There had always been a torment in Doriel, but around her there had been a sort of armored penumbra which, I had felt, would never let her demons out or others in.

"Come out of it, old boy," said Mike, running a long hand through his crew-cut gray hair. "Something like this was bound to happen, or she would have burst at the typewriter. Let's have a few pipes while waiting for her."

Numb with the realization that Doriel, like so many other good friends, had found no refuge but such as this in our bloody world without a roof, I walked stolidly beside Mike to the door of the fumerie, The Door, I thought. When I had been younger there had been the Door of sunset leading to golden sheltered worlds, and later the Doors of planes and battle tents leading to a personal peace.

As there was peace here, a pseudo-peace, a polite apology for peace which would smack you in the eye once you closed your eye. It was a long room, freshly walled with green bamboo and furnished only with a continuous bed of red mahogany around three walls. The foot of it was about three inches lower than the head where were

410

little square pillows of straw. The hush of it was hypnotic. As in the war years, no one was permitted here who was not impeccably dressed. It was more proper than a swank British club, and its members lay gracefully, discreetly apart, whispering, sleeping, beckoning with a slim white hand for a new pipe.

Mike and I spread out our tough old carcasses with dignity as a minute Cambodian girl, wearing black pajama trousers but with her full breasts bared, came in with the pipes and the pear-shaped little opium lamps. They and the fat candles threw the shadow of her high against the fluted bamboo wall, like the menace which all beauty may become. The shadow would move, diminish, grow great again with preposterous breasts which no opium addict wanted, for the drug attenuates lust. The exquisite prostitutes from the front rooms would stride through nude, their skins the color of jonquils, firm and taut to bursting, and the quiet men would look up from them to their grotesque but by now more familiar and easy shadows on the wall. And the quiet women beside their men would tranquilly go to sleep.

Once an explosion followed by the shatter of machine-gun fire resounded down the quais not far from us. Only Mike and I were startled, although we were on our sixth pipes now. Someone said languidly, "Those Vietminh are so annoying. . . ."

Leaning toward each other on our elbows, we talked in the hush of trenches about the renascent war of Indo-China since my old Leclerc had left to be killed in a plane crash. Red China's Communists were abetting the Vietminh troops, and Vietnam and the French volunteers were buckling to the north. Red agitation had spread like a cancer through Saigon itself, as demonstrated just now by the racket in the streets. Why the hell, asked Mike justly, should the United States have accepted the Korean action, which proved nothing whatsoever, when they could effectively have buffered Indo-China? The gentle theocracy of Tibet was already lost to the Reds. If Indo-China were to go, so, probably, would Singapore. And across the way was Indonesia, a fence-walker still. And Nehru's India. The entire East was slipping through our fuddled fingers.

We were now on our eleventh pipes, which was pretty good for amateurs. The little Cambodian girl squatted on the mahogany between us. She twirled the tarlike opium on a long needle above the flame and popped it into the little mouths of our pipes. We breathed deep, holding the sweet smoke in our lungs as long as possible, and leaned back hopefully.

"Am I talking particularly brilliantly, old boy?" Mike asked.

"You always were a wag," I remarked. "Will you remind me of what you were saying?"

"Christ!" said Mike, sitting up with some slight dizziness, as did I. "Let's get the hell out of here and have a drink!"

It was just at that moment that there came the snicking of what I judged a tommy gun outside and the bamboo wall in front of us zipped open across its top, its shreds hanging down like bangs before our ducking shadows. I think I saw the top of my shadow's head cut off. No one moved but we, who moved with commando celerity through the door.

"Where's Madame Doriel?" I demanded of a whiskery little servant.

"She say good-by. Good-by you both. She gone. She kiss you both." He pulled down both our foreheads to kiss them. "No charge." He pushed us to the slimy steps of the quai.

The good ship *Tofevo,* a better tranquilizer than opium, slid through green seas along the coast of Annam, but we were not tranquil, for we had been warned to stay on the seaward side of the deck, as the Vietminh along these shores were conscientious with their target practice. We sailed through one of the world's fairylands in the Baie d'Along, jutting with extraordinary islands, narrow at their bases, rising to narrow green spires like fairy cathedrals. You could imagine great halls beneath the bay and submarine passages from one to another for the travel of the many monkeys, who don't swim but nonetheless inhabit the peaks. It was as appealing a notion as the legend, which had always fascinated me, of the undersea passage between Morocco and Gibraltar for the transit of the Barbary apes which are identical on both sides of the strait.

At Haiphong we picked up cargo and orders to go to Borneo for refueling. There at Tarakan I had the first intimation of the tragedy which Indonesia has brought to the once magnificent Dutch East Indies. It was as though children had taken over their father's estate, the splendid roads cracking for lack of upkeep, the walls of the schools

412

and hospitals fissured, the library decayed, the canals of the Dutch filled with refuse. The people were unchanged, except that the progressive government had now obliged the women, under that sweltering sun, to cover their breasts with either the beautiful batik sarongs or the ugly modern blouses. Ah, my Bali, I sighed, you will be in a Mother Hubbard soon, and soon you will be playing boogie-woogie and be-bop on chrome-plated electrically operated gamelans. And then there will be no music in you but the grunt of bulldozers chomping on those exquisite old-fashioned temples.

Down the seas we sailed, in a new direction now, past the Great Barrier Reef of Australia and to Sydney, which I had not seen since I was twenty-one. I was impressed anew by the gray conservatism and blazing individualism of it, the bland buildings, and the luminous lavender jacaranda trees, the bars closing at an hour inhumane, and fat dock workers who could go on personal strike at the drop of a mood.

And there was Ron Monson, one of the best and wildest correspondents of the war, with whom I had done dour battle in the garden of Public Relations; no friendship is so sweet as one founded on the fair battering of each other's heads. Ron was domesticated by now, a suburbanite with wife and children, garden and dogs, but we had a few short snorts and talked the wild poetry of the war we had shamefully loved, and poked each other in the ribs for auld lang syne. And Ron led me to the editors of the town who bought a ream of fantasy manuscripts I had never been able to sell in New York. And he took me to the Royal Geographical Society, which made me an honorary life member. At the end of my talk to them, the chairman asked what I should like as a souvenir of Australia.

"You have a dwarf kangaroo," I said, "which I should love to have hopping around my flat in New York." That wasn't good enough. When I returned to my ship there was a cage as large as your bathroom with a giant kangaroo named Joey in it. He was happy to see me, but the captain wasn't.

Joey, however, was the joy of the ship on the long journey around the southern tip of Australia, past Tasmania, and across the Indian Ocean where we traveled for a month without putting foot on land. Joey would welcome you to his cage in a boxing posture, lick your

413

ear politely, then give you a clout to the midriff. You would retaliate with a Judas kiss to Joey and a slap, and the bout was on. This was great sport until you saw the first drops of sweat between his eyes, which meant he was becoming riled and would soon lift his feet to supplement his arms. It is with these ponderous feet and their talons that kangaroos eviscerate the wild dingo dogs. We solved that one. We held down his feet with our own and hugged him tight while he hopped with us about the cage. Only a banana would make it safe to break the clinch.

"Joey I love," said the chief mate, a Marseillais, "but I wish he were a girl. I've always wanted to go through that pouch they wear. Imagine what you might find there: old keys, a flower pressed in a kangaroo bible, love letters tied up in pink ribbon—" Joey is now one of the friendliest members of the New York Zoological Gardens.

The only land between us and Arabia now, on August first, was the Chagos Archipelago, one of the most lonely in the world. No one goes there, and only a small supply of copra, from which is squeezed coconut oil, comes out. But when James Norman Hall and I had talked in Tahiti of his adventures in solitude I had dreamed of Chagos. I could actually see it now, its wreaths of green palm atolls enclosing golden water. We were passing within a few hundred yards of it, and through the binoculars I could see a dark-skinned people waving. Here was the real Chagos, but Chagos was also, happily, a state of mind.

Now a weird thing occurred to me. I wanted more than anything in the world to reach Chagos—urgently—now. I might convince the captain to put me ashore, or I could swim for it. I would be returning to and surpassing the Tahiti of my early dreams, full cycle and beyond, and there would surely be a book in it, of absolute withdrawal to utter isolation, and the killing or the curing of the fever that had all my life sent me somersaulting in pursuit, primarily, of my own shadow which raced ahead.

Now the captain of this ship was a perspicacious character, of whom the men stood somewhat in awe. The krewmen of French West Africa had attributed second sight to him, for he could tell the thieves among them and those who were falsely sick when cargo was to be loaded. All I had noticed was the seemingly clairvoyant speed with

414

which he could join picture puzzles, which helped pass our long hours at sea, from the vermiculate pieces of cardboard.

His shoulder touched mine at the rail, and his dry gray profile looked at Chagos. "I was just reading my old logs," he said, "and thinking of the several people, passengers and seamen, who had had the whim to jump overboard. Most of them were malcontents whom I wished well, but, mon Dieu, what a nuisance they were! I would have to turn the ship around to look for them—only one I found— and telegraph the countries nearest to us, and the head office of our line, which would give me hell for the delay on a schedule which was tightly plotted. Always it was I to blame."

"Strange. I was just wondering—"

"I was, too. Can you use a hypodermic? Good. We have three men who need penicillin. Come along." Firmly I was led from Chagos.

We went through the Red Sea and the Suez Canal which was already brooding with some mad bomber's mine in it. Apparently we missed the mine by inches, and it held up traffic for a day until it could be brought ashore. It had probably not been placed for us. What seemed clear was that then, in 1954, Egypt considered the canal her own. This mine was no accident; it could have fallen out of no one's pocket.

We put foot to land at last in Genoa, which wasn't very stable after a month at sea, and were wandering among the dozens of tiny ancient churches around the port when a sailor from the ship came rushing after us with the mail which had just arrived. The captain's orders were among it and several letters for me, including one from Judy.

"I had the damnedest dream," she wrote, "on August first. I was on an island and up a tree (don't laugh, because I'm always up a tree!) and a white ship passed, with you, of all things, at the railing of it. Will you never come home to my bright island?"

Home was now as much Paris as New York, and I returned to my little apartment with the glassed-in terrace on Rue Roquepine, over-looking the mansard roofs and twisted chimney pots. On the top floor opposite me was the same theater of neighbors whom somehow I

415

never met on the street. There was the brawny-bearded old fellow in love with his bicycle which he carried up and down six flights of stairs. He slept with it beside his bed. There was the grim gray dentist in the apartment beside him. I was so close that I could see his hand tremble as he filled teeth, until he would knock off for a moment, reappear with a bottle at his other window, and return heartened to his drill. And there was the concierge of the building, diagonally across. She was my great love, in her sixties, I'd say, round as an apple and with apple cheeks.

I had with me, of course, the old slingshot which had been so useful in impressing the natives with its superiority over their unfletched arrows. Now on a golden afternoon, when I knew that Madame la Concierge would soon be returning to her room to water her ragged plant and take a nap, I wrote a note saying, *"Il y a quelqu'un qui t'aime—Monsieur X,"* and wrapped it around a marble and shot it straight into her room. It was not long before she appeared at the window, wearing her steel-rimmed glasses to read the note. She shook her head, puzzled but pleased.

The next day I pipped in a note saying, *"Bons baisers—Monsieur X,"* and when she read it I was leaning over my terrace, smoking thoughtfully. She called to me. "How can it be, monsieur, that I receive billets-doux in my room which is locked? Can they be brought by a homing pigeon, a dove of love?" I let a week go by while my sweet old lady simmered in anticipation, coming frequently to the window looking for her love dove, and then I began a furious attack with hard candies wrapped in silver foil. Now she had always one or both cheeks puffed out like a squirrel as she nodded good day to me. It was on a hot evening, when I had zipped over a weighted rose with a note saying, *"Pour mon amour!—Monsieur X,"* that she came to the window with a glass of wine as I stood on the terrace with my favorite drink, half vodka, half champagne, a dash of angostura, and the twist of a lemon peel with a couple of cubes of ice.

She looked at me cunningly, putting her forefinger to a lower eyelid and pulling it down, which is a French gesture for skepticism. "Now if I only had ice," she said, "for this warm wine . . . if only my dove—"

The jig was up. She was on to me, and she danced like a demoiselle to catch the foil-wrapped ice cubes which I shot over to her. *"Je*

416

t'aimerai toute ma vie—pour un rêve!" she called, as we raised our tinkling glasses.

42 ~~~~~~~~~~~~~~~~~~~~

The world, the singing place—the
senses of Paris—Gri-gri finds my Doriel

I SPENT TWO YEARS in Paris now, with some of my oldest and dearest friends. Here nearby were the Princesses Dadiani, refugees from Georgia, U.S.S.R., whose brother-in-law, Prince Amilakvari, had been "twice killed" beside me in Libya, and Cas Edmonds, whom I had known in Tahiti, with his gem of a wife, Sheila, living like regal vagabonds on their yacht moored near the Place de la Concorde. Tales of wonder and mystery were told around their tall candles as the passage of little ships rocked us gently on the Seine. And I went to Düsseldorf in Germany for the publication of my books there, but most to see Barrows Mussey, magician and author extraordinary, whom I had known at the age of ten. With him now was Jane, irradiating that city of fogs where once The Vampire lived. And Charles de Breteuil, who had been my captain in the Italian and French campaigns, bore me off to Morocco where he had bought the fabulous Villa Tailor that had lodged Roosevelt and Churchill during the war, and we wandered quite safely, during these new times of stress, late at night through the corkscrew alleys, caressed by whispers.

Here in Morocco was a proper war between the French and the *fellagha,* continuing throughout North Africa, supposedly for native independence, and as an old colonial I was sickened by it. Before the progressive administration of Marshal Lyautey in the first quarter of this century the Hamitic culture had been slopping toward complete desuetude. Agronomy did not exist. Hygiene was unknown and international commerce insignificant. Now in Casablanca and Marrakesh there were broad-windowed white skyscrapers devoted equally to the interests of the French and the Berbers. Fields of grain were being harvested scientifically by the dimmest-witted rustics, obviously to their profit as much as that of the French who bought their produce. And on the road from Casablanca to Marrakesh were deserts which hundreds of years ago had been forested, now bravely blooming again with the thousands of transplanted saplings of the French reforestation program. The negative Will of Allah had been vitalized by French colonials who, in contrast to the natives, were willing to work.

There was a fetid wind blowing through Marrakesh, and in spite of the fabulous hospitality of the De Breteuils in their walled palatial estate and the delight of hunting dinosaurs beneath the orange trees with young Jean, I was happy to return to Paris again.

Life was wonderful. I could fail at nothing. With the help of Marie Schebeko, the world's most beautiful literary agent, I lodged my books with publishers in six foreign countries and placed articles in France's magazines. Oddly, my writing was doing better abroad than at home, and in anticipation of Europe as my future major market I slugged away cheerfully on my tale of the Ivory Coast, thinking that the keys of a happy typewriter should have bells in them to sing.

The world was a singing place. The laughter of friends was good song, and the colors of vegetables in the street markets made chromatic music. A beggar's bleat echoed the note of a coin falling in a tin cup, and the husky proposals of the prostitutes in the dark streets near the Madeleine were like fingers brushing over taught little drums. Everything smelled good, during these two years of Parisian euphoria, people, steaming horses, the electricity of subways. Everything felt good, skin, rude linen sheets, and iced flagon.

And, of course, though the French cuisine had signally declined since about the end of World War I, there were still little restaurants of clandestine renown beneath a bridge or in the Algerian quarter where a frog's leg in your teeth was nearly prize enough to slit your throat for. One of my favorites was the Kortchma in an alley near the Place Pigalle, where there were seven tables only, and the gentle or the roaring songs of White Russia were chanted so close to your ear that you could think in peace with the liveliest companion, for conversation was impossible. And as a penthouse on an old ladies' home in Auteuil, with a view of the Bois, was the capacious and snazzy Chinese restaurant of Mr. T. F. Liou. And for French food of the old days when it merited its reputation there was the Auberge de la Truite, where the chicken was roasted perpendicularly before you, spinning on a string. And a very naughty restaurant, and swank and dear indeed, was the Mouton de Panurge with its Rabelaisian murals and erotically sculptured breads and the live sheep that brought flowers to your lady while she chose from a menu which would make Rabelais blush.

Ah, the senses were served well in Paris, and mine were in danger of settling forever for her blandishments when there came a letter from an old friend, Karl Jensen, head of Public Relations for Lederle Laboratories in New York. His proposal was, as usual, explosive. He had talked Lederle into offering one hundred thousand dollars' worth of antibiotics to medical missions in Africa, regardless of nationality or creed and Sikorsky Aircraft into renting him one of their own helicopters from the Belgian Congo. Karl asked me to join him on the first helicopter flight across Africa, to distribute these essential drugs.

Here was the wind again, the cleansing wind, and I remembered Mongo in Africa, an ambulant village which was hard to trace, for its people worshiped the wind and moved where the wind urged them. If it came from the east they would go to the west with it until it subsided and they could replant their homes. And if it came from the west they would swerve back faithfully with it. They were a tall, lean, pliant people, tattooed with lines fluent as the wind. They would sit in their huts' doorways talking a lullaby language to one another, but you would never know when, with a dark wind blowing, they would whip off like baboons on camels to massacre a caravan.

There was barely time for me to drive to Spain and back again before joining Karl and the African expedition, but Barcelona was publishing two of my books and I should be there to talk with my film about them. It was a mystic journey, no wind in it but a constant fog from Paris to Perpignan. My little Renault nosed into it like a dog seeking bones in a snowbank. Never a château of the Loire did I see but as a ghostly blue shadow spiking the fog. Like a general reviewing troops I moved through the regiment of witches, the poplars, lining the road, and would have been off it often had it not been for their guardian shadows.

Gri-gri, the giant chameleon I had found in the Atlas Mountains on the trip with De Breteuil, rode quietly on my shoulder, nuzzling my ear occasionally with his cold scaly nose, rolling his telescopic eyes from witch to witch along the way. One eye could look forward, the other back, simultaneously, combining images in hellish concord on his mental screen. I was a little afraid of Gri-gri; he scared men to sobriety when I placed him on a bar, and when women wore him in their hair at dinner, happy in that warm nest, he would be remarked by the smart set as "what an unusual hat" until one of his eyes would swivel. Another of his talents was in his tongue, which he carried rolled up and could slish out nearly the length of his ten-inch body, for catching flies or flicking your nose if you came too close to his master. Of all the dragons I have had on my back, Gri-gri was quite the brightest. Nothing would put me to work so promptly as Gri-gri swiveling at me from the typewriter's edge, trying to catch with his long tongue the words snarled just back of my fingertips.

The car lights were no help in the fog, which became a very odd fog as we entered the Gorges of the Tarn. The precipitous drop to the river was veiled, but the heights of the cliffs on both sides were brazen in sunlight, and clinging to them like wasp nests were little hermitages which had been incredibly inhabited several hundred years ago, although there wasn't a bush or a berry on those sheer walls. Gri-gri telescoped an eye at them and blinked; they resembled his home in the mountains of Morocco.

It was late on an afternoon and toward the end of the Gorges that a whining sound came seemingly from the heart of my car. I stopped, backed up. There it was, "Whaang-whaang." I went forward, and it was repeated. Dimly I saw a house through the fog on my left, and drove to it while I felt my motor eating its heart away, and miraculously there was a rustic garage. Pushing out of it, as though doing a breast stroke in the fog, came the garagiste. He called me "thee" as these friendly lone folk are likely to do. "Would it be worth ten francs to thee," he asked, his beard thrusting like a sea growth through turbid water, "if I cured the malady of thy motor in just ten seconds?"

420

"The gods of the Tarn be with thee," I said, "and here's a cigarette and a cognac from a silver cup as well."

"The sound ye heard was of the buzz-saw," he said. "I was slicing wood with it! God speed thee to a sunny day! . . . Christ, is that the fiend on thy shoulder?"

"Is there an inn hereabouts?" I asked the beard, which had retreated to a wisp now.

"Across the way!" he yelled. "Beyond the pearly gates of hell across the way."

I turned and drove across the road to where there was indeed a nearly invisible inn, all rock and timber crisscrossed, with a sign stating "Aux Portes Nacrées de l'Enfer." I pushed open the heavy door and had it half-closed behind me when I caught the aroma, sickly sweet, reminiscent of Saigon. It was opium, opium in a lost rural area of France. I closed the door gently and leaned my back to it while my eyes became accustomed to the darkness. There was a small fire on the hearth, two candles on a long good refectory table, and a small opium lamp on the floor beside a couch. Now I saw the heads of two great dogs, like Danes, raised to me against the firelight. One of them barked, and a tall woman dressed in black rose slowly from the couch. I had time only to note that her white hair, long to her shoulders, was neatly curled under in what I think is called a page-boy bob.

She moved toward me, very tall, her hands held to me like a somnambulist's. "Hello, old Bill," she said. "Sorry to have missed you in Saigon."

"Christ, it's not you, Doriel?"

"Christ, it is. Will you have a pipe or a foul drink?"

I sat on a bench before the fire with a dog's head on each of my knees, while Doriel stood tall and proud, her elbow on the mantelpiece, talking quite without wonder of her coming here. Her fumerie had been destroyed by the Vietminh on the night when Mike and I had hurriedly left it. With the fortune she had made there she had come to Paris and written a very popular book about her war years in Indo-China, as seen from the radio tower, where I had worked with her, from the paddy fields between the lines where she was one of our spies, from the shadows of her brothel and fumerie.

Her success in Paris had wearied Doriel, a grande dame with a nun's mute yearnings, so she had chosen the semisolitude of this inn among the Gorges. It was hers. The dogs were hers. The silence of the fog was hers. The inn had little trade, nor did she want it. Her life was in the poetry of seclusion now, and she wrote poetry which she leaned down to tell me secretly, holding Gri-gri to her breast. It was Dali in poetry, of twisted jewels and tormented torsos against hopeless space:

> Tomorrow is the screaming tree
> to shelter us, if we can deafen
> all the dreams we dreamed to be . . .

I poured out the rich red wine from a Spanish bottle with a glass spout. The taut stream of it across the fire seemed to have a core of gold.

"And of course," said Doriel, "I who live in the dark grow the fruit of darkness to sell quite profitably. Look." She slid open a door in the back of the tavern and held the two candles before a galaxy of what looked like little planets against the black earth. They seemed to glow with a fire of their own in that cavern. They were mushrooms. Doriel pointed a candle toward a group of them to one side, forming a sort of fairy ring. "Those are mine," she said, "the Amanita, the deadly ones. Probably I won't need them for some time, so I pickle them; one never knows. . . . Let's have dinner."

It was a fabulous one. Doriel, after a quick gardening by candlelight, sautéed mushrooms—and I raised an eyebrow akimbo at that —over the open fire. On one side of the hearth she roasted great hunks of skewered Swiss cheese which had been dipped in fritter batter. On the other side was a skewer of ham cubes which had been stirred in a mixture of honey and wine. Both her hands were active turning the skewers and tossing the skillet until simultaneously all was done and on our plates. The mushrooms, flavored with chives, were delicious, and benign.

Gri-gri, like an infant succubus, was still nuzzling Doriel's breast. "May I have him, old friend?"

Hesitantly, looking at the opium lamp and the door to the good and the evil mushrooms, and Gri-gri whom I loved, and Doriel standing straight before me as I put my hand on the latch to the road, I said yes, Gri-gri was hers. The night outside was crystal pure.

"Witch of a Doriel, you have lifted my fog," I said.

"And you have lifted mine. *A Dieu*," she said.

43

Medical mission through Africa—
the high hippo—the gorilla and
the nice old maid—Chagos, 1957

BARCELONA DID ME proud with the translations of my books and a good press and lectures arranged for my bronchial, sepulchral voice coming straight from the Gorges of the Tarn. The Catalans, a wild, industrious, and always revolutionary people, were unlike other Spaniards, as they were proud to be. They would swoop me to their buttressed hills around the city and make me inhale their special air—which was not of Spain, mind you—and rush me down to great dinners which were never served before ten o'clock. The odd thing was that the food was bland, unpeppered, quite un-Catalonian. Their spicing was spiritual.

It buoyed me back to Paris, full of a tingling warmth, as fast as the little Renault would go. Karl's telegram awaited me: "Brussels Wednesday," which was tomorrow, and here before me was a fine example of mechanized adventure. It dizzied an old explorer (late in his forties now) who was accustomed to the contemplative long journeys, by canoe in the swamps, by foot in the mountains, by the frequent adherence of his tail to a stump on an island so he could lean back and travel in time along the economic and cultural and ethnic trails to this island, this stump.

Karl Jensen and I, with a newspaper correspondent and a Sikorsky representative, took off by plane across Europe and the Sahara for

423

Léopoldville, Belgian Congo. And there we were, with nothing but ourselves seen en route. I scarcely recognized Léopoldville of my war years from the window of my air-conditioned hotel room. Here was a modern city, sired by Uranium on the body of that rollicking old whore, the Congo. No one used mosquito nets now; there wasn't a fly in the open fish market, for the region had been sprayed with DDT from just such a helicopter as the one we should employ.

Here was a city of busy people who had earned their right to be snobs. At their dinners you could count on the meat, eggs, vegetables, and even flowers being imported by air from Europe; the glorious hibiscus and orchids of the country were too commonplace. As it seemed that we were, crass Americans, who couldn't even appreciate the imported synthetic orangeade labeled "SPIT." We were worse; we were suspect, we learned as the days went by. One rumor was that we were uranium spies, another that the hundred thousand dollars' worth of drugs we were distributing were leftovers. Vainly we explained to the man, actually named Major Dieu, who held our project in his hands, that this altruistic mission of ours was to supply all missions, Belgian, French, American, English, Swiss, with aureomycin, stylomycin, and other antibiotics.

Our Major God said this first helicopter flight across Africa would be planned by him, and that we would not be permitted to deviate by an inch from the ordinary airplane lanes and landing strips. He exploded our whole purpose of doing with a helicopter what a plane could not do, of landing in the small jungle mission clearings where supplies must be brought by man back. He also forbade us to take aerial photos, an order which was quickly rescinded with the help of the governor's press attaché.

Chafing with delay, Karl and I took the periodic launch to the French shore of Brazzaville, twisting our way through the massive floating islands of hyacinth. Old friends of the war days were still there, Governor Cédile, General Diot, and Radio Brazzaville, where this time I broadcast a message of peace, of free drugs to whatever missions might request them.

"One mission which will welcome you here," said Dr. Grosperrin, also a Free French veteran, "is the one at Linzolo. They have almost nothing."

424

"And on the way," said the governor, "you might stop in at the little inn of your old friend Milo. You will find it considerably changed."

The Djoue River is a confluent of the Congo, and upon its banks, overlooking cataracts and crocodiles, is the charming thatched inn of La Gasconne. It had been our quiet refuge from the bureaux during the early days of the war. Now when we came to it near dark along the jungle paths it was making a tremendous noise, with its radio on full blast and a blahting, hiccuping howl coming out of the river.

"That would be Sulphite," said Milo, welcoming us amid a crowd of guests, "our hippo, gentle but entirely free to go and come as she likes. She's taken to drink, fortunately for me, as she attracts clients. I doubt that you have ever seen an alcoholic hippo. Watch!" Out of the river came Sulphite, yawning with sound, and appraising the crowd for its potential in drink. She must have weighed nearly a ton, with liquor bloat, for she was only about six years old.

The first to receive her was the barman with half a bottle of red wine. Then the clients bought her drink, Coca-Cola, at which she snorted, and rum, at which she smiled. With dignity she made her way up the stairs of the porch and into the bar, where she bellowed for grog which was copiously spilled into her. As the afternoon wore on Sulphite became progressively tighter, doing an occasional little dance step to the peril of the furniture.

Milo explained that his hunting dog, Varga, had first made friends with Suphite five months ago, and had lured her to shore to play tag with him. Varga, in exchange, learned to swim. The bartenders won the hippo's confidence by spreading bread upon the waters and then upon the bank. Varga had gradually led her up the garden path until she timidly met her human benefactors who offered her first soft drinks, then harder brews. Regardless of what the S.P.C.A. and the W.C.T.U. may think, she became a very happy hippo, with an unquenchable thirst. Tourists flocked to see and indulge her, and the inn of La Gasconne flourished.

Sulphite was already three sheets to the wind, when Karl, large of heart as a hippo, offered her Scotch which she had never had from that meanie clientele. She loved it. She kissed him up and down, but it was the straw that broke the hippo's back, for she passed out

425

cold beneath a table, a sweet grin on her pretty face, and slept it off for an hour when she rose, roared, and titubated like a drunk who pretends he's sober—back to the Congo to soak her head.

"Sweetest hippo there ever was," said Milo, *"and* devoted. A two-tonner Belgian hippo, twice her size, came roaring out of the Congo a few weeks back to try to steal Sulphite's pitch. Sulphite tossed him back. There was a hell of a battle. The river boiled with it, and Sulphite won. Chased that interloper to the Belgian shore. She accepted our victory champagne, of course. . . ."

All right, said Major God, we could take off, but we must abide by the flight schedule he had drawn up, and by the decisions of the pilot who quaked before him. No nonsense now. It was true that Sikorsky had paid the rental of the helicopter and that Lederle had insured it, but we were to take no chances in visiting mission stations off the beaten track. It might take six months for Sikorsky to build him a new helicopter, because of its contracts with the United States armed forces. Eagerly but humbly now, we agreed to make the first helicopter flight across Africa, stopping only for determined minutes where we had to. Lederle must pay for the gasoline, of course, and the return trip from Tanganyika must start precisely three weeks from now.

At last, with Dr. Kinany, an Egyptian expert on tropical diseases, we climbed into the gaping belly of the helicopter, and took off in the wrong direction, west to Boma on the Atlantic Coast, for Karl was intent on making the complete flight from one coast to the other. The helicopter is a great vehicle, when allowed to do what it was built for, to travel slowly and surely, to hover like a bat above its prey, but despite the padding of its cabin it still rattles your teeth. Conversation, even shoulder to shoulder with your neighbor, is impossible without earphones and microphones. The broad door to the cabin remains open to diminish pressure, and you can hang on to the net across it for photography.

The missions at Boma received us with the token drugs we brought them. The rest would be sent from New York. It was a very zoo of a mission project, with snakes and rats to study for the evil in them, and captive fish to indicate which ate which mosquito larvae.

426

Spinning to our proper course, we came down to the Thysville and Kimpeshi missions, where bilhariasis, malaria, and dysentery were rife, and approximately eight thousand new cases of sleeping sickness a year. Our stylomycin was for them, streptomycin for the astounding number of gonorrheal patients. The natives might not want the so-called exploiting colonist, but they could not deny that their live birth rate was increasing by thousands each year, even though Caesarian operations were common (performed by the white man only), due to superior nutrition but not equivalent pelvis growth.

The Congo passed beneath us, spuming violent water, hurtling bulbs of it like atomic explosions into the air, and we landed at French Brazzaville on the way to our goal, by truck, to the mission station of Linzolo. High on a dusty hill it stood, a chapel, a dozen white-washed huts, a disheartened surgery surrounding the greensward where in 1883 Monseigneur Angouard and the chief of the tribe had buried their only rifles to promote a Christian mission. Now one old Negro medical father and a few nurses were in charge of the few patients who would trust Christ and his modern miracle drugs. The dark sick people turned on their cots to look at our pale faces, and went to sleep again. A woman, her belly swollen and nude, knees spread, waited for childbirth, cocking a skeptic eye at our passage. Karl tossed her an orchid, which landed neatly on her navel. She smiled. This was better medicine than drugs.

Linzolo was the first of several of the missions of the Holy Ghost Fathers we should find across Africa, and, like the others, as if in a spirit of self-immolation, it had found a difficult site for its work, high and close to God. There was no water here, no good wood, but continually up the foggy path of the hill came women bearing them. It was a happy settlement, under the charge of an agile and witty father who sat on the stone steps with us, cuddling Lederle's munificence to his heart. At home you could get it for a fancy price at the corner drugstore. At Brazzaville or Léopoldville it would cost a fortune which missions don't have. Sixty per cent of the medical work in the Congo was done by the government, 25 per cent by the missionaries, and 15 per cent by the large European companies for their own workers. Rarely could any of them afford the wonder drugs.

"What is your mortality here, Father?"

His wise eyes twinkled. "Where do you come from, son?"

I told him. "Ah," he said, "I believe that our mortality here is just about the same as in your home town. That is—one decease per capita."

The helicopter flapped the three long ears of its rotor. It was incredible that these flexible blades of metal should sufficiently stiffen to support us in flight, that the twenty-two dials in the cockpit should, with their fragile needles, control the mastodon of the sky. We traveled slowly, at about seventy-five miles per hour and about five hundred feet from the ground. This was the way to see Africa. By foot, car, train, or river boat you were submerged in jungle; you couldn't see the forest for the trees; and by plane you flew so high that you saw nothing below but African clouds, which are quite like other clouds. Now we could perceive the infinite variety of Africa, the bare brown hills, the small green clots of jungle, the rusty gold roads, the thin, lemon-colored trails, miles long, leading from nowhere to nowhere with neither man nor beast on them.

From the Congo we followed the Kwango River, exploding with cataracts and whirlpools, hurtling over cliffs, jutting high in spume, a Narcissus of a river performing for itself alone, as no man would live by its terrible arrogance. Swooping away from it we slid low over the villages where the people rushed to wave at us and the dogs to bark at us. Only the hens would flutter away in panic; they were supersonic, said our pilot, susceptible to a plane's sound waves which affect the ears of only birds. An agony, said the pilot, shouting through the microphone to our earphones in the back seats. We nodded through our microphones; we sympathized with the hens. Once we passed low over a native couple in a field, both with pots on their heads, very cleverly embracing. The pilot decently cut off the engine while we glided beyond their dreams.

But mostly we rushed. We had that damned schedule to meet. We plopped into Banningville, tossed our bounty at the missionaries, noted that there were one hundred whites, eight thousand blacks, proportionately as much venereal disease among whites as blacks, that there was 5 per cent miscarriage here, largely due to malaria, that, as elsewhere in this most disease-ridden area of the world, between ten degrees north and ten south of the equator, simple lack of protein was one of the great killers. In Tarzan country there were few animals. The carnivore were mostly in the form of bugs which ate men.

The Belgian Congo, one third the size of the United States, is rich in malaria, yaws, filariasis, trachoma, and dysentery. A great part of Tanganyika, which we were soon to enter, was uninhabitable because of the tsetse fly which carries trypanosomiasis or sleeping sickness. Kenya, still within our funereal region, had, in the way of germ progress, developed snail fever, or schistomiasis, which attacked honest bathers in the streams. It became clear to us that the miracles of curative medicine were less important than the prophylaxis of disease. Our generous giving of drugs was very decent, but the teaching of hygiene to the natives, and often the ignorant white colonists, was the essential.

The town of Kikwit was a haunted and silent place, but aware of our coming. From the windows of the helicopter we could see thousands of natives streaming down the hill paths toward the little airfield. Slowly we descended, chose a landing spot, hovered stationary above it ten feet from the ground, then spun half-circle on our axis and landed gently, facing the other way. This should have drawn some applause from the usual crowd, but not in Kikwit. It gaped and didn't say a word as we emerged from our aluminum cocoon, smiling politely without response as we made our way to the sleepy village and its one hotel.

The dining room of it was solemn, hushed, brightened only by dozens of parrots which didn't say a word and a few starched colonials eating quietly. There wasn't even ice to make a tinkle in our glasses, and the plates were of plastic so our knives and forks didn't clink. The manager, a portly Portuguese, drew up his armchair to our table and talked with us quietly while we ate. He was frowned upon by the parrots and the colonials.

"Odd thing," he said, "we had two other Europeans today. Came walking out of the bush with the remains of strange uniforms on them. Mad as hatters. What occurred to us first was the disappearance of a Belgian plane ten years ago. But they couldn't help us for they were completely incoherent. They babbled at the natives, who couldn't understand them. They babbled at us, who spoke several languages, and we couldn't catch on to a word of their monkey talk. But they talked to each other easily while I gave them lunch. They had no money. When they finished eating they each put down a little twisted root beside their plates and walked off into the bush again. Christ! Now here comes the ephemerae!"

Around the Coleman lanterns were clouds of these strange insects, like small white moths, thickening, curdling, till the lights were blurred, till the whole room was filled with them and the floor carpeted with their corpses. They were born and died within five minutes. They filled our glasses, coated our hair, clogged our nostrils. We wore masks of these insects, ecstatic with their few minutes of life. We rushed to the dark corridors, breathing out plumes of ephemerae, and suddenly they all were dead in a silent, downy blanket upon everything they touched, and we walked like ghosts to our beds.

Now I had a cat again, named Congo. For my sins I am always being obliged, by some force stronger than I, to adopt cats, which I don't understand, or horses which bite me. Cats choose and destroy with great accuracy that page of manuscript behind which I have put the carbon paper wrong side to, and a lesson it is to me; horses, even with blinders on them, will instinctively turn to chew on me as I pass their curb. Congo was a cat of the American consulate at Léopoldville, and he had no love for helicopters. He would hang for hours on the canvas net before the open door, as we flew over Port Franqui, Lulua-bourg, Kabinda, threatening to jump out of our thunder, and it was somewhere above a plunging, terrified elephant herd between Kongolo and Kabalo that Congo, probably thinking them mice, made a leap to the end of her leash into space and was nearly hanged.

Nothing daunted, an American consular cat with all that implies of independence, Congo now stalked the pilots in their lair and went hurtling and howling like a banshee from one of their shoulders to the other. The plane dipped dangerously. We fastened our safety belts and came down at Albertville on Lake Tanganyika.

The pilots said with a single voice, "Either that Congo cat goes or we!" It seemed prophetic of what soon and inevitably must happen to the Belgian Congo, as it already has to the Gold Coast, the return to savage control.

430

"Pity that Congo can't navigate," said Karl. We had to leave him with the gentle kitchen folk of our hotel.

Ah no, said our Belgian pilots, we couldn't fly over Lake Tanganyika, despite our pontoons, to Dar-es-Salaam. We couldn't hop over the narrow straight to Zanzibar. Ah no, something might happen to this precious helicopter, so we must waste days going around the lake through Ruanda-Urundi, and stay with the well-filmed giant dancers, the Tutsi, inaccurately called Watussi. Proud and immensely tall, probably descendants of Ethiopians and Egyptians mixed with the darker races, they met us in tweed jackets and sun goggles left over from the film, *King Solomon's Mines,* and danced for us for a fat fee. It was a very odd tribe, largely homosexual, although the women were stately and lovely, splitting their hair-do in the middle to indicate celibacy, wearing a fiber band around it triumphantly to show they were mothers.

Theirs was a feudal organization. They had no villages composed entirely of themselves, but lived in those of their tribal inferiors, mostly Batwa. They gave cattle to their vassals in exchange for work. The offspring of the cattle belonged to the villagers, but the hides went to the Tutsi lords. They had a strange reverence, similar to that of the Hindus, for beef, and would eat it only if it had died a natural death. During the great famine a few years ago they, but not the Batwa, had starved rather than eat their cows.

All this area was beautiful. Lake Kivu and its surrounding volcanic peaks made Switzerland and the United States national parks look like scratched old photos seen through the stereopticons of our youth. The air was like a silver breeze. There were no mosquitoes. The gorillas were so friendly that I regretted we had not time enough at Bukavu to follow up a weird tale told us by a bookseller there.

I had come to his shop to buy what the British so charmingly call a "penny dreadful," a mystery story, to take my mind off the frustrations of our flight, when suddenly I saw a title familiar to me, *The Jungle and the Damned*. Mightily pleased at being on sale in the jungle, I bought the book, autographed it to the bookseller, and invited him to lunch.

"You're interested in natural things, sir," he said over coffee. "If

431

your plane weren't leaving in the morning I'd drive you out to see the girl in the tree. Farmer Bruyns' daughter she is, and up in that tree she's lived with a gorilla these last three weeks. It started gradually, sir. Farmer Bruyns was always a timid man with wild animals, didn't like to shoot them, and he lived alone with this daughter called Elsie, an old maid of about thirty-five, I guess. Well, sir, a couple of months ago old Bruyns was in the forest looking for oranges when suddenly he saw the emperor of all gorillas coming toward him. He was so scared that all he could do was put his hands over his eyes and hide behind a tree. When, finally, he had the courage to peak around it the gorilla was gone, although there were sounds of its passage through the trees. Bruyns followed it timidly, and it would stop, start, teasing him, like in a game of hide-and-seek.

"Well, the next morning he and his old-maid daughter went out and what should they see but the gorilla hiding behind a tree with his hands clasped over his eyes. He'd caught on to the game, see? Old Bruyns walked up to him carefully and was about to tag him to say he was It, when the beast hopped high in the tree and made its 'whoo-whoo-whoo' sound as chimps and gorillas do when they are friendly. But it beat its chest, said the old man, and looked rather piercingly at the girl.

"Next day the farmer and the girl hid behind a tree with their eyes closed, and sure enough there came the rush of the gorilla to tag them, which they barely escaped by beating it indoors."

A Belgian policeman had sat down at our table now and was nodding in confirmation of this fantastic tale. "Gorillas are valuable," he said, "and the old guy thought he'd catch this one alive. According to Bruyns, the ape had learned thoroughly the rules of the game, and on alternate mornings he hid and closed his eyes honestly, while the farmer tried to sneak up on him with a rope."

The little bookseller was not going to lose his story. "There came a morning when farmer Bruyns didn't find his little old-maid daughter in the house. And where was she? High in the treetops with that bloody ape, and not scared or anything. The gorilla was feeding the farmer's bananas to her, and she lolled out on a limb as happy as be damned!"

The policeman nodded. "Bruyns can't shoot the ape for fear of hitting her, and anyway she says she's quite happy there. 'Just leave a little food at the base of the tree,' tied to a liana vine which she lets down. She's even got her old man to send her up some lipstick which she hadn't worn for years. Happiest couple you ever saw, though I think that one or both of them is a little touched in the head."

Roaring like a flatulent hornet, we swooped down upon Nyanza to break up a dance class of the White Fathers. These sensible fellows not only encouraged the native arts and crafts, but even their tribal dancing, as few missionaries do, and it was a gay thing to see an old father in his long white gown leaping with an imaginary spear—the spear of God, be it understood—before the young half-heathens. We were served a Christian rum, and Father Klep came out to the garden with me so I might photograph his magnificent beard.

"It's a second growth," he apologized. "I sold the original."

So, indeed, he had, and built a chapel with the million francs it earned him. He had sat at dinner some years ago with a newspaperman and bemoaned the fact that he had no money to build a chapel. He'd do anything this side of perdition to raise money for the chapel. He'd sell his heritage of a property in France, he'd sell his clothes and walk naked like an Indian saddhu. . . . Would he sell his great beard? asked the newspaperman.

By the living Jesus, that he would! he shouted, tugging at the treasure which had taken forty years to raise. And the newspaperman went back to Brussels and published the offer of the great Christly man, and lo, there was a miracle. A letter came to him with a check from a Belgian financier, with a self-addressed envelope enclosed, and into it carefully, losing not a hair, Father Klep sheared his beard. He felt twenty years younger, he said, as he started the foundations of the chapel with his own hands.

Now we had with us an exciting letter which we received at Ujiji, where Stanley met Livingstone on the tenth of November, 1871. Here, too, were the White Fathers, grateful for our drugs, and happy to pass on to us the letter which their American colleagues, the Holy Ghost Fathers on Mount Kilomeni, Tanganyika, had sent to them. They had heard of our mission, they wrote, and could we not drop

433

on to their mountaintop where they had a playground which could serve as a landing field? They would mark across it on white rocks the name Kilomeni. They were but two missionaries in this eagle's nest, Father McCraley and Father Kelly. The nearest village was forty miles away, and all the sick were transported by themselves and their flock up the mountain on their own shoulders.

This was what we wanted, but while the missionaries of Ujiji were telling us that in Livingstone's time there was little malaria, bilharzia, or sleeping sickness because of smaller concentrations of natives, our Belgian pilots shook their heads.

"Why don't you shake your heads up and down for once?" I demanded impatiently. Every time we had a useful job to perform off the beaten track these fellows would veto it. "Look, let down that ladder and I'll jump into the Kilomeni mission." They had forgotten the ladder. This was moral sabotage and we all knew it, but it was agreed that we should fly over the mission grounds.

It was a brave little place, neat and trim, perched, God knows why, on the mountainside, a precipitous path leading to it, with the jungle surrounding it like a green hand to crumble it if the work of the good men there was for a moment relaxed. Slowly we circled over it and the hundreds of black faces turned up to us, and there, almost within a hand's grasp, were the two missionaries in working khaki, waving to us eagerly, and I could almost feel the drums throughout the mountain range signaling our approach, "The Holy Ghost has come! The great Dove has come!"

"For God's sake, why don't you land?" Karl shouted at the pilot through our cabin microphone.

"Impossible. Updrafts," came the Belgian voice. He had his orders and he wouldn't depart from them. I tossed overboard a weighted note saying we would be back tomorrow.

We were glum on the hotel terrace of romantic old Dar-es-Salaam that night. The pilots sat apart. Karl and Dr. Kinany were busy chewing American and Egyptian oaths. I was busy devising a parachute from the landlady's pink plastic parasol and strapping to it a plastic Tupperware container filled with our miracle drugs. A miracle drug to end bureaucracy was what I wanted.

434

"You know you can't drop anything," said the chief pilot, while I was busy with my Christian weaving.

But in the morning we were in the clouds again, prodding, seeking among them for the little patch of white that was Kilomeni, and then lower through the infinite green of the mountains where, somewhere, two great lonely men were fighting death with little more than their bare hands. These were the true explorers, I thought, I who was without formal religion, who didn't believe that any white-bearded god was the superior of an African's naked sacred tree. Then I saw the space where the mission was, and I no longer thought of the hand of green strangling it, but of the mission's hand opening across the jungle to make a waltzing place for frightened people.

I dropped my parachute into it, and we swung off, straight toward the white cone of Mount Kilimanjaro.

All around me was my Paris again, and I went hurtling from the heart of it, by car, by foot, by scooter, by spiritual somersaults from the Île St. Louis to the cavernous alleys, to the high forests of Meudon where the "Rabbit Who Smokes" served me fabulous omelettes protected from the wind in the garden by golden autumn leaves, to the little mill near Chantilly where Yvonne and André Wick lived so graciously on the willow-sheltered banks of the stream, the Nonette.

There was Roussik, whom I loved, marrying my former captain, and Pierre, a sudden suicide, and Notre Dame infirm with the same scaffolding it had supported like witch-nurse bones these many years. And old men fished for dream fish along the Seine, and the bookstalls sold books so senile they could only gabble now. And the tourists around the Madeleine, the Concorde, and the Etoile walked in wonderment that such beauty should be vital still.

I wakened, one dark night, to find my head on the windshield sparkling with pain and half my car stove in to my ribs. And the hospital received me with my detached bones and a fine case of pneumonia. Before I quite passed out I could hear the doctor saying, "Better warn the family," a gay message to take to sleep. Dimly I saw the swimming faces of Armand and Dinorah who had brought me here, to lay me, like Hemingway's leopard, on the Kilimanjaro of my life. Through the last of vision I could see their unquiet faces, the

435

telephone, the lavabo, the pretty nurse with a white cone like Kilimanjaro on her head, the brutal tanks of oxygen which were being shoved into my nose, the mask descending like a ripped cliff over me. There was a jab in my arm; that would be penicillin; and an oil well drilling through my back to bring out the pleural fluid.

This might happen to others, not to me, who had never been seriously sick in my life, but I rather enjoyed the blind dependence at last upon the good other people, the need not to fight any more, to lie quiet with a mountaintop air being fed me without having to reach for it. That was the night I was to die, and I saw death very clearly. It wasn't an old man with a scythe or a skeleton beckoning. It was, and I remember accurately, simply a gray wall of what seemed sponge rubber. I lunged at it, trying to break open a door to death, and elasticly it flung me back into life again. And I lunged and lunged at it, laughing because it was as hard to fight for death as life, and each time I was bounced back into life again. But now I had torn a hole in the wall, and Kilimanjaro soared in snow before me. Furious with this wall of gray sponge-rubber death, I tore at it with my hands and my teeth, to spread the little door.

And I was puzzled by Aline's voice saying, "I'll see you on Chagos," and I turned to see the atolls of Chagos, green and gold, just over there on my side of the gray wall. Simplest thing in the world; I could swim to it. And Judy was saying, "See you on Chagos." And General Leclerc was saying, peremptorily, "Chagos." And Cas and Sheila and Dick and Zuila and my blind dog Bill and my fair Lucille were chanting, "See you on Chagos . . . Chagos . . . Chagos. . . ."

I turned my back to the wall and started swimming.

Chagos, 1957

436